Qualitative Research in
EDUCATION

Edition 2

Qualitative Research in
EDUCATION
A User's Guide

Edition 2

Marilyn Lichtman
Virginia Tech

Los Angeles • London • New Delhi • Singapore • Washington DC

For information:

SAGE Publications, Inc.
2455 Teller Road
Thousand Oaks, California 91320
E-mail: order@sagepub.com

SAGE Publications Ltd.
1 Oliver's Yard
55 City Road
London EC1Y 1SP
United Kingdom

SAGE Publications India Pvt. Ltd.
B 1/I 1 Mohan Cooperative Industrial Area
Mathura Road, New Delhi 110 044
India

SAGE Publications Asia-Pacific Pte. Ltd.
33 Pekin Street #02-01
Far East Square
Singapore 048763

Printed in the United States of America

Library of Congress Cataloging-in-Publication Data

Lichtman, Marilyn.
Qualitative research in education: A user's guide/Marilyn Lichtman. — 2nd ed.
    p. cm.
Includes bibliographical references and index.
ISBN 978-1-4129-7052-5 (pbk.)

    1. Education—Research—Handbooks, manuals, etc. I. Title.

LB1028.L436 2009
370.7′2—dc22   2008044868

Printed on acid-free paper.

09   10   11   12   13   10   9   8   7   6   5   4   3   2   1

Acquiring Editor:	Diane McDaniel
Associate Editor:	Deya Saoud
Editorial Assistant:	Ashley Conlon
Production Editor:	Sarah K. Quesenberry
Copy Editor:	Diana Breti
Proofreader:	Wendy Jo Dymond
Indexer:	Michael Ferreira
Typesetter:	C&M Digitals (P) Ltd.
Cover Designer:	Janet Foulger
Marketing Manager:	Christy Guilbault

Brief Contents

Preface   xiii

Acknowledgments   xx

PART I: TRADITIONS AND INFLUENCES   1

Chapter 1:   Introduction and Overview of the Field   3

Chapter 2:   Insights From the Past   24

Chapter 3:   Learning How to Be a Qualitative Researcher   37

Chapter 4:   Ethical Issues in Qualitative Research   51

Chapter 5:   Designing Your Research: Choosing From
             a Variety of Approaches   68

PART II: GATHERING, ORGANIZING, AND ANALYZING   93

Chapter 6:   Embarking on Qualitative Research   95

Chapter 7:   Self-Reflexivity and Subjectivity   115

Chapter 8:   The Role and Function of a Literature Review   124

Chapter 9:   Learning About Others Through Interviewing   138

Chapter 10: Learning About Others Through Observations
             and Other Techniques   163

PART III: PUTTING IT ALL TOGETHER   185

Chapter 11: Making Meaning From Your Data   187

Chapter 12: Communicating Your Ideas   205

Chapter 13: Judging and Evaluating   221

Chapter 14: Thinking About the Future   235

Glossary   243

References   247

Index   259

About the Author   265

Detailed Contents

Preface   **xiii**

    The Early Days   xiv

    Late 1990s and Beyond   xvi

    Current Challenges   xvii

    Structure of This Book   xviii

    Becoming a Savvy Learner   xix

Acknowledgments   **xx**

PART I: TRADITIONS AND INFLUENCES   **1**

Chapter 1: Introduction and Overview of the Field   **3**

    Definitions and Illustrative Examples   5

    A Brief Background   7

    Some Basic Comparisons Between Quantitative and Qualitative Research   9

    Ten Critical Elements of Qualitative Research   12

        1. Description, Understanding, and Interpretation   12

        2. Dynamic   13

        3. No Single Way of Doing Something   13

        4. Inductive Thinking   14

        5. Holistic   15

        6. Variety of Data in Natural Settings   15

        7. Role of the Researcher   16

        8. In-Depth Study   17

        9. Words, Themes, and Writing   18

        10. Nonlinear   19

    Additional Issues   19

        Objectivity as Fiction   19

        Critical Role of the Researcher   20

        Role of Those Studied   20

        The Nature of Reality (Ontology)   20

        Values and Ethics (Axiology)   20

        How Can Various Paradigms Accommodate Each Other?   21

        What Role Does Action Play in Research?   21

Issues About Who Is in Control 21
Self-Reflection 22
Challenge of Doing Qualitative Research 22
Summary 22
Group Activity 23
Individual Activity 23

Chapter 2: Insights From the Past   **24**

Educational Research Prior to the 1980s 26
The 1980s to 2000 31
2000 and Beyond 32
Speculations for the Future 33
Summary 35
Group Activity 35
Individual Activity 35

Chapter 3: Learning How to Be a Qualitative Researcher   **37**

General Ideas 38
So You Want to Be a Qualitative Researcher? 41
Qualitative Questions 42
Getting Started 46
Summary 49
Group Activity 50
Individual Activity 50

Chapter 4: Ethical Issues in Qualitative Research   **51**

Ethical Behavior: Definitions and Background 53
Major Principles Associated With Ethical Conduct 54
Problems With the Standards 58
Alleged Misconduct in the General Scientific Community 59
Misconduct in the Qualitative Research Arena 60
What Are the Special Problems for the Qualitative Researcher? 61
Setting and Maintaining Standards 63
Problems With Review Boards 65
Summary 66
Individual Activity 67

Chapter 5: Designing Your Research: Choosing From a Variety of Approaches   **68**

Ethnography: Studying Cultures 70
Introduction 70
History and Meaning of Anthropology and Ethnography 70
Examples From the Field 72

Grounded Theory: Placing Theory in Its Context 72

    Introduction 72

    History and Meaning of Grounded Theory 73

    Examples From the Field 74

Our Lived Experiences: Phenomenological Inquiry as a Philosophy
and Method of Study 75

    Introduction 75

    History and Meaning of Phenomenology 76

    Phenomenology in Today's World 77

    Phenomenology as a Philosophy and as a Method 79

Case Study: A Look at the Particular 81

    Introduction 81

    History and Meaning of Case Studies 81

    Selecting a Case 82

    Examples From the Field 83

Mixed Methods 84

    Introduction 84

    History and Meaning of Mixed Methods 85

    Examples From the Field 85

Feminist Research and Feminist Theory 85

    Introduction 86

    History and Meaning of Feminist Research 86

    Examples From the Field 87

Generic Approach to Doing Qualitative Research 87

Additional Approaches to Qualitative Research 88

Summary 89

Group Activity 89

Individual Activity 90

**PART II: GATHERING, ORGANIZING,
AND ANALYZING**　　　　　　　　　　　　　　　　　**93**

Chapter 6: Embarking on Qualitative Research　　　　**95**

Twenty Questions 96

My Life as a Graduate Student 99

    Phase 1: Getting Started 100

    Phase 2: Modeling Good Practices 100

    Phase 3: Practicing Interviewing and Debriefing 101

    Phase 4: Conducting Outside Interviews 102

    Phase 5: Doing Preliminary Analyses as a Group 107

    Phase 6: Doing Analyses as an Individual 108

    Phase 7: Preparing Individual Papers 108

My Perspective on the Graduate School Experience   113
Summary   113
Group Activity   114
Individual Activity   114

Chapter 7: Self-Reflexivity and Subjectivity   115

Personal Journey   117
Role of Self   121
Reflexivity   121
Self-Awareness and Growth   122
Summary   123
Individual Activity   123

Chapter 8: The Role and Function of a Literature Review   124

What Is a Literature Review?   126
Importance of a Literature Review   127
Theory in Qualitative Research   128
Sources of the Literature for a Review   128
Steps in Conducting a Literature Review   129
   Identifying and Limiting the Research Topic   129
   Locating What Is Out There   130
   Deciding What Is Relevant and Critical   131
   Sorting, Selecting, and Organizing the Information   131
   Writing the Review   132
Examples From the Field   132
Practical Suggestions for Keeping Track of Things   136
Summary   137
Group Activity   137
Individual Activity   137

Chapter 9: Learning About Others Through Interviewing   138

Qualitative Interviewing   139
   The Purpose of Interviewing   140
   General Issues in Interviewing   141
In-depth Interviewing   143
   The Interview Process   143
   Interviewing Techniques   145
   Some Dos and Don'ts of In-Depth Interviewing   151
Focus Group Interviewing   152
   The Purpose of Focus Group Interviewing   153
   Issues Regarding Focus Groups   154
   Example of a Focus Group Interview   156

Online Interviewing   157
    The Purpose of Online Interviewing   157
    Issues and Challenges With Online Interviewing   158
    Focus Groups on the Internet   159
Summary   161
Group Activity   161
Individual Activity   162

Chapter 10: Learning About Others Through Observations and Other Techniques   163

Observing in Natural Settings   164
    The Purpose of Observations   165
    Issues Regarding Observations   166
    How to Conduct an Observation   168
    Examples of Observations   170
Existing Writing, Your Writing, and Writing You Generate   173
    The Purpose of Written Material   173
    Issues Regarding Written Material   173
    Extracting the Essence   174
Images   175
    The Purpose of Images   175
    Examples of Images   176
    Issues Regarding Images   176
Using the Internet in Qualitative Research   177
    Persistent Online Environments   177
    Chat Rooms and Discussion Groups   177
    Focus Groups   178
    Online Teaching   178
    Visual Diaries, Wikis, Blogs, and Vlogs   181
    Available Data and Communication   182
Summary   182
Group Activity   183
Individual Activity   183

PART III: PUTTING IT ALL TOGETHER   185

Chapter 11: Making Meaning From Your Data   187

Myriad Techniques or Procedures   189
The Process   190
    What Is Qualitative Data?   192
    Process and Traditions   192

What About Transcribing? 193
When Should You Do Your Analysis? 193
Coding and Themes or Concepts 194
Narratives or Stories 194
How Do You Know When You Are Finished? 194
Philosophical Stance 195
Conducting an Analysis 195
Getting Started 195
Preparing and Organizing Your Data 196
Reviewing and Recording Your Thoughts 197
The Three Cs: Coding, Categorizing, and Identifying Concepts 197
Additional Ideas 200
Data Analysis With Computers 200
New Trends 203
Summary 204
Group Activity 204
Individual Activity 204

Chapter 12: Communicating Your Ideas   205

First Steps 206
Guidelines for Writing and Presenting Qualitative Research 208
Your Audience: What Do They Expect? 208
What Are You Trying to Say? 208
The First Person 208
The Voices of Others 209
The Use of Metaphors 210
Creative Nonfiction 210
Structure Is a Good Thing 213
Writing a Qualitative Research Proposal 215
Alternative Forms of Presentation 217
Qualitative Writing 217
Summary 219
Group Activity 219
Individual Activity 220

Chapter 13: Judging and Evaluating   221

Personal Criteria 224
Researcher's Role: Revealing the Self and Other Connection 224
Convincing Arguments: What Was Studied and What Was Found 225
Rich in Detail: How the Study Was Done 226
Communication: Are You Convinced by the Presentation? 226

What Do Others Have to Say? 227
    Prior to 1990 227
    The 1990s 228
    2000 to Present 229
    2008 and Beyond 231
Journals and Editorial Board Criteria 233
Summary 233
Group Activity 233
Individual Activity 234

Chapter 14: Thinking About the Future　　　　　　　　　　**235**

Trends 235
    Sustained Growth, Yet Skepticism 235
    Creativity Abounds 236
The Internet 237
    Access to Information 237
    Communication With Everyone 238
    New Ideas 238
Greater Acceptance by the Field 239
About Theory 239
About Practice 240
Journals With a Qualitative Focus 240
For the Future 242

Glossary　　　　　　　　　　**243**

References　　　　　　　　　　**247**

Index　　　　　　　　　　**259**

About the Author　　　　　　　　　　**265**

Preface

Providing public education through high school has been a goal in this democracy since the first settlers landed on Plymouth Rock in the 1600s. Since the United States was established, education has been the responsibility of individual states and local school districts. We have Thomas Jefferson and Horace Mann to thank for helping create a public school system. By the end of the 19th century, free public education became available to all. Since the civil rights movement, the federal government has taken an increasing role in schools. Today, schools face such challenges as school violence, drug and alcohol abuse, and poor achievement, especially among minorities.

As students in education, you have the responsibility and opportunity to influence our schools. One way to do this is to identify questions that still need to be studied. Qualitative research strategies offer opportunities to examine issues in depth that may yield a clearer understanding of what is happening in certain circumstances and how changes can be made to meet the needs of all students. I am especially drawn to qualitative research because I think we can gain insights that statistics and numbers might not yield. I urge you to identify questions related to issues of importance to you and those with whom you live and work. Small steps toward answering these questions can serve as building blocks for the future.

I revisited this book in the summer of 2008. My goal was to add a chapter on ethics and to redo the epilogue on current issues and trends. In fact, each chapter was revisited and updated with new examples and references. As you read about designing and conducting qualitative research, I urge you to connect these skills with your role in education. Whether you are a teacher of young children or work with adults in prisons, I believe that qualitative research can be used to answer many of the questions you have about learning and teaching. I recall when I began my career in the field of education. Through a variety of circumstances, I moved, changed universities, and found myself without a major. So I decided to earn a degree in education so that I could become a teacher. It was during a time when few opportunities were available to women. In my mind, my career path was going to take me into teaching, so I registered for an education class. Its title was "Teaching and Learning." I still remember that class, in which we learned 16 principles on the topic of teaching. To this day, I don't know who came up with the principles, but they were considered gospel. "Begin where the learner is; suit methods to the learner; mesh the new with the old." How interesting. They are still important principles. I am sure I did not question them. Why did we learn them? Who decided? Was research a part of this? It was not until much later that I began to think about how education could be guided and informed by conducting research on important topics. In this book, I provide you with a combination of practical and theoretical information that will assist you as you advance in your educational pursuits. But first, here is a little background you might find interesting.

The study of education at the college and university level became popular in the United States during the mid- to late 1800s. Universities opened departments of education, and separate normal schools were established. Their purpose was to train teachers to work at the elementary or grammar school levels. Courses were of a practical nature. It was not until the 1890s that Josiah Royce asked whether education was based on science. Lagemann (2000) provides a fascinating account of how education research became a profession. She attributes much of the movement to John Dewey at the Laboratory School of the University of Chicago. (As an aside, I am not sure whether I was drawn to the field of education research because I spent the formative years of my own education at this same Laboratory School.) In the next century, especially after World War I, the education community adopted the stance that a scientific approach to the study of education, with an emphasis on quantitative measurement, would take the field to a higher level. Colleges and universities required education students to take courses in research methods and statistics and to read research studies that emphasized experiments and complex statistical analyses. Federal government funding of educational research was directed at studies with a scientific underpinning. Journals published articles based on quantitative research.

However, in spite of their best intentions, many educators found they were still unclear about some basic questions: What are the best practices for teaching reading? How should classroom discipline be managed? How should teachers work with disadvantaged youth? How could teachers working with adults provide appropriate training? There was a large chasm between the teachers in the schools and the researchers and professors in the universities, whose mission was to educate school teachers. During the 1980s, educational researchers began to use alternative approaches to answering questions. Today, the literature is enormous and growing exponentially.

Several factors led colleges and departments of education to begin to look at the value of the scientific approach to the study of education. Some thought that adoption of the scientific method did not make sense when so many variables were outside the control of the researcher. Lagemann (2000) speaks of a misguided attempt to be scientific. In addition, many teachers found statistical modeling and experimental research foreign to their experience and difficult to grasp and implement. Teachers began to take ownership of research conducted in schools, and the teacher researcher and **action research** movements moved the central focus from the universities to the schools. Action research is a type of qualitative research that focuses on a solution to a specific local problem. Finally, more women and minorities entered the educational research community and brought new ways of thinking and a different sensibility to the endeavor.

I do not want to mislead you, however. Many education schools still expect you to be well-versed in the scientific method. But if you are reading this book, you are in a program where alternative ways of answering questions are considered.

■ The Early Days

Although anthropologists and sociologists have used qualitative methods for about 100 years, researchers in the field of education adopted methods drawn from the natural sciences and psychology. You can read this history in detail, with many interesting photographs, in the first chapter of Bogdan and Biklen's (1992) book on the foundations of qualitative research. These approaches tended to be quantitative in nature and involved hypothesis testing and generalizations. It was not until the 1980s that anthropologists began to work in educational arenas to any great extent

(Spradley, 1979). Lincoln and Guba (1985) suggested studies be conducted in natural settings rather than in laboratories. They referred to this as **naturalistic inquiry**. But the primary mode of conducting educational research remained experimental in nature. Students were expected to become conversant in behavioral science and statistics. Most research courses and programs were dominated by the scientific method.

Qualitative research is a relatively new field in educational research. It was not until the 1990s that scholars, publishers, journals, and government agencies began to think about qualitative research. *The Handbook of Qualitative Research* (Denzin & Lincoln, 1994) led the way. The University of Georgia had its first Qualitative Interest Group (QUIG) conference in 1992 and continues to this day as a leader in the field. *The Qualitative Report* issued its first paper journal in 1990 and went online in 1994. Free online distribution made the information accessible worldwide.

Just as qualitative research in education has witnessed a phenomenal growth, so, too, have changes in approaches to research been seen in other disciplines and in other parts of the world. Psychology, often the last bastion of the scientific approach, has seen increased interest in the field. The American Psychological Association issued *Qualitative Research in Psychology* (Camic, Rhodes, & Yardley, 2003), a series of edited papers expanding perspectives in methodology and design. Volume 5 of *Qualitative Research in Psychology* is devoted to teaching qualitative methods; it includes five original papers (Hansen & Rapley, 2008). *Forum Qualitative Social Research* publishes articles and reviews reflecting this more open perspective from a Western European point of view (see Lichtman, 2005, for my review of the proceedings of a conference on qualitative psychology). Parker (2003) and Harré (2004) suggested that psychologists might even consider that qualitative research is scientific.

There are several reasons for the increased interest in qualitative research that began in the 1990s. First, the opening up of the educational research field to women and people of color led to alternative sensibilities and alternative voices. No longer were quantitative studies (developed by white European men) the only choice of research methods; other ways of knowing might be considered just as legitimate. Second, there was a growing dissatisfaction with educational research findings based on quantitative studies alone. Educational research findings were often vague, subject to many problems in implementation, poorly disseminated, and often irrelevant. The public school community made decisions based on many factors other than research results. Third, teachers demanded a larger role in design and conduct of research and were drawn more to action research projects. Finally, publishers broadened the base of their offerings, and methods drawn from many disciplines were disseminated to a much greater extent than previously.

In these early days, most of us were not really sure what qualitative research was. Was it ethnography? Yes, said some. Was it having findings emerge from the data using a grounded theory approach? Yes, said some. Was it phenomenology or hermeneutics? Yes, said some. Was it an approach, a method, a philosophy, a science? All of the above and more, said some.

As for universities, there were few courses in qualitative research in the early 1990s. Many educational research departments offered none or devoted one lecture in a survey of methods to qualitative research. Faculty who taught qualitative research either came from the discipline of anthropology or were self-taught. I recall feeling very much like an outsider in my own department of educational research when I decided I wanted to learn about this field. One colleague described what he knew about qualitative research as fitting on the nail of his little finger. Others denigrated the field. It was seen as a field for those who were not objective, who were soft, or, worse yet, who were incapable of doing "the really hard stuff" that involved statistics. Because many research faculty, as well as other education faculty, had little or no training or experience, they often did not know how to react to what they read. They looked for research that fit the mold of quantitative research. When it didn't, they were unsure what to ask for and what to expect.

Publishers of qualitative research textbooks were very few in the early 1990s. Most books that were published were devoted to a particular discipline. For example, Glaser and Strauss' *The Discovery of Grounded Theory* appeared in 1967, but this book dealt with only a small portion of the field. Bogdan and Biklen's *Qualitative Research for Education* appeared first in 1982, but it was written from an ethnographer's point of view.

Journals that either published articles written from a qualitative perspective or were devoted primarily to qualitative articles were rare in the early 1990s. Many of these journals struggled with establishing appropriate criteria for judging qualitative work and locating reviewers who were appropriately trained.

Professional associations, such as The American Educational Research Association, barely recognized the field of qualitative research. A few special interest groups existed in the early 1990s, and a few presentations were given. For the most part, however, they were relegated to a minor role.

Communication between and among qualitative researchers both in education and in the larger social science arena was rare in the early 1990s. There were few avenues for researchers to find each other, to share ideas, and to discuss common issues.

As for teaching, I found it very difficult to find appropriate materials in the early 1990s. I searched journals for articles that were on target and combined them in textbook format, issued by our bookstore. The Internet was not readily available to most students or faculty, so it was difficult to get access to new material and make it available to students.

In those early days, if you were interested in teaching about or doing qualitative research, you were often criticized. Criteria for determining quality were nonexistent, thought some. This couldn't be science because you did not test hypotheses. This couldn't be science because it wasn't objective. This couldn't be science because only a few were studied.

■ Late 1990s and Beyond

In less than 10 years, this field has exploded. Denzin and Lincoln's *Handbook of Qualitative Research,* first issued in 1994, was completely restructured and a second edition was published in 2000; a third edition was published in 2005. Additional online journals came into being. *Forum Qualitative Social Research* (*FQS*) was established in 1999. Based in Berlin, it is a multilingual online journal for qualitative research. It includes articles, reviews, debates, interviews, and special topics. QUIG and *The Qualitative Report* expanded greatly. Listservs devoted to discussions of qualitative topics were developed, such as qualrs-l@listserv.uga.edu. Sophisticated qualitative research software was developed with a Listserv available to provide assistance (qsr.news@qsr.com.au).

Qualitative research became an umbrella under which many different types of information were included. It used a feminist perspective. It became postmodern. It became structural. It used case studies, action research, or mixed methods. It included various ways of gathering data. Many disciplines adopted qualitative research ideas.

Some sought a compromise position by using quantitative and qualitative methods in the same research study. Bergman (2005) spelled out the central issues. Beginning about the mid-1980s, much of the writing suggested that researchers should choose either one or the other approach because their philosophical underpinnings were incompatible with each other. Some 25 years later, he suggested that there is a "wealth of possibilities in relation to data collection and data analysis techniques" (Abstract, p. 1; see also Creswell, 2007).

Qualitative courses were offered at many universities and in many different departments. Online teaching became available. More dissertations and theses were written and accepted. More faculty became interested in the field.

The publishing field exploded. Journals devoted specifically to qualitative research were published. It became very difficult to capture the essence of the field. The Internet entered the scene, so information became instantly available. Researchers beyond the United States and Great Britain began to make contributions.

Professional associations, government agencies, and universities acknowledged the field and broadened the scope of the scientific community.

The marginalized voices that previously had no arena began to make contributions. People of color and women addressed issues of power and disenfranchisement.

■ Current Challenges

Today, the field is booming. New books, new Web sites, new journals, new conferences, and new faces appear almost daily. I find it difficult to keep up with all that is out there. But lest you think that all is rosy, I want to highlight a few challenges that this field faces.

Preparation of Students and Faculty. Although many new courses are being offered, much still needs to be done. Faculty who teach in the field need ways to stay current; faculty who work in other fields need to be educated. Issues that appear to have been put to rest reemerge. Many students speak of having difficulty pleasing their advisers. In response to the No Child Left Behind initiative, some advisers have become more conservative and unwilling to let students move in alternative directions. Students suggest to others that they need to jump through appropriate hoops to receive their degrees and that they should not make this their battlefield. Of course, many other areas are still subject to question and debate.

Criteria for Evaluation. I think this is an area that remains challenging and conflicted. I do not believe we need to find parallel criteria to those used in quantitative research. At the same time, however, the field needs to stake a legitimate place in the scholarly community. The debate continues as to how qualitative research should be evaluated. Journal editors and Institutional Review Boards recognize these challenges but do not agree on how to evaluate qualitative research.

Rigidity, Structure, and Conservatism. I worry that as we become fixed and rigid, we move toward conservatism. Those opportunities for other voices to be heard, for other means of sharing what we learn, and for creativity and new ideas to emerge may be stifled in the interest of wide acceptance. Once we become mainstream, do we lose what we have been looking for?

Managing Information Overload. It is not just the domain of qualitative research that faces this problem. We are constantly bombarded with information in the field. Some of it conflicts with other ideas. It reminds me of the dilemma we face about our health. Should we drink a glass of wine at dinner? Should it be red or white? Should we eat carbs or not? Is being slightly over the optimum weight good for you?

How Do We Balance Acceptance of Various Alternatives With a Sense of Scholarship and Rigor? Should there be rigor at all? How can we dispel the idea that anything goes? Can we say that some ways of gathering material are better than others? Can we say that some writing is more convincing than others? There is still a debate about what constitutes scientific rigor. Maxwell (2004) suggested that qualitative research can offer a "legitimate scientific approach to causal explanation" (p. 3). Perhaps not completely tongue in cheek, one blogger cites a violation of the "Iron Law" in qualitative research: The number of participants in the study should exceed the number of writers of the article.

These are all ideas to think about as you begin to learn how to be a qualitative researcher.

■ Structure of This Book

I have divided this book into three parts.

In Part I: Traditions and Influences, I provide a blend of history, approaches, influences, and specifics. My intention is to put you immediately into the setting. Many readers of this book have heard about qualitative research and find themselves attracted to it. You may like the fact that it usually does not involve numbers or statistics. You may like the idea of personal stories, or you may be taking a qualitative research class to fulfill a requirement. By blending history and tradition with some practical ideas, I hope to provide you with a framework to continue your studies. Chapter 1 identifies 10 critical elements that are part of the new paradigms of qualitative research. It also addresses such issues as objectivity and the researcher's role. I conclude this and every chapter with group and individual activities. In Chapter 2, I look at the past and toward the future to give you a sense of the field and how it has changed. I believe that one of the best ways to become a qualitative researcher is to become actively engaged in doing. As such, Chapter 3 provides some suggestions about learning to be a qualitative researcher. Chapter 4 is a new chapter that confronts ethical issues. I end Part I with Chapter 5, in which I provide you with details about how different traditions and approaches inform the field. This last chapter is very challenging. You may find that you will need to read it more than once.

Part II: Gathering, Organizing, and Analyzing is designed to provide you with practical information on doing qualitative research. Although there are many traditions and approaches on which qualitative researchers may base their work, when it comes to methods for gathering data, there is much agreement. Chapter 6 is concrete and based on my many years of experience working with students. After I ask and answer 20 questions about qualitative research, I provide you with a detailed example I have used in my classes, and I include examples from student writing. In Chapter 7, I introduce an idea that might be unfamiliar to you: self-reflection. Chapter 8 addresses some new ideas about doing a literature review and offers steps in doing such a review. Chapter 9 and Chapter 10 deal with learning about others. In Chapter 9, I focus on qualitative interviewing and focus groups. In Chapter 10, I examine other ways of learning about others, including observations, document reviews, using images, and finding information online.

Part III: Putting It All Together contains four chapters. In this section, I take you from collecting data and analyzing it to thinking about how you can draw meaning from what you have gathered and subsequently how to say it. I deal with drawing meaning from your data in Chapter 11.

Chapter 12 addresses issues of communication: how to write and present a qualitative research study. Chapter 13 addresses how qualitative research is judged by others and by ourselves. Part III concludes with Chapter 14, in which I discuss keeping abreast of an evolving field.

At http://www.sagepub.com/lichtman2estudy, you will find a resource titled "Teaching Qualitative Research Online." This resource presents a detailed online interchange that occurred in one of my classes. The material is about phenomenology, but the process can be adapted to any topic. The Web site includes Web resources, links to journal articles, and research proposals.

■ Becoming a Savvy Learner

I have tried to provide you with tools to facilitate your learning this complex material. The quotations that are presented as you begin each chapter help you see other influences and ways of thinking. I suggest you do a quick read of each chapter before you begin to study it. In this way, you will have an overall view before you get bogged down in details. The images presented at the beginning of each chapter provide a visual alternative introduction for what is to come. The group and individual activities that conclude each chapter have been used in my classes over the years; most students find them helpful. I hope you will have a chance to use some of them. I suggest that you keep a journal of your thoughts and ideas about becoming a qualitative researcher throughout the time you study this material. It should be your personal journal, but in keeping with my philosophy of self-reflection, I hope you will share it with your peers and your professors.

You will be faced with much material that is new to you. You will need to decide what is important and what you accept. Because qualitative research has no right answers, this puts you in a state of flux. I know that some students like to be told what to learn and memorize. I do not intend for you to learn that way. I want you to begin to think about what research is, what qualitative research is for the field and for yourself, and how you might make contributions as you pursue your personal goals.

Acknowledgments

Since completing the first edition of this book in 2005, I retired from full-time teaching at Virginia Tech. My last doctoral student defended her dissertation approximately two years ago. But these activities are always with me. When Diane McDaniel from SAGE and I discussed revising this book to reflect the latest thinking, I welcomed the opportunity. This latest edition reflects my thinking and the current state of the field. I have tried to present a variety of viewpoints. At the same time, I want to acknowledge my personal viewpoint about the field. This is in keeping with the acknowledged role of the researcher in qualitative research.

Since my retirement, I have become immersed in the study of art. Traveling on the Grand Tour in the summer of 2007 and visiting Art Basel in Switzerland; Documenta 12 in Kassel, Germany; and the Venice Biennale in Italy certainly opened my eyes to new ways of seeing and doing. Certainly, what was quality in art could no longer be judged by one group of people or placed in a certain domain. Artists were free to try anything—and they certainly did. We saw William Hamilton emerge from a car filled with water in a performance piece in Switzerland. In Kassel, we saw towering structures by Ai Wei Wei built of reutilized pieces of ancient Chinese buildings. In Venice, we viewed and sometimes ate a floor sculpture built of licorice candy by Gonzalez-Torres. When viewers ate some of the pieces, more were added. If you want to know about this journey, read my blog at http://thegrandtour07.blogspot.com/2007_05_01_archive.html.

I also took two courses in contemporary art—one in writing art criticism. I learned how to look closely and carefully at things I thought I knew so well. And I learned how to write and communicate my ideas in a clear and pointed manner.

How does this all fit into qualitative research? I continue to be open and astounded by the creativity of the individual. I continue to believe that there is no right or best way. I hope as you read this book you will find yourself open to new ideas. You will be all the wiser for it.

I began this project in 2002 when Art Pomponio from SAGE called me to explore my interest in writing a text aimed at education students taking a first course in qualitative research. He had read my work and was interested in some of my ideas. At that time, I was teaching a graduate class at Virginia Tech that combined online teaching with face-to-face teaching. I was exploring several strategies for presenting material online to students. After several phone discussions and an outline had been submitted to SAGE, I was offered a contract to write a textbook that targeted the education field. I developed an extensive outline and wrote several chapters. You may wonder why it took so long to bring this project to fruition. My husband, Martin Gerstein, became ill and died in May, 2003. By then, Art had moved on and Diane McDaniel took over. She provided a seamless transition to the first edition and made this revision go smoothly.

To My Students. I want to thank all my students who, over many years, taught me perhaps as much as I taught them. We challenged each other to think outside the box. We valued each other's creativity. We questioned each other's ways of thinking and of knowing. To all of you, a special thanks. It is always a risk to provide a list of names because it is so easy to leave someone out, but a special word of thanks to Freddie Cross, Gohar Farahani, Paul Glass, Donna Joy, Paul Parker, Judy Smith, Warren Snyder, Satomi Izumi Taylor, Leanne Wells, and Frank Wong. Mary Repass, your support and encouragement meant a lot to me.

To My Colleagues. Ron Chenail: We began our discussions about qualitative research almost two decades ago. Your continued help and ideas always challenge me to think about this topic in new ways. Günter Mey and Katja Mruck: Your openness and support have broadened my knowledge base extensively and I value your friendship. My colleagues at Virginia Tech, both in Blacksburg and Falls Church: Thanks for all the good years together. Diane McDaniel from SAGE, who took over editorial work on this book: Your feedback and organizational ability are wonderful. Deya Saoud from SAGE: I appreciate so much your attention to the myriad details involved in making this book happen. Diana Breti, copy editor, and Sarah Quesenberry, production editor: You have made bringing this book to fruition all the easier by your insightful comments.

Also, I would like to thank the peer reviewers of this project for their helpful feedback and suggestions: Alberto M. Bursztyn, Brooklyn College and The Graduate Center; Joe Bishop, Eastern Michigan University; Sharon Anderson Dannels, The George Washington University; Lee S. Duemer, Texas Tech University; Christie Eppler, Seattle Pacific University; Jennifer Esposito, Georgia State University; Douglas Fisher, San Diego State University; Kathy K. Franklin, East Tennessee State University; Robert Hampel, University of Delaware; David R. Holliway, Washington State University; S. Kim MacGregor, Louisiana State University; Steve Siera, Saint Martin's University; Stephen A. Sivo, University of Central Florida; Lucille B. Strain, Bowie State University; Charles Tesconi, American University; and James R. Valadez, California Lutheran University.

Thanks also to Steve Siera at Saint Martin's University, who created the end-of-chapter summary for each chapter. He did a great job of providing succinct summaries that readers will find helpful.

To My Family. My daughters, Ellen and Judy: Thanks for being my sounding board and providing me with challenges and ideas and for listening to my gripes. My son, David: I always know I can count on you for anything. My brother, Lee: Thanks for worrying about me and always being there. Jim, my son-in-law: Our talks about art continue to get me to think about things in different ways. To the rest of my family—Claire, Margaret, Anath, Michael, and Lilah—you provide nourishment and encouragement to all. I couldn't have done this without all your support. To my ever-extended family, Judy Barokas, Louise Appell, Joan Blitman, Rita and Karl Girshman, Ruth Bell and all the other bridge buddies, and Shari and Curly Johnson. To my wonderful Corcoran Gallery of Art family who have helped me think so differently about art, research, and life. I value your thinking and ideas greatly. And finally, to my late husband and best friend, Marty. I know you are proud of this effort. I love you all.

—Marilyn Lichtman

PART I

Traditions and Influences

I have organized this book in three parts. In Part I, I introduce you to the very exciting field of qualitative research. Chapter 1 provides an introduction and overview of the field. Chapter 2 presents insights from the past. Learning how to be a qualitative researcher is covered in Chapter 3. Chapter 4 is a new chapter addressing ethical issues in qualitative research. Chapter 5 examines a variety of approaches to conducting qualitative research. If this is your first course in qualitative research, you probably have little knowledge or experience. These five chapters combine and interweave both practical experience and historical traditions. You might find it interesting that the field has grown so rapidly over the past 20 years. Many voices have shaped the field. Ultimately it is hoped that the knowledge gained from this kind of research can inform educators of both children and adults to provide a more meaningful educational experience for all.

My intention is to provide a balance of practical experience and knowledge about the past and the various approaches that have shaped the field. I believe that active participation will help you internalize some of the more abstract ideas you will face.

Each chapter concludes with a group activity and an individual activity. I have used many of these activities in my own teaching. I urge you to try some of them to fix the information in your mind.

Chapter 1

Introduction and Overview of the Field

FOCUS YOUR READING

- Qualitative research is a general term that describes research about humans in which the researcher is key to all.

- There are 10 critical elements of qualitative research.

Anyone who isn't confused here doesn't really understand what's going on.

—Anonymous

As a doctoral student who had returned to the academic world much later in life than most students, I wanted to pursue a dissertation topic that was relevant to me and to develop a research project where I could bring my personal experiences and explore a subject that was intriguing. After all, I realized that writing a dissertation was a project that was going to consume months of my life, and if I was to dedicate this time to active research and creating a product that would be useful in the future, it should be a subject for which I had a passion and a desire to learn more.

—Mary Repass

This is a book about the systematic investigation of phenomena using **research**. For some of you, the term **research** is intimidating, off-putting, and far removed from your life as a professional. Yet, as you glance through this book, you see some major differences between this and most research books.

There are no numbers or statistical formulae. It is written in a conversational and accessible style. It includes visuals. My purpose is to draw you into the qualitative research field. When you complete the book, you should be able to design and conduct a qualitative research study. I do not suggest that the task is simple, for you will find ambiguities and lack of precision and even inconsistencies in what you read and encounter. I hope that the information I provide will take you far along the path.

No doubt many of you who read these pages currently work in schools, have done so in the past, or are contemplating doing so. Much of your professional experience targets the here and now. Your focus is usually on teaching, counseling, or administration. You might work with adults or children. Most of your time is spent getting through the day, and you have not had the inclination or time to do more than reflect on practices. You might not have actually planned or conducted any research in the field. Now you have the opportunity to engage in systematic and planned investigations about questions you may find interesting. I pose some below.

As you think about students, you might ask yourself these questions: How do I get my students to apply themselves, to pay attention, or to enjoy learning? Why is it that some students seem to learn more quickly than others? How should I motivate students to learn? How can I account for individual differences among my students? How can I understand those students who are different from me? How is my class similar to or different from others around me? What about students who have had few home experiences that foster learning? Why can I reach some students but not others?

As you think about teachers or other adults, you might consider different questions. What is it like to be a teacher? Why do so many who are initially attracted to teaching decide to leave the profession? What could schools do to retain talented professionals? What could schools do to help teachers who are having difficulties but still want to remain in the profession?

You might find yourself interested in looking at specific groups of individuals in the educational field. What challenges do women face as they seek to move up the ladder? How do minority teachers express their views and share elements of their social group? Or, you might consider how adults navigate in online learning environments. I suspect you can add to this list by thinking about the problems and challenges you face each day while working in the educational arena.

Why do I pose these questions, and what do they have to do with qualitative research? I put forth these examples because they are important to consider but are not often addressed from a research perspective. Many approaches to educational research typically involve conducting a survey of a large group. The focus of such surveys is often quantitative: how many graduate from high school, how many pass the state standards, or how much money is spent for books in the library. Other research designs are experimental; they compare one method of teaching to another and evaluate how well students perform on standardized tests. While this information can be valuable, it does not provide answers to the kinds of questions I posed earlier. The questions above are more suitable for qualitative research designs.

Many of you are unfamiliar with qualitative research. You may have heard the term but do not really know what it means. In this book, I introduce you to many aspects of qualitative research. I discuss ethical issues involved in planning and conducting such research. I talk about various research approaches from which qualitative research has evolved. I ask you to reflect on how you affect and are affected by qualitative research. I provide specific ideas about how to do qualitative interviewing and observations. I consider the challenge of organizing and of making sense of the data that you collect. I introduce you to current thinking about how to evaluate a qualitative research study. Throughout this book, I provide you with many examples that will help as you embark on this very interesting journey of thinking about conducting research in a new way.

Did You Know

Two journals publish exclusively online: *The Qualitative Report,* published by Nova Southeastern University, start date 1990, and *Forum: Qualitative Social Research,* published in Berlin, start date 1999. Both are free. Two journals (published by Sage) are issued in hard copy and can be accessed online via appropriate permission: *Qualitative Inquiry,* with U.S. editors, start date 1995, and *Qualitative Research,* with editors from Wales, start date 2001.

I want to convey a general understanding of what qualitative research is all about. It is multidimensional and fluid. Certain kinds of questions are more suitable than others. It relies heavily on the voices of humans. It uses **inductive reasoning**, moving from the specific to the general. Novice researchers are sometimes frustrated and challenged but, at the same time, exhilarated. You can learn how to do this kind of research. You are about to embark on a challenging and exciting way of thinking about important questions. The path is no doubt different from one you have followed previously, and therein lies the challenge.

■ Definitions and Illustrative Examples

I find myself struggling to provide you with a definition that is meaningful, inclusive, and yet conveys the diversity within the broad term qualitative research. Among the first to write about the field extensively were Lincoln and Guba (1985). By the time the first *Handbook of Qualitative Research* was published (Denzin & Lincoln, 1994), definitions included "multimethod in focus," "interpretive," and "naturalistic approach to subject matter." Some take a very narrow view, while others give it a broad brush. In fact, there is no clear agreement on a definition. Some even speak of a lack of a coherent definition (Olson, 1995) or one that is difficult to get (Simmons-Mackie & Damico, 2003). Even Schwandt (2007), in his recently revised *Dictionary of Qualitative Inquiry,* does not provide a specific definition of the term. A 2008 Google search yielded diverse ideas: "research techniques which seek in-depth insights," "explores and tries to understand people's beliefs," "follows an inductive research process," or "a study of people or systems by interacting with them."

For our purposes, I would like you to consider this definition:

Qualitative research is a general term. It is a way of knowing in which a researcher gathers, organizes, and interprets information obtained from humans using his or her eyes and ears as filters. It often involves in-depth interviews and/or observations of humans in natural and social settings. It can be contrasted with quantitative research, which relies heavily on hypothesis testing, cause and effect, and statistical analyses.

Perhaps some examples will help you to get a clearer picture of what qualitative research is. Mary, a student in her early thirties, was particularly interested in young children. Throughout her life, she had been a "loner" with few friends. She wondered about other children who seemed like her. Mary decided she wanted to study the informal ways young children form friendships or find themselves outside the mainstream. Because she volunteered in a preschool, she asked permission to observe several classes. She developed a schedule to spend at least four hours per week in the school. She decided it would be wise to observe at different times of the day. Initially, she did not know quite what she was looking for. She decided to look both at students who always seemed to be part of a group and at students who stayed by themselves. She thought she knew what was meant by friendship, but she decided not to review the literature at this point. Rather, she made an explicit statement in her journal of what friendship meant to her and what she remembered about forming friendships (or not) when she was younger. During the course of her three-month study, she took extensive notes. Sometimes she took photographs or videos. She also decided that she would speak to the teacher and aides about their ideas of friendship. In a few cases, she decided to approach some of the children individually. Eventually, she recorded all her information in a database. She began her analysis by **coding** the notes she had made; that is, she sorted and organized the text to identify recurrent themes and concepts. For example, if one student always hung around with another student, she highlighted the entry in red. If one student offered to assist another student, she highlighted the note in blue. If one student was always alone, she chose a third color for that note. At this point, she decided to examine what others had written about friendships among young children. Eventually, she was able to organize her **codes**—the terms she used to identify chunks of the data—into categories and develop some themes from them. I have just given you a bare outline of the study, but I hope you get the idea. The study built on Mary's personal interests and her professional experience. If you wanted to give this type of study a label, you might call it classroom ethnography.

Steven was also interested in the topic of friendship. He was a retired military enlisted man. He had decided to return to school and to explore working with seniors. His area of expertise and interest was the elderly. He gained access to a seniors' home and received permission to conduct extensive interviews with those residents who were willing to participate. He, too, began by making explicit his own view of friendship. Writing in his journal, Steven found himself thinking back over the years. Who had his friends been? How long had the friendships lasted? What kind of person did he choose? Who chose him? He was a little confused by the many questions. His general design involved extensive interviews with several residents of the home. He was concerned that the residents might not be able to maintain interest for too long, so he planned to conduct at least two shorter interviews with each of 10 residents. Since Steven had some knowledge of qualitative computer software, he began by putting his notes into the computer. He also transcribed each interview after completion. He then began to look for common elements among the interviews. He found himself working back and forth between coding and questioning. In this way, he refined his questions, picked up missing information from some residents, and got a better feel for his data. This type of study relied heavily on in-depth interviews and might be labeled a case study of friendships as seen by seniors.

A third example shows yet another way to consider the topic of friendship. Alice was especially interested in teenage girls. She volunteered at an afterschool program that served many girls. She had begun to notice certain cliques forming and decided she wanted to investigate the nature of these cliques; how the girls formed friendships within the cliques; and how others were invited into, or excluded from, the cliques. Alice had some experience conducting focus groups, so her main avenue to gain information was focus groups. She also decided that she wanted to use the computer chat rooms that the girls had formed. Alice also added video clips of club meetings and informal gatherings to her database. This type of study, which examined the lived experiences of these teenagers, might be called a phenomenology.

In these three examples, you can see that each investigator approached the topic of friendship somewhat differently. Each made use of professional contacts to obtain access to certain groups. Each tried to narrow the scope of the investigation by looking at a particular type or class of individual (e.g., young children, seniors, teenagers). They chose data collection methods with which they were comfortable and that afforded them rich data. One relied on computers to assist in data analysis. Some performed a study that fit a particular type of qualitative research (e.g., ethnography), while others operated from a more eclectic mode. Let's return to the definition from above: Qualitative research is a way of knowing that assumes that the researcher gathers, organizes, and interprets information with his or her eyes and ears as a filter. It is a way of doing that often involves in-depth interviews and/or observations of humans in natural and social settings. It can be contrasted with **quantitative research**, which relies heavily on hypothesis testing, cause and effect, and statistical analyses.

Each type of study met the criteria outlined in the definition. As you read examples of other studies, you should decide to what extent they meet the criteria. It should be clear to you that there is no single way to conduct a qualitative research study. Throughout this text, I offer you many examples that will help you gain a clearer understanding of what qualitative research is.

■ A Brief Background

You might find it helpful to know a little history of how the field developed. When preparation for a degree in education expanded beyond the study of teaching techniques, many institutions of higher learning added a research component. These institutions were faced with a challenge: What were the best ways for educators to conduct research? The answer appeared straightforward. They would adopt research methods associated with the scientific world. By using such methods, they reasoned, the field of education would be elevated to a high level.

The **scientific method** is a systematic way of testing hypotheses and determining cause and effect. It involves several basic steps: develop a question, identify related research, develop a **hypothesis** (a formal statement about the relationship between variables), design an experiment, analyze the data to test the hypothesis, and present results. One very important characteristic is that the data gathered and the methods of analysis are quantitative. The scientific method relies heavily on numbers and statistics. Different terms are often used to describe the scientific method. In this book, I have used them interchangeably. I might talk about the scientific method; quantitative methods; experimental research; traditional paradigms; **foundationalist** (traditional experimental research) paradigms; **positivism,** which deals only with observable entities and objective reality; or traditional research paradigms. While there are subtle differences among the terms, for your purposes, those differences are not critical because my focus here is to consider alternative approaches to conducting research.

Traditional research **paradigms**, or ways of seeing the world, make certain assumptions about the world. They assume that there is an objective reality that researchers should try to uncover as they conduct their research. Further, they assume that the role of the researcher is neutral; his or her purpose is to describe an objective reality. These paradigms are called *positivist,* a term associated with Auguste Comte, who wrote in the first half of the 19th century. In his development of the field of **sociology**, the study of social lives and behaviors, he suggested that we should look for observable facts and apply methods of the natural sciences to the social sciences. He actually called himself the Pope of Positivism. This positivist tradition dominated the way research was done in education for many years.

It became evident that capturing a reality that was "out there" was difficult, if not impossible, to achieve. As a consequence, postpositivist ideas emerged around the end of World War II as the assumptions of positivism were questioned. A postpositivist point of view held that researchers should strive to capture reality by using multiple methods. In such a way, reality would be approximated (see Trochim, 2001, for greater detail about the differences between positivism and **postpositivism**).

Traditional ways of doing research (positivism and postpositivism) dominated the field of research in education until the 1980s. For a variety of reasons that I discuss in detail in Chapter 2, alternative approaches to conducting research began to surface. Much of the influence came from the field of anthropology, in which ethnographic research was preferred. We began to see ethnographies about schools (for a detailed history, see Zou & Trueba, 2002). At times, some anthropologists doing ethnographies called themselves *qualitative researchers*—no doubt to distinguish themselves from those doing traditional quantitative research. You might find it interesting to read Eisenhart's (2001) overview of educational ethnography. She writes about three "muddles" that confront her as an ethnographer: the meaning of culture, the conflicting acceptance regarding ethnography, and the responsibility to those being studied. During this period, many qualitative researchers tried to meet the criteria of quantitative research and adopt methods that relied on validity, high structure, and computer analysis to count and tabulate data. Some even said that qualitative research "attempted to do good positivist research with less rigorous methods and procedures" (Denzin & Lincoln, 2000, p. 9).

It became clear to other qualitative researchers that striving to be positivists or postpositivists and accepting the assumptions of these perspectives was not what they wanted to do or to be. New generations of qualitative researchers adopted a poststructural or postmodern point of view (see, e.g., Koro-Ljungberg, 2008; Mazzei, 2007). Some said that a positivist or postpositivist stance was no longer the only acceptable way to conduct research. Multiple realities constructed by the researcher replaced the traditional single approximation of an objective reality. This group of people also rejected the traditional criteria associated with judging quantitative research. They were concerned that a traditional view of scientific research kept the voices of many silenced. Some were interested in personal responsibility, multiple voices, and verisimilitude, instead of objectivity and validity.

In the first decade of the 2000s, it is evident to me that research has taken on a political agenda. One camp would have us believe that we need to return to traditional research models—what Patton (2002) and others call the "gold standard," or randomized control trials (see also Eisenhart, 2006). For example, Constas (2007), in his study of journal articles published in 2001 (prior to the move toward standardized tests and accountability) and again in 2005, demonstrated a decrease in nonexperimental research. Torrance (2008) spoke of the movement in the United States for randomized control trials and the (unfortunate, in my view) development of standards and guidelines to control the production of qualitative research. Further, Torrance commented that this movement, which he calls *neopositivist,* has reached the United Kingdom. His suggestion is to engage with policymakers, even at the same time recognizing the possibility of co-option and collusion. I do not think that all is lost, however, because we see some organizations take an activist posture and see research that advocates for human rights (see, e.g., the program announcement of the Fifth International Congress of Qualitative Inquiry 2009 at http://www.icqi.org/). You can read more of my thoughts on this topic in Chapter 14.

■ **Some Basic Comparisons Between
Quantitative and Qualitative Research**

I think it might help you to understand these two different philosophical and methodological ways of knowing if I make some basic comparisons. I do this to assist your understanding; however, I want you to recognize that the lines between the two are not completely fixed, and overlap is often possible. In fact, one accommodation to the overlap is what is known as the mixed methods approach. I discuss more about mixed methods in Chapter 5. At this point in your learning, however, I draw some major distinctions by looking at the assumptions that each method makes. In Table 1.1a and b, I compare and contrast these two ways of thinking about and doing research from both a theoretical and practical perspective.

Table 1.1a Comparison of Qualitative and Quantitative Methods of Research

Theoretical	Qualitative	Quantitative	Comments
Nature of Reality	Multiple realities. Reality is constructed by the observer.	Single reality. In a well-designed study, a reasonable approximation of reality can be observed.	These two ideas are not as far apart as they seem. Most qualitative researchers do not take the position that any reality is a reasonable one. Many quantitative researchers acknowledge the influence of the observer, even while trying to limit it.
Objectivity/ Subjectivity Dichotomy	Subjectivity based on role of researcher is expected. Objectivity is inconsistent with the idea of a constructed reality.	Objectivity is critical in a scientific approach to acquiring knowledge.	Quantitative researchers acknowledge difficulties in reaching objectivity. Many qualitative researchers still hold on to the objectivity stance.
Role of Researcher	Researcher is central to any study. Interpretations are based on researcher's experience and background.	Researcher tries to remain outside of the system, keeping biases to a minimum.	In fact, both acknowledge that researcher cannot stay outside the system. Double blind experiments are designed to do this, but other factors may compromise things.
Generalizability, Cause and Effect	Not interested in cause and effect or generalizing, but want people to apply to own situations.	Goal to apply to other situations.	Quantitative researchers more successful in cause/effect than in generalizing, since samples are often limited.
Ways of Knowing	Multiple ways of knowing. We can learn about something in many ways.	Best way of knowing is through the process of science.	But science is not so pristine.

Now I want you to think about some of the practical distinctions.

Table 1.1b Comparison of Qualitative and Quantitative Methods of Research

Practical	Qualitative	Quantitative	Comments
Purpose	Understand and interpret social interactions.	Test hypotheses. Look at cause and effect. Prediction.	In general, most qualitative research is not interested in hypothesis testing and most quantitative research is. However, survey research using quantitative techniques describes without testing hypotheses.
Group Studied	Tends to be smaller, nonrandom. Researchers may get involved in lives of those studied.	Tends to be larger, randomly selected. Anonymity important.	Many quantitative researchers not able to randomly select.
Variables	Study of the whole rather than specific variables.	A few variables studied.	Quantitative researchers are limited to variables measured by a test.
Type of Data Collected	Emphasis is on words. Increasing interest in visual data.	Emphasis is on numbers.	Sometimes qualitative researchers use numbers and quantitative researchers use interviews.
Type of Data Analysis	Coding and themes. Some use computers.	Statistical analysis. Computers.	Both might use computer programs, but quantitative researchers use statistics.
Writing Style	Less formal, more personal.	Scientific and impersonal.	Informal style of qualitative may suggest less value to traditionalists.

You can read many references on this topic. A traditional view holds that quantitative research is better and leads to results that are more believable. Others argue that we are making too much out of the differences. One of the best sources of this latter idea can be found in Trochim (2001). The topic, he says, is so important that "there has probably been more energy expended on debating the differences between and relative advantages of qualitative and quantitative methods than almost any other methodological topic in social research." His view is that it is much ado about nothing.

In a sense, Parker (2003) agreed with Trochim (2001), but takes a slightly different position. Most traditionalists argue that the only proper or real scientific research is quantitative research. However, I want you to think about these issues in a different way. Suppose that qualitative research is seen as science (Harré, 2004; Parker, 2003). According to Parker's interpretation of Harré, laboratory experiments are actually prescientific, and quantitative researchers need to account for "the reflexive capacity of human beings, the meaningful nature of the data they produce, and the way that claims are made about individuals from aggregated descriptions of behaviour from particular populations" (p. 4). Parker continued forcefully as he discusses questions about quality. Parker did not answer these questions. He posed them for you to consider.

It is crucial to the enterprise of scientific work generally, and qualitative research in particular, that the way we go about it is open to debate. Parker (2003) presented some questions for which there are no clear answers and much disagreement.

1. *What counts as good?* (a) It corresponds to the norms of established scientific study. (b) It will improve the lives of those who participated. (c) It is intrinsically interesting and will provoke and satisfy those who are curious about the questions posed.

2. *Who should it be for?* (a) It should be directly accessible to ordinary people outside psychology. (b) It should contribute to the accumulating body of knowledge for the use of other researchers. (c) Those who participated should gain something from it in exchange for their time.

3. *What counts as analysis?* (a) A careful redescription using some categories from a particular framework. (b) The discovery of something that can be empirically confirmed as true. (c) The emergence of a new meaning that was entirely unexpected.

4. *What is the role of theory?* (a) Mystification by those versed in jargon at the expense of those who participated. (b) A necessary antidote to the commonsense and often mistaken explanations for human behaviour. (c) The space for thinking afresh about something. (p. 5)

The questions Parker (2003) proposed are quite different from traditional ideas. I offer them to you so that you can begin to really think about the activities in which you are involved. I don't mean to imply that there are right or wrong answers. That would be presumptuous. Nor are there right or wrong questions. As you continue with your learning, keep in mind that things are not always as they seem or as they once were. Whatever your views are, it is important that you are aware that the comparisons and judgment about which type of research is better continues to be a controversy even as you read this chapter.

Up to this point, I have asked you to compare qualitative research with traditional quantitative research. Table 1.1 a and b suggest many of these differences. But you can also think about qualitative research in terms of worldview, traditions, or methods. Some people think of qualitative research in terms of the way they know or understand the world. While quantitative researchers think about the world as having an objective reality, many qualitative researchers speak about a worldview in which reality is constructed by the researcher. As such, there is no single reality that exists independent of the researcher. Rather, the researcher constructs multiple realities. For example, in postmodern thinking, subjectivism and constructivism are two terms that are often used to describe how people see the world. **Constructivism** is a **theory**, or proposed explanation of a phenomenon, that says that knowledge is constructed by the researcher and is affected by his or her context. Crotty (2003) suggested a subjective stance: We see the world through our own construction of it. You can understand this more clearly if you think about the idea that "the subject is the meaning maker, and whatever meaning is imposed may come from a seemingly endless source of experiences" (Faux, 2005, ¶ 5).

Lincoln and Guba (2000) used the term *constructivism* when they write about how the world is viewed. Similar to Crotty (2003), their writing suggested that realities are socially constructed.

It should be clear to you that the researcher's role in qualitative research is critical because he or she makes sense of, or constructs, a view of the world.

Others associate qualitative research with methodologies rather than views of the world. They consider how to conduct qualitative interviews or observations. They analyze data and look for themes. Still others associate qualitative research with various research approaches or paradigms that inform their work. They look for an approach that will provide a theoretical basis for their thinking. They might decide to do a case study or a phenomenology, for example.

All these ideas are important. How is a worldview determined or constructed? What methodologies are used to learn about the world? What approaches serve as a theoretical basis for the research? It is critical for you to know that there is no "right" way to think about qualitative research. It is a way of knowing and a way of doing.

In this chapter, I identify 10 critical elements that apply to research that is qualitative and ask that you think about each one. In subsequent chapters, I discuss in greater depth methodologies, approaches, and philosophy. I hope you will find this journey challenging, stimulating, and fun.

■ Ten Critical Elements of Qualitative Research

1. Description, Understanding, and Interpretation

In general, the main purpose of qualitative research—whatever kind—is to provide an in-depth description and understanding of the human experience. It is about humans. The purpose of qualitative research is to describe and understand human phenomena, human interaction, or human discourse. When we speak about phenomena we often think of lived experiences of humans. When we speak about human interaction we often think of how humans interact with each other, especially in terms of their culture. When we speak about human discourse we think of humans communicating with each other or communicating ideas. Sometimes phenomena, interaction, and discourse are intertwined.

Qualitative researchers tend to ask "why" questions and questions that lead to a particular meaning (Hollway & Jefferson, 2000). Because qualitative researchers are interested in meaning and interpretation, they typically do not deal with hypotheses. Quantitative research is designed to test hypotheses. But no type of qualitative research is designed to test hypotheses or to generalize beyond the particular group at hand.[1] While early efforts at qualitative research might have stopped at description, it is now more generally accepted that a qualitative researcher adds understanding and interpretation to the description. You may know of some early work that sets forth things that happen to a particular group, group member, or subculture. Wolcott (1973) gave a detailed account of a principal after following him for a year. His emphasis is a descriptive account rather than an interpretation.

But many believe that it is the role of the researcher to bring understanding, interpretation, and meaning to mere description. An example might help you to see this more clearly. Richardson (2008) wrote a humorous ethnographic account of her dinner with Lord Esqy and other prominent figures on the occasion of her giving a lecture at the University of Melbourne. In this account, she moves beyond simple description and leads us to greater insight about the culture that is so different from hers.

You will see as you become familiar with qualitative research that most writers focus on description and interpretation. However, some feminist researchers and some postmodernists take a political stance as well and have an agenda that places the researcher in an activist posture. These researchers often become quite involved with the individuals they study and try to improve their human condition. Some even contribute a portion of their royalties to those they studied.

2. Dynamic

In general, qualitative research is thought to be fluid and ever changing. As such, it doesn't follow one particular way of doing things. There are many traditions that inform qualitative research. Often, qualitative researchers pose new kinds of questions and explore new ways of answering them.

Here are some examples that will help you see how dynamic qualitative research has become. In the past, ethnographers traveled to countries and cultures different from their own. They immersed themselves in the culture for an extended period and attempted to understand the culture. You may have read of Margaret Mead's trip to Samoa or Oscar Lewis' visit with five families in Mexico. Some sociologists (the Chicago School) tended to study immigrants and their life experiences (see, e.g., Bulmer, 1984, for a detailed account of sociology in Chicago). Even today, some ethnographers take field trips with their students; Wallace (2003) conducted fieldwork with his students in Guatemala. But many have moved to the Internet to study cultures. For example, Markham (1998) studied themes of life in cyberspace.

Qualitative researchers often conduct interviews in which the participants tell their stories and do not follow a predetermined format or set of questions. Rubin and Rubin (2005) spoke about interviewees, informants, or conversational partners rather than subjects or sample. They suggest that in qualitative interviewing "you can understand experiences in which you did not participate" (p. 3). Because much of the interviewing can be unstructured, they suggest that qualitative interviewers "explore new areas and discover and unravel intriguing puzzles" (p. 4). I know that this dynamic nature of qualitative interviewing is a critical element in the development of a successful qualitative study.

Qualitative researchers do not always know who they will study or what they will study. Qualitative researchers feel free to modify protocols as they progress through the ever-changing landscape of those they study. They sometimes rely on some of their participants to identify others who might be studied by using a snowball sampling technique (Atkinson & Flint, 2001), or they might ask key informants to nominate others who can be studied.

Qualitative researchers do not always begin with a detailed and concrete plan for how they will conduct their research. They may find that the questions they investigate evolve as they begin to gather and analyze their data. In keeping with the dynamic nature of qualitative research, you will discover that "qualitative research characteristically does not use standardized procedures—and this is a main reason for the low reputation of qualitative research in some social disciplinary 'communities.' Doing qualitative research makes the impact of the researcher far more obvious than in its quantitative counterpart" (Breuer, Mruck, & Roth, 2002, ¶ 3).

3. No Single Way of Doing Something

There is not just one way of doing qualitative research. When qualitative research began to take hold in education, many equated qualitative research with ethnography and saw extensive fieldwork as the way (and, for some, the only way) to conduct research. Bogdan and Biklen's (1992) work makes this quite clear. Although its title is *Qualitative Research for Education,* its content is limited to a discussion of ethnography and related methods. I am not sure whether later editions take a more comprehensive approach. Some identify **symbolic interactionism**[2] with qualitative research (Blumer, 1969). Others equate qualitative research with grounded theory (Glaser & Strauss, 1967; Strauss & Corbin, 1990). Still others see qualitative research as being case studies (e.g., Merriam, 1988; Yin, 2002). You will read more about some of these approaches in Chapter 5.

I think the fact that there is no specific or best way to conduct qualitative research is one of the reasons students sometimes have difficulty understanding what qualitative research is. They want it to be a single thing. "Tell me how to do it," they say. After all, if I do scientific research and conduct an experiment, I know what makes a true experiment (D. Campbell & Stanley, 1963). I know what difficulties there are in conducting an experiment in a real-world setting and how to approximate a true experiment (Cook & Campbell, 1979; Trochim, 2001). I know how to conduct a survey (Dillman, 1978). Why can't I have the "right" or "best" way to conduct qualitative research? As consumers and conductors of research, we are so often wedded to our old positivist or postpositivist paradigms, and we know that old ways are hard to discard.

Of course, we are all aware that there is no one way to do something; there is no right way to do something; there is no best way to do something. You might come to appreciate this idea if you move out of the discipline of research and into the field of art. What is "the way art should be"? The Church used to set the standard for good art. There was only one way. But then some artists tried new ideas. People laughed at Impressionists like Monet, but now their work is appreciated by many. People jeered the Cubists (Picasso and Braque), and yet they are seen as opening the doors to so many other ways of making art. People said modern art was not art, and now much of it commands millions of dollars. So I urge you to keep your minds open as you explore alternative ways of doing research.

Multiple realities is an expression I touched on earlier. Can you accept that there is no single reality that exists independent of your interpretation? I am not talking about the philosophical question of whether a branch dropping from a tree in the forest makes a sound. I am talking about social interactions among humans, or thoughts individuals have about a topic, or the inner workings of a unit in a small company. There are potentially several ways to interpret what you see or hear. As the researcher, you do the interpretation. Of course, your interpretation will carry more weight if the data you gather, the manner in which you organize the data, and the vehicle you use to present your interpretation support it. For more information on credibility and legitimacy of your research, see Chapter 13.

4. Inductive Thinking

A traditional approach to research follows a deductive approach. **Deductive reasoning** works from the general to the specific. In contrast, qualitative research deals with specifics and moves to the general. You can think of this as going from the bottom up, by using observations to generate hypotheses, if indeed there are any hypotheses. Qualitative research moves from the concrete to the abstract. Researchers begin with data and use the data to gain an understanding of phenomena and interactions. They do not test hypotheses, as is typical in experimental research. Because qualitative research employs inductive thinking, I have used an inductive way of writing and presenting the material in this book. I suggest that you begin by collecting data for some kind of research project. This inductive approach is the opposite of a deductive approach to doing research. In the latter type, you would do a considerable amount of planning and write a proposal for research, rather than actually conduct research. You have heard the term inductive approach often throughout your school experience. But what does it really mean?

When using an inductive approach, one thing leads to another, like scaffolding. You begin by gathering a considerable amount of data. You then go through your data to see whether you can find many examples of a particular thing, in order to identify a central issue or idea (a **concept** or **theme**). Of course, you might find some statements that do not support the theme. As you collect and simultaneously look at your data, you begin to move to more general statements or ideas based on the specifics found in your data.

5. Holistic

Qualitative research involves the study of a situation or thing in its entirety, rather than identification of specific variables. Gunzenhauser (personal communication, 2005) speaks about the particular, contextual, and holistic characteristics of qualitative research. You can think of it this way: Qualitative researchers want to study how something is and understand it. They are not interested in breaking down components into separate variables. Many of you who have studied the scientific method of research are used to looking at how one variable is caused by another, or how several variables are related to each other. This approach is used in order to test hypotheses. But in qualitative research, we are not interested in testing hypotheses. In fact, most qualitative research traditions aim for description, understanding, and interpretation and not examinations of cause and effect. Let's look at an example. Sharon has been working with young females who have returned to complete a high school education after having a baby. She meets with them once a week in the evening at a local high school. Although Sharon feels that she knows something about their basic skills in reading and math, she does not understand other aspects of these students' lives. She decides to try to determine what life is like for these students. She is not interested in looking at various factors that might predict their poor performance; she feels that she knows some of this already. Rather, she wants to know what they are like as individuals. How is their life now, and how do they think it will be when they complete high school? I think this is an ideal situation to do a qualitative study from a feminist perspective. The students are available, she has access to them, and she hopes to empower them to take charge of their lives in a more meaningful manner.

6. Variety of Data in Natural Settings

Qualitative research typically involves studying things as they exist, rather than contriving artificial situations or experiments. So a qualitative researcher might be interested in looking at a particular classroom, rather than having a teacher change her classroom to see how something she does might affect how the students learn. I recall a student of mine who was interested in studying how kindergarten students develop formal and informal rules of conduct. She observed a class each day for several months. She also joined the class occasionally and participated in some of their activities. In these ways, she was able to learn how children established rules. She did not ask the teacher to change the way she was doing anything.

Natural settings are preferred when talking to people or observing them. Interviews can be conducted in the home or office of the participant, or by phone, or in cyberspace. **Observation** of the interaction of individuals in natural settings can be conducted in classrooms, in homes, in the school yard, or at a parent-teacher meeting. I had a student who observed an online chat room of middle school girls (Robbins, 2001). I have interviewed people in school libraries, at fast-food restaurants, online, and even in a custodian's closet.

Natural settings also are desirable when collecting other types of data, such as photographs, videos, or pictures created by the participants or of the environment in which the participants live or work. I have seen family portraits used as data. I have seen drawings made by children used as data. Notes taken by the researcher, either at the time of an observation or as soon thereafter as possible, are also data.

Here is an example of the use of a variety of data in a natural setting. Don was interested in studying teenagers away from their school setting. He decided that an excellent place to do this was at a local mall. He gathered his notebook and digital camera and set out for the mall. Of course, he had been there many times before and knew that teens often congregated at the food court. He bought a soda and settled down at a table near some teenagers. Because these teenagers were in a public place, he did not need to ask their permission. But he needed to be cautious about being observed himself, and he decided that he would be direct if anyone asked him what he was doing. He sat for about an hour and watched and listened. He took notes and used his camera. These data obtained in natural settings formed the basis for Don's study.

7. Role of the Researcher

The researcher plays a pivotal role in the qualitative research process. Data are collected, information is gathered, settings are viewed, and realities are constructed through his or her eyes and ears. Further, the qualitative researcher is responsible for analyzing the data through an iterative process that moves back and forth between data collected and data analyzed. And finally, the qualitative researcher interprets and makes sense of the data (Coffey & Atkinson, 1996). Quantitative researchers are more likely to select a statistic that is appropriate to the hypothesis being tested. Their role in the actual analysis is, therefore, limited. Of course, how they interpret the statistical data and how they organize and report it are critical.

I know I have said this before, but it is important to remember that the researcher is the primary instrument of data collection and analysis. Unlike doing an experimental study, in which scientific scales or measuring instruments are often used, when doing qualitative research the researcher decides what information to gather. All information is filtered through the researcher's eyes and ears and is influenced by his or her experience, knowledge, skill, and background. Most qualitative researchers acknowledge the dilemma of trying to be unbiased and objective. In fact, postmodernists, interpretivists, constructivists, and feminists acknowledge that the elusive objectivity often sought in traditional or scientific research is inappropriate in the qualitative research arena. They have come to believe that what exists out in the world can be understood as it is mediated through the one doing the observing. I want to be very clear about this idea. There is no "getting it right" because there could be many "rights." Descriptions, understandings, and interpretations are based on the data you collect and your ability to organize and integrate them to make a meaningful whole.

A **bias** is a preference that inhibits impartial judgment. Bias and qualitative research is a topic that challenges both students and their professors. One view is that bias can be eliminated, or at least controlled, by careful work, triangulation, and multiple sources. I do not believe this is true. Bias is a concept that is related to foundationalist, traditional, or postpositivist thinking. The position I take here is that striving for objectivity by reducing bias is not important for much of qualitative research. I think that some are reluctant to adopt a qualitative research approach because they think the researcher is biased. Well, of course, the researcher has views on the topic. After all, she probably would not be investigating a particular topic if she had not thought about the topic. There is no single or simple answer to this dilemma. I think the following viewpoint is instructive.

> The (social) sciences usually try to create the impression that the results of their research have *objective* character. In this view, scientific results are—or at least should be—independent from the person who produced the knowledge, e.g., from the single researcher. According to this perspective objectivity is what makes the difference between valid scientific knowledge and other outcomes of human endeavors and mind. On the one hand, there are many efforts to justify this perspective on epistemological and philosophical grounds. On the other hand, various practices are used to support and produce this idea of objectivity (a rather well-known and mundane example is the rhetorical strategy of avoiding the use of the first-person pronouns in scientific texts). In their everyday scientific life almost all (experienced) researchers nevertheless "know" about the impact of personal and situational influences on their research work and its results. "Officially" and in publications these influences are usually covered up— they are treated as defaults that are to be avoided. (Breuer et al., 2002, ¶ 1)

Researchers know that they influence the research and results. But some researchers, those who still hold on to a positivist or postpositivist position about objectivity, maintaining distance, and the need to reduce bias that Breuer and his colleagues (2002) cite above, try to identify ways to reduce the "subjectivity" of the qualitative researcher. There are several stances taken. Some qualitative researchers, who see themselves as phenomenologists, use a technique they call bracketing. I will talk more about this later, but for now, think of bracketing as trying to identify your views on the topic and then putting them aside. Other qualitative researchers take the view that they can verify their interpretations by having others look at the data and go through the same process. They refer to this process as *member checks* or *inter-rater reliability.* Other qualitative researchers take the view that if they collect data from multiple sources, they will have a more accurate picture and thus remain less biased. They refer to this as triangulation. At this point, you are probably beginning to question some of your basic assumptions about doing research. Can we really take an objective stance? Should we want to? Why should we want to?

8. In-Depth Study

Another critical element of qualitative research involves looking deeply at a few things rather than looking at the surface of many things. An important aspect of the investigation is to look at the whole rather than isolate variables in a reductionistic manner. If we want to understand something fully, we need to look at it much more completely. Some have said it is like opening up an artichoke and looking at the layers upon layers until you reach the core. There are often gems hidden deep inside, but there is a struggle along the way to get there.

So much of qualitative research involves studying and looking at a few individuals, sometimes just one person. The study of Jermaine (Hébert, 2001) illustrated this principle well. Hébert and his colleague spent a considerable amount of time in Jermaine's environment and collected documents, talked to others, and learned about him. Richardson (2008) studied Lord Esqy, and Wolcott (1973) studied a single principal. More often, however, qualitative researchers study individuals or groups who have similar characteristics. Glass (2001) studied families of autistic children. Repass (2002) studied professional women preparing to retire.

Others tend to study small groups as they interact with each other in a particular setting. Some of these groups may be highly structured and others loosely structured. Kidder (1989) studied a fifth-grade class. The number of individuals you study is not critical; rather, it is the nature of the study and the degree to which you explore complex in-depth phenomena that distinguishes qualitative research.

9. Words, Themes, and Writing

Words, rather than numbers, characterize qualitative research. Quite often, direct quotes from the participants are included to illustrate a certain point. Details are often included about those studied or the setting in which a study is conducted. Those who studied cultures, the ethnographers, took the position that **thick description**, a detailed description of a culture (Geertz, 1973; Ryle, 1949), is desirable in order to see underlying meanings and understandings. The idea of thick description has been adopted by many different kinds of qualitative researchers. You will often read details about the setting in which a study was conducted, how the participants looked, or even the nonverbal gestures used by respondents.

I suspect that almost any qualitative research study that you read will have used either interviews, observations, or both as a major source of data. But most of you think of data as numbers, not words. As you begin to think about any kind of qualitative research, try to remember that data do not have to be numbers; data can be words and visual representations as well. For example, Diane was studying women principals and how they dealt with issues of power. She interviewed 10 principals. She also observed them in their offices, at faculty meetings, and at school board meetings. In addition, she reviewed their written memos to faculty. It should be clear that she obtained her data from interviews, from observation, and by reviewing written material. The kind of data she collected were the principals' thoughts about interacting with superiors and subordinates, the observations she made of how the principals interacted with these two groups at meetings, general observations of the physical surroundings in which they worked, and written material provided by the principals. As you read the information in later chapters, you will find some differences in the kind of data that are collected by the various traditions. For example, ethnographers tend to spend more time immersed in the cultural environment, while phenomenologists are more likely to talk at length to participants. Contemporary ethnographers often study online culture, so the data they collect may come from e-mails or chat rooms.

Themes are developed from the data. All of the traditions and approaches eventually lead to your taking the large amount of data you collect and making sense of it. Grounded theory uses a structured approach to data analysis and offers specific steps to follow in order to organize and synthesize data. Most of the other approaches are very general in terms of how to make meaning from data. Computer software programs facilitate organizing, searching, combining, processing, and locating data. Unlike a statistical package, however, qualitative software requires your input and decision making.

Qualitative research is also characterized by a style of writing that is less technical and formal than is used in more traditional research. Additionally, qualitative researchers often write in the first person (Hamill, 1999; Intrator, 2000) or active voice. Such active voice often leads to greater trust and accountability and is more forceful. Intrator (2000) suggests several text devices writers can use to get the audience to trust the author and to show how description and interpretation are intertwined. Colyar (2008) believes that writing should be taught in qualitative research courses.

Rather than writing a report or an account as a vehicle for disseminating information, some avant-garde researchers take the output of qualitative research to a different level. They publish poetry (Weems, 2003), look at contemporary photographs or videos of significant events (Ratcliff, 2003; Robertson, 2003), or perform a dance (Blumenfeld-Jones, 1995). Moreira (2008b) presented a performance ethnography. Caulley (2008) urged us to write creative nonfiction using fiction techniques.

10. Nonlinear

We often think of traditional research as following a c
research question, conduct a review of the literature, gather d
clusions. The order is relatively fixed. In contrast, qualitative
nonlinear, with multiple beginning points. You could start
individual. You could begin with an observation about how
could begin with an interest in something you read. In add
the sequence of data collection followed by data analysis,
ferent approach. In qualitative research, the researcher m
ing/collection and data analysis, rather than in a linear fash...
Imagine that you are weaving back and forth between gathering data and an...,
contrast to what you would do if you were conducting an experimental study.

Here is an illustration of how Glass (2001) may have progressed through his study of families of
autistic children. He identified a number of families who fit the criterion of having an autistic child.
He scheduled his first appointment and visited the family in their home for one afternoon. Following
his visit, he transcribed the interview he conducted with the mother, recorded his observations of the
family, and began his journal. All data were entered into a database or a word processing program. He
subsequently imported these files into **NVivo** (a computer software program for storing, organizing,
and managing complex qualitative data) and began initial coding. He knew the codes were tentative
and served as guidelines. Next, he scheduled a visit with a second family. He refined his questions to
these new family members based on his initial coding and his thinking about what he had learned so
far. He went back to his journal and his observational record. He also returned to importing his data
into the software program, processed the second set of materials, and reviewed everything. This back
and forth nature of the process is what I mean by iterative and nonlinear.

■ Additional Issues

In addition to the 10 critical elements outlined above, I want to expose you to some other important and basic considerations. I don't want to confuse you with too much technical language, but
you need to be aware of important current issues. I want you to understand that what you read
here may have changed between the time I write and the time you read.

I have drawn much of my material from Lincoln and Guba (2000), who address a variety of
issues. I have included those I find to be critical, but you can read details of their thinking in their
chapter in the *Handbook of Qualitative Research*.

Objectivity as Fiction

If you have received any training in research methods, you will have been exposed to the
idea that research should be designed to yield objective and scientific evidence. This is a tenet
of positivist research.[3] In order to accomplish this, the positivists suggest that the researcher
needs to remain outside the system and strive to be objective. However, the postpositivist movement acknowledged that it is not possible for the researcher to be separate from the system or
society he is studying. Instead, objective reality is approximated rather than achieved. The
underlying assumption, however, is that if we had the correct tools, we could characterize our
reality objectively.

me of the subsets of qualitative research, such as **interpretivism** (a doctrine that empha-
analyzing meanings people confer on their own actions), constructivism, and critical theory,
cept that reality is virtual and is shaped by various forces. Further, findings are value-laden
rather than value-free. In **postmodernism** and poststructuralism, inquiry is value-determined.
Given these changes, I want you to begin to think about research in a new way, one that acknowledges the role of the researcher and his or her belief system. Objectivity should not be considered
bad; rather, it is just another way of thinking about how we gain knowledge and what knowledge
is. So, for now, try to open your mind to the idea that designing a study to provide data that is
objective and factual is not part of your goal. And you are to disabuse yourself of the need to be
sorry that you are not quite sufficiently objective.

Critical Role of the Researcher

Given what I have said above, you must know by now that the researcher's role is critical to qualitative research. She is the one who asks the questions. She is the one who conducts the analyses. She
is the one who decides who to study and what to study. The researcher is the conduit through which
information is gathered and filtered. It is imperative, then, that the researcher has experience and
understanding about the problem, the issues, and the procedures.

Role of Those Studied

Traditional research often refers to those studied as *subjects*. More recently, the term *participants* has been used. But whatever term is used, quantitative researchers tend to treat those they
study as anonymous objects to be measured and observed. In qualitative research, we refer to
individuals who provide information for the research as participants, informants,
or coresearchers. As such, those studied become the experts on the topic. Some qualitative
researchers think of them as co-investigators.

The Nature of Reality (Ontology)

Although Lincoln and Guba (2000) no longer included the term **ontology** as one of the key
issues, I think you will encounter it quite often. Ontology is concerned with what is real or the
nature of reality. Alternative paradigms take different views of what is real. A traditional scientific
paradigm (positivist) would accept an objective reality. A postpositivist view would accept that
reality can only be reached in an imperfect manner but nevertheless would anticipate a researcher
striving to reach it. Those espousing a critical theory paradigm consider historical realism, while
those who see themselves as constructivists speak of relativism and constructed realities.
Paradigms that are participatory speak of realities that are created by both the participants and
the researcher. So the nature of reality means different things to qualitative researchers.

Values and Ethics (Axiology)[4]

I would suggest that it is neither possible nor desirable for researchers to keep their values
from influencing aspects of the research study. I find some qualitative researchers apologizing
for their beliefs and talking about how they try to keep their beliefs out of a study. Both qualitative researchers and quantitative researchers operate within a certain belief system; however,
quantitative researchers strive for a position that is value-free rather than value-laden. A second

issue regarding values relates to the role of the research participants. As participants, what level of involvement can and should they have in the research and how do you protect them? I want you to think about these ideas. For the moment, suspend your judgment about the issue. However, be aware that it influences much that is new in qualitative research.

How Can Various Paradigms Accommodate Each Other?

Lincoln and Guba (2000) suggested that certain paradigms can accommodate each other, but that there are fundamental differences between positivist and other models and that "the axioms are contradictory and mutually exclusive" (p. 174). I think some examples might help you to understand this idea. If you accept a traditional scientific approach to research, you are looking for a single correct answer. It might be a statistical test that helps you decide whether or not to reject a null hypothesis. In traditional thinking, you either reject or fail to reject a hypothesis. While you might have a choice of which statistical test to use, you would accept the finding of the analysis.

In contrast, in a number of qualitative paradigms, you are looking for a way to understand and interpret the meaning of human interaction or human views. The information you receive, filtered through your own lens, is subject to a multitude of interpretations. There is no single interpretation that is better than another. You are not necessarily better at interpretation than someone else. Your faculty mentor is no better than you. Using a computer program does not make your interpretation more correct. So, because some paradigms look for a single right answer while others do not, some paradigms cannot accommodate the assumptions taken by others. But others see a way to handle quantitative and qualitative paradigms in the same study. B. Johnson and Christensen (2008) and Tashakkori and Teddlie (2003) spoke about a mixed methods approach, which uses elements from both qualitative and quantitative research.

What Role Does Action Play in Research?

Trained as a traditional researcher, you would take the position that action is not part of your responsibility. You do the work; someone else uses it.

> Action has become a major controversy that limns the ongoing debates among practitioners of the various paradigms. . . . The mandate for social action, especially action designed and created by and for research participants with the aid and cooperation of researchers, can be most sharply delineated between positivist/postpositivist and new-paradigm inquirers. (Lincoln & Guba, 2000, p. 175)

I suspect these are ideas new to many of you. I do not believe that you are required to do something with each piece of research you do, but perhaps you can at least think about why you are doing what you are doing and what you hope to do with the information.

Issues About Who Is in Control

Suffice it to say that traditional inquiry places control in the hands of the researcher. However, in some new paradigms, control issues are intertwined with **voice** (privileged position and self-disclosure), **reflexivity** (a researcher's capacity to reflect on his or her values), and textual representation. I agree with Lincoln and Guba (2000) when they say that "nowhere can the conversation about paradigm differences be more fertile than in the extended controversy about validity" (p. 178). You will read about this topic in greater detail in Chapter 13. At this point, I want you to be aware of the issues. What are the criteria for judging the worth of something? Who should set the criteria? Should there be any? How do the criteria differ or compare to those for traditional research? Is one way better than another? These are all issues being debated even as I write this book. There are three additional issues: voice, reflexivity, and postmodern textual representation. Researchers who adopted new paradigms became aware of how critical it was to have informants speak in their own voice. Most of you are familiar with reading quotes from participants. Some of the newer avenues for voice are in the form of plays or town meetings. Reflexivity can be many things about the self. You are the researcher as well as the learner. You might change the experience or be changed by it. Ultimately, you come to know yourself. How we represent what we learn and know is also at issue.

Self-Reflection

Qualitative researchers often include a section on **self-reflection** to indicate their awareness of self and their influence on the research process: How have my background, concerns, and interests affected the project at its various stages? How might somebody else have gone about it? For example, what questions might he or she have asked? How might he or she have interpreted these passages differently? How have I changed as a consequence of learning about others? This self-reflection can be carried out to varying degrees. You may use it to assure yourself as a quality control indicator for a particular interview, or you may wish to modify parts of your write-up in light of it. You may even wish to document this self-reflection as a section in the written report, that is, as an account of your own part in the construction of the project and its results.

Breuer et al. (2002) devoted two issues of an online journal to the topic of subjectivity and reflexivity. Such issues as the construction of a narratory self (Day, 2002), or the way in which a hermeneutic procedure for interpreting narratives helps us understand real psychological meanings (Ratner, 2002), or the postmodern view that subjectivity is assumed and appreciated (Russell & Kelly, 2002) point to the view that not only do subjectivity and reflexivity exist in qualitative research, but they also should be there.

Challenge of Doing Qualitative Research

I have heard some people say that doing qualitative research is appealing because you don't have to deal with numbers, statistics, and tables. But often, I believe, the lack of rules, the vast amounts of data to process, and the tasks of writing are baffling to some. If you are uncomfortable with ambiguity, have difficulty putting words on paper, and need high structure, you might find qualitative research frustrating.

You no doubt might also find yourself keeping a journal, engaging in self-reflection, writing extensive notes, taking videos or photographs, filling your kitchen table with note cards and colored pencils, learning how to store and retrieve information on your personal computer, learning how to access chat rooms and download conversations, writing drafts of your project, meeting with your faculty advisers, commiserating with fellow students, ignoring your family and social life, feeling the joys and hardships of your participants, and traveling on a journey of growth, frustration, and accomplishment.

■ Summary

Although there is not a consensus on the definition of qualitative research, in this chapter, I provided a working definition. Examples revealed that qualitative research deals with questions about how and why; involves extended data collection (usually including observation or interviews); requires the researcher to organize data using coding, themes, or other tools; and engages the researcher in interpreting the meaning of the data.

Ten critical elements of qualitative research were introduced: it involves description, understanding, and interpretation; it is dynamic; different methods may be employed in conducting qualitative research; it involves an inductive approach; it is holistic, viewing the situation in its entirety; data is typically gathered in natural settings; the researcher is instrumental in constructing an interpretation of reality; limited phenomena are studied in depth; reporting is characterized by thick description, often using the words of participants; and qualitative research frequently proceeds in a nonlinear fashion.

GROUP ACTIVITY

Purpose: To become familiar with critical elements of qualitative research.

Activity: During the first or second week of class, select a partner and choose one idea from the "Ten Critical Elements" listed above. Discuss how this element might be contrasted with an element from traditional research. Write a one-paragraph summary of your ideas and present it to the class.

Evaluation: Determine to what extent students are able to compare ideas about qualitative research with those of traditional quantitative research.

INDIVIDUAL ACTIVITY

Purpose: To involve students in thinking about qualitative research and recording their thoughts and ideas.

Activity: Begin your journal, either in a notebook or on the computer. The advantage of a notebook is that you can write anytime. The advantage of the computer is that your ideas are already in the computer and you will be able to share with others. Throughout the semester, continue making journal entries.

Evaluation: This activity models the dynamic and iterative nature of qualitative research. Students can review it to determine how their ideas progress over time.

Instructor's Note: One activity I have used in a semester class is to import journal entries from each student into a computer software program, such as NVivo, and then use those data to practice coding, forming nodes, and identifying themes.

■ Notes

1. One exception is a type of qualitative research called *grounded theory,* in which hypotheses may emerge from the study.

2. *Symbolic interaction* refers to the nature of the interaction between humans. Interpretation of the interaction is based on the meaning attached to actions. With humans, actions are mediated through symbols.

3. Rusu-Toderean (n.d.) provided a detailed background of the various movements, beginning with Comte's positivism up to the positivism of the 1950s and 1960s that dominated social science research.

4. **Axiology** is a branch of philosophy that deals with values and judgments; the term comes from the Greek word *axios,* meaning worth.

Chapter 2

Insights From the Past

FOCUS YOUR READING

- Early teacher preparation was for women and was based on models from the French.

- The scientific method was predominant in educational research until the 1980s.

- Other voices and approaches have expanded the field.

- Qualitative research has a place as a viable alternative.

- Many research approaches can coexist, although a vocal group still believes that experimental research represents the "gold standard."

A work of art must balance three elements: Does it understand the past? Does it elucidate the present? Does it reflect a personal vision?

—Jake Biddington

I was a bit naïve when I started my doctoral degree journey. I thought the most difficult part would be to complete the course work, rather than the dissertation. I was wrong. As a full-time researcher for more than 20 years, I thought I had the skills to accomplish the task. However, the process was long. It took one and a half years to complete my dissertation. The process taught me a systematic way of thinking about the research question, having a focus, deciding on a research method, and sticking to it. Also, I learned that different audiences (in this case, committee members) may perceive the same research question differently depending on their backgrounds and expertise. Consequently, the research direction(s) might be impacted by that perception. Therefore, I learned that clear communication to the audience about the purpose of the research is vital.

—Gohar Farahani

In this chapter, I set the stage for the field of qualitative research. I begin with a discussion of educational research in general. Then, I include a history of how the field of qualitative research developed. Emphasis is on the last century and, in particular, on the burgeoning growth and changes in the field since the 1980s.

The education of teachers in the United States began with teacher training offered by normal schools designed to teach young women how to work with children of elementary school age.[1] The first state-supported normal school was opened in Massachusetts in 1839. These individuals received training in child development and pedagogy. Universities were not involved in teacher training until around the turn of the 20th century. The first schools of education were developed at New York University and Columbia University in 1887; Teachers College at Columbia granted its first PhD in 1899 and the first EdD in 1935.

In addition to offering training in child development, these new programs began to expand their curriculum. The faculty knew that for the university to grant higher degrees, students needed to conduct original research, as was required in other disciplines. The universities were faced with a challenge. How should they prepare their students to conduct research? In what ways should the research be designed? You might think that there were numerous ways open to those planning the programs; no doubt there were. But the times dictated that the most desirable approach to conducting research was that used by the natural sciences. I think it is helpful for you to remember that although the students were almost exclusively female, those who planned the programs were almost exclusively male. These male-dominated departments operated under the assumption that they knew best. And for many years, women had no power in the academy. Lagemann's (2000) excellent historical account will help you see some of the issues more clearly. She suggests that the entire field was marginalized and seen as second class. Her reason: It was women's work.

From the scientific movement and testing that began in the 1920s, educational research adopted a stance that was scientific, objective, and rigorous. Breuer et al. (2002) remind us that "the (social) sciences usually try to create the impression that the results of their research have objective character" (¶ 1). There was little room for other disciplines that seemed to be "soft" or "subjective." Thus, anthropology, sociology (unless it was statistical), phenomenology, or other approaches to answering questions were seen as somewhat lesser. These would not be approaches that could be used to answer important questions in education or to provide us with pure factual information. At least until the 1980s, it was accepted practice to conduct educational research using the scientific method. Experimental designs and statistics were emphasized. Hypothesis testing was expected. Objectivity and rigor were considered critical. Men who valued the approach of the natural sciences dominated the field. I think this subservient position in which women found themselves resulted in their accepting what was being done to and for them. I know that was true for me.

The best source of documentation for this early period is the *Review of Educational Research,* a journal from the American Educational Research Association summarizing published research. The foreword of the first issue, published in 1931, tells the story clearly: "This is the first number of the *Review of Educational Research.* . . . The following review of the scientific work in the field of curriculum illustrates the method that will be followed in the entire series" (Foreword, p. 2). It goes on to say that the review will be restricted to all the scientific studies related to the topic. The first issue was devoted to research on curriculum, of which there was a large amount of available work. What is quite fascinating about this issue is that there are no authors noted. The reviews are written as though they are part of a book. For example, "Chapter II: Investigations of the Objectives of a Curriculum" (1931) is 11 pages long. It includes 116 references. The foreword indicates that the Editorial Committee (chaired by Frank N. Freeman) prepared the review.[2] The second issue (March, 1931) was devoted to issues related to teachers. The Table of Contents for that issue could just as easily have been written today. Issues include supply and demand, preparation, salaries, load, tenure, and legal status. In fact, the only topic that surprised me was the article on the health of teachers. The September 1931 issue is devoted to research on different disciplines, such as the teaching of reading, handwriting, and spelling. I strongly encourage you to take some time to look at these early reviews of research because you can get a clear sense of the type of research that was valued and encouraged during the early 20th century. If you are able to obtain access through your library, you can find the full text of all issues by going to the *Review of Educational Research* Web site (http://rer.sagepub.com/).

Did You Know

More than 90% of elementary school teachers are women. Of the three million teachers in the United States, only 25% are men. Educational research departments and professional organizations used to be dominated by men. Today, this is no longer the case; women play a major role.

I can remember back in my graduate school days (in the mid-1960s) I was a firm believer in a traditionalist viewpoint. I did not question why; I seemed to just follow along. I never really thought about whether white men dominated the field. What did I know? I was learning but not really questioning. It seemed like a status thing to me. If we could get the "real" or "true" data, we could find the answers. This view was fueled by the increasing availability of computer programs and advanced statistical techniques: More numbers meant better answers. I have to say that I bought into this completely. Now, I ask myself what I was thinking, but then, things were really different.

The emphasis on the scientific method persisted for decades. However, by the 1980s, the scientific method was no longer considered to be the only way to conduct research. Other voices began to be heard. Women were crying out for an opportunity to influence what was studied and what methods were being used. It had taken some 80 years for women to question why; anthropologists, phenomenologists, and others wanted their views heard. In the sections that follow, I discuss these changes in greater depth.

■ Educational Research Prior to the 1980s

Imagine that it is 100 years ago and you are working as a teacher. Because women are excluded from preparatory schools, education at a normal school is the only form of advanced education you can receive. In normal schools, the study of child development is emphasized, and the curriculum does not include anything about research. You have just barely completed your own education.

You are probably unmarried. Your primary focus is on trying to get your little charges to learn. While you have studied how children develop, you really don't know much about how to teach reading, spelling, or math. You probably do not know how to answer questions in a formal or scientific manner, but you may have thought of some questions you could explore. What is the best way to teach spelling? Should you have your students memorize words and then recite them back? You could design a simple study comparing two different ways of teaching spelling and see which way students learn better. If you did something like this, you would have designed a simple experimental research study. If you are studying at an advanced level, you might submit a study like this in order to obtain your degree. Colleges are just beginning to develop programs to prepare people like you. They know they need to add the study of research methods to the curriculum and define the questions to ask about schools. However, they are not considering the needs of teachers when they plan the curriculum. Instead, administrators in charge of the school systems determine what questions are raised.

Two factors influenced the way in which educational research developed in higher education. First, teacher training moved from normal schools to colleges and universities. Second, graduate degree programs were developed. Additional courses were needed, and questions were asked about how students learned, what curricula should be offered, and how teachers should be evaluated. The colleges needed to develop a curriculum that would incorporate research methods so that students could be prepared to design and conduct their own research.

I suspect that there was not too much discussion about what research paradigm to use because the scientific method favored by the natural sciences was seen as the highest form of research. Educators were quick to follow in the footsteps of the disciplines that were considered more rigorous. Thus, they were strongly influenced by psychology and the testing movement, which, too, had adopted the scientific method. Many of these early educators came from the field of educational psychology. You might be familiar with some of the leaders. G. Stanley Hall (1844–1924) was the first president of the American Psychological Association and a founder of *The American Journal of Psychology*. As president of Clark University, he was instrumental in bringing Freud to Clark in 1909 for a series of seminal lectures. John Dewey (1859–1952) was also a psychologist and educational reformer. He came to the University of Chicago in 1894, where he founded the Laboratory Schools, but he left some 10 years later for Columbia. I know you could identify many other prominent men, most of whom trained as psychologists, who provided the backbone of our schools of education.

I think it is interesting that in these early years, there was some collaboration between school administrators and professors. Topics of interest generally were developed from the needs and concerns of the schools. As I studied this early literature, I came across one topic that both groups found important. Given that there were so many small high schools, the question on the minds of some was the adequacy of the education small high schools offered. Administrators, principals, and teachers were concerned that students were not receiving proper training to enter college. One idea was to offer students correspondence courses through universities, which raised the following question: Do students who take correspondence courses learn at the same level as those exposed to regular classes? If the answer was yes, then educators could close small schools without jeopardizing students.

One of the first dissertations was written by Rufi in 1926. He wrote on the inadequacy of the small high school. Influenced by his findings, Wooden and Mort (1929) conducted a study of supervised correspondence study for high school pupils. Wooden was a superintendent of schools, and Mort was a professor of education at Columbia. Wooden and Mort took a real problem that had surfaced in other research and attempted to conduct a systematic investigation. By today's standards, one might say that their study did not constitute experimental research: It is basically a description of how a small high school can make course material available to its students. But I think this study is important for two reasons. It demonstrates that school and university people worked together in the early years on problems of common interest. Second, it shows that decisions in education can be based on systematic investigation and study.

Very little of this early research was experimental in nature, although Crump (1928) wrote about correspondence and class extension work in Oklahoma for his doctoral research at Teachers College. He concluded that there were no significant differences between those studying in regular classrooms and those who studied by correspondence. This is one of the earliest experimental research studies conducted in the United States. On a national scale, one of the first major educational studies was begun in 1930. It involved 30 secondary schools and 300 colleges. Known as the Eight-Year Study, it was designed to examine how high schools prepared students for college. It was led by Ralph Tyler (1902–1994), who was considered one of the strongest advocates of the scientific study of education. Unfortunately, World War II minimized the impact of the study. Tyler (who received his PhD in educational psychology) left Ohio State to return to the University of Chicago. where he became head of the Department of Education and then the Division of Social Sciences.

It is somewhat surprising to me that the Department of Sociology at the University of Chicago did not have a stronger influence on the research methods adopted by other colleges. It was the first sociology department established in the United States. Its approach to sociology, which became known as the Chicago School, was popular from the end of the Depression until about the end of the 1950s. The Chicago School was a reaction to sociology departments elsewhere, which were more subjective. While the concerns of the Chicago School were related to urban growth and decay, crime, and the family, the methods were more formal and systematic. I see the Chicago School as a combination of qualitative and quantitative approaches: qualitative in that data were collected in the field, but quantitative in that methods were formal and scientific. One member of what is known as the second generation of the Chicago School was Anselm Strauss, who, you will learn later, was a proponent of an approach called grounded theory.

These sociologists emphasized going into the field and collecting data about life in the city. Because there were so many immigrants to the United States during the early years of the 20th century, these scholars became vitally interested in studying their behaviors. They relied on in-depth interviews and life histories. I know firsthand about various immigrant groups, such as the Polish, because I grew up in Chicago.[3] Chicago was one of the great cities, with immigrant populations who lived in virtual ghettos throughout the city. To this day, you can find many ethnic restaurants reflecting these groups.

I suspect that you can find other studies from this period that address problems facing the schools. But you need to remember that very few educators were trained to design and conduct research; the majority of the professors were trained as psychologists or measurement specialists. Again, I want to stress how important the scientific movement and scientific thinking were to this newly emerging discipline of education. Educators adopted the method of science as a method that was suitable to the study of education. After all, this method had been used by psychologists such as B. F. Skinner, who contributed so much to our thinking about teaching and learning. Although Skinner studied rats and pigeons, his conclusions were widely applied to teaching. He was a behaviorist and believed that children could be conditioned to learn a certain way through operant conditioning.[4] You may not be aware that one of Skinner's first books on how organisms behave became the model for experimental research. As recently as 2001, Bissell suggested that the theoretical constructs and experimental results presented by Skinner had a critical influence on education and teaching. Today, almost no undergraduate student in education is exposed to research design and practice. Many graduate students receive a research methods course, but overwhelmingly the emphasis is on traditional research paradigms. Increasingly, these courses are expanding to include work in qualitative research methods.

I planned to provide the names of the leaders and innovators who became synonymous with educational research. This turned into a much more difficult task than I had envisioned. Although I wanted to tell you who the father of educational research was, I was not able to find anyone who was clearly acknowledged as such. As I said earlier, I think that is because much of research was intertwined with measurement and psychology. If you are interested, you can read about the father of modern testing, of the testing movement, of creativity, and of educational psychology.[5] I think it would be fair to conclude that the discipline of educational research developed after universities became involved in advanced training of those going into education.

Psychology and the testing movement played a pivotal role in guiding what should be studied and how it should be studied. The field was completely dominated by men, and the scientific movement was the preferred, if not the only, mode of investigation. As more universities developed doctoral programs in education, this view permeated approaches to the conduct of research and training of researchers. Few women studied research methods or made contributions to the field.[6]

You cannot ignore the impact of World War II. Thousands of men inducted into the military needed to be tested, and test development became highly specialized. Educators addressed these issues. By the 1950s, the era of Sputnik, American educators moved even more rapidly into a scientific stance. Federal funding for research in the 1960s also encouraged and stressed scientific approaches to the field of research. The widespread use of computers by the 1970s enabled advanced statistical analyses to be conducted, which also reinforced this scientific bent. So you should not be surprised that there was little room for a discipline that seemed antithetical to what so many believed.

The application of ethnographic methods to the study of educational topics has existed for some time. In my experience, however, these studies were conducted by anthropologists trained as ethnographers who found their way to a study of education, rather than by educational researchers who were steeped in the traditions of the scientific method. In many universities, educational ethnographers were not in departments of educational research, whose domain was statistics and experimental design. Yon (2003) reviews the growth of educational ethnography as a subset of anthropology.

I do not think there was just one event that led researchers to move beyond the positivism and postpositivism that pervaded the field. One attempt to open the field to new ideas was the establishment of the *Review of Research in Education.* As you read the account, you will see that they were not entirely successful because they still held many of the assumptions of the scientific method. Kerlinger, a major educational researcher, introduced the *Review of Research in Education* (not to be confused with the *Review of Educational Research,* about which I wrote earlier) in 1973. According to his stated goal, this journal was trying to open things up somewhat. They wanted to survey "disciplined inquiry" in education through critical and synthesizing essays. He acknowledged that they wanted to look at theory in other fields in the behavioral sciences (e.g., sociology, psychology, anthropology). On the one hand, he said they wanted to take a critical look at education. And while he stated they were not focused on "exclusively empirical research" and that they wanted to be open to different approaches, in almost the next sentence he contradicted himself and commented that the primary emphasis would be on the empirical evidence in the scientific tradition. And then again he repeated they wanted to encourage going beyond the scientific and empirical (Kerlinger, 1973, p. v). Yes. You read this correctly. We value the scientific and empirical, but perhaps we know that we really need to go beyond it, but we still value it. I am so disappointed to reread these words by a leader in the field of behavioral science. Who are the contributors to this first issue? All the favored men in the field. Perhaps I shouldn't be surprised, but here they all are. By 1976, Kerlinger was no longer the editor, but the style remained consistent. I think this new journal was trying to open up the educational field somewhat. But old habits die hard, and getting rid of the scientific aspect of research was not something that Kerlinger would have been able to do.[7]

Qualitative research as a field did not exist in education until the 1980s. In 1985, the Qualitative Interest Group (QUIG) at the University of Georgia was the first group devoted primarily to qualitative research. The annual conference began in 1988 and the listserv in 1991. QUIG is very active today. As I mentioned, prior to that time educational research was guided by research from the natural sciences. Students learned experimental design and statistics. Faculty wrote articles that were of an experimental nature. Sometimes surveys were conducted, but because they were not about hypothesis testing and generalizing, they were not seen to be as high quality as those that were experimental. Students across the country were trained to conduct scientific experiments and to think about hypothesis testing and generalization. The professional organizations, like the American Educational Research Association (founded in 1916), did not have a special interest group that was interested in qualitative research. Little was available in terms of textbooks or printed material. Most publishers were not interested in publishing books about qualitative research.

I do not mean to suggest that there was no research that could be characterized as qualitative prior to the 1980s. Ethnographies became popular. Some researchers came to the field of education from anthropology and began to conduct ethnographies in schools and classrooms. Although these ethnographies were often on topics of interest to educators, few were specifically about education.[8] Ethnographers tended to study entire cultures and immerse themselves in the topic for extended periods. Even in 1982, Fetterman reminded us that ethnography has been misunderstood and misused in education. As an adaptation and recognition of the difficulties of conducting such ethnographies, some researchers adopted a case study approach. Thus, by looking at a smaller part of an entire culture, an ethnographic stance could be adopted yet made manageable. Denny (1978) suggested that this kind of case study in education was growing in popularity.

While Bogdan and Biklen (1992) agreed that the dominant research paradigm was hypothesis testing and measurement, they acknowledge that prior to 1980, there were other traditions that influenced the development of research methods in education. Denzin and Lincoln (2000) characterized the period from the early 1900s until the end of World War II as a traditional period. They said that those individuals who were conducting qualitative research wrote "objective" accounts and were practicing in a positivist mode. In spite of these modest attempts to introduce alternative research approaches, they did not catch on to any great extent, and the field continued to be dominated by the traditional paradigm.[9]

Denzin and Lincoln (2000) spoke about how the "modernist ethnographer and sociological participant observer attempted rigorous qualitative studies of important social processes" (p. 14).

Bogdan and Biklen (1992) suggested that although not in a central position, methods that were labeled qualitative could no longer be considered fringe efforts. And Denzin and Lincoln (2000) spoke of the "golden age" of rigorous qualitative analysis. As I see it, qualitative research until the late 1980s was striving to fit into a traditional, quantitative paradigm. I am not sure that they actually recognized that they were trying to put a square peg into a round hole. I would disagree with the view offered by some that qualitative approaches mushroomed in education. Eisner and Peshkin (1990) echo my sentiments: "To conduct experiments and surveys was to be scientific; to do otherwise . . . was to be soft-, wrong- or muddle-headed" (p. 1). In my experience, those who were involved in qualitative research were often discounted and seen as soft or aberrant. I remember one colleague who asked me whether I had lost my mind when I said I was interested in qualitative research methods.

■ The 1980s to 2000

By the 1980s, many more people were being trained as educational researchers. Some were beginning to question the dominant traditional paradigms of experimental research and hypothesis testing. Ethnographers were increasingly making their presence felt in the field of education. Rist (1980) wrote of blitzkrieg ethnography: the transformation of a method into a movement. However, many researchers equated qualitative and ethnographic.[10] By the middle of the 1980s, approaches other than ethnography began to take hold in the educational community.

It was no longer sufficient to say that qualitative research was the same as doing ethnography or a modified ethnography/case study. The idea of doing research in a naturalistic setting began to surface (Custer, 1996; Lincoln & Guba, 1985), although, as Custer acknowledged, it was by no means accepted as a better alternative to traditional work. Voices of feminists began to be heard as well (Harding, 1987; Reinharz, 1992; Roman & Apple, 1990).

This was a time when researchers tried to clarify what research approaches to take and how to legitimize their alternative ways of thinking, and the road was somewhat rocky. I agree with Eisner and Peshkin (1990) when they stated, "There were no accepted models to which educational researchers with a qualitative bent could turn for direction" (p. 1). Crabtree and Miller (1992) concurred: "No prepackaged designs exist from which to choose" (p. xiv).

Denzin and Lincoln (2000) saw this period as a time of blurred genres. It seemed as though almost anything fit. They acknowledged that the "naturalistic, postpositivist, and constructionist" paradigms gained power during this period. They spoke about the crisis of representation during the mid-1980s and suggested that in the 1990s, "the ethnographer's authority remains under assault" (p. 17). Yon (2003) mapped the transition from modernist formulations of the field in its formative days, when ethnographies laid claim to being sealed and scientific texts, to the more recent formulations shaped by postmodern and poststructural ideas that undermine earlier meanings of culture and call attention to the explanatory limits of ethnography.

According to B. Campbell (n.d.),

the research paradigm shift has to do with major shifts in the way knowledge is constructed and created. Associated with this is the further question of whose interests are served by the dominant paradigm? Research has been dominated in the last hundred years or more by what is commonly known as the scientific method. Also known as positivist or quantitative research, its emphasis is on objectivity, neutrality, measurement, and validity. To live in the scientific method means to live within an understanding of the beliefs, values, and techniques that guide scientific inquiry (Lather, 1991). Those working within the scientific framework also accept the conventions, language, and methods of carrying out research in this way. Those living within the scientific paradigm judge other ways of carrying out investigations as too open to multiple interpretations, too biased, too subjective, simply not scientific or rigorous enough. (¶ 5)

Denzin and Lincoln (2000) characterized this latter period as a time of crisis. One crisis is what they refer to as the representational crisis. They questioned the assumption that qualitative researchers can capture lived experience. They argued that such experience is created in the "social text written by the researcher" (p. 17). For them, this is the crisis of representation. The other crisis they posed is the question of legitimation. They commented that traditional criteria for evaluating and interpreting qualitative research need to be rethought. They also briefly mentioned new ways of writing and representing information. They acknowledged that "fictional ethnographies, ethnographic poetry, and multimedia texts are today taken for granted" (p. 17).

At the end of the 100 years or so during which education training moved from being dominated by the training of women teachers, through the adoption of the scientific method to lend an air of legitimacy to research, to a questioning of traditional approaches, educational researchers and those who describe themselves as qualitative researchers find themselves in somewhat of a dilemma. No longer are the rules clear. No longer can they feel secure in how to conduct research. No longer do they know how to evaluate research. They have opened themselves to new ideas, to new paradigms, to new ways of thinking, and to the creativity of those who follow.

■ 2000 and Beyond

As I write this book in 2008, I find myself wondering what I should tell you about the state of qualitative research today. I recognize that by the time you read this material, "today" may be quite different from what we know now. This is interesting because for many years, educational research was fairly predictable and consistent. We knew what to do and how to do it. And now, I am not sure what we know except that we don't agree on what to do and how to do it. In Chapter 14, you will be exposed to the very latest thinking on the topic.

Things have flipped 180 degrees in a very short time. It has become almost impossible to keep up with the writing and publishing in the field. No longer is qualitative research dominated by the anthropologists and ethnographers. Many disciplines and subdisciplines inform the field. Creswell (2007) singled out five approaches to discuss, although he acknowledges others as well. B. Johnson and Christensen (2008) emphasized also looking at a mixed methods approach, in which elements of both qualitative and quantitative research are combined to enlarge an investigation. Merriam (2002) and Patton (2002) also acknowledged various approaches and methodologies. Denzin and Lincoln's *Handbook of Qualitative Research,* first published in 1994, added other ideas. The second edition of the *Handbook,* issued in 2000, introduced still more ideas, and the third edition, published in 2005, expanded our horizons even further. Now it seems that almost anything can be labeled qualitative research. I talk later about how this is confusing for you as a student and how you can begin to make judgments about which way works for you.

■ Speculations for the Future

I have been in the field for a long time. I have seen many things become popular. Education is a discipline replete with fads. We tend to react to and are often driven by forces beyond our immediate range. I suspect this will be true for qualitative research as well, but here are some trends that I see.

Greater Diversity and Creativity. This new millennium will be a time for greater diversity and creativity in answering questions about human interaction and in representing information. The doors have been opened, and I believe we will see creativity unlike anything we can imagine. I know the art and music worlds have gone in directions we could not expect. Why not the world of research and education?

I think we have just begun to scratch the surface in terms of our thinking about how research will be done and who will be doing it. The field has opened up dramatically since the 1980s. Women have taken leadership roles in all aspects of the profession. I remember clearly the mid-1970s, when I was interviewed for a position at a university in a department of educational research. The chairman of the search committee said he was especially pleased that I was a woman; I would be joining a department of almost a dozen men. Today, that department is almost exclusively women. People of color have made contributions to the field and heightened awareness of issues. These voices were not heard in the past; now they are a force.

How research will be done and how it will be transmitted will continue to be examined. Representations will not be strictly textual. I hope we will move more toward the visual because it is well known that so many gain their information through television, the Internet, social networks, DVDs, and other visual media. I wonder why we think it is important to convey our information solely through words and traditional text?

Greater Access and Availability. The revolution of the Internet has affected all aspects of our lives. Instantaneous communication around the world is now available to almost everyone. One way this will continue to affect qualitative research is to make information readily available through online journals and discussion groups. No longer do we have to wait until a journal is published in hard copy. This means what you read is current, not a year old or more. Another fact of instant worldwide communication is worldwide influence. In 2005, when I wrote the first edition, I commented that the United States or Europe would no longer be the driving force from which our ideas about research would come. I suggested that we would see new ideas from Asia, Africa, and South America. We certainly have seen China emerging in many arenas. They now are a force in the contemporary art world; perhaps they will become so in the world of qualitative research.

More Voices Heard. Educational research began with voices of men. They were remote, objective, and scientific. You may know that research in the medical field began the same way. In fact, in medicine, much of the research was done on white men (usually doctors) and extrapolated to other groups. Once women became a greater force, both men and women began to design studies and conduct them on women. The qualitative research field has opened up to many voices. But, although we have a greater representation of women and minorities than ever before, we still hear from those with more education and traditional schooling. Because much research emanates from universities—either by professors or by students—this is not surprising. But I wonder if there is not a way to include a broader perspective of education and experience in the planning and design of our research. I predict that this will be so and in ways we can't now imagine.

Creative Flow That Does Not Follow Any One Pattern. If we look at the field of art, we have seen a variety of movements since the center of art moved from Paris to New York. Just as in research, men initially dominated the art world. Now we see women and minorities making enormous contributions. Their creative ideas are astounding. In 2004, for example, I visited an exhibit at the Saatchi Gallery in London of Richard Wilson's *20:50,* which is an installation of a lake of sump oil that reflects the ceiling and completely disorients the viewer. It was quite fantastic. Some would probably say this is not art, but I do not agree. Installation art is not new, but reusing oil probably is. In 2007, I visited *Art 38 Basel* in Switzerland. I saw William Hunt immersed in a car full of water. He was surrounded by dozens of people. When he emerged from the open top, he made some comments about his experience (see the YouTube video at http://www.youtube.com/watch?v=Wqf96VznMeU). I am not sure I know what it meant, but it made a distinct impression on me.

What else can we expect of qualitative researchers? We have performance art, dance, play reading, and blogs. I believe that multimedia will be used to a much greater extent. Chenail speaks about a research park similar to Disneyland (Lichtman, 2004). Without rules and restrictions, who knows where we will go?

Is It Good Enough? As researchers grapple with what qualitative research is, what it should be, how it should be done, and what it should look like, I suspect we might see conservatives moving to more traditional approaches. These were my comments in 2005. In 2008, I am afraid my speculation has come true. The conservative movement in education has stressed accountability and proof through quantifiable test scores. They have moved toward randomized control group studies. Some will ask what the rules are and will begin to set rules that will follow a traditional paradigm. Davis (2002), in an editorial in the *Journal of Curriculum and Supervision,* spoke about the future of educational research:

> It seeks new ends, for example, reliable research conclusions, causal relationships, and replicable "best practices." At first blush, its aim appears to represent a political "back to the future" policy in which a "new educational scientism" will flourish. This educational research policy, however, differs profoundly from the multiple approaches, even the "scientific" rationale, used by researchers during most of the 20th century. In the past, educational researchers adopted and shifted their research paradigms and techniques on the bases of scholarly exposition, demonstration, and persuasion. In the current scene, on the other hand, bureaucratic mandates supersede the reasonableness of research options. (p. 175)

From Davis' viewpoint, bureaucracy and politics take a more prominent role in determining research agendas. I, for one, hope he is in error.

A related issue is a concern by some that qualitative research will not be taken seriously because the rules are not hard and fast and therefore it is difficult to judge what is "good" or of high "quality." I think there will still be those who are of this view.

Keeping Up With the Explosion. Information access and retrieval is a challenging pursuit. I suspect that by the time you read this book, you will be able to access an enormous amount of material on the Internet. Some of it will be scholarly; some of it will be personal and specific to an individual. I don't hold to the admonition that the only good material needs to be peer-reviewed. I know there are politics that affect much of what we hear and say and of what gets printed. It will be your challenge to locate information, judge its merit, and integrate it with what you already know. This will be a greater challenge than ever before because the Internet makes so much material instantly available and retrievable. This is true for you and for the students you might teach and for their parents. Ten years ago, Denzin and Lincoln (1994) wrote about the concept of the qualitative researcher as a *bricoleur,* a French term that suggests someone who has the tools to get the job done. According to McLeod (2000), a bricoleur's image is a tension between creativity and conformity. He saw creativity as one of the core characteristics of a good qualitative researcher. How the new qualitative researcher will be creative is a matter of speculation. I believe we will continue to see creativity and resourcefulness, and those characteristics will overcome the need by some to move into a more traditional and conservative posture.

■ Summary

In this chapter, I traced the early development of educational research and the transition of teacher preparation in normal schools to colleges and universities. Universities needed to include research in the curriculum, so they borrowed from other disciplines, especially psychology and its research paradigm based on the scientific approach. Early 20th-century research often involved school/university efforts to address issues of practical concern and borrowed **methodology**, or research techniques, from psychology and related fields. Consequently, research using qualitative approaches was often viewed as soft or inferior.

Conceptions of research in education opened up in the 1970s, and by the 1980s, qualitative research in education emerged as a separate field. Originally based primarily on case study and ethnography, approaches to qualitative research now incorporate multiple approaches. Because of this, there remain diverse views of exactly what to do and how to do it among qualitative researchers. I concluded the chapter with several likely trends for the future.

■

GROUP ACTIVITY

Purpose: To identify the latest trends in the field.

Activity: Join a team of two other students. Identify possible new trends—I suggest many will involve technology and the Internet. Prepare a one-page synopsis of what you think you know about the topic. Now you are going to find out what else is out there. Use a search engine (e.g., Google) to search the Internet. Allow at least two hours for your search. Save your information in a word processing program and be prepared to send it to your teammates. You may engage in a discussion via e-mail before your next class meeting. Prepare a summary to send to each other and to other class members.

Evaluation: Determine whether you have located new information that supports, adds to, or contradicts what you know so far.

■

INDIVIDUAL ACTIVITY

Purpose: To examine your views on the appropriateness of qualitative research as a tool for answering questions in education.

Activity: This is a self-reflexive, introspective activity in which you will write in your qualitative research journal. The topic to think about is how you view the field based on what you know so far and how it fits with your belief system.

Evaluation: Determine to what extent you are able to examine your motivations and thoughts. Decide what additional information you need to obtain a clearer understanding.

■ Notes

1. The term *normal* is used because the schools were designed to establish standards or norms. These schools in the United States were modeled on the French Écoles Normale. The town of Normal, Illinois, founded in 1865, was so named in order to attract money from the state to build a normal school there. Eventually, normal schools disappeared, and the task of educating teachers was taken over by colleges and universities. The town of Normal, Illinois, still exists, however.

2. One of the first references I found to Freeman (1880–1961) is a book review he published in 1922 in the *Journal of Educational Research* (published by the American Educational Research Association). Freeman was at the University of Chicago. He was trained in philosophy, but after receiving his degree, he shifted to the then-new field of psychology. One of his first published experiments was a study of handwriting that appeared in 1914.

3. I had the good fortune to attend The Laboratory School at the University of Chicago while Tyler and others were conducting research on the students. We used to move to the "Experimental Lab–Room 400" during certain periods each week. We were told they were studying us. I think most of us tried to mug for the cameras, as pictures were taken. You can read more about the Eight-Year Study at http://fcis.oise.utoronto.ca/~daniel_schugurensky/assignment1/1930eight.html or http://www.coe.uh.edu/courses/cuin6373/idhistory/8year.html.

4. You can read more about Skinner in his 1938 work *The Behavior of Organisms*. Skinner died in 1990 after a long career at the University of Minnesota, Indiana University, and Harvard. Skinner also studied his daughter, whom he raised for a time in a box called the Skinner box.

5. Frederic Lord, who died at age 87 in 2000, is said to be the father of modern testing. G. Stanley Hall (1844–1924) was an American psychologist and founder of the testing movement. He also founded the American Psychological Association and *The American Journal of Psychology*. E. Paul Torrance, who died at age 87 in 2003, is said to be the father of creativity. E. L. Thorndike, who died at age 98 in 1998, was known as the father of educational psychology. But no one was named the father of educational research. Lewis Terman, a professor of education and psychology at Stanford between 1910 and 1946, was instrumental in bringing the scientific approach both to research studies and to the training of researchers. He became president of the American Psychological Association in 1923.

6. How ironic, though, that in 2008, the majority of the more than 20,000 members of the American Educational Research Association are female. The president of the organization is female as well.

7. Kerlinger's *Foundations of Educational Research,* originally published in 1964, was considered a major text in the field. The fourth edition appeared in 2000.

8. See Becker's (1976) study of medical students, Liebow's (1967) study of street corner men in Washington, D.C., and Agar's (1973) study of urban heroin addicts.

9. For an excellent account of the history, read Chapter 1 in Bogdan and Biklen's (1992) *Foundations of Qualitative Research in Education.*

10. You can read ethnographies on such topics as drug dealing, girl gangs, or psychiatric clients. Few ethnographies were actually conducted in schools.

Chapter 3

Learning How to Be a Qualitative Researcher

FOCUS YOUR READING

- Clarify the research question.
- Get practice by doing simple studies with real people.
- Explore your own style.

Education is a kind of continuing dialogue, and a dialogue assumes, in the nature of the case, different points of view.

—Robert Hutchins

It was also very helpful to work closely with the school system where I planned to do the research. In the end, we formed an excellent match for doing qualitative research. The school system has a very comprehensive mentoring program for beginning teachers. They had substantial survey data, given annually to all mentors and beginning teachers, which documents the value of this program. However, there had been no inquiry into how the mentor/mentee relationships are operating at the local school level. This helped to solidify the research questions.

—Judy Smith

I have found over the years that sometimes it is best *to do* something rather than *to plan to do* something. In 1990, while attending my son's graduation from business school, I heard Tom Peters speak to the newly minted MBAs from UC-Berkeley. We were sitting outside in the Greek Theater. Peters advised them: Ready, Fire, Aim. Almost 20 years later, these words stay with me. Get out and do something, he advised the graduates. You can make adjustments and corrections later (see Peters, 2007, or Schrage, 1999, for their comments on Peters' advice). I couldn't agree with him more. In my experience, many students get turned off when they have to write draft upon draft of plans for a qualitative research study. They like to jump in with both feet and begin the process, rather than plan and ponder. For the most part, I agree with this idea.

Graduation advice from outside-the-box thinkers can be instructive when we think about doing research in a nontraditional manner. In 2005, Steve Jobs, CEO of Apple Computers, offered this advice to the new graduates of Stanford University. After telling the students that he had dropped out of college but stayed around anyway, he talked about taking a calligraphy class, in which he learned about different typefaces and fonts. He said that if he had not dropped out, he wouldn't have taken the class, and personal computers wouldn't look the way they do. Here is the important advice for you: "You can't connect the dots looking forward; you can only connect them looking backwards. So you have to trust that the dots will somehow connect in your future. You have to trust in something" ("You've got to find what you love," 2005). Although I didn't personally hear this speech, I find that it resonates strongly. Trust that what you are doing will work, and pursue what you believe in.

You have now read some of the history of the development of qualitative research in education, but you may still not really be sure what it is about. This small excerpt, taken from a much longer interview by a student on the topic "what life is like as a graduate student," should help you see how qualitative research reveals much about participants.

Paul: Tell me about a recent experience you've had at Tech.

Pablo: There are many. One of them is the recent statistics course I am taking at Tech. In the case of here, compared to what I had in Venezuela, I feel like it is really kind of easy. You can see how the teacher is trying to help you, kind of all the time. It is completely different. The teachers are more concerned with demonstrations, or not even thinking that you need to understand stuff. It's like they want to screw you, instead of helping you. Something like that.

Well, you might ask what you can learn about Pablo from this story and what else you would like to know. Can you see how appealing it is to let people talk to you in their own words? One thing you can definitely say about qualitative research is that it is about listening, thinking, and making meaning from what you hear and what you see.

■ General Ideas

Research is a process by which we seek answers to questions. The kinds of questions and the ways we seek answers are up to the researcher. If our question has to do with the relationship between money spent in a school system and student performance, we would not want to

Did You Know

You can find the 50 most frequently cited and read articles each month in the U.K. journal *Qualitative Research* by going to Sage Journals Online (http://qrj.sagepub .com/) and choosing "Article Statistics."

conduct qualitative research. We might get much more reliable answers to this question by conducting a simple survey. If our question has to do with examining the effectiveness of two kinds of reading programs, we would not want to conduct qualitative research. We could get much more reliable answers to this question by designing an experiment and seeing which program yielded higher test scores. But suppose the questions posed have to do with looking at how rules are developed by kindergarten children, or experiences of families who have suffered a death of a child, or how school atmosphere and style are exhibited in a small rural school, or how school leaders develop, or what it is like to plan for retirement. A survey or an experiment won't provide very insightful answers to these questions. This is where qualitative research comes in. These are different kinds of questions. They do not ask us to look for relationships among variables. They do not ask us to test hypotheses. They ask us to think about the whole and about the ways humans interact. Now, we have to look for ways to answer them.

As a novice researcher, you might say, "Well, why don't I just go and talk to the people and see what they have to say?" You can probably imagine that to conduct your research, you need a plan that follows a particular research design. In a broad sense, you can think of either a quantitative research design or a qualitative research design. I am only going to discuss qualitative research designs. Within the general category of qualitative research designs, there are a number of approaches to choose from. Sometimes it will be very clear to you which approach you will want to follow. Other times, it seems as though you choose elements from more than one approach. That is all right as well. Sometimes you are not quite sure whether you are using any specific research approach at all. In Chapter 5, I review some of the major qualitative research approaches in depth. Now, I want you to direct your attention to the kinds of questions and problems you want to address.

You might ask, what makes a piece of research qualitative? How do you know? In general, qualitative research involves looking at things in their natural settings or talking to individuals about a particular topic, or investigating individuals who have experienced a particular phenomenon.

What do you think the field is about? It may be too early in your exploration to have formulated clear ideas to answer this question, but many students new to the field of qualitative research have some terms they identify with the field. They know about doing interviews, case studies, small samples, and looking at a natural setting. They are usually very attracted to what they read and identify with much of the style of writing used in qualitative research. They question how they can be objective and unbiased in conducting qualitative research. They express concern that the research doesn't appear to be very scientific and wonder whether it is legitimate. They may have heard from some professors that qualitative research takes too long or is not real research. However, the academic and research communities have come to accept alternative ways of conducting research. No longer is quantitative or experimental research the only or best way to answer questions.

You can sort out your own ideas about qualitative research by reading, thinking, and talking with others. Be open to new ideas. Be willing to step outside the box. Be prepared for ambiguity. You are on a fascinating adventure.

So much of qualitative research depends on what people have to say. After all, we come to understand people by listening to them, watching them interact, and thinking about the meaning beyond, beneath, and around the words. No matter what approach you take or what group you study or what topic you consider, you will gather some information that is represented by what your respondents tell you. This might be supplemented with pictures, observations, artifacts, videos, or notes, but you cannot get away from the fact that to learn about people you have to listen to them.

I know that when students start going out and listening to others, they sometimes feel unprepared. They don't quite know how to do it. I discuss these issues in Chapter 9, but for now, I want to tell you about some techniques that work very well for me and for my students.

One of the best techniques to get people started during an interview is to ask them to tell a story about something that happened to them last week (at school, at work, at home, on the street). In this way, you can delve immediately into something specific, concrete, and meaningful to the person doing the talking. While it may not be quite what you, the interviewer, have in mind, you will be very surprised at how it sets the stage for what is to come.

It takes the speaker and the listener right into the nitty-gritty of their lives. And, after all, isn't that a part of what qualitative research is about? You'll find that it is very easy for people to talk about themselves. You need to set the stage, be accepting and open to what they have to say, and be nonjudgmental. This is not always easy, but it comes with practice, I assure you.

You don't have to stay in the immediate present for individuals to open up to you. Sometimes stories can be from the past. I recall many years ago when I asked my father-in-law to come and speak to my classroom of teachers about his early days in school. At that time, he was well into his nineties; he had attended school in New York City as a young child. He was very reluctant, at first, to come to my class; I suspect he was afraid that he would not do the right thing. However, when I arrived at his home to transport him to my class, I found him all dressed up in a shirt, tie, and sport coat. I knew he was ready. When he got to my class, I began interviewing him about his earliest memories of school. He spoke about first grade.

Initially, he said he didn't know what I wanted him to say. I replied that I wanted him to say what he knew and remembered. He said that perhaps he wasn't doing the right thing. I assured him he was. What things he remembered! The most meaningful event was being sent to the "rat cellar" with the janitor if you somehow behaved inappropriately. I asked him if he had ever been sent there. He replied, "Just once." He smiled and my class burst into laughter. Well, I opened up a flood of memories and learned much about schooling in the early 1900s, about my father-in-law, about how young people react to those generations removed from them, and about myself. I was fortunate that I had the foresight to tape-record this interview because he is no longer here to tell these stories.

I use these illustrations to help you see what qualitative research is and can be. Qualitative research has as one of its central goals to describe and understand human behavior. Qualitative research relies heavily on words. Qualitative research seeks to capture voices of individuals as they are. These examples reveal how much individuals have to say if the stage is set for them to speak. It takes skill and practice to interview someone. Neophyte researchers are often nervous when they begin conducting qualitative interviews. Talisha, one of my graduate students, summed this up quite well in her journal entry:

I thought the interview process was going to be a lot easier than it actually was. I felt unprepared and unorganized because I did not have any set questions in front of me to ask. I was surprised because I am usually someone that enjoys carrying on conversations and I found it difficult to "go with the flow." There was one point in the interview when I had to turn off the recorder to gather my thoughts and come up with another question. I also felt pressured to meet the 30–45 minute suggested interview time. Before I could ask a question, the interviewee had already answered the question in a previous response. So, it was really hard for me to come up with other questions. After conducting this interview, I realized why I prefer having set questions. In my opinion, it helps the interview to flow smoother.

If you experience these same feelings, you should know that they are very common. Like learning any new skill, you get better with practice.

■ So You Want to Be a Qualitative Researcher?

At this point, you have a taste of qualitative research. Many of you will be intrigued. It sounds like something that is interesting to you and something that you can manage to do. If you are working on a degree, you know that any discipline is informed by research efforts and findings. As a practitioner, you can learn how to do something, but what works and why are what we gain from conducting research.

Use this checklist to see whether being a qualitative researcher seems right for you.

1. You are interested in people and empathetic toward them, their situations, and the environment around them.

2. You are interested in real people in natural settings.

3. You are interested in looking at behaviors, thoughts, or feelings of individuals with certain traits or characteristics.

4. You like the opportunity to explore ideas in depth.

5. You want to study questions about how people interact, how social networks develop, or how cultures are nurtured.

6. You are a good judge of self and others and you have an introspective viewpoint.

7. You like to be with people and see how they tick.

8. You are attracted to what people say, how they portray themselves, or how they talk to each other.

9. You are interested in studying schools and classrooms and kids.

10. You see value in going beyond facts and tables.

11. You like new ways of doing things and are innovative.

12. You are a good listener and good at asking questions.

13. You are willing to deal with ambiguity.

14. You have a tolerance for lack of structure.

15. You like to write and are good at it.

16. You have to write a research paper, a thesis, or a dissertation.

17. You are willing to see research as more than hypothesis testing.

18. You are open to new ideas.

19. You recognize that all research is complex and challenging, and you are not necessarily looking for an easy way out.

I offer this checklist so that you can gauge how comfortable you are with qualitative research approaches. In my experience, some students like the rules laid out for them in advance, while others are challenged by lack of structure and ambiguity. To begin doing qualitative research, you must have an open mind.

I want to begin with an example. Sandra is just beginning her advanced degree in education. She hopes to obtain an endorsement in special education. She has worked with children in her rural hometown and in the adjacent city where she attended college. She found the work stimulating and challenging, but she continued to ask questions about what she was doing. She wanted to know about ways to work with these challenging children. She especially wanted to explore ways to socialize them into the larger school community. She began taking notes about how these kids behaved when they were having lunch and passing through the halls. She often thought about what she might do to help them feel more comfortable.

Sandra sounds like a good candidate to begin to learn some of the skills of doing qualitative research. She asks questions about her own practice. She has had several types of experiences and remains open to improving her own teaching. And she is a careful observer and recorder. I see her as someone who would benefit tremendously by jumping into the field. From those experiences, she can begin to build her repertoire of qualitative research skills.

Why does she want to do qualitative research? I suspect Sandra doesn't know explicitly that she wants to do qualitative research. She probably has heard the term but doesn't have a clear understanding of what it is. In this chapter, I offer some advice about when you might want to do qualitative research, and I provide you with some practical suggestions to get started.

Why would someone want to do qualitative research? One way to think about qualitative research is that it is a way to answer questions. In fact, most research deals with finding answers to questions. But the kinds of questions qualitative research tends to focus on are those that take place in real settings and not in a laboratory. They are not contrived or manipulated by the researcher. The questions are often about human or social interaction. They are often somewhat general and not always well thought out. They may even evolve; qualitative research is a cyclical and dynamic process, rather than one that is linear and static.

■ Qualitative Questions

Some questions seem to fit well into the qualitative domain. Others fit neatly into a quantitative approach. Still others seem to fit into some combined niche. Qualitative questions address meaning or understanding or interpretation. Qualitative questions address sociological, psycho-logical, or political aspects. Qualitative questions are those that focus on human beings and how they interact in social settings or how they see themselves or aspects of their environment. Qualitative questions tend to ask *why* and *how,* rather than *what* and *how many.* Qualitative questions tend to be general and broad.

Take a look at the topics of some recent research conducted in the field.

- Exploring online teaching

- Planning for retirement: A perspective from professional women

- Questions and issues of Alzheimer's patients' family caregivers

- Gender, power, and the television remote control

- What is it like to be an occupational therapist practicing in a rural area?

- Voices from the margins

- Mentoring pregnant adolescents

- Exploring the personal in qualitative research

- Personal narratives of elite college athletes: Stories of career-ending injuries

- Always single and single again women

- Change from teachers' perspectives: A model of personal change

- The triangulation of researcher interpretations of interview data: Cross-gender friendships

- School, family, and community context of African American children in South Carolina

- Marks on paper: Exploring literacy through theatre

- Marco said I looked like charcoal: A Puerto Rican's exploration of her ethnic identity

- Telling tales out of school: Connecting the prose and the passion in the learning and teach-ing of English

- "If you know our names it helps!" Students' perspectives about "good" teaching

- A good teacher

- Madhubani art: A journey of an education researcher seeking self-development answers through art and self-study

Although the titles do not tell you about the research approach, they suggest questions that ask *why* rather than *what* and *how many.* You can see that these kinds of questions are quite dif-ferent from those that ask you to look at the relationship between variables, or ask you to test hypotheses, or ask you to make generalizations.

I know how very difficult it is to come up with a suitable research question. Here are some ways that might be helpful to you. I have constructed Table 3.1 so you can think about this more clearly. Begin by thinking about different categories: people, concepts, places, and events. Let's look more closely at each of these categories.

Table 3.1 Formulating Research Questions

People	Concepts	Places	Events
students	power	classrooms	hurricanes
teachers	leadership	playgrounds	pep rallies
parents	loneliness	malls	parties
adult students	mentoring	coffee houses	athletic events
administrators	gender differences	homes	assemblies
high-achieving girls	violence	lunchrooms	concerts
children at risk	cooperation	schools	parades
gangs	friendships	adult centers	flood
pregnant teens	mentoring relationship	places of worship	holidays
beginning teachers	teacher burnout	online chat rooms	mealtimes
students in same-sex classes	aggression	rural classrooms	elections

People. Many qualitative researchers begin with the type or kind of person they want to study. Sometimes qualitative researchers are interested in exploring individuals who are disadvantaged, or homeless, or deviant, or in trouble. In a very early qualitative dissertation, Liebow (1967) studied men who were unemployed and living on a street corner in Washington, D.C. Several decades later, Liebow (1993) studied women who lived in a homeless shelter. Some do ethnographies on specific groups of individuals. Correll (1995) studied a lesbian online "bar." Although you would expect that the general research question dictates who is studied, in my experience, qualitative researchers often decide they want to study individuals with whom they identify. Repass (2002), thinking about retiring herself, studied professional women as they planned their retirement. Glass (2001), a parent of a child with autism, studied families with an autistic child. Snyder (2003), a consultant to the military, studied a military organization's adoption of an innovative technique. Rodriguez (2006) studied African American and Latina women in the academy. Others may choose to examine people different from themselves. This is not always easy, as Butera (2006) discovered. She described the extreme challenge she encountered in getting men to participate in a study of cross-gender friendship.

Concepts. Another way to develop a potential research question is to think about concepts or topics of interest. Concepts that researchers address are very wide ranging. Qualitative researchers have studied surviving a heart attack, living with AIDS, power in hospitals and schools, music teachers' personal traits, and experiences of female school superintendents. They have asked questions about forming friendships, about successful minority students, about

reading programs that work, and about the politics of identity. The topics are very often clo..
their hearts. In keeping with the newer participatory paradigms of qualitative research, some
have chosen areas in which they could intervene and make social change. Some have chosen
topics that lead to political action.

Places. I believe that most researchers begin either with the people they want to study or the
concept they want to investigate. Yet, I think it is important to also consider where a study might
take place. For ease of discussion, I have not differentiated between open or closed places.
Without getting too complicated, you can think about it in this way. If your study is conducted
in an open and public place, you do not need permission to conduct your study nor do you need
to provide anonymity. For example, if you decide to conduct a study in a shopping mall and you
choose to sit in an open corridor and observe people around you, you should be able to do this
without encountering a problem. I warn you, however, that in this time of heightened awareness
and security, you might be approached by someone from the facility and be asked to identify
yourself and what you are doing. To the extent that the place in which you plan to conduct your
study is open to all, you should not face any problems. Places that fit into this category include
sporting arenas, libraries, playgrounds, amusement parks, beaches, fast-food restaurants,
museums—in other words, places where adults and/or children gather that are open to all. If
the place in which you plan to conduct your study is more private, you will need to obtain permission to conduct the study from both the organization and the individuals within it. Some
challenges to conducting qualitative research in certain settings are the result of specific situations. Belousov and his colleagues (2007) describe the incredible difficulties they faced in a
study of health and safety regulatory enforcement in the shipping industry in Russia. Sadly, one
of the fieldworkers was murdered. They talk specifically about particular social spaces and the
frontier-like nature of certain settings.

Events. The last category you might consider as you think about formulating a research question
is either a unique event (such as 9/11, or Hurricane Katrina, or the closing of the Prince Edward,
Virginia, school system to avoid integration) or a more general event such as a holiday celebration
or a Fourth of July parade. For the most part, you will find it easier to concentrate on more general
events. But if you happen to be in a position to study a major and possibly unique event, I encourage you to think about that. As I write this book in the summer of 2008, I think about the upcom-
ing national elections. It will be the first time in the history of the United States that a major
political party has an African American candidate running as president. If you work in a school
system, this might be the perfect time for you to engage in investigating questions of race, power,
and access among young people.

    Of course, the examples under each category are those I have thought about. You can substi-
tute any you wish. Very often, researchers begin by identifying individuals of interest to them.
Some find it helpful to select a particular concept to study. I think this helps you to focus your ideas
as you begin your research. Once you have selected who and what you plan to study, you need to
determine where the study will take place. In Table 3.1, I have listed some places for you to consider. Finally, some people find that they are motivated by a particular event and want to study the
event itself. The event can be unique, such as a hurricane or disaster, or more common, such as a
sporting event or assembly.

■ Getting Started

One of the best ways to learn about various qualitative approaches is to practice. So, get your notebook and pen ready, charge the battery in your digital camera, get your laptop out, and embark on this new adventure. You are going to do a very small qualitative study with a coresearcher. I promise you that you will learn something; you will enjoy yourself; and, most important, you will gain some insight into being a qualitative researcher. In this first attempt, you are going to rely on your skills of observation.

Jump right in. Here is something that you can do to follow Tom Peters' admonition "Ready, Fire, Aim." By now, you might be ready to think about how you would plan a qualitative research study. I think too many people spend a lot of time planning, making sure that everything is just so, and perhaps avoiding the actual task of collecting and analyzing data.

- Select a partner from your class. Doing research can often be a very lonely task, and here you are asked to do something you don't really know how to do. Remember, there is no right way to do something; there are many ways. You will have to identify what works best for you, but in my experience, it is a good idea to work with someone else. It is not necessary to be interested in the same topic or to have the same major. In fact, I suspect you might learn more from someone who is quite different from yourself.

- Select something, some place, and someone to study. Most people like to begin by selecting something to study. Because you are doing this just for practice, I think it is advisable to select something that is immediate, accessible, and of interest to you. I've made some suggestions below. Because you are going to a public place, you do not have to seek permission, worry about privacy, or otherwise get bogged down in technicalities. Remember, your purpose is just to practice and begin to think and act like a qualitative researcher. Your next step is to consider from whom you might gather information on the topic. At this point, it is easier if you can avoid obtaining permission through Institutional Review Boards, which is often time consuming and counterproductive. You might consider studying adults—coworkers, relatives, or friends. Usually, they are willing to be studied and you can work out a time to meet with them.

  o Select something or someone to study in your college setting. You can study people in the library, individuals at a sporting event, students as they interact between classes, students at coffee breaks, or small group work efforts. You can position yourself in the lounge areas of buildings and watch as students leave and return to their classes. I had a student who studied an aspect of personal space (she was getting her degree in architecture) by observing in the campus library for an extended period. She was interested in the physical use of space, how students surrounded themselves with books, whether they sat near others, and so on.

  o Venture outside your immediate campus and study social interaction in fast-food places (e.g., McDonald's, Burger King, or Starbucks). I often get my best practice watching and listening to people in public places. You will find that if you frequent one of these places at about the same time each day, you will see the same people. You can look from afar, or you can interact with them more directly. I have studied retirees, young mothers, and young professionals. By the way, the crowd is different during the week than on weekends.

○ Identify other places where groups of people tend to congregate: parks, playgrounds, grocery stores, malls, airports, or train stations. Malls are a great place to study teenagers. If you live in a suburban area or a city, these places offer insight into a contemporary society that may be quite different from when you were a teenager. At the airport, it is especially interesting to see how different cultures greet one another.

- Get yourself ready. Allow at least 30 minutes for your observations. Bring a notepad and pen with you to take notes. You might also do some thinking in advance about what you will be looking for. I do not recommend that you look at what others have studied at this point. I find that it tends to close you off and dictate what you will look for, rather than let the data emerge from the setting.

- Decide what kind of data you will gather. For this task, you will be concentrating on gathering data through observation. You might also talk to some people, but only if they seem to want to interact with you.

- Now go out there to observe. Depending on which place you select, you might have to figure out where to sit or stand, whether you really want to take notes or not, and how you will position yourself so that others will not become wary or suspicious. If you are on a college campus, you might find it easy to observe in the library or at a coffee house. Both locations will provide you access to a variety of people. Because many people stay in these places for a long time, you will be able to work on your skills easily. You can take notes about how people are dressed, how frequently they interact with others, whether they use their cell phones or text message, or the extent to which they are aware of others in their surroundings. Your note taking should be inconspicuous because others will be writing as well.

- For additional practice, interview your partner or coresearcher. Arrange a quiet meeting place. Limit your interview to three open-ended questions: "Tell me about yourself." "What do you think about X?" "Tell me something that happened to you recently that concerns X." X might be any general topic about which no special knowledge is needed. For example, X could be working spouses, single-sex education, teacher burnout, home schooling, or outsider students.

- Debrief with your partner. After you finish your 30 minutes of observation, meet with your partner for at least 30 additional minutes. Have a general discussion about what you did, what you noticed, what seemed important, how you felt, and what you think you learned. This session will be invaluable as you will see what someone else thought and did in the same setting. Your purpose is to talk about process, not necessarily about what the findings are. But I know that you will begin your discussion talking about what you saw and what it meant. That is only human nature.

- Organize and make meaning from your observation data. You will need to perform some kind of analysis of the data you have collected. In its simplest form, this might involve reviewing the material you have and identifying some themes. You and your partner can write a joint two- to three-page paper on what you found, or you can each write a short paper and then compare them.

- Try to write your data in an entirely different way. Can you create a poem or play? How about writing your interpretation and interspersing that of your partner? Think about what you found and how you might communicate it to an audience. Try to write two papers that are different in style and format and contrast with traditional scholarly writing.

Practice, practice, practice. You can never get enough practice. You know that professional athletes practice every day. For you, qualitative research is new and perhaps somewhat foreign to your daily behavior. You might be more likely to do something rather than to study how others are acting or doing. If you are a counselor, you might be more likely to want to help someone you see in trouble. If you are a special education teacher, you might want to provide additional assistance to a needy student. If you are working as an administrator, your inclination might be to just get the job done. But you are training to be a researcher, and that is something with which you have little or no experience. So I suggest you continue your practice. You might want to refine what you did in your first practice session. Perhaps, as a result of your dialogue with your partner, you get the idea that it would be good to focus on one particular aspect of what you observe. Maybe you decide that you want to look at the interaction between teenage boys and girls in the mall. Maybe you want to focus just on how they talk to each other and the informal body language they demonstrate. Do you see what you have done? You have begun to work your ideas around to something that you find interesting, unique, or unusual. That is what qualitative researchers tend to do. So let's look at some ways you can practice and build your repertoire and your confidence.

- Look at the same or a similar site. Use the same partner. Try to identify at least one thing that you will do differently from your first time out. It might be to focus on a particular aspect of the interaction, as I suggested above, it might be to take more extensive notes than you did the first time, or it might be to actually talk to someone you are observing.

- Choose a different kind of site, one where the people you are observing are of a different age, involved in different kinds of activities, or are in a very different setting. Do the same thing at the new site that you did at the previous site.

- Select a different partner. You might get some new insights by talking to someone else.

Work with others. We can learn so much by working with others. That is why I stress that you should begin with a partner. There are a number of things that you can do with a partner or with a larger group.

- Plan together what you will look at or how you will look at something. Alternatively, work separately and then compare what you have done afterward.

- Work with others on data analysis. Although there is no one right way of making sense of your data, sometimes it is helpful to see others' response to your ideas.

Read work by others. There are different kinds of material you can read. All are helpful, but I don't think it is critical to read before you set out into the field for your practice work.

- Read what others have to say about the topic. How do teenagers interact with each other? What are effective ways of working with students with special needs?

- Read what others have to say about doing qualitative research. You can read about how to do qualitative interviewing, how to observe, what kind of data analysis to do, and you can read about theory. What are qualitative research traditions? What is grounded theory? What is phenomenology?

To make your life easier, I suggest you begin by reading material that is free and readily available. Two good sources are *The Qualitative Report* (http://www.nova.edu/ssss/QR/) and *Forum: Qualitative Social Research* (http://www.qualitative-research.net/fqs/fqs-eng.htm).

Don't be afraid. At this point, you cannot make a mistake. Remember, you are not writing a journal article or your thesis; you are developing skills. Because there is no one right way of doing something, you need to experiment with what works best for you. Your creative juices will flow when you go into the field. It is often the case that new researchers try to write down everything they see and hear, but quickly they will notice how difficult this is to do. What should they write down? What if they miss something? What is important and what is not? I suggest that you also need to rely on what you see, so I like people to write a detailed description of the setting. If you have a digital camera, you might want to take pictures of what you see. This combination of visuals and words often leads to a much richer set of data with which you can work.

Keep a journal. Write early and often. I cannot emphasize this enough. You need to write down your reflections. They can be about the process, they can be about what you are thinking, or they can be about what you found. I suggest you take a laptop with you to any site. If convenient, you can write while you are observing. If this is too cumbersome, you need to allocate some time in the following day or so to write your reflections.

Join an online discussion. There are a number of online discussions that are often very helpful. Many of them are supportive of questions from students. One Listserv that has become very useful emanates from the University of Georgia. You can join it by going to listserv@listserv.uga.edu.

Seek out others with similar interests. Learning to become a qualitative researcher sometimes places you out of the mainstream of other researchers. If you are taking a qualitative research class, find others in the class with whom you seem compatible and form a small discussion group. If you are taking the class online, initiate a chat room or other discussion forum. If you are reading the material and not enrolled in a course, use an online discussion.

Be an advocate, not an apologist. In the early days of qualitative research practice, I found that students would say something like, "I am doing qualitative research. I know it is not as good as quantitative, but that is what I want to do." Qualitative research has an important and legitimate role in the research community. You can contribute to this growing field by accepting what you are doing and being positive about it.

Believe in what you are doing. I am a firm believer that qualitative research can be used to answer questions that other approaches cannot. This does not mean that other forms of research are wrong or bad, but certain kinds of questions lend themselves to be answered by looking and listening.

■ Summary

In this chapter, I introduced you to some general ideas about doing qualitative research. I provided a checklist of characteristics commonly found among qualitative researchers to assess your fit as a qualitative researcher. Qualitative and quantitative research questions were contrasted, by pointing out that qualitative research questions usually are broad questions dealing with why or how things occur. I suggested that in seeking to identify a research question, you might consider people, concepts, places, or events as a starting point.

A strategy for jumping into the qualitative research process to develop skills was introduced. The strategy guides the hands-on introduction to the required skills, which lead the novice to proceed by selecting a partner, selecting something or someone to study, identifying a setting, deciding what data to gather, and analyzing the data to make meaning.

GROUP ACTIVITY

Purpose: To explore alternative ways of gathering information.

Activity: Identify a television program that focuses on family or friend interaction. Many programs are available to watch in reruns or on the Internet. Decide on a particular aspect of the interaction that you find interesting. It might be looking at gender differences, interplay of parents and children, or couple interaction. I like to use the topic of power.

Watch the program in class; alternatively, watch it outside of class and be prepared to discuss it when the class meets. Following the viewing, each person should prepare a written statement of examples of how power is displayed between individuals.

Evaluation: Look at the variety of responses people offer. This activity should help people to see how one's perspective influences interpretations.

INDIVIDUAL ACTIVITY

Purpose: To continue practicing alternative ways to gather data.

Activity: In your home, identify pictures, photos, or other symbols that describe who you are. Select several to bring to class. In class, explain what you chose and why you chose it. Then participate in a discussion of how others learn about you.

Evaluation: This will help you move away from the literal into the meaning behind what you see.

Of course, you need to keep up your journal writing. Your question this week might be "What else can I do to get myself ready? How do I feel about where I am so far?"

Chapter 4

Ethical Issues in Qualitative Research

FOCUS YOUR READING

■ Researchers are responsible for ensuring that participants are not harmed, privacy is maintained, and the participants have provided informed consent.

■ Qualitative researchers do not have clear standards governing their activities.

■ Universities rely on review boards to decide which research activities to approve.

If it is not right do not do it; if it is not true do not say it.

—Marcus Aurelius

A few years ago, I was doing a phenomenological study of teenage girls. I was interested in learning how they coped with conflicting messages about doing well in school and not being seen as "too smart." The school system had approved my proposal, and I had also received permission from the parents of the girls. I promised confidentiality to the girls. My plan called for me to do a minimum of two interviews with each girl. I was well into my second interview with Susan when the tears started to slowly roll down her cheeks. We were talking about how she wanted to do well, but she sensed that the boys might not like her if she was too "brainy." But then she switched topics and really opened up. She started to tell me about how her stepfather was getting too friendly with her and had touched her in those "special places." I knew then that I was on very sensitive ground. Fortunately, or perhaps not so, our scheduled time together was coming to an end. I completed the interview and told her I would be in touch. Now I was in quite a dilemma. What was I to do? I had promised to keep all information confidential, but if her stepfather was sexually abusing her, was I obligated to report it? And to whom? Was she telling me the truth or just trying to "con" me? What would you do?

I tell you this story not to shock you but to get you thinking about the kinds of dilemmas in which you might find yourself when doing qualitative research. Even though I had followed all procedures, received permissions, informed my participants, and promised confidentiality, I had learned some information that troubled me. I felt I had a responsibility to Susan not to reveal the confidence. I also felt I had a responsibility to her if she was being abused. However, I really did not know whether the story she told me was true. Because I was not part of the school system and had no supervisor there, I did not know what to do with the information.

This story illustrates a delicate balance you might face between trying to do what is right in terms of maintaining privacy and, at the same time, recognizing that you have received information that might be damaging to the participant. Should you tell someone? If so, who? What about the promise you made to maintain privacy?

You might not have thought about ethics while you were planning your research. Yet, recently, much has been written on the topic. I want you to think about what kinds of issues you might face and how you would handle them. In this chapter, I introduce you to some of the basic principles associated with ethics and recent controversies concerning universities and monitoring of qualitative research plans. I know you will find the information challenging. I hope it will cause you to think carefully about your research and about the people you study.

The scenario I described above is not something you will encounter on a regular basis. But I began with it to point out that you might find yourself in a situation that is unexpected and for which you will need to use judgment and good sense.

You know that much of qualitative research involves interactions with individuals. As a consequence of developing rapport with participants and getting them to trust you, you may find they open up to you in very personal ways. When this happens, you face an ethical challenge. What should you do with information you obtain that might be damaging to the individual or to others?

You might think that there are clear guidelines available to you as a researcher to assist you if you encounter such challenges, but this is not the case. In your role as a teacher, counselor, administrator, or therapist, you are guided by a code of conduct or set of ethics established by licensing boards or by the organization for which you work. In contrast, researchers do not have a formal licensing body. A number of organizations offer guidelines about ethical standards, but many lack an enforcement mechanism. The *Ethical Standards of the American Educational Research Association* were adopted in 1992 and revised in 2000 to "evoke voluntary compliance by moral persuasion" (American Educational Research Association, 2005). Many universities use review boards to set and enforce standards. Many large school systems have guidelines.

In this chapter, I begin with definitions of ethical behavior. Next, I look at the major principles associated with the ethics of conducting research. I also address problems with the standards. Following, I review some significant examples of unethical behavior in the general scientific community as well as examine inappropriate behavior in the field of qualitative research. I look next at some special problems faced by qualitative researchers. I conclude with the issues of setting and enforcing standards of behavior.

Did You Know

It was in 1906, when the Pure Food and Drug Act was passed, that regulations regarding the use of human subjects in research came into being.

■ Ethical Behavior: Definitions and Background

As I began this chapter, I asked myself, "What is the meaning of ethics and ethical behavior?" Seems straightforward, doesn't it? In laymen's terms, we all know what we mean when we say ethics or ethical behavior. I think there are various commonsense responses to the question. It means doing what is right. It means treating people fairly. It means not hurting anyone.

We deal with ethical issues on a daily basis. Should you report someone who cheats on an exam or copies someone else's writing? Should you return that extra dollar given to you by a clerk or keep a wallet found on the street? Should you give children additional time to finish an exam or provide answers to difficult questions on a test?

Randy Cohen, who writes a weekly column—The Ethicist—for *The New York Times*, provides a popular and accessible vehicle for us to examine our belief system. Here is a recent problem and his response; his tone is wonderful.

One of my grad students copied a term paper from the Internet, cutting and pasting from various uncredited sources. The university's rules say expulsion or an F in the course is appropriate, but I proposed that she search out the several dozen articles she used to "compose" her paper and write each author an apology. I will mail the letters. My department chair thinks this is unethical—a cruel and unusual punishment. You?

—P. R., Houston

Unusual? Quite likely, but that's not necessarily a bad thing. A roomy and inexpensive Manhattan apartment is unusual. Cruel? I think not. This cheater is even spared the torment of visiting the post office to mail the apologies. But effectual? I doubt it. And that is key. Your task as a professor is to reinforce a respect for academic integrity and to preserve it in your classroom. I'm skeptical that your method will do either (R. Cohen, 2007).

Cohen's weekly column illustrates the public's need for guidance in handling issues they face daily. What Cohen does so well is to present the issue and his response in a no-nonsense, easy-to-understand manner. I do not know who sets his moral compass, but I suspect he does. You can learn more about him through various National Public Radio (NPR) interviews (http://www.npr.org/programs/atc/ethicist/). There is no Cohen around for the ethical dilemmas researchers face. We need to rely on various guidelines from several sources. Ultimately, we need to rely on our own moral compass.

Here is a general definition: Ethical behavior represents a set of moral principles, rules, or standards governing a person or a profession. We understand that to be ethical is to "do good and avoid evil."

This general definition is helpful as we try to understand research ethics. Below, I discuss what I consider to be the major principles of ethical behavior associated with research that involves human subjects, rather than research on animals. In particular, I am interested in qualitative research, although I offer you some background on unethical conduct in general.

Although research on human subjects has been conducted since the Middle Ages, codes of conduct regarding appropriate researcher behavior did not emerge until the 20th century. It was not until the 1960s, when federal government funding became available, that more researchers became interested in school-based research. At first, there were no clear guidelines. But as more research was conducted in schools, it became necessary for many institutions to establish review boards. Universities followed suit and set up procedures to review student research.

■ Major Principles Associated With Ethical Conduct

The principles of ethical conduct that I identify below represent an amalgam gleaned from many sources.

- **Do No Harm**. Of all the principles associated with research ethics, I think it is safe to say that this admonition is the cornerstone of ethical conduct. There should be a reasonable expectation by those participating in a research study that they will not be involved in any situation in which they might be harmed. Although this is the standard we are most concerned about violating, I think it is fairly safe to assume that the research you plan and conduct will not be harmful to participants. This principle is often applied to studies involving drugs or a treatment that might be harmful to participants. You might have read about mistreatment during experiments. The 1971 Stanford Prison Experiment, in which students played the role of guards and prisoners, is one example. When it was found that the guards became increasingly sadistic, the study was terminated. Of course, the kind of qualitative research you plan will not be of this nature. We have become well aware of the potential damage caused by such studies. It is still important, however, for you to make explicit any possible adverse effects of your research.

Bottom Line: It is best to safeguard against doing anything that will harm the participants in your study. If you begin a study and you find that some of your participants seem to have adverse reactions, it is best to discontinue the study, even if it means foregoing your research plan.

- **Privacy and Anonymity**. Any individual participating in a research study has a reasonable expectation that privacy will be guaranteed. Consequently, no identifying information about the individual should be revealed in written or other communication. Further, any group or organization participating in a research study has a reasonable expectation that its identity will not be revealed. I would like you to think about privacy of two kinds: institutional and individual. If you study an institution, how do you keep the information you learn private? Suppose you take pictures of places in the institution and want to include them in your written product. Suppose the institution you study is sufficiently unusual that it can be identified from a description or from photographs. If you study individuals, you are faced with other challenges. Suppose you have recorded interviews and want to place a hyperlink in your report to the person being interviewed. Will the voice be recognized? Suppose you collaborate with others and maintain files in a database that can be accessed via the Internet, and others gain access. Suppose you use a computer software program that has links to video and audio. How do you guarantee privacy in these cases? Suppose you study individuals of some prominence, and their identities cannot readily be disguised. One idea to consider is to obtain a signed release authorizing you to use such information in your research. With the availability of so much information on the Internet (e.g., YouTube, Facebook), you are faced with challenges that were never considered when the original privacy statements were written. Conversely, you might find yourself facing the opposite problem: Your participants may want their identities revealed. They may want to be acknowledged in your written product. Perhaps they see it as their "15 minutes of fame." Can you reveal their identities?

Bottom Line: Remove identifying information from your records. Seek permission from the participants if you wish to make public information that might reveal who they are or who the organization is. Use caution in publishing long verbatim quotes, especially if they are damaging to the organization or people in it. Often, these quotes can be located on the Internet and traced to the speaker or author.

- **Confidentiality**. Any individual participating in a research study has a reasonable expectation that information provided to the researcher will be treated in a confidential manner. Consequently, the participant is entitled to expect that such information will not be given to anyone else. Think back to the case of Susan that I presented at the beginning of this chapter. Although I had promised her confidentiality and I had gotten her to open up to me, I now had to deal with information that might prove damaging to her or to others. I chose to investigate the situation further to try to determine the truthfulness of her allegations. Fortunately, she eventually told me that she made the story up to get my attention. During your research, you might learn a considerable amount of personal information because many of the interviews you conduct will be open ended and may move in various directions. As a researcher, you are in a situation that you control. If you sense an interview might be moving in a personal direction, you might have to stop the interview and suggest to the participant that she talk to a counselor or other trusted support person.

Bottom Line: It is your responsibility to keep the information you learn confidential. If you sense that an individual is in an emergency situation, you might decide that you can waive your promise for the good of the individual or of others. You need to be much more sensitive to information that you obtain from minors and others who might be in a vulnerable position.

- **Informed Consent**. Individuals participating in a research study have a reasonable expectation that they will be informed of the nature of the study and may choose whether or not to participate. They also have a reasonable expectation that they will not be coerced into participation. On the face of it, this might seem to be relatively easy to follow. But if a study is to be done in an organization, individuals within that group (e.g., students, workers) might feel that they cannot refuse when asked. There might be pressure placed on them by peers or by superiors. Although the idea of informed consent appears to be straightforward, there are situations in which informed consent may not possible. For example, it is more difficult to obtain consent from minors or individuals who do not have a clear understanding of written English or those who are mentally disabled or emotionally fragile. Another issue regarding obtaining informed consent is that your research study—because it is dynamic and subject to twists and turns—might diverge in a direction that causes participants to become uncomfortable or unwilling to continue. Because of this, I believe that the consent people give in advance may not really be "informed." Recently, researchers have expressed concerns about studying people on the Internet. I have read accounts of individuals who became angry that a researcher was using their discussion board or Listserv for data collection. Whether you lurk in chat rooms or on Listservs or you enter domains of YouTube or Facebook, you are exploring Internet cultures. There is no general procedure to seek consent in these arenas. Researchers are now beginning to explore ways of obtaining consent from such groups.

Bottom Line: Your responsibility is to make sure that participants are informed, to the extent possible, about the nature of your study. Even though it is not always possible to describe the direction your study might take, it is your responsibility to do the best you can to provide complete information. If participants decide to withdraw from the study, they should not feel penalized for so doing. Second, you need to be aware of special problems when you study people online. For example, one concern might be vulnerability of group participants. Another is the level of intrusiveness of the researcher. McCleary (2007) discusses many of these issues from the perspective of social workers; many of these concerns can be transferred to educators.

- **Rapport and Friendship**. Once participants agree to be part of a study, the researcher develops rapport in order to get them to disclose information. I recall when Alice, a student of mine from China, studied the wives of Chinese graduate students who had relocated to a rural college campus. She found herself getting too close to the women she studied. She was concerned about their language difficulties and problems they had adjusting to Western society. Yet, as she became close to these women, she became sad and frustrated that she couldn't do anything about their situation. She was somewhere between rapport and a faked friendship. Duncombe and Jessop (2005) bring out issues related to what they call faking friendship. From their feminist perspective, they suggest that the interviewer might put herself in the position of being a friend so as to get participants to disclose more information than they really want to (pp. 120–121). I think there is a difference between developing rapport and becoming a friend.

Bottom Line: Researchers should make sure that they provide an environment that is trustworthy. At the same time, they need to be sensitive to the power that they hold over participants. Researchers need to avoid setting up a situation in which participants think they are friends with the researcher.

- **Intrusiveness**. Individuals participating in a research study have a reasonable expectation that the conduct of the researcher will not be excessively intrusive. Intrusiveness can mean intruding on their time, intruding on their space, and intruding on their personal lives. As you design a research study, you ought to be able to make a reasonable estimate of the amount of time participation will take. I remember Mary's study of senior female executives with very busy schedules. She needed to make sure that her study would not intrude on their work lives. She scheduled interviews at their offices and tried to limit her interviews to a maximum of one hour. Intrusion into personal space might be an issue for some individuals; they may not want you in their homes or classrooms. You might have to negotiate a neutral location for a discussion. Although you may forgo some important information, the trade-off is worthwhile. Invading personal lives is a very real problem when you are studying the lives of others. Sometimes the conversation gets very personal. I recall a class in which we were practicing interviewing techniques—getting participants to open up and talk to each other. One situation became quite sensitive and one of the class members began to cry. I quickly ended the demonstration, but my eyes were opened to what can happen when rapport develops quickly and when participants have sensitive issues they wish to discuss.

Bottom Line: I don't think there are any easy answers here either. Experience and caution are the watchwords. You might find it difficult to shift roles to neutral researcher, especially if your field is counseling or a related helping profession.

- **Inappropriate Behavior**. Individuals participating in a research study have a reasonable expectation that the researcher will not engage in conduct of a personal or sexual nature. Here, researchers might find themselves getting too close to the participants and blurring boundaries between themselves and others. We probably all know what we mean by inappropriate behavior. We know it should be avoided. Yet, there are documented examples of inappropriate behaviors between teachers and their minor students, between therapists and their patients, and between researchers and their participants.

Bottom Line: If you think you are getting too close to those you are studying, you probably are. Back off and remember that you are a researcher and bound by your code of conduct to treat those you study with respect.

- **Data Interpretation**. A researcher is expected to analyze data in a manner that avoids misstatements, misinterpretations, or fraudulent analysis. The other principles I have discussed involve your interaction with individuals in your study. This principle represents something different. It guides you to use your data to fairly represent what you see and hear. Of course, your own lens will influence you. I am not suggesting that you strive for an objective stance. I think that is more the province of traditional approaches to research. Rather, I am pointing out the potential pitfalls of overinterpreting or misinterpreting the data you collect to present a picture that is not supported by data and evidence.

Bottom Line: You have a responsibility to interpret your data and present evidence so that others can decide to what extent your interpretation is believable.

- **Data Ownership and Rewards**. In general, the researcher owns the work generated. Some researchers choose to archive data and make them available through databanks. Questions have been raised as to who actually owns such data. Some have questioned whether the participants should share in the financial rewards of publishing. Several ethnographers have shared a portion of their royalties with participants. Parry and Mauthner (2004) discuss this issue in their article on the practical, legal, and ethical questions surrounding archived data. They suggest that because qualitative data might be a joint construction between researcher and respondent, there are unique issues related to confidentiality, anonymity, and consent.

Bottom Line: In fact, most researchers do not benefit financially from their writing. It is rare that your work will turn into a bestseller or even be published outside your university. But, if you have a winner on hand, you might think about sharing some of the financial benefits with others.

- **Other Issues**. As you plan your research, you might consider several additional principles raised by some. Roth (2004b) talks about the politics of research application approval and how those who make judgments about research applications are influenced by power and control. The feminist perspective is concerned, to a much greater extent, with power, respect, and risk. Others might take exception to this list. They state the main concern is the ethics of care for our participants and that these traditional ethical standards may not always be appropriate.

■ Problems With the Standards

Enumerating the list of standards is one thing; monitoring and enforcement is another. Governing bodies purport to be neutral and objective in these latter pursuits. However, some believe that applying these criteria to qualitative research is difficult because the standards were originally developed for scientific research. Universities differ considerably in the extent to which they apply the criteria to qualitative research proposals. Many members of these boards have little or no experience with qualitative research. Canella and Lincoln (2007) suggest that regulatory boards create "an illusion of the ethical practice of research" (p. 316). They suggest contradictory positions between a regulatory agency, on the one hand, and a philosophical disposition, on the other (p. 317). Their challenging paper introduces various complex issues. It seems clear to me that the more dynamic and fluid the research, the more difficult it is for review committees to determine whether the proposed research will meet the standards.

Here are some questions to consider.

- Can a written proposal convey a sense of the research to such an extent that a review panel can determine whether the standards will be met?

- How is a review panel to judge a qualitative research proposal in which the researcher is the instrument of research? In which questioning is fluid and dynamic, rather than fixed and static? In which the researcher may modify the plan as she proceeds?

- What happens when the standards are violated?

- How does a review panel that represents the dominant culture at a university evaluate a proposal that does not fit the usual mode? Feminist researchers, among others, are particularly sensitive to the politics of the review process.

You need to be aware of these potential pitfalls as you read the standards and think about your own research plans.

It seems obvious that researchers should pay attention to the principles outlined above. At this point in your reading, I think you will find it helpful to review some of the violations of these principles. First, I look at a few examples of misconduct in the general field of scientific research. Next, I highlight some of the cases in the field of qualitative research.

■ Alleged Misconduct in the General Scientific Community

We would like to believe that all people behave in an ethical manner. In practice, we know this is not true. From the politicians who take bribes, to the clergy who have inappropriate relationships with their parishioners, to the teachers who change grades when pressured, there are all too many examples of individuals who have behaved in unethical ways. While it is true that the vast majority behave ethically, we are no longer shocked or surprised when instances of unethical or inappropriate behavior occur.

Individuals who work in the research field are no different from those in other fields. Most behave ethically, but some do not. Here is an example of an experiment that went drastically astray. The principle of Do No Harm was ignored, overlooked, or forgotten in what is known as the Tuskegee Experiment. In 1972, details of this experiment run by the U.S. Public Health Service became known. The experiment actually began in 1932, when about 400 poor black men with syphilis from Tuskegee, Alabama, were identified for a study about the effects of penicillin on the disease. Even when the drug proved to be a cure in the 1940s, treatment was withheld. The experiment continued for 40 years, and not until the NAACP won a lawsuit in 1973 was some restitution paid. A public apology was finally delivered by President Clinton in 1997. This egregious example, in the name of scientific research, highlights many issues: Individuals without power or status can be mistreated for political or economic reasons; treatment can be denied even when it is shown to be efficacious; government safeguards are not always effective. Several factors are especially troubling about this landmark case: The individuals studied were poor, black men; the study was funded and sanctioned by the government; it took a lawsuit to bring the information to public awareness; the experiment lasted for 40 years; and finally, a public apology to the men in the study and their families was not issued until 65 years later. (For a full account, see National Public Radio's 2002 description of these experiments at http://www.npr.org/programs/morning/features/2002/jul/tuskegee/.)

Another principle of ethical behavior is related to data interpretation. You are probably aware of admonitions to interpret data conservatively and not go beyond what the numbers or facts show. Misleading statements are also to be avoided. But what about the researcher who falsifies or manufactures data? What strikes me as so distressing about the following two examples is that the individuals involved were prominent: one a Nobel Prize winner and the other a knighted British psychologist. In his 1992 book *Impure Science,* Bell wrote of the competition for research funds from government and industry and how researchers have falsified data to obtain or keep funding. The case of David Baltimore is especially interesting. As president of the Rockefeller University in the early 1990s, Baltimore, a 1975 Nobel Prize recipient, was accused of research misconduct and cover-up. The allegations were not proven, and Baltimore went on to become president of Cal Tech and the 2007 president of the American Association of the Advancement of Science. His coauthor was accused of fabricating data; the case ultimately went before the U.S. Congress, and she was barred from receiving grants for 10 years. In 1996, however, the charges were dismissed. What seems clear to me is that high stakes, power, and influence may lead to corruption or the appearance of corruption. Falsifying data or misrepresenting it may seem minor when so much is at stake. For details about the case, read the compelling 1998 account by Kevles. Another example is that of renowned British psychologist Sir Cyril O. Burt. Born in Stratford-upon-Avon in 1883, Burt attended Oxford, worked on intelligence tests, and was chairman of the Psychology Department at University College in London. He was knighted in 1946. Much of his research involved studies of identical twins, and he rose to prominence for the conclusion that identical twins reared apart were closer in intelligence than nonidentical twins reared together. It was not until after his death that others studied his data and concluded that the data were falsified to advance his hypothesis. This case is not completely clear-cut, however, because others reviewed his diaries and did not find any evidence of misrepresentation. Whether or not Burt falsified his data to support his conclusions is unknown. However, it is clear that temptations are there to manipulate data.

While the examples cited are extreme, I bring them to your attention because the researchers who were involved were considered preeminent in their fields. Rather than serving as role models for those in the ranks, these people were alleged to have violated important ethical principles. What seems clear to me from these examples is that when the stakes are high, our ethical compass sometimes goes off kilter.

■ Misconduct in the Qualitative Research Arena

Qualitative researchers have their share of unethical conduct. One case that has recently come to light concerns inappropriate behavior on the part of the researcher. Harry Wolcott, a longtime ethnographer, wrote a case study of a Kwakiutl village and school in 1967, and he has written extensively about qualitative research over the years. In 2002, he wrote about Brad, a young man he studied and befriended. *The Sneaky Kid and Its Aftermath* chronicles his "intimate and tumultuous" relationship with Brad. We learned from Roth's 2003 review that this book is actually a first-person account of the sexual intimacy between the researcher and the research participant. Subsequently, we learned that the young man beat up the researcher and set fire to his house (see also Plummer's 2004 review). That Wolcott continues to make contributions to the field of qualitative research is quite a puzzle to me. While Baltimore and Burt seemed to have weathered the storms surrounding their alleged data falsification, Wolcott himself admitted to the behavior and wrote about it publicly.

Another interesting case is that of Laud Humphreys. This case involves the principles of confidentiality and informed consent. During the 1970s, Humphreys acted as a lookout in a study of homosexuals in public places. He took information about them, especially their license plate numbers. Using this information, he later visited these men, saying they were selected for a random survey. While he violated the two principles mentioned above, some believe that the greatest damage had to do with violation of the Do No Harm principle.

Tolich (2002) discussed issues regarding internal confidentiality. In particular, he talked about confidentiality within connected groups. These groups might be families, couples, or mentors and apprentices. When various informants who are members of a particular group become aware of what other insiders are saying, confidentiality might be compromised. Although Tolich himself didn't violate codes of ethical conduct, he argued that institutional committees need to be aware of internal confidentiality to the same extent that they are aware of external confidentiality.

What appears clear is that researchers may find themselves knowingly or unknowingly violating research codes of ethics. In this next section, I discuss special problems associated with qualitative research and ethical conduct.

■ What Are the Special Problems for the Qualitative Researcher?

Principles and theory are good, as far as they go. But it is now time for me to get practical. I'd like to consider several different kinds of research projects in which you might become involved. The first issue concerns potential difficulties in maintaining privacy and keeping information confidential. This example comes from a study a student of mine conducted several years ago. Judy and several of her colleagues had taken the initiative to start a preschool in a poor area in a large city adjacent to the suburb in which they lived. They had worked for several years, raising funds and getting the school operational. Data were gathered, primarily through interviews with the five founders of the organization. She went through the appropriate channels to receive approval. Now, some years later, I think about the potential ethical issues regarding this study. I see a possible dilemma for Judy. While she had promised the organization privacy, it was common knowledge in Judy's community and the community in which the school existed that she had started this school. When she published her findings, even though she disguised names and locations, how could it be expected that many would not know which school and which leaders were interviewed? How could she reasonably maintain privacy and confidentiality in this situation?

I suspect this might happen fairly often when case studies are conducted. Imagine that you are located in a very remote area. If you study a particular school or classroom, it might be impossible to disguise the identity of the school. Is this a serious violation? Perhaps the problem only arises if the results turn out to be negative in some way. If not, I think the researcher needs to take extra precautions to try to avoid revealing identifying characteristics about the case.

Another student of mine designed a phenomenological study of the lived experiences of families with autistic children. In 2008, as I write this chapter, the issue of autism dominates the news. Estimates on the number of autistic children have risen dramatically. But in the year 2000, when Paul conceived of this study, autism was not talked about very much. Those who had studied the topic focused on the children, but Paul had another idea in mind. He wanted to study family life. He was the president of a school for autistic children. His research involved studying the lived experiences of the families. His participants were recruited from the school he directed. When he wrote his findings, he needed to disguise identifiable information about the school. In fact, those who knew him were well aware of his role at that school. Paul's study is another example of problems of maintaining privacy. A second issue with his study was how to ensure that participation was voluntary. And finally, because he planned to go into homes, he needed to make sure to avoid being intrusive. I do not think participants were unwilling to be studied, but if they did not want to, I think it might have been difficult for them to deny his request, given his relationship to the school. You can see that because of Paul's position in the organization, families whose children were at the school might have felt that they could not say no. As I remember, however, Paul had quite the opposite situation. Because he was the father of an autistic child, other families felt comfortable opening up to him. Paul was able to avoid ethical dilemmas and instead presented a candid and revealing picture of their lives. I remember Paul sitting in my office in awe of the cooperation he received from these families and the insight he gained into their lives and his own.

These real-life examples should help you see that the divide between what is written on paper and what you encounter is sometimes great. So much of qualitative research evolves as you proceed with data collection and analysis. Plans that you make in your office or at your computer in the quiet of your own space may shift and turn as you proceed in the real world. As you learn about being a qualitative researcher, you might find yourself facing many dilemmas. McGinn and Bosacki (2004) supported the idea of addressing ethical issues in research courses. Here are some questions you should think about.

How do you balance the need to respect those you study and not see them as just objects or subjects? Much of experimental research talks about drawing random samples of subjects. These nameless and faceless individuals are only there to serve as representatives of larger populations, to which you will draw inferences. But qualitative research is not like that. In fact, that is why I keep using the term *participant* rather than *subject.* That is by design. The people you study are real people. Unless you are on the Internet, you will see them. You might even take a liking to them. You might see their personal plights, as Alice did when she studied the wives of Chinese students. But you need to be very cautious about getting too close to the people you study. You cannot save them if they are sick. You cannot offer them counseling if they are troubled.

How do you deal with the politics of review boards? Roth (2004a) cited four fictional case studies related to ethics, politics, and power. He argued, in fact, that he couldn't really write about actual case studies because he would need institutional approval. He concluded that ethics and politics are inseparable. You probably never really thought that research and politics were connected. As I sat at my computer in June 2008, I was reminded only too vividly of the discussions concerning the "gold standard" of research studies (i.e., randomized double-blind experiments). One writer on a qualitative Listserv suggests it is the qualitative research community that needs to demonstrate the appropriateness and rigor of our designs to the larger community. So it is that review boards struggle to determine how best to judge qualitative research proposals. You need to be aware of this as you proceed.

Much of qualitative research involves observing individuals in their natural settings. You can think of these observations as occurring in public spaces. I remember a student who studied how students arranged their physical space in a large university library. She was interested in the extent to which they exhibited open tendencies or closed themselves off by surrounding themselves with books, coats, and papers. She did not obtain consent from these individuals because they were in view of everyone. Maybe she was invading their privacy. You can imagine all kinds of public spaces in which you might want to study people: people at sporting events, schoolchildren on a playground, parents and children interacting at McDonald's. I have spent quite a bit of time observing discipline strategies of young mothers as they interact with their children in various public spaces. I do not think you need to obtain consent in these situations. If you approach the people you are studying, they might think you are crazy. Anthropologists often traveled to exotic lands to study cultures other than their own. Today, researchers are more likely to study Internet cultures. When you are in cyberspace, you don't necessarily know who else is there. And they may not know that you are there.

I have mentioned special problems with regard to conducting studies on the Internet. We know that some people resent others using their discussion groups or other communities as "data" to be mined, as though the writers are not really people. Seeking permission is often problematic. Sometimes you don't know who the people are. Other times, people report that they feel violated. I think we have much more to learn about this.

Technology seems so wonderful. Writing our papers on computers seems to be the desired approach. I can't imagine going back to a typewriter or a pad and pen. Yet, with these technological advances come so many responsibilities. Here are some things to think about when doing qualitative research. Many of us use videos, cell phones, or digital cameras to capture the environments we study. But when you publish your study, how do you preserve anonymity when using video? Prettyman and Jackson (2006) highlighted some important ethical questions. For example, how do they guarantee anonymity when using videos and when linking data through a software program that links audio and video in presentations? New technology lets you link quotes directly back to data, which makes it increasingly easy to find where data come from.

You may wonder how you can possibly manage all these issues. In the next section, I provide you with information about how many universities handle the research conducted by faculty and students.

■ Setting and Maintaining Standards

As students, you are bound by the code of conduct and ethical standards imposed by your college or university. Most colleges or universities have established Institutional Review Boards (IRBs). An IRB is a committee whose job is to review, approve, and monitor research involving human subjects. It is designed to provide critical oversight. Actually, IRBs are governed by a federal regulation under The Research Act of 1974. All institutions that receive federal funds, whether directly or indirectly, require IRB approval for all research. When the legislation was passed, research was considered to be of a biomedical or laboratory nature. As social science research has moved away from the purely experimental, review boards have offered interpretations of the rules. You can read examples of the interpretations, as well as some vignettes, at the National Science Foundation (n.d.) Web site. IRBs wield considerable power within a university. It will be your responsibility to prepare a research proposal in such a manner that an IRB will be able to determine whether human subjects are protected from many of the violations mentioned earlier. Many have developed comprehensive instructions and procedures for conducting research.

Typically, an IRB will ask you to prepare a research proposal explaining your study. In addition to preparing a proposal, the board will usually want you to prepare an informed consent letter or form to be signed by all participants. Participation in a research study should be voluntary. Typically, your research will involve either identifying an organization or group you wish to study or identifying individuals who represent a particular group or have a particular characteristic. In the first case, you might gain approval from the organization. However, you must also obtain approval from individuals within the organization. Individuals should not feel as though they are coerced and must participate in a particular study. This may seem straightforward, but the voluntary nature of participation needs to be stressed by you. On the other hand, you might be studying individuals with certain characteristics or traits. In such cases, you would identify them from various sources and then seek their consent.

Here are two examples that might help you see this more clearly. You plan to study educational programs in an adult training facility. You seek approval from the director of the facility. He gives his approval. All participants in the facility are volunteers. Everyone will have to complete an informed consent letter. Or, you decide to investigate teacher interaction within several schools. You receive approval from the school district and from the principals of the several schools. You will still need to obtain signed informed consent letters from the individuals at those facilities.

If your study involves non-English speakers or those with certain disabilities that might make reading difficult, a responsible adult would need to sign the consent.

In some cases, researchers choose an "opt-out" letter rather than an informed consent letter. Such a letter would say something like this: We plan to conduct research at your school on the topic of forming friendships. Your child might be chosen to participate. The time involved will be less than one hour. If you do not want your child to participate, please sign the attached and return it to the school office.

If your research involves studying people who are in public spaces, obtaining informed consent becomes quite tricky. I recall taking my class to study parent-child interactions in a large supermarket. I instructed them to enter the grocery store, obtain a cart, and pretend to be shopping. They were then to find a parent and child together and surreptitiously follow them. We did not get consent because we were in a public space. This entire class project backfired, however. The store manager noticed me lurking at the front of the store, and he thought I was someone from the central office observing him. Eventually, he came up to me and asked what I was doing. One of my students came to me and told me that he had seen a shoplifter but did not confront him. In hindsight, I believe I should have notified the manager of what we were doing. Whether or not we need to obtain informed consent to observe individual behaviors or listen to other people's conversations is somewhat open to question.

Studying individuals on the Internet has also been the subject of some discussion. We can think of the Internet as either public or private space. I do not believe that IRBs have come to a clear decision on how to treat this kind of data. Increasingly, qualitative researchers have developed projects that involve studying individuals they encounter on the Internet. They might want to study people on MySpace or YouTube, or they might want to study individuals who participate in chat rooms. Whether this is public or private space is unclear. But when a researcher intrudes into private space, resentment may occur. One member of a group said in anger: "I certainly don't feel . . . it is a safe environment . . . and I will not open myself up to be dissected by students or scientists." Eysenbach and Till (2001) raised questions about privacy and informed consent. In discussing informed consent, they talked about both passive and active research strategies. Passive research might involve observing communication patterns. Obtaining permission is not needed. In contrast, active research might involve more direct involvement of the researcher. They cautioned that those on the Internet do not expect to be participants in research studies and might even resent a researcher "lurking" in their online community. They offered two suggestions for obtaining informed consent. First, they suggested sending an e-mail giving people the opportunity to withdraw from the list. Alternatively, they talked about asking individuals retroactively if they want to withdraw from the analysis. They did not think obtaining permission from the list owner is adequate. This is similar to getting permission from the head of an organization to have people in the organization participate.

Researchers and institutional review boards must primarily consider whether research is intrusive and has potential for harm, whether the venue is perceived as "private" or "public" space, how confidentiality can be protected, and whether and how informed consent should be obtained.

Eysenbach and Till (2001) also raised questions with regard to privacy. Quoting the exact words of a participant in a newsgroup may violate privacy and confidentiality even if identifying information is removed. You might wonder how this is the case. They suggest that powerful search engines might enable someone to identify the original source, even if the researcher is not able to. It is actually not so simple to distinguish between public and private space.

■ Problems With Review Boards

It seemed so simple. Universities would establish boards to review research conducted by faculty and students. The boards would develop a set of standards for research. When IRBs came into being in the 1970s, there was general agreement about what constituted solid scientific research, so most boards adopted standards to monitor research of that type. But as I have discussed throughout this book, many types of qualitative research take a philosophically different position from traditional research. Many individuals who serve on IRBs are not trained in this type of research and may find it inadequate. Many IRBs have been slow to change. Hemmings (2006) added the point that there are different ethical frameworks and orientations toward what she calls "ethical principles of respect for persons, beneficence, and justice" (p. 12). Finally, Cannella (2004) suggested that qualitative researchers should become activists with regard to such boards.

Because a qualitative research proposal often lacks specificity with regard to questions to be asked or observations to be made, some boards find it difficult to determine whether violations might occur. There is some controversy in the field as to whether, and in what ways, IRBs can remain objective, while at the same time recognizing that qualitative research is, of necessity, fluid and dynamic.

In fact, some lament that IRBs struggle with finding ways to accommodate qualitative research modes, while at the same time enforcing what they perceive to be standards of appropriate conduct for all research. In much the same manner that I suggest that we need to modify our evaluation standards, here, too, I suggest that IRBs should find ways to accommodate what Mauthner et al. (2005) called "qualitative research that is characterized by fluidity and inductive uncertainty" (p. 2). They continue, "most ethical judgments applied to qualitative research designs are negotiated within an organisation's own internal regulatory body" (p. 4).

Lincoln and Tierney (2004) discussed how IRBs can impede the conduct of qualitative research. They suggested that proposals for such studies often have to be revised numerous times to move them in a more conventional direction. They believed this demonstrates either lack of understanding or prejudice toward nontraditional research. Tierney and Corwin (2007) suggested that IRB regulations are becoming stricter as universities anticipate litigation. They believe that these increased restrictions may impinge on the academic freedom of the researcher. T. Johnson's

(2008) personal narrative about her difficulty receiving IRB approval for her dissertation is extremely revealing. She had planned to study the phenomenon of sexual dynamics in the classroom. Of course, she knew this was a sensitive topic, but she had the backing of her committee. She quickly learned that she had "forgotten the necessity of performing docility" (p. 213). I think she felt betrayed by her institution that, she said, "had once set me free" (p. 213). She noted that one reason she faced so much difficulty is that her work did not fit the standard concept of scientific methodology.

Ultimately, we are our own monitors and judges of appropriate behavior. Guidelines are helpful; they remind us of the areas to concentrate on. They pinpoint specific principles we might not have considered. IRBs serve as monitors for universities, but they also are political beings. Requirements set by government agencies, private organizations, or school systems also attempt to keep us on track. As a researcher entering the field, you have an obligation to those who provide the valuable information for your study. It is easy to focus on your study and what you need; those you study are equally important. Koro-Ljungberg, Gemignani, Brodeur, and Kmiec (2007) suggested "researchers' ethical decision making and freedom of choice need to be separate from discussions related to researchers' compliance, duties, and institutional responsibilities" (Abstract). Boman and Jevne (2000), in their narrative about being charged with an ethical violation, offered this suggestion: "The stories about the dilemmas and the conflicts of our research experiences, often left untold, are paramount to advancing our notions about what constitutes ethical and unethical conduct in qualitative research endeavors" (p. 554).

You might be interested to learn what happened to Susan. She contacted me the next time I was at the school and asked to speak to me. She assured me that she was just testing me to see whether I kept my word. After further questioning, I came to believe that she was now telling me the truth. I only wish all dilemmas would end so easily. Of course, I will never really know which version of the truth Susan was telling.

■ Summary

Ethical behavior is defined as "a set of moral principles, rules, or standards governing a person or profession." Major principles of ethical conduct include that the researcher should do no harm, that privacy and anonymity of participants must be protected, that confidentiality of information must be maintained, that informed consent of participants needs to be obtained (including assurance that participation is voluntary, with the opportunity to withdraw from the research), that inappropriate behavior must be avoided, and that data must be interpreted honestly without distortion. Finally, the extent to which participants are to share in data ownership and any benefits from the research must be considered.

Although the principles seem straightforward, a series of examples were provided that illustrate the difficulty in adhering to the principles, often because situations may have a complex array of conflicting interests. The role of the IRB was discussed, along with the dilemmas sometimes faced by qualitative researchers in meeting the requirements of the IRB.

INDIVIDUAL ACTIVITY

Purpose: To examine the major principles of ethical conduct.

Activity: Answer the following questions, then share your ideas with the class.

1. *Dealing With Confidentiality.* You conduct a phenomenological study of teenage students from a suburban school system. You conduct an in-depth interview with a teenager to whom you have promised confidentiality. She tells you she is depressed and plans to commit suicide. You believe she means it. Can you break your promise? If so, who do you tell?

2. *Dealing With Anonymity.* You conduct a case study on a small school in a remote location. When you write up the results, it is almost impossible to disguise the school, yet you promised you would treat the data anonymously. How should you deal with this?

3. *Dealing With Inappropriate Relationships.* You conduct an ethnographic study of a young adult over a long period. Your fieldwork takes you to his home, his school, the bars he frequents, his church, and so on. Over time, you become very attached to him. You find your friendship leads to feelings toward him that you cannot control. You know that getting too close is inappropriate, but you find it difficult to control your feelings. What should you do?

4. *Dealing With Informed Consent.* Your plan is to study educational practice among a particular tribe of Native Americans. You approach the leader of the school on the reservation. He gives his permission to study students and teachers. However, when you attempt to get the participation of these groups, no one is willing to sign your permission form. They are willing to talk to you, but they do not trust what you might do with the form. Even though you assure them that you will keep the information private, they see you as someone who represents the leadership and thus are mistrustful. What should you do? How do you convince them that they need to sign the form for you to continue?

5. *Dealing With a Reluctant IRB.* You attend a state school in the Midwest. You have heard that the IRB is quite traditional, yet your study is about teenagers and illegal substances. You have access to a number of individuals through a recreational center. You feel sure that you can get participants to be in your study and open up to you, but you do not want to plan a detailed list of questions because you want the conversation to evolve. You receive support from your advisor and encouragement from your committee members. How do you write a proposal that will get approved?

6. *Dealing With Privacy.* You interview college students about life on campus. One student tells you that his roommate seems seriously depressed and spends much time on the Internet looking at sites for making bombs. Do you tell someone?

Evaluation: Look at how students are able to resolve ethical dilemmas.

Chapter 5

Designing Your Research

Choosing From a Variety of Approaches

FOCUS YOUR READING

- Qualitative research designs include various approaches.

- No one approach is better than another.

- Several approaches can be combined in one study.

Those who cannot remember the past are condemned to repeat it.

—George Santayana

The next step was how to approach qualitative research. Learning the experiences that are "lived" and "felt" led me to the phenomenological aspect of research. This directed me to intense reading and inner searching as to how to conduct my research. I needed to divorce myself of my personal thoughts about retirement, my viewpoints, and biases. I had to listen to the story that the professional women would tell me. I could not embellish or put words in their mouths. This would be the study of their stories and experiences.

—Mary Repass

There are many ways to think about doing qualitative research. You can think about what sort of **research approach,** or plan for conducting research, you might use. Some researchers choose a phenomenological approach, in which they study the lived experiences of individuals with the primary goal of describing the experience. Other researchers choose an ethnographic approach; they are interested in sociocultural phenomena and how humans interact within a culture. Some rely on doing case studies of a particular event or setting or of particular people. Still other researchers have considered using a mixed methods approach, rather than relying on purely qualitative research.

You can also think about *who* is studied. In some cases, researchers select individuals different from themselves. Filmer (2007), an Anglo-American, focused on immersion into a Mexican and Spanish culture and deals with issues of the linguistic experiences of these students. Westrick (2005) studied secondary students and their understanding of intercultural sensitivity. Kozleski et al. (2008) studied special education students in several countries. In addition to focusing on students, researchers also study teachers, parents, or administrators. You might find yourself drawn to one or another group of individuals to study, either because you can gain access to them or because you have a research question that pertains to one or another group.

You can also think about *what topics* are being studied. I presented a variety of research questions in Chapter 1. Here are other examples drawn from recently published studies. Luykx, Lee, and Edwards (2008) examined how teachers and students in one science classroom carried out their "communicative work" in the context of certain policy constraints. As ethnographers, Golden and Mayseless (2008) are primarily concerned with the ways in which teachers seek to nurture and inculcate a deep sense of cultural, social, and political values in their young students.

Whether a researcher begins with a research approach, participants to be studied, or a topic, these three areas are intertwined, as depicted in Figure 5.1. In fact, you can plan your own research by entering the process in any of the three places, individually or in combination.

Recall that earlier I described qualitative research as an umbrella term. Some people who conduct qualitative research do not appear to select any one particular approach but follow general principles that include hearing the voices of those studied, using the researcher as a conduit for the information, studying things in a naturalistic manner, looking at the whole of things, and avoiding testing hypotheses. Results rely heavily on words, and often quotations from those studied are included in the document. In fact, these characteristics are common to all kinds of qualitative research. Others who conduct

Figure 5.1   Interrelated Factors in a Qualitative Research Study

qualitative research choose an approach that serves as a guide and helps define how the study is to be conducted. In the sections that follow, I discuss these approaches in depth. It is clear that there is not general agreement about which approach represents the best qualitative research design, even though some claim that they know the best way to conduct research. The variety of approaches to qualitative research presents a challenge both to the novice and experienced researcher. See Starks and Trinidad (2007) or Creswell, Hanson, Clark, and Morales (2007) for comparisons of the different approaches.

Did You Know

Many of the research approaches come from disciplines other than education, but since the 1980s, qualitative designs have been applied to study questions related to students, teachers, and ways of learning.

■ Ethnography: Studying Cultures

The purpose of **ethnography** is to describe the culture and social interactions of a particular group or subgroup. It involves extensive immersion in a setting (e.g., a school, classroom, playing field, lunchroom, bus, nurses' station, or airport). Offshoots of the ethnographic method that you may come across are autoethnography, photoethnography, and microethnography. In some cases, researchers conduct studies that are ethnographic in nature but do not involve extensive interactions or immersion. The ethnographic approach, long a mainstay of anthropologists, has been widely used in education, especially since the 1980s.

Introduction

Ethnography is one of the qualitative research designs that became popular in education in the 1980s. Initially, ethnographers immersed themselves in different cultures for extended periods. School ethnographies usually involve researcher immersion for a much shorter time. Ethnographies of online communities have become popular today. This approach to research has moved from a scientific model to one that is more open to hearing the voices of others. Offshoots of an ethnographic approach include critical ethnography and feminist anthropology.

History and Meaning of Anthropology and Ethnography

Anthropology and ethnography are two related terms. **Anthropology** is a general term used to describe the study of cultures. Ethnography refers to a systematic description of a culture that is based on direct observation of a particular group. Such observation usually involves a detailed study of physical characteristics and social customs. The field of anthropology began at the end of the 19th century. Originally from England and Europe, it was brought to the United States at the beginning of the 20th century. British anthropologist E. B. Taylor (1832–1917) is considered the father of anthropology.[1] He and the American scientist Lewis Henry Morgan (1818–1881) were considered the founders of the study of cultural or social dimensions. Franz Boas (1858–1942)[2] and Bronislaw Malinowski (1884–1942),[3] together with Ruth Benedict (1887–1948)[4] and Margaret Mead (1901–1978), were identified with anthropology and ethnography. Boas contributed the idea of cultural relativism to the literature. Boas' approach was to utilize documents and informants, while Malinowski believed that a researcher must become immersed for long periods in the field. He urged ethnographers to live with their informants, learn the language, and participate as allowed. From him, we get the idea of interpretive anthropology since it was the viewpoint of the "native" that was important. This is the origin of fieldwork and **field methods**, the procedures used to collect and analyze data.

From the latter part of the 19th century until the 1950s, anthropology was aligned with a strong scientific foundation. As the field developed, one concern was the power relationship between anthropologists and those they studied. As colonialism ended, new ways of conceptualizing anthropology emerged. In the 1960s, the climate shifted toward acknowledging that the scientific study of culture might not be possible. It was acknowledged that change and conflict might be as prevalent as stability and harmony. By the 1970s, postmodernism and feminist anthropology became popular.[5]

Although anthropology as a discipline has been around for well over one hundred years, the field of educational research did not adopt ethnography to any great extent until the 1980s. Metz (1983) set the stage: "Qualitative research, or more narrowly ethnography, has recently [early 1980s] enjoyed a sudden burst of moral and financial support in educational research" (p. 391). Yon (2003) suggested that

> the growth of educational ethnography as a subfield within anthropology reflects a growing focus on prescriptive, applied, and reformist research within urban contexts. It maps the transition from modernist formulations of the field in its formative days, when ethnographies laid claim to being sealed and scientific texts, to the more recent formulations shaped by postmodern and poststructural ideas that undermine earlier meanings of culture and call attention to the explanatory limits of ethnography. (p. 411)

Yon (2003) argued that these developments are not distinct phases but overlapping moments in the evolution of the field of study. In particular, he notes a move toward reflexivity in educational ethnography. Actually, this move toward reflexivity permeates many traditions in qualitative research.[6]

Offshoots of ethnography/anthropology include autoethnography (Bochner & Ellis, 2001; Childers, 2008; Ellis, 1995; Holman Jones, 2004; Jewett, 2004; Slattery, 2001) and photoethnography (Aldridge, 1995; Harper, 2003), which is said to be the art and science of representing other cultures through visual means. Ellis and Bochner (2000) describe autoethnography as a "systematic sociological introspection and emotional recall" as a way to understand personal experiences (p. 737). A related area is visual anthropology, which is premised on the belief that other cultures can be understood through the visual symbols they use, based on an analysis derived from long-term participant observation of that culture. Photographs and films of other cultures have a seemingly objective explanatory power that masks the subjectivity implicit in their making (Nakamura, 2003).

Examples From the Field

Much of the ethnographic writing comes from sociology or anthropology departments rather than from departments of education. Ethnographers often choose as their area of study subgroups within their own culture that operate outside the mainstream, so you might encounter studies of gangs, of special education students, of ESL (English as a Second Language) learners, or of people with disabilities. Frank and Uy (2004) taught preservice teachers ethnographic practices. A. Campbell (1984) and Schalet, Hunt, and Joe-Laidler (2003) wrote about girls in gangs; Armstrong (1998) provided a portrait of football (soccer) hooligans; and Goode (1994) described the social construction of children who are born deaf and blind.

Some ethnographies are about schools or school children. Aggleton (1987) informed us about middle-class youth in transition from school to work in his book *Rebels Without a Cause;* Hey (1997) described girls' friendships in *The Company She Keeps;* and B. Thorne (1993) selected the topic *Gender Play: Girls and Boys in School.* Conteh (2003) wrote about a group of bilingual learners in the United Kingdom who have achieved success. Ulichny (1997) combined critical ethnography with praxis in a study of the restructuring of an urban high school. Creese, Bhatt, Bhojani, and Martin (2008) used a team ethnographic approach in a study of different types of schools. The study of cultures is an approach to research that educators find attractive (Fetterman, 1998). Schools and classes are studied extensively. Subgroups of students, especially those who have a particular behavior or characteristic or trait in common, appeal to researchers. Becoming immersed in a classroom is highly interesting to many researchers, who are too often put off by test scores and surveys. Ethnography has become a popular approach adopted by some qualitative researchers. Ellis and Bochner (2008) serve as the editors of a series on ethnographic lives. Eight titles are available as of 2008. A word of caution, however: De Welde (2003) reminded us "it is in fact ethnographers themselves who are battling it out over what ethnography should look like, how it should be done, how it should be presented, and what the goals should be" (p. 233).

■ Grounded Theory: Placing Theory in Its Context

> The purpose of **grounded theory** is to generate theory that is grounded in or emerges from the field. Two key ideas relate to grounded theory. One important hallmark is the use of theoretical sampling techniques—a concept that involves drawing repeated samples until no new concepts emerge. A second hallmark is the constant-comparative method of coding. This approach was developed in the 1960s (Glaser & Strauss, 1967) and is used in education. You will also find many interesting research studies in the field of nursing.

Introduction

Grounded theory is a relative newcomer to the field of qualitative research in education. You might be surprised to learn that Glaser and Strauss wrote *The Discovery of Grounded Theory* in 1967. As its name implies, this book dealt with theory, but not in the traditional sense. The authors suggest that using this way of doing research, theory emanates from the data, rather than the more typical view that data are used to test a particular theory. I believe that some researchers are attracted to grounded theory because the research being conducted could be taken beyond a particular data set and applied to theoretical issues. Others are attracted because its methodology is closer to the scientific rigor of quantitative approaches than some other qualitative research designs.

Glaser and Strauss came to see grounded theory in different ways as their thinking developed. Strauss, writing with Corbin in 1990, took a somewhat different approach, and Glaser (1992, 1998; Glaser & Holton, 2004) responded to Strauss' views. I will talk about a few of these differences subsequently; however, I don't think it is critical that you understand the nuances of the differences between these two writers. Rather, I would like to stress what I see is the essence of the approach.

Theoretical sampling, the constant-comparative method, and specific ways of coding are key elements of grounded theory. Theoretical sampling involves an iterative process of selecting a series of samples and analyzing data simultaneously until no new ideas emerge and the sample is said to be saturated (Draucker, Martsolf, Ross, & Rusk, 2007). Bowen (2008) described the process in detail. Unlike phenomenology or ethnography, grounded theory emphasizes a specific approach to coding the data. Three terms you often will encounter are *open coding, axial coding,* and *selective coding.* Davidson (2002) explained coding as follows:

> There are three distinct yet overlapping processes of analysis involved in grounded theory. . . . These are: open coding, axial coding, and selective coding. Open coding is based on the concept of data being cracked open as a means of identifying relevant categories. Axial coding is most often used when categories are in an advanced stage of development; and selective coding is used when the "core category," or central category that correlates all other categories in the theory, is identified and related to other categories. (¶ 4)

I believe that a number of people are attracted to grounded theory because the coding process is systematic and described in detail. McCarthy (1999) suggested that it was the rigor of grounded theory that led her to that approach for her dissertation. It works well for those who like structure. Coyne and Cowley (2006) provided a clear example of the steps you might follow in two critical elements of grounded theory: theoretical sampling and the constant comparison method of coding. Much of the published research using a grounded theory approach is related to nursing and health fields, rather than education.

History and Meaning of Grounded Theory

In the 1960s, positivism dominated the social sciences. Many researchers were drawn to methods that involved hypothesis testing, statistical manipulations, and computer analyses. I think this is because the scientific method was thought to be the sine qua non of methods. Those in the social sciences—who were often seen by other disciplines as "soft" and "lesser" and sometimes saw themselves in that vein—either believed that they were practicing "true" science or thought that they could convince others that they were. They believed that by using statistics and experimental designs, they were exercising rigor and searching for the truth. Like many of my colleagues, I adopted that view.

And although some educational researchers were attracted to ethnography or phenomenology, by far, they were in the minority. These approaches did not have the scientific rigor that was thought to be part of positivism and postpositivism. Words like "touchy-feely" and "soft" were bandied about.

So who should come on the scene but Anselm Strauss? Strauss was involved in studying death and dying and the care of the chronically ill. After earning his degree, he went to San Francisco to head a new sociology department as part of the school of nursing. He did extensive writing prior to his work on grounded theory. I suspect that he found quantitative methods lacking in terms of understanding the needs of the physically ill.[7]

What emerged was his seminal work (with Barney Glaser) on grounded theory (Glaser & Strauss, 1967). Initially it was directed at sociologists and accepted by many because it offered an element of scientific rigor and intellectual rationale. Haig (1995) concurred with this view and suggests that Glaser and Strauss thought the approach met accepted standards for good science. Haig argued that grounded theory "offers us an attractive conception of scientific method." Grounded theory appealed to those in higher education, adult education, and nursing education for these same reasons (Daalen-Smith, 2008; Eich, 2008; Reid & Moore, 2008).

As I said above, after their initial writing, Glaser and Strauss took disparate views of what they meant by grounded theory. Glaser's view is that grounded theory looks at a particular situation and tries to understand what is going on. As with other qualitative approaches, data are gathered, typically through observations and interviews. The researcher jots down the key issues as data collection proceeds. What distinguishes Glaser's view is the constant comparative method. This data analysis technique involves comparing data from one interview (or observation) with data from another interview or observation. He suggests that theory quickly emerges.

Imagine that you are studying teachers from urban school settings. You are interested in investigating how administrative support enhances teaching. As you collect data from Teacher 1 and then Teacher 2, you write down the issues they present and compare the two interviews. You would then follow with additional interviews and compare what you learned with what you already have. You would make note of—or insert in your database—some simple codes that express what you think each is saying. This first step is open coding. You would then move from these specific codes to more general categories or themes. This is the step called axial coding. From these themes, you begin to develop a working theory to help explain the key concepts of administrative support, teaching, and urban settings. This last step is called selective coding.

Now, how does this process lead to theory? I think Dick (2002) said it very nicely.

> As you code, certain theoretical propositions will occur to you. These may be about links between categories, or about a core category: a category which appears central to the study. As the categories and properties emerge, they and their links to the core category provide the theory.

Glaser and Holton (2004) despaired that grounded theory has eroded with the remodeling used in qualitative data analysis. They reminded us that grounded theory actually emerged from doing research on dying patients in the 1960s. Consequently, they suggested, it was discovered and not invented.[8]

Examples From the Field

I have selected a variety of examples of grounded theory so that you can see the range of topics covered. McCarthy (2001) studied parents from various socioeconomic backgrounds to gain an understanding of the process they go through to make school choices. Petrie (2003) used grounded theory to study ESL teachers' views on the innovation of visual language. Starbuck (2003) relied on data from the Internet in her unusual dissertation about art and collage. Here is an example taken from her work. This dramatic and unusual dissertation offers insight into as yet rarely tapped sources.

> You enter an artist's studio outside of Paris to find an animated group of artists. A heated conversation is in full swing. A dramatic French woman looks around the room and passionately exclaims, "Mail art must move, change like the world. Mail art is just at his [*sic*] starting, we have to re-invent it." . . . Message boards are an art supply in the studio of the networking artists. Artists use message boards to achieve a continuation of correspondence art networking goals. However, in many cases, artists feel that the real communication still takes place in the mail. (pp. 27, 34)

Brown, Stevens, Troino, and Schneider (2002) suggested that by using grounded theory they can increase understanding of the college student experience. They also provided a detailed explanation of the coding process as well as how to enhance credibility.

Grounded theory has become a popular paradigm for many who value structure and order. I believe it is closest to using a quantitative approach of all the research designs. Some students are attracted to it because they can offer a logical and coherent, if somewhat cumbersome, method of data analysis. On the other hand, those very characteristics seem to limit its usefulness, in my view. I wonder how much of what is found in the field contributes to theory.

■ Our Lived Experiences: Phenomenological Inquiry as a Philosophy and Method of Study

The purpose of **phenomenology** is to describe and understand the essence of lived experiences of individuals who have experienced a particular phenomenon. This tradition is closely tied to existential philosophy. Originally proposed by Husserl (1917/1981) and predominant in Europe in the 1930s, it has been reinterpreted by a variety of writers and extended to the United States. Bracketing is a key concept. In the last few years, with the wide availability of the Internet, phenomenology has become prominent in diverse areas of the world. In the 1990s, nursing researchers and educators were among the first to make use of phenomenological approaches. Hermeneutics is closely associated with phenomenology; its purpose is to interpret text. It originally was associated with interpretation of the Bible.

Introduction

I want to begin with a story. I have been a teacher for many years. I have thought a lot about what it is to teach, what I am trying to get across, how to assist my students to find their own way of raising questions and finding answers. I have also thought about how I should do this in the context of a university. Should I provide detailed lectures? Should I have students engage in small-group discussions? Should I ask students to read everything about a topic and then write a paper? Should I ask students to find an expert and pick his or her brain? Should I have students do a project reflective of what they understand? You can see that these questions that I raise are not about content per se; rather, they center on the pedagogy of teaching.

Now, not all of you have been teachers. But what you each have in common is that you have been students—prior to formal schooling (from the time you played school with your siblings and friends or from the time your parent tried to teach you the names of colors and parts of your body), during your elementary and high school years (in classes with others of your own age or peer group), during your college years (in classes or increasingly mediated with the Internet and computers), and even at this moment. As you continue to read, I would like you to try to recall what it was like to be a student.

So, back to my story. For the last few years, I have been engaged in teaching with the new technology facilitated by the Internet. When I began, I wondered how to do it. Were the questions I raised earlier the appropriate ones? Were there other things I needed to consider? I lived through this transition for several years, and I wanted to know more about it. Was I alone in my questioning? What did others think? How could I find out?

I had the perfect topic for a phenomenological study. At least, so I thought. I was very interested in the increased activity of online teaching. I recruited one of my doctoral students to conduct the study. She liked the idea; it seemed so simple and straightforward to her. Her committee accepted her idea. We were ready to go.

And now my challenge came. This student had been in one of my qualitative research classes several years prior to her conducting the study. Based on that information, I assumed she had quite a good grasp of the major traditions in qualitative research as well as some knowledge of phenomenology. I suggested to her that the study of online teaching might appropriately be done using a phenomenological approach. I offered the idea to her and she seemed to be taken with it. I thought she understood phenomenology. After all, she just had to go to a few references (e.g., Husserl or Heidegger or van Manen), figure out how to bracket her thoughts, decide what *epoche* means, and be on her way.

As I worked with her, I came to see that what seemed so simple—studying the lived experiences of individuals who had experienced the same phenomenon—was indeed quite complex. I found myself extremely challenged in trying to make sense of all these complex ideas and bring them to a practical understanding. At the same time, I did not want to "dumb down" or "make trivial" the philosophical or existentialist underpinnings. In this next section, I try to take you on the same journey that I took my student.

History and Meaning of Phenomenology

It is generally acknowledged that Edmund Husserl[9] is the father of phenomenology, although Priest (2002) suggested that it was Kant who first used the Greek term in 1764. I found it instructive to read from Husserl's inaugural lecture at Freiburg im Breslau in 1917: "A new fundamental science, pure phenomenology, has developed within philosophy. . . . It is inferior in methodological rigor to none of the modern sciences" (Husserl, 1917/1981, p. 10). Husserl continued somewhat later in his talk to acknowledge that empirical science is not "the only kind of science possible" (p. 14). I think this issue is important because it highlights the idea that an approach other than a pure science is an acceptable alternative.

Husserl's writings on phenomenology served as the impetus as this philosophical movement spread throughout Europe. Heidegger (a German) and Merleau-Ponty (from France) were leading proponents of the philosophical concept of phenomenology. Sartre's writings on existentialism were closely related.[10] European writers and philosophers were critical influences on phenomenology, unlike other qualitative research approaches.

Phenomenology in Today's World

You might be wondering why you are reading about a movement that had its origins in Germany around World War I and was not practiced much in the United States. What does that have to do with studying one's lived experiences? What kinds of links can be made to the use of phenomenology in the current climate?

Phenomenology is not an easy concept to understand. It is said to be both a philosophy and an approach. My intention here is to first tell you about key elements of phenomenology and then to introduce you to some of the newer thinking. Researchers, philosophers, and writers do not agree on what phenomenology is. So how do you, as a new learner, come to understand this field?

Phenomenology, as an approach, looks at the lived experiences of those who have experienced a certain phenomenon. Suppose you have selected some experience that you want to study and you have located individuals who have lived that experience. Let's follow my earlier example with my student. She decides that she is interested in studying the experience or phenomenon of teaching online. She identifies individuals who she knows have taught online. She places her own thoughts on the topic in brackets so as not to influence or color her thinking as she continues her investigation. She interviews a number of people who taught online. After transcribing her data, she moves on with the process of reducing the data so that ultimately she is able to discern the essence of the phenomenon. Think of it as moving from very specific and detailed statements about the phenomenon, or even examples of the phenomenon, ultimately to the essence of the phenomenon. One way to think of it is that we begin to stretch our understanding of something into an interpretation of it, and the researcher is the interpreter of the data.

The process is completed when you reduce the data you have to its essence. I often see people begin with 25 themes. By the time the reductive process is complete, there might only be three essential components to describe the lived experience. In a later section, I talk more about phenomenology and its methodological process.

I want you to appreciate that phenomenology, as an approach, has taken hold worldwide. From its roots in Europe it has now spread broadly into the United States, Canada, and parts of Asia. I want to talk about three trends: first, the use of a phenomenological method in a variety of disciplines including, but not limited to, education, nursing, adult learning, allied health fields, art education, and special education; second, the broadening scope of interest in phenomenology worldwide facilitated, in part, by the Internet and the opening up of travel throughout the world; and, third, the expansion, modification, and in some instances reinterpretations of the application of a phenomenological method.[11]

A Variety of Disciplines

The use of a phenomenological approach has taken hold, especially in education and nursing. Beginning in the 1990s, phenomenology in education became fairly widespread (Barnacle, 2001; Vandenberg, 1996; van Manen, 1997).

Examples of phenomenological studies in education and related fields include Nielsen (2000), who wrote about using a hermeneutical phenomenological approach in art education; Stanage (1995), who explored adult education and phenomenological research; Westrick (2005) who was interested in international secondary school students and their understanding of cultural differences; and McPhail (1995), who wrote about phenomenology in remedial and special education and why it is an appropriate approach. Robinson (2000) reported on her study of students who are involved in online learning and presents an alternative to traditional linear writing by using what she calls a "Web-based spatial dissertation."

With the development of postpositivist approaches, phenomenology has been adopted by different disciplines as an appropriate way to explore research questions, which leads to a different way to construct knowledge. Rose (1993), in a book called *Feminism and Geography,* described how she saw the discipline of geography being influenced by feminist studies and phenomenology. In particular, phenomenology has become a way to research the gaps in the discipline, those areas that previously were not considered important to research because they had little to do with the public and patriarchal world of geography. Nursing education, in recent moves to define itself as a separate and different discipline from the rational, scientific medical model, has adopted phenomenology as a way to research previously uninvestigated areas, in order to inform the theory of nursing practice on which nurse education is based. LeVasseur (2003) provided insight into the issues regarding bracketing.

Growth Worldwide

There has been an enormous resurgence of the study and use of phenomenology worldwide. Embree (2003) spoke about phenomenology in the 21st century. He suggested that the resurgence is due to the collapse of the Soviet Union, increased international travel, and the Internet. It is interesting to see how this resurgence has developed. A 2002 conference in Prague on issues confronting the post-European world led to the founding of The Organization of Phenomenological Organizations. In an essay published to celebrate that event, Embree (2003) informed us that there are at least 20 countries with traditions of phenomenology and 22 disciplines other than philosophy that have conducted phenomenological investigations.

Embree (2003) offered a number of reasons to explain the worldwide growth. Colleagues with no personal experience of World War II are coming into leadership positions, so phenomenology has been restored since the end of fascism in Germany. You will recall that I said earlier that Heidegger was a strong proponent of phenomenology, but his fascist persuasion put him in disfavor with many academics. Embree also suggested that while no tradition in philosophy prior to the 1970s was generally receptive to women, there are now many women new to the field. Although the center of the phenomenological movement is still in the West (remember that its center had been in Europe for long periods of time), greater international travel and the Internet and the widespread use of English have led to a greater interconnectedness among countries.

There are many recent writings in phenomenology, especially from the Far East, that represent a much larger viewpoint. From Malaysia, Scown (2003) studied the process of phenomenological inquiry into the lived experience of being an academic. You can read about reflective analysis in the phenomenology of photography by a Chinese colleague in Korea (in Embree, 2003). In the *Finnish Journal of Education,* Perttula (2000) wrote about transforming experience into knowledge using a phenomenological approach. There is also the *Journal of Phenomenology and Education,* published in Italian.[12]

Reinterpretations of Phenomenology

You have read above about the burgeoning of the phenomenological movement worldwide. I imagine that you will not be surprised, then, to discover that there is no one thing that is considered phenomenology. Although most acknowledge Husserl and his influence, what you will find in the research and writing today is that many things, many ways, and many approaches take on the phenomenology label. These approaches range from very strict, conservative, traditional approaches to very broad interpretations and applications to the study of lived experiences, the thread that holds the various applications together. It is unclear how phenomenology evolved from a rigorous science to an antifoundationalist position. Ihde (1995) discussed postphenomenology in his essays in the postmodern context.

Phenomenology as a Philosophy and as a Method

You can also consider phenomenology to be a philosophy. Dermot (2000) suggested that the phenomenological movement reflects European philosophy in the 20th century. Husserl's idea was that phenomenology was a new way of thinking about philosophy; rather than being esoteric and metaphysical, phenomenology would enable the philosopher (and phenomenologist) to come into contact with matters, the actual lived experiences. It is quite beyond the scope of this book to get into the philosophical voyage that Dermot takes.[13] The philosophical underpinnings are very complex and are not necessary for you to understand as you begin to learn the elements of phenomenology as a method.

As I said earlier, we can think of phenomenology as a philosophy and we can think of it as an approach. I don't think you can begin to understand one without the other, which is why I have tried to give you some key elements of the philosophy. Now we turn to phenomenology as an approach. If the philosophy is about the lived experiences, and the essence of these lived experiences, how is it that we should go about "doing" a phenomenology? I have gone into the method of phenomenology in some depth because at times it is somewhat confusing. You know that it is a study of lived experience. But it is more than that because ultimately the researcher's role is to extract the essence of that experience by means of a reductionist process.

1. *What do we mean by the lived experience?* The lived experience is a term from Husserl.[14] Lived experiences, or life experiences, are those in which we are all involved. Often, a researcher selects a particular experience or event on which to focus. In the adult education field, one might study the lived experience of professional women as they plan for retirement (Repass, 2002). The individuals who are studied have been involved in the experience. In education, one might study the experiences of families living with a child with autism (Glass, 2001) or one might study educational leadership (Van der Mescht, 2004). Boeree (1998) offers some insight into understanding the lived experience. Think of it this way: Every experience has an objective and a subjective component; thus, you must understand all aspects of a phenomenon.[15]

2. *What is meant by the essence of the experience?* On a deeper, more philosophical level, we can ask, How does the nature of the experience indicate the nature of the human being's existence? I agree with Bottorff (2003) that when we consider the essence of the experience, we are moving to a deeper level of understanding. It is this last part that gets a little difficult to understand

and that is related more to the philosophical underpinnings. You can see that a description of an experience, while interesting, is not the full intent of the research. I believe, however, that you will encounter a number of studies that are phenomenological in intent but do not go to a deeper level of understanding. Perhaps that is because some are reluctant to bring too much interpretation to the data they have. Or perhaps it is because we do not trust ourselves to move to an understanding of the inner self.

3. *What is the reductionist process?* How are bracketing and epoche related to it? Phenomenological reduction is the process that is used to facilitate seeking the essence of a phenomenon. It is here that bracketing, epoche, or eidetic reduction (terms often used interchangeably) describe the change in attitude that is necessary for the philosophical reduction. **Bracketing** involves placing one's own thoughts about the topic in suspense or out of question. Epoche involves the deliberate suspension of judgment.[16] Giorgi (1989) suggested that the researcher should search for all possible meanings of the phenomenon.

Husserl suggested that a researcher could set aside his or her own views about the phenomenon by using a process of bracketing. As a mathematician, he was interested in objective and logical approaches, so he thought that this act of setting aside would accomplish objectivity. It has been almost 100 years since Husserl gave us this idea of bracketing. Gearing (2004) provided detailed information about six distinct forms of this concept—ideal, descriptive, existential, analytical, reflexive, and pragmatic—as well as a very clear account of phenomenology. I have found in my own experience that it is too simplistic to think that a researcher can set aside his or her own ideas about a phenomenon. I like to think of making explicit one's ideas on the topic. This is accomplished by writing down one's ideas, preferably prior to immersion in the literature on the topic. The mere task of writing puts the researcher in a mind-set that forces him or her to make explicit his or her ideas.

Hermeneutics is a term related to phenomenology.[17] Hermeneutics is generally thought to be the science of interpretation and explanation. In the hermeneutical process, there is an interaction or link between the researcher and what is being interpreted. I don't want to get involved in too much detail, but you should know that hermeneutics was originally associated with interpretation of textual material, especially the Bible. Byrne (1998) suggested that hermeneutics and phenomenology are often used interchangeably. She reminded us, however, that phenomenologists focus on lived experiences and hermeneutics refers to interpretation of language. Two assumptions of hermeneutics are that humans use language to experience the world and that we obtain understanding and knowledge through our language. The word derives from the Greek god Hermes, a son of Zeus and the fastest of the gods.

You have read about the philosophy and methodology of phenomenology. With an almost 100-year history, this tradition has become widely used in education. Starting in Europe and transported to the United States, it has now become a dominant tradition worldwide. I think you will find yourself very attracted to the elements of the tradition. However, as with many of the other approaches to research, details of how to do a phenomenology are not readily available. Further, current writers do not agree on what phenomenology is and even how to do it. You would be well advised to read some completed phenomenological studies to decide whether this tradition is right for you.

■ Case Study: A Look at the Particular

A **case study** approach is an in-depth examination of a particular case or several cases. You may be familiar with case studies in psychology or counseling; doing case study research is somewhat similar. But instead of focusing on one individual, a case often is identified as a particular program, or project, or setting. It is up to the researcher to identify the case and to set limits or boundaries. As with several other approaches, this came to education in the late 1980s.

Introduction

Case study is another approach to qualitative research. Case study seems to be primarily an approach without any philosophical underpinnings. In many instances, when researchers say they are doing case study research, they are most likely identifying a single entity to study. The entity could be as small as one individual or as large as an entire school. It is quite common to encounter case study methods combined with some of the other paradigms I described earlier, so you might come across a phenomenological case study or an ethnographic case study.

History and Meaning of Case Studies

No doubt you have heard of case studies in many disciplines. Business schools use case studies from real life. Psychologists use case studies of individual patients or families. Product designers use case studies to examine new products. Case studies were used fairly often in the early days of sociology, when an interest developed in studying various groups or programs. But case study research approaches were not accepted by many, who saw them as less rigorous and not scientific. According to Tellis (1997), the history of case study research is marked by periods of activity and inertia. He attributes early use in the United States to the Chicago School of Sociology. The study of immigrants presented ready-made cases for researchers. However, in a move to make research more scientific, sociologists at Columbia University began to discredit case study methodology. For many years, the Columbia view was predominant. However, a resurgence of interest in case study research emerged as qualitative methods began to be accepted in education.[18]

Case study as an approach to qualitative research involves the specific and detailed study of a case or cases. I recall a student of mine who studied the case of the development of a nursery school in an urban neighborhood of Washington, D.C. For years, the community was interested in building a school for the children, many of whom were non-English speaking. But most who lived in the immediate area did not have the experience or means to tackle the assignment. It took an outside group of concerned citizens, working together with the clergy and members of the local community, to secure a location, build a staff, and develop a program. Her research documented this process and the program. Case studies are often of this type.

What is a case? What do we mean when we talk about a case? Here are some ideas that might help you sort through this murky area. A case can be limited to a characteristic, trait, or behavior.

You might study a child (or children) with a particular type of learning disability (characteristic). Or you might study an administrator who exhibits particular behaviors, such as cooperative or collegial interactions (behaviors). Or you might study a teacher who is outgoing (trait). The key to this kind of case study is that you identify the characteristic, trait, or behavior in advance and then identify individuals who have or are thought to have the characteristic. This is a somewhat narrow view of case study and might result in missing the very information that would be enriching or informative.

More often, a case is limited to a particular entity, for example, Mr. Brown's special education classroom, Ms. Hernandez's honors English class, or an athletic team with the highest win/loss record. By extension, more than one case could be studied.

A case can be limited to one type of situation. These situations are often special or even unique. For example, you might come across a case study of the experience of 9/11. Or you might come across a case study of those who lived in Prince Edward, Virginia, when the public schools closed to avoid integration. Or you might read about a case study of individuals who attend year-round schools.

So we might have cases that are designed to study behaviors, traits, or characteristics. We might have cases that are designed to study a particular program or classroom. Or we might have cases that are designed to study a particular situation. You can see in all of these examples that what is studied is critical to the design, analysis, and interpretation.

Selecting a Case

How do you select a case? I propose you consider one of three types of cases: the typical, the exemplary or model, or the unusual or unique. Other kinds of cases you might select could be the constructed or the borderline. One of the most common methods is to select a case that is considered *typical* of others in the same set. For example, if you want to study fourth-grade classrooms, you can ask someone knowledgeable in a school system to nominate a typical class or classes. What is typical? It is up to you, the researcher, to think about the criteria you want to use. You might give some guidelines; for example, you could decide that the class test scores should be average for that school system or the racial composition should be similar to that of the school system, and so on. It is usually a good idea to identify more than one case because it is possible that a particular case does not want to participate, or you find you need additional information. Of course, you might have decided to do a multiple case study, so you would need to have several cases. What I want to stress here is that the case you study is considered typical. Since you are not trying to generalize to other fourth grades, it is not important that you cover the range of possible fourth grades. Patton (2002) and Donmoyer (1990) reminded us that we are more interested in the richness of the information we generate from the case than the ability to generalize.

Another approach is to select a case that might be considered *exemplary*. For example, you might want to study the best or the most outstanding fourth-grade classroom in a specific area or system. Again, you would have to rely on nominations from knowledgeable individuals to get the appropriate case. For an unusual exemplary case study, you can read an account of football in Bath, England, in the late Victorian era that was designed to illustrate cultural imperialism (Henson, 2001). A third type of case you might select is one that is considered *unusual, unique,* or *special* in some way. While this sounds somewhat similar to an exemplar, it does not have to be. For example, you might ask for nominations of a sixth-grade class that is doing something unusual or creative or groundbreaking.

Often, students think they have to identify a case that is representative of all cases of a particular type. This kind of thinking occurs because the novice researcher is thinking about making generalizations to other cases. In qualitative research, this is definitely not so because you do not have sufficient breadth to make generalizations. So, it is not important to get a case that represents all other cases. Your goal is to get detailed and rich descriptions of the case you select.

We can look at some examples from education as well. If you wanted to study reading programs serving urban youth, you might come up with the following:

Typical case: A program that exists in a school division with average test scores.

Exemplary or model case: A program nominated by a school division with high test scores.

Unusual or unique case: A program identified by a school division using special materials.

Of course, you could select criteria other than test scores. There are several important ideas to remember. Your case does not have to be one type or another, nor must you include all types of cases.

Still another take on selecting cases is one offered by Jensen and Rodgers (2001). They mention snapshot case studies, longitudinal case studies, pre-post case studies, patchwork case studies, and comparative case studies.

While most suggest selecting cases using the methods I describe above, Garson (2002) took the position that the selection of a case should be theory driven. This is in keeping with his scientific orientation. His views represent a more scientific, traditionalist view of research. I think you would find his views are in the minority, however.[19]

Examples From the Field

There are many different kinds of case studies. Typically, researchers study a program or project on which they have been working. I find it interesting that case studies of online programs or multimedia are readily available. Kearsley (2002) is an example of a typical case study of students in an online masters program in engineering. Piper (n.d.) conducted a case study of her own interactive and multimedia dissertation. C. Smith (1996) reported on a case study of corporal punishment in public education and discusses the difficulties of applying research findings in local policy situations. Bennett's (2002) case study of ways in which a university tried to increase enrollment of minorities in teacher education programs illustrates a study of a case close to the researcher. O'Brien's (2007) case study of a black school founder provided insight into African American schooling.

Together with Izumi Taylor, I conducted a case study of the Kawasaki Kindergarten (Lichtman & Taylor, 1993). Izumi Taylor, originally from Japan, had studied the school on several occasions and had close contact with the principal. I traveled to the site and spent several days observing classes, interviewing the principal and teachers, and photographing various situations. We addressed typical case study issues, including identifying a single unit, developing boundaries, the larger context of the case, the in-depth and longitudinal nature of the case, and, finally, the process we followed. We selected a case study approach because we were interested in the particularistic and descriptive nature of the case.

I use this example to illustrate the power of working together and working apart. In our presentation, we emphasized the use of multiple perspectives. Our own backgrounds—one Japanese and one American—enabled us to see things through different lenses. In our paper, we interwove our different perspectives to describe the school. We began with no particular ideas in mind. Our major findings identified the importance of rituals, especially at mealtimes. We also noted group effort and cooperation as important components of this modern Japanese preschool.

The use of case studies has had a resurgence of interest along with other approaches to qualitative research. The process is similar to many other approaches. I think you will find it helpful to remember that information from case studies provides rich and detailed insight into the case or cases being studied. As with other approaches to qualitative research, generalization is not expected or viable. You will probably locate case studies that also are referred to as ethnography, grounded theory, or phenomenology.

■ Mixed Methods

The purpose of a **mixed methods** approach is to intertwine both qualitative and quantitative methods in a single study. Many students are drawn to mixed methods because they learn that professors like the more structured approach of statistics but acknowledge that data from observations or interviews yield rich information. Creswell (2003), in his book *Research Design: Qualitative, Quantitative and Mixed Methods Approaches,* provided some details on how to conduct a mixed methods study. You can also read Tashakkori and Teddlie (2003) or B. Johnson and Christensen (2008) on the same topic.

Introduction

Although, in practice, researchers have tended to take elements from both quantitative and qualitative research paradigms, methodologists have argued that to be true to the assumptions of either a qualitative or a quantitative research design, the two designs should not be mixed. The idea of combining quantitative and qualitative research designs into a third design or paradigm is a fairly recent phenomenon. When qualitative research in education began to be adopted by some, the assumptions under which these early writers operated (e.g., Lincoln & Guba, 1985) precluded combining elements from quantitative designs. Beginning in the 1990s, some researchers looked to combine the best elements of the two paradigms. For a full discussion of the issues and analyses of the strengths and weaknesses of the two paradigms, you can read R. Johnson and Onwuegbuzie's (2004) very informative journal article. They argue that mixed methods should be seen as a third paradigm (quantitative and qualitative being the other two).

History and Meaning of Mixed Methods

It is difficult to locate references prior to the late 1980s that combined quantitative and qualitative research designs. Tashakkori and Creswell (2007) agreed; in the first issue of a new journal on mixed methods, they commented that "The issues have been debated for almost three decades" (p. 3). When elements from both models were joined in research studies, it was often to accommodate the idea of triangulation. By gathering data using questionnaires and tests with interviews or observations, researchers would be able to make a stronger case for the quality of their research. In these early times, researchers felt bound to try to meet criteria of sound research that involved objectivity and numbers. Today, the field has changed to the extent that using elements of both in a mixed design model has become quite popular. After reviewing the results of more than 200 studies, Bryman (2006) suggested that researchers should be explicit about when to use such a model and that "the outcomes may not be predictable" (p. 111).

Not all who write about mixed methods support its use. Giddings (2006) warned that "Rather than the promotion of more co-operative and complex designs for increasingly complex social and health issues, economic and administrative pressures may lead to demands for the 'quick fix' that mixed methods appears to offer" (p. 195).

Examples From the Field

Sosu, McWilliam, and Gray (2008) studied teacher commitment to environmental education, following what Creswell (2003) called sequential and concurrent procedures that involve a quantitative approach to test theories and a qualitative approach to examine a number of individuals in depth. In this type of design, data are collected in sequence rather than concurrently. The quantitative analysis is heavily statistical while the analysis of qualitative data involves looking for themes. Results are reported separately as well. Jang, McDougall, Pollon, Herbert, and Russell (2008) reported on research about school success under challenging circumstances. In contrast to the Sosu et al. study, these researchers collect data concurrently. Data analysis is heavily statistical, and the style of writing in both articles is very traditional.

Mixed methods is not parallel to the other research approaches that fit under the umbrella of qualitative research. Rather, it is an attempt, as some say, to take the best of quantitative and qualitative research designs. There are some differences in the way it is applied when conducting research, however, and if you decide to combine elements from both qualitative and quantitative research designs, you will need to read in much greater depth.

■ Feminist Research and Feminist Theory

The purpose of feminist research is to use a feminist perspective in conducting research. Although not exactly a research approach or tradition, **feminist theory** is a movement that arose in the 1980s. In part, it was a reaction to the disparate power, politics, and equality between those conducting the research (typically white men) and those who were being studied (often women, minorities, or those with disabilities). Feminist theory is also related to postmodernism, postcolonialism, and

(Continued)

(Continued)

post-Freudian psychoanalysis. This movement and more contemporary feminist approaches have a stronghold in Canada and Australia as well as in the United States. Geiger (1986) argued that feminism depends on women's point of view, and the meaning of their life experiences and histories provides important insights.

Although not always seen as a research approach, feminist research is included so that you can see approaches that take a more active stance. It is often closely associated with critical theory and structuralism.

Introduction

Feminist research emerged as a reaction to approaches described earlier. As the field of research began to be open to female scholars, there were numerous questions about the appropriateness and adequacy of prevailing approaches. In particular, questions of power disparities were on the minds of many women. This field actually has many principles in common with critical theory; **queer theory**, which treats sexual and gender identity as social constructs; and postmodernism. But like many of the other approaches I have discussed, there is not general agreement on what is meant by feminist research.

History and Meaning of Feminist Research

Harding (1998) is one of the key figures in this movement. She combines elements of feminist, postmodern, and postcolonial critiques of modern science. Brayton (1997) suggests that what makes feminist research uniquely feminine are "the motives, concerns, and knowledge" brought to the research process (¶ 1). Brayton suggested that it differs from traditional research for three reasons: it removes the imbalance of power (Fine, 1992), it is politically motivated and concerned with social inequality, and it addresses experiences of women. Maguire (1987) defined feminism as

(a) a belief that women universally face some form of oppression or exploitation; (b) a commitment to uncover and understand what causes and sustains oppression, in all its forms; and (c) a commitment to work individually and collectively in everyday life to end all forms of oppression. (p. 79)

Fine (1992) identified other aspects of feminist research as well. I see many of these as being common to all qualitative research. I wonder whether these principles were identified first by qualitative researchers and then feminist researchers, or whether the reverse is true. In any event, Fine identified the unequal power issue and the need to eliminate it. She talked about making research participants true participants by calling them coresearchers. Others speak to eliminating the word *subject* because it is a masculine term. Related to letting participants share in the research is the view that they are experts about their own experiences. Fine also spoke about the researcher taking an active role, rather than being a detached and objective observer. Related, then, is the need to address the actual and apparent inequalities between those being studied and those who are doing the study. Research as consciousness raising and transforming is another element. I recall hearing a researcher at a conference speak about sharing the proceeds of her book with the participants. Social change is also important to feminist research. Rosenberg (1999) described how a feminist research circle promotes changing power relationships and contributes to social change.

Scheurich (1997) said there are four parts to feminist research. Feminist research aims to create social change; it strives to represent human diversity; it is a perspective, not a research method; and it frequently includes the researcher as a person. English and Irving (2008) wrote of feminist poststructural issues related to power as they studied gender and learning.

Examples From the Field

Here are some studies you might find interesting. Clinchy (n.d.) wrote about women's reflections on their undergraduate experience. Jackson (2001) wrote from a feminist poststructural theory of subjectivity. In her article, she presented the story of a young woman who worked with two cooperating teachers with opposing philosophies. LePage-Lees (1997) studied academically successful women from disadvantaged backgrounds. Aparicio (1999) presented a video project about women of color. Deutsch (2004) reflected on the process of becoming a feminist researcher and writer. I think you will enjoy reading Vargas' (2008) personal account that deals with race, ethnicity, and the power of interpretation. Lather's 2007 follow-up to an earlier experimental ethnography addresses what it means to do feminist poststructural work. Childers' (2008) thoughtful review commented that the book "puts a mark on what it means to practice at this historical moment in feminist research" (p. 301). These examples highlight how feminist research topics address social change and power relationships.

Feminist research methods and theories acknowledge disparities in power between those who are studied and those who study. They are also interested in issues about women and women's ways of knowing. Like some of the other new approaches, they are critical of the presumed objectivity and remoteness that characterizes traditional methodologies. They align themselves closely with critical theory and postmodernism. New on the horizon are some postfeminist approaches, which suggest that there be a reexamination of the premises of feminist theory.

■ Generic Approach to Doing Qualitative Research

> The purpose of a **generic approach** is to use qualitative methodologies to collect and analyze data (Lichtman, 2004; Sprenkle & Piercy, 2005). Users do not subscribe to any one of the approaches mentioned above; they often select elements from many of them. The use of a generic approach has gained fairly wide acceptance in the last decade.

You have read in depth about a number of approaches in qualitative research. Many have been used in education and serve as a guiding force for those beginning a research project. Sometimes a researcher selects a single approach; often, a researcher combines several qualitative approaches. Sometimes a researcher combines both qualitative and quantitative approaches. I want you to understand, however, that you can do qualitative research and not choose one of the approaches you have just read about. If you decide to take that path, you will be following in the footsteps of many others.

Although many researchers choose a particular orientation or combination of approaches, others do not make such a choice; rather, they take a generic approach. Chenail discusses this idea in an interview (Lichtman, 2004). While many may have operated this way, only fairly recently has it been articulated as a generic approach (Caelli, Ray, & Mill, 2003). Further, Caelli et al. see this as a trend that is growing. If the researcher takes a generic viewpoint, it is not necessary to adopt any one approach to doing qualitative research. Although Caelli and her colleagues suggested that this presents a challenge in terms of evaluating a study, they acknowledged that people are conducting studies that do not adopt any single methodology. The issue of evaluating the worth of a study is certainly not limited to evaluating generic studies. I have devoted an entire chapter to this topic (see Chapter 13). Caelli et al. expressed the view that evaluation is challenging because there is little in the literature about how to do a "generic" study well. They offered four areas that could be considered in evaluation of generic qualitative research: noting the researchers' position, distinguishing method and methodology, making explicit the approach to rigor, and identifying the researchers' analytic lens.

Merriam (2002) discussed a basic interpretive qualitative study. Such a design is used when the goal of the researcher is to understand how participants make meaning of a situation or a phenomenon. The researcher serves as the filter for the meaning, using inductive strategies with a descriptive outcome (Imel, Kerka, & Wonacott, 2002; Merriam, 2002). Of course, these ideas are prevalent in almost all approaches to qualitative research.

■ Additional Approaches to Qualitative Research

While I have talked in detail about a number of approaches, there are others you might encounter.

Narrative Analysis, Discourse Analysis, Biography, Autobiography, Narrative Storytelling Analysis, Life History. The purpose is to tell a story using the written or spoken word. Often, an epiphany is interpreted from the story. Denzin (1989) described several steps: collect an objective set of experiences, either chronologically or in life stages; gather actual stories; organize stories into pivotal events or epiphanies; search for meaning in the stories; look for larger structures to help explain the meaning in the stories. Goodson (1992) wrote about teachers' life histories. I have grouped these oral traditions together because they rely so heavily on narrative and stories. Narrative analysis is a general term that incorporates first-person accounts in story form, biography, autobiography, life history, oral history, autoethnography, pathography, discourse analysis (Lemke, 2003), or life narratives. Although life history as a technique (developed in the Chicago school) was popular from the 1920s, the technique came under fire when the debate between statistics and case studies became more intense and participant observation took on a greater predominance compared to life histories. But there has been increased use of biographical methods and life histories since the late 1980s (Bertaux & Delacroix, 2000; Chamberlayne, Bornat, & Wengraf, 2000; Creswell, 1997; Denzin, 1989).

Postmodernism and Critical Theory/Research. These approaches represent more of a philosophy and intellectual movement than a research method or theory.[20] According to Lemke (2003), postmodernism derives from **poststructuralism** and deconstructionism, which were initially criticisms of the structuralist movement of the 1960s. **Critical theory** derives from neo-Marxism and feminist theory, extended to include postcolonial theory and queer theory.

Perhaps the most characteristic tenet of postmodern critical work is that everything that European philosophy and science has held to be fundamentally true at an abstract or programmatic level is in fact a contingent, historically specific cultural construction, which has often served the covert function of empowering members of a dominant social caste at the expense of Others.[21]

Critical qualitative research, or critical theory, is related to postmodern research. Its purpose is to change the social context. Tripp (1992) argued that socially critical research in education is informed by principles of social justice.[22] Other key concepts associated with critical theory are sexuality and gender. You can see how closely related these ideas are to feminist theory.

Post-Postmodernism. The purpose of post-postmodernism is to react to "postmodernism's monstrous balloon of misconceptions" (S. Steinberg, 2000). Postmodern research, a trend popularized in the 1990s, challenges other forms of research. This is an outgrowth of the challenge to the modern world offered by the postmodern movement (Imel, 1998). I see this as primarily a philosophical movement and beyond the scope of our thinking here. You will find that the newest challenge is post-postmodernism. Many of the contributors to this movement are associated with phenomenology and hermeneutics. Diekelmann (2002) pointed out that

> Postmodern discourses share a commitment to egalitarianism and emancipation through deconstruction of the subject as opposed to recognition of its social and historical dimensions. The metanarrative, or grand stories of the culture, are considered discursive regimes of power and are deconstructed to reveal new thinking and possibilities. (¶ 1)

■ Summary

Different approaches to qualitative research were presented and described. An ethnography describes the culture of a group using direct observation. Grounded theory research generates theory that emerges from, or is grounded in, the field. It is characterized by the use of theoretical sampling, the constant comparative method, and specific coding methods (open, axial, and selective coding). Phenomenology is based on description and understanding of the lived experience of one or more individuals who have undergone a particular experience. In this approach, the researcher brackets, or attempts to set aside, her own thoughts on the topic; suspends judgment; and focuses on inductively understanding the meaning of the experience to the one(s) studied. A case study is an in-depth investigation of an individual or group with a primary purpose of describing one or more characteristics, behaviors, or traits. In feminist research, the purpose is to use a feminist perspective in conducting the research, which often involves an activist role to foster change. Finally, mixed methods research combines approaches from quantitative and qualitative traditions.

GROUP ACTIVITY

Purpose: To organize your ideas. You need to extract the essential elements about the various approaches.

Activity: Develop a series of questions and answers that would be suitable for a *Jeopardy* game. Work with three or four other students. Put your questions on cards with the answers on the reverse side. Play the game with volunteers from the class.

Evaluation: Determine to what extent your questions get at key elements and how your responses reflect your new knowledge.

───────────────── ■ ─────────────────

INDIVIDUAL ACTIVITY

Purpose: To design your own research study.

Activity: Identify at least three research questions that lend themselves to qualitative research. Write a one-page outline of how you would answer the questions. See whether you can determine which approach would be most appropriate for each of the questions.

Evaluation: Assess the extent to which you believe you have captured the essence of the approach.

■ Notes

1. In 1871, Taylor defined culture as "that complex whole which includes knowledge, belief, art, morals, law, customs, and many other capabilities and habits acquired by members of society" (p. 1).

2. Boas worked at Columbia University, which was thought to be the seat of the anthropological movement.

3. Bronislaw Malinowski, a prominent anthropologist who lived from 1884 to 1942, founded the field of social anthropology. During World War I, he studied Trobriand Islanders of New Guinea. Subsequently, he came to the United States, where he held prominent positions at Cornell and Harvard.

4. After earning her PhD under Boas, Benedict went to Barnard. Mead became one of her students. Benedict's *Patterns of Culture* and Mead's writing were significant contributions.

5. See Barrett (1996).

6. In recent years, the swing has been back to broader theoretical models. Most influential over the past 20 years has been Lévi-Strauss' (1968) structural model, which seeks to look below the surface of culture to identify the mental structures of human thought that underlie all cultures.

7. Strauss died in 1996. Strauss was trained as a sociologist at the University of Chicago but established his career as the founder of the Department of Social and Behavioral Sciences in the School of Nursing at San Francisco State. Glaser was part of his research team. Strauss' initial writings were in medical sociology; he studied chronically ill and dying patients. Glaser continues to work in the field. His book discusses the remodeling of grounded theory methodology by ascendant methods of qualitative analysis. There is also an international journal called the *Grounded Theory Review,* edited by Glaser.

8. You can read Glaser's current thinking on the topic in his comprehensive article titled *Remodeling Grounded Theory,* available at http://www.qualitative-research.net/fqstexte/2–04/ 2–04glaser-e.htm.

9. Husserl, born in Czechoslovakia in 1859, studied mathematics and astronomy in Berlin and Vienna. Brentano, an Austrian philosopher, led him toward philosophy and away from mathematics. In 1907, he gave five lectures on phenomenology. Although he planned to come to California in the mid-1930s, he became ill and died in 1938.

10. Other leaders include Levinas, who studied with Husserl and developed a philosophy of ethics, and Derrida, a French philosopher, whose contribution concerns the idea that there is no single meaning to language or text. He suggested that language is constantly shifting.

11. Go to the Center for Advanced Research in Phenomenology to read the latest ideas. They can be found online at http://www.phenomenologycenter.org.

12. If you read Italian, it is online at http://www.encyclopaideia.it/.

13. Dermot (2000) and Dillon (1997) provide additional and clear information on Husserl, Heidegger, Brentano, Sartre, Merleau-Ponty, Gadamer, Arendt, and Derrida. See also Sokolowski (2000) and Hopkins and Crowell (2003).

14. In its original German, *Lebenswelt,* or the world of lived experience, comes from Husserl's last work.

15. For more information, see Byers (2003) and Moustakis (1994).

16. Heidegger provides an alternative to bracketing. He acknowledged that our own culture, background, and gender influence our experience. He did not think bracketing was possible. Instead, he talked about authentic reflection that would enable us to know our own assumptions about a phenomenon.

17. Byrne (1998) offered a clear explanation of various aspects of hermeneutics. Lye (1996) also identified some basic principles of phenomenological hermeneutics.

18. You will learn something about the history of this field by reading Yin (2002), Merriam (2002), and Stake (1995).

19. Soy (2006) provided some specific directions on how to do a case study.

20. Postmodernist is the term used to refer to sociopolitical analysts known as the Frankfurt School, including Adorno, Marcuse, and Habermas. Freire has taken the movement into education in his work with oppressed minorities. See also Michael Apple and Henry Giroux.

21. It dismantles the most foundational procedures and assumptions whereby prior European philosophical traditions sought to establish universal truths or principles. It is fundamentally a revolutionary political movement, argued in intellectual terms. For a rather casual introduction to some of these issues, see Lemke (1994).

22. Tripp continued, saying "It involves strategic pedagogic action on the part of classroom teachers, aimed at emancipation from overt and covert forms of domination. In practical terms, it is not simply a matter of challenging the existing practices of the system, but of seeking to understand what makes the system be the way it is, and challenging that, whilst remaining conscious that one's own sense of justice and equality are themselves open to question" (Tripp, 1993, p. 114). According to Tripp, there are a number of methodological principles associated with the theory. They include participation by mutually supporting groups, consciousness that influences the way we teach and conduct research, and meaning that suggests that knowledge is not "subjectively neutral objectively verified facts." Rather, knowledge is socially constructed facts that are artificial and held differently by different groups.

PART II

Gathering, Organizing, and Analyzing

The five chapters in this part focus on the methodology of qualitative research. Chapter 6 addresses embarking on qualitative research. Chapter 7 is devoted to reflexivity and subjectivity. Chapter 8 deals with the role and function of a literature review. In Chapters 9 and 10, I offer you many practical suggestions on how to collect data through interviewing, observing, and other techniques.

I have said several times that qualitative research follows an inductive approach. I follow this principle in this book. I ask you to begin with the particular and move to the general.

Many of the suggestions I make are based on practical experience. I ask you to use the suggestions as you practice gathering data.

When you finish this Part, you should have collected a considerable amount of data. You will then need to turn your attention to deciding what to do with the data. That information is contained in Part III.

Chapter 6

Embarking on Qualitative Research

FOCUS YOUR READING

■ Think about what role you will play in conducting qualitative research. Are you suited to it?

■ Explore various steps to follow in conducting a group project on what it means to be a graduate student.

The position of the artist is humble. He is essentially a channel.

—Piet Mondrian

I was initially excited about the idea of doing a qualitative study. Though I had very little background, I knew that I was much more interested in qualitative research than quantitative research. Even though I had a strong background in math and statistics, I never quite bought into the quantitative techniques. I guess this is so for me because as an individual, I never quite fit into any of the stereotypes or norms that statistics claimed. I always thought that we could learn so much more in some cases by going out into the environment and investigating for ourselves.

—Donna Joy

In this chapter, I provide you with a concrete example of an extensive study that I have conducted with several of my classes. This study uses in-depth interviewing as the primary source of information. I use it for illustrative purposes only. Of course, other studies often rely on other methods of gathering information including observation, examining records, or collecting visual data. I begin the chapter with 20 questions that students typically ask. Then I lay out in detail the elements of the study and include much information drawn from student output. I hope you will find this interesting and that it will give you some ideas that you and your colleagues can use.

■ Twenty Questions

Did you know that *Twenty Questions* began in the 1950s as a BBC radio game show? The premise was that the host was thinking of something that could be animal, vegetable, or mineral. The questioners had 20 chances to ask the host "yes" or "no" questions about the object. At the end of the allotted number of questions, or earlier if a questioner wanted, a guess was made. If the guess was correct, prizes were awarded. When it was a game show, the audience was told by a mystery voice what the object was; the questioners could not hear. The phrase "twenty questions" became very popular. I want to begin with a variation of this game. I have chosen 20 questions that students typically ask me or that are asked by others, and I have provided my responses.

Q.1. How do I convince my adviser that doing a qualitative study will be worthwhile?

A.1. Prepare. If you come to a meeting with knowledge, you are always in a one-up position. So, read this book, read other material, and read qualitative proposals and completed qualitative research studies.

Q.2. How many research questions should I have?

A.2. Usually you have only one or two main questions. The questions you ask your participants are not considered your research questions.

Q.3. Since I only talked to three people, how can I generalize to similar individuals?

A.3. Generalization is a concept used in scientific research when you draw random samples from populations and generalize back to the populations; in that type of research, you test hypotheses. In qualitative research, you do not generalize or test hypotheses. Rather, you describe, understand, and interpret.

Q.4. How do I keep going when I do not seem to be getting anywhere?

A.4. Find a support group. Your fellow students are often the best source of support. If they are not available, rely on your faculty mentors or other supportive faculty. Try to locate a chat room on the topic. Develop your own blog. Remind yourself why you are in school and the goals you plan to achieve. Take a break and treat yourself to something that does not have anything to do with school.

Q.5. How do I form a good committee who will understand what I am doing and assist me in the process?

A.5. Rely on your advisor to guide you. Fellow students are also very helpful.

Did You Know

Many graduate students have posted blogs about their experiences. A student from Tunisia wrote about studying in Japan. A PhD biochemistry student wrote about his life and his lack of personal time. A father wrote about caring for two young children while being a student. This one is particularly amusing to me because almost all the women students I know have had to do just this. Another even wrote about her life after graduate school.

Q.6. Why won't they tell me how to do it?

A.6. I know how frustrated you are, but because this field is dynamic and creative, there is no right way to do something. There are several ways, and new ways emerge all the time. Use your creativity and talents here.

Q.7. What should I do with all the data I collect?

A.7. Well, you should have thought about that before you started, but I would strongly suggest you rely on the computer. You need to develop a system to organize and manage your information. At the very least, you should become familiar with a word processing program and a filing system. If you decide to use a computer software program, you will need to invest a considerable amount of time in learning the program.

Q.8. Do I need to back things up?

A.8. How often have I heard students say their computer died, the hard drive crashed, it rained on their files, and so on? I can't urge you enough to save your work often and in at least two locations. There are many easy storage systems available for use on your computer. Make sure you are familiar with them. You should probably invest in an external hard drive.

Q.9. I plan to do interviews. Should I develop a detailed interview script?

A.9. I expect you are used to having questions written out in advance and that you want to follow the same format for each participant. I would state an emphatic "no" about doing this. Your interview should be more like a conversation that you guide. You need to provide a chance for participants to tell their story in their own way and their own words.

Q.10. Which is easier to do—quantitative or qualitative research?

A.10. I would say that ease is not a deciding factor. What research questions do you have? Are you trying to study people, their lives, and their interactions? If so, qualitative research might be suitable. That is what you need to think about.

Q.11. I have read about triangulation. What is it and should I use it?

A.11. Triangulation is based on the idea that something (e.g., a submarine, a cell phone) can be located by measuring the radial distance or direction from three different points. Some writers hold the view that triangulating data, investigators, and methodologies can establish validity. I believe, however, that the concept is more appropriate to traditional or positivist paradigms and is not necessary in the newer forms of qualitative research.

Q.12. What style of writing should I use?

A.12. It is strongly recommended that you use a narrative, first person style. In that way, your story has more impact. Some resist this, but I do not. You can read Holliday (2007) or Wolcott (2001), who provide good resources for writing up your work and recommend using first person.

Q.13. I want to do something different. What else can I do?

A.13. There are many new ideas out there. I like the idea of using images to convey messages, and I strongly urge you to explore alternative means of presenting information.

Q.14. Why should I waste my time keeping a journal?

A.14. Self-reflection is critical in the new qualitative traditions. By keeping a journal, you will be able to examine your thinking and motivations and how they influence and are influenced by the work you do.

Q.15. I have read about feminist research, but I am a man. Am I precluded from this methodology?

A.15. As with most questions, it depends on whom you ask. I would say that sensitivity to feminist issues is critical. I suggest you explore with your female colleagues their reaction.

Q.16. This seems overwhelming to me. How can I do all of this and still live my life?

A.16. My two watchwords are priorities and balance. I often tell my students that they need to take time for themselves and build it into each day. I know so many of them have family and work responsibilities and often feel cut into many pieces. Of course, it helps to have supportive and understanding friends and family.

Q.17. How will I know when I am finished?

A.17. This is not an easy question to answer. You need to remember that you are capturing a slice in time and space of thoughts, actions, and beliefs. From a practical standpoint, finishing often relates to deadlines imposed by your institution or yourself.

Q.18. How do I learn about computer software packages, and should I use them?

A.18. You actually have two questions here. In my experience, the more sophisticated packages are quite difficult to learn on your own. If possible, you should attend a training workshop. You can also join a Listserv so you can ask others questions. But the learning curve is steep, and you may decide it is not worth the trouble. So you might have to revert to the colored pencils and note cards. I remember one student of mine used tape and poster board and had things pinned up all over her basement. I wonder how her family managed.

Q.19. How do I know whether my work is worthwhile?

A.19. This is a question that is relevant to anything you do. From doing laundry to making decisions about war, we strive for the best and put forth our best efforts. Qualitative research is no exception, but judging is quite complicated. Who is the judge? On what basis does he or she judge? You know whether the pillowcase is clean. Do you know whether going to war is right? And because one of the vexing questions now about qualitative research is its merit or worth, it is incumbent on you to be prepared to document what you did, how you did it, and what you found.

Q.20. So, I'm ready for my first steps. How do I begin?

A.20. I have included many suggestions throughout this book. Read below for a detailed account of a study conducted in my classes. Its topic—My Life as a Graduate Student—should be near and dear to you.

■ My Life as a Graduate Student

This project began with my desire to have students practice interviewing. It evolved into a complex, multiyear project with many documents. I have chosen to include some of the material that was developed by my classes over several years.

Let me tell you briefly what we did so you can get an overview. I identified the parameters of the project: We would explore life as a graduate student. I chose this topic because I knew that everyone in the class was going through the experience at that very moment. I could not think of another more pertinent topic than this. We would begin by discussing what interviewing was and then practice interviewing each other in class. In this way, we would be able to immediately identify a participant who met the criterion. We did not have to seek permission or go through an institutional review board. Next, we would identify someone else to interview. Our interviews would be recorded and transcribed, and we would bring in copies for all other students or post them as attachments to be accessed online. We would work in teams practicing data analysis, first by hand and later using computer programs (such as NVivo). Finally, we would each write up our interpretation based on our own data and the data of others. We would also keep a journal of our experiences. I, too, wrote up my interpretation of the process and the findings.

What follows is a detailed account of what we did at each phase of the project, why we did it, and some examples. These are the phases of the project:

Phase 1: Getting Started

Phase 2: Modeling Good Practices

Phase 3: Practicing Interviewing and Debriefing

Phase 4: Conducting Outside Interviews

Phase 5: Doing Preliminary Analyses as a Group

Phase 6: Doing Analyses as an Individual

Phase 7: Preparing Individual Papers

Phase 1: Getting Started

If you want to do qualitative research, it is critical that you get involved in a qualitative research project and actually collect and analyze data and write about what you learned. I decided that it would be valuable for my class to become involved in a group research project. In this way, I could deal with some common questions, some common data, and a topic that would be interesting to students. I don't remember precisely when I came up with the idea that the best topic would be to study the lived experiences of graduate students. I don't recall telling them that they were doing a phenomenological study. I thought that would be too complicated. I didn't ask them to do a literature review. But I knew they had a wealth of experience and thoughts on the topic.

Like much of qualitative research, the details were not all worked out before we began the project. But I knew there were certain things that I wanted them to do. My three main goals were for the students to practice interviewing, practice coding, and practice writing up results. We were on our way. I developed a set of materials for the interviews, worked out the details of the assignment, and introduced the project.

Phase 2: Modeling Good Practices

The first step in Phase 2 was to record our views about the topic. I knew that talking about them was not sufficient; we had to write our thoughts down. We took some class time to do this. I did not tell them that we were bracketing. Bracketing, as I discussed in the section on phenomenology in Chapter 5, is a concept that comes from Husserl (1917/1981) and Moustakis (1994). Its purpose is to set aside our views on a topic that we are studying so that our beliefs will not have undue influence on what we ask and what we learn. Actually, I don't really believe that you can set your views aside. Rather, I take the position that by making them explicit and overt, you will be well on your way to accomplishing the same purpose.

I did not give students specific questions to follow. I wanted them to practice the interview as conversation (Rubin & Rubin, 1995, 2005), but I knew that they would feel more comfortable if they had some general topic areas. So I asked them to write down what areas they thought they might find interesting. We discussed these thoughts in class prior to doing our interviews.

I encourage questions that are of a "how" and "why" nature. I also encourage questions that are neutral. I avoid questions that are "who" and "what." These latter kinds of questions lead to very specific answers and then just stop. They do not lead to a conversation.

The first thing I did was to demonstrate how to conduct such an interview. I asked for a student volunteer and I began my interview. Although I knew these students, I still wanted to model appropriate behaviors. I asked permission to record, gathered my paper and pen, and placed myself in the center of the classroom with onlookers on all sides. I began by making the participant feel at ease. We talked about her family and school in general. I asked what her major was and what kind of work she did. She seemed ready to begin. Now I was ready to conduct the interview.

I have two favorite ways to begin an interview. I either begin with a Grand Tour question (Spradley, 1979) or ask the participant to tell a specific and concrete story about the topic—something that happened to her last week or last month. I find these concrete stories very meaningful and reflective of underlying thoughts. They are especially useful for getting material that is not full of jargon. Grand Tour questions usually begin with something like, "Tell me what it is like . . ." In this case, I asked, "Tell me about your being a graduate student." Notice that the question is neutral and nondirective. I don't want to ask, "Tell me about the difficulties you face as a graduate student." I continued my interview for some time. I asked specific story questions, such as "Tell me something that happened to you last week while you were in school." Due to time limitations, I tried to illustrate different aspects of interviewing strategies, so I asked questions that permitted comparisons and contrasts. I asked questions that probed more fully. In Chapter 9, you will see my complete Interview Guide that illustrates various principles.

The next step in my modeling was to debrief with class members. I do this in several ways. I ask questions that try to get at points I was intending to illustrate. For example, what behaviors did they notice that showed my neutral stance? How did I provide wait time for the respondent to answer? How did I let the respondent's story come out in his or her own language?

Phase 3: Practicing Interviewing and Debriefing

We were ready to begin our practice interviews. Tape recorders were assembled, teams of three were chosen, and places selected for the interviews. The students were told they had about 30 minutes for the task. One was to conduct the interview, a second was to take notes and observe, and a third was to be interviewed. If time permitted, they could trade places so that each would get an opportunity to do each thing. During the interviews, I moved among teams and made notes of practices that illustrated certain points. I tried to operate in a positive manner and point out things that were done correctly, rather than dwell on mistakes made.

As I recall, this task took quite a long time, and some of the actual practice time had to be cut short. Different classes operate differently. Some get right to it while others seem to get lost in trivia or just take a much-needed break from their studies. In an ideal world, I think I would allocate two or three class sessions to practicing interviewing techniques. But given the reality of much material to cover and too little time, I suspect that some people did not get as much time as they needed.

We concluded with a debriefing time. I called for volunteers. The observer/recorder commented on what was done. The other two members of the team talked about their experience. If time permitted, we listened to the tape. We discussed the merits of doing an unstructured interview and why I thought it was so important. I remember more than one student expressed a concern that she or he did not really know quite what to ask and what to do without formal questions. We discussed how important it was to think about the topic in advance and to get their thoughts clear in their minds. I recommend using a general outline of potential topics to cover. I reiterated the idea that the interview was a conversation and thus not meant to be planned in advance. While I knew that everyone was not ready, time was passing, and I decided to ask them to commence with their outside interviews.

At this point, it is important to know that individual **in-depth interviews** are a type of qualitative interview that is described as a conversation between interviewer and participant (Kvale, 1996; McCracken, 1988; Rubin & Rubin, 1995, 2005; Spradley, 1979). Our purpose in using this style of interview is to hear what participants have to say in their own words, in their voice, with their language and narrative. In this way, participants can share what they know and have learned and can add a dimension to our understanding of the situation that questionnaire data does not reveal.

Individual in-depth interviewing is a process, not just a predetermined list of questions. The process builds in several stages. It begins with developing rapport and getting the participant to trust you and to open up to you. It is advisable to talk about why you are there, why they have been selected to be interviewed, and how you will use what you learn from them.

Although this class example involved adult students, I want to mention some issues that might develop when interviewing younger students. Although procedures are quite well established for interviewing adults, they need to be modified somewhat when interviewing students, especially those who might be suspicious of adults in formal school situations. Students might be reluctant to answer questions if they are not sure how the information will be used.

Once rapport has been established, it is desirable to find a way to connect with the student and his or her experiences. One way that works well is to have a student relate stories about his or her school successes. This use of the concrete guarantees rich data and is well documented in the literature on qualitative research.

Phase 4: Conducting Outside Interviews

Students were asked to identify someone who would be willing to be interviewed. They were left on their own to schedule appointments, conduct the interview, transcribe the interview, and prepare copies for classmates. As students became more technologically savvy, they transmitted material via e-mail attachments. Initially, however, I remember that they brought me a diskette and hard copies for classmates. In 2008, I suspect that all or almost all students send and receive material via e-mail.

Before we began any analysis, we debriefed our experience. These are some of the comments I recall: "I really liked doing this. I learned so much from talking to someone else." "I felt uncomfortable when I asked a question and it was not answered. I did not know where to go next." "I found transcribing took so much time. Is there an easier way? Why can't I just summarize what I learned?" "I could identify with things that others told me." You can see quite a range of reactions.

Now, let's take a look at some of these interviews. I have chosen excerpts from a number of interviews and have modified the interviews to shorten them, to remove personal information, and to provide uniformity of presentation. Although I modified some of the interviews, I did leave much information intact. I want you to see that often the information you gather may not be directly on point or provide insight into what your participant thinks about the topic. My comments should help you to see how you might formulate your questions and how you might follow up based on the responses you receive.

Although each student had the same assignment, they approached things differently. Some clearly had predetermined questions; others were more open in their approach. Some elicited responses that were more informative, while others were less successful.

This particular activity is one that can be used in any situation. Its main advantages are that it is easy to locate respondents and to select questions about which each has some thoughts and knowledge (because they are currently in school). By using this common activity, students begin on a similar footing and can practice technique and skill with less emphasis on the questions.

INTERVIEW A: JON INTERVIEWS PAUL

I am here with Paul, who is a second-year Adult Learning and Human Resource Development PhD candidate. The purpose of this interview is to find out how the graduate student experience has been for Paul and to perhaps gain some insight into how students balance their work, family, and school commitments.

Q1:   *Paul, are we ready to start the interview?*

A1:   Absolutely. Let's go for it.

Q2:   *I wanted to thank you for taking the time to talk with me. As you know, we both started the program at the same time, and I'm curious as to how we both perceive the graduate student process. Paul, how is it that we have gotten so far that now we are looking at the dissertation in the next year?*

A2:   (Laughs) I have no idea, Jon. It just seems like yesterday that we started this program. It has been a real adventure so far.

Q3:   *Well, Paul, why don't you tell me a little bit about your general experience here as a graduate student at Virginia Tech?*

A3:   Well, my experience has been one of . . . change.

Q4:   *Change?*

A4:   Yes, change. We both started in Fall of '98, and the whole experience has been hard at times, eye-opening at times . . . you know, it's hard to juggle family, work, and school, taking quite a load every semester, and it's starting to wear on me now. By May, I will have taken over 60 credit hours of coursework. At times, I can see glimpses of the end, and at others, it's hard to see the end.

Q18:   *As a graduate student now, going through what you have gone through, how would you improve your experience as a graduate student for others?*

A18:   For myself, I would gear my core Foundational courses toward the Cognate, which would determine what my interests and coursework would be. I would definitely get a good overview during the first Foundations courses, and then move toward fleshing out the requirements and targeting the coursework toward the Cognate as soon as possible.

Interview A: My Comments

These two students were friends outside class. Notice Jon's introduction prior to the interview. He talks about his purpose and sets the stage. His Q3 reflects a general Grand Tour question. His Q4 reflects a probing or "tell me more" question. Q18 is more directive, but it is not leading.

Now, I want you to learn different techniques you can use as you embark on your research. I want you to think about how you might go about gathering your data.

There are a variety of methods used by qualitative researchers to gather data. In this chapter, I describe qualitative interviewing (on a continuum from high structure to low or no structure), focus group interviewing (again on a continuum), and online interviewing. In Chapter 10, I discuss observing in natural settings, using images (created by informants or created by the researcher), accessing chat rooms and online discussion groups (created by informants or created by the researcher), and using diaries and written material from informants (created by informants or stimulated by the researcher).

Before elaborating on the details of each technique, I provide you with a brief overview of different types of interviewing. Each is designed to let you get "the story" from the point of view of the participant. As the researcher, you become the instrument or tool through which participants tell their stories.

Qualitative interviewing is a general term used to describe a group of methods that permit you to engage in a dialogue or conversation with the participant. Although it is a conversation, it is usually orchestrated and directed by you. This can be considered a conversation with a purpose. The interview format can range from highly structured to one with little or no structure. Some type of interviewing is used in almost all types of qualitative research. There are several types of interviews, including the structured interview, the guided (semistructured) interview, the in-depth interview, and casual or unplanned interviews.

Focus group interviewing provides opportunities for members of a group to interact with each other and stimulate each other's thinking. It is not desirable or necessary for the group to reach consensus in their discussion.

Online interviewing can run the gamut from informal chat rooms or Listservs to organized and planned e-mail interviews with a single individual. Its purpose is similar to other forms of interviewing.

■ Qualitative Interviewing

There is so much to tell you about interviewing. It seems so easy. "Just a little conversation between two people. I can do that," you will say to yourself. In this section, I talk about the purpose of interviewing, provide you with a specific interview protocol that I have developed, and offer some examples of interviews. By the time you finish reading this section, you will be well on your way to conducting a successful interview.

Interviewing is the most common form of data collection in qualitative research. We have all experienced being interviewed or interviewing another person. You are interviewed when you visit your doctor and she asks how you feel and follows up with additional questions. You are interviewed when you apply for a job, participate in therapy, or talk on the telephone to a marketer. You were interviewed when you entered graduate school. Many of you have also had experience conducting interviews. As a counselor, you might have interviewed a client or a parent in a special education planning meeting. You might have interviewed a fellow teacher to learn about new techniques. I want to emphasize, however, that whether you adopt a formal, structured approach or take an unstructured view, there still must be planning and thought in advance of the interview.

Did You Know

Interviews of many famous people from music, politics, and pop culture have been published by *Rolling Stone*. If you are more interested in literary figures, check out interviews published by *The Paris Review*.

The Purpose of Interviewing

The purpose of conducting an interview is the same whether you use a structured and formal style or select an unstructured, conversational style. You are gathering information from your participant about the topic you are studying. What does she think about the new reading program? How does he feel about the new grading policy in your county? What is the culture of the participant's organization, and how does it relate to her individual needs? These are all topics you might study.

Your goal might be to learn what your interviewee thinks or feels about certain things, or your goal might be to explore the shared meanings of people who live or work together (Rubin & Rubin, 2005). In either case, you need to think about an interview in this way. You, as the interviewer and researcher, are trying to set up a situation in which the individual being interviewed will reveal to you his or her feelings, intentions, meanings, subcontexts, or thoughts on a topic, situation, or idea. It is critical to remember that you are not trying to determine these things as if you did not exist or were some kind of fly on the wall that could transmit the ideas directly. In qualitative research, each idea, interpretation, and plan is filtered through your eyes, through your mind, and through your point of view. You are not trying to do away with your role, as you would if you were conducting traditional experimental research. You are not trying to be objective. You adopt the role of constructing and subsequently interpreting the reality of the person being interviewed, but your own lens is critical. I think the most difficult task a novice researcher faces is what to do about his or her own role. Should she strive to approximate objectivity? Should he gather multiple sources and use triangulation to make sure that what he says is right? Should she get others—especially those with higher status or authority—to verify that what she writes is the way it is? I would answer all these questions with a resounding NO. I want you to reexamine the assumptions I mention earlier in the book. Accept that there is no single objective reality that you strive for. Accept that you, as the researcher, serve as the filter through which information is gathered, processed, and organized.

You may have heard a number of different terms used to describe the individual you interview. In traditional experimental research, the person being studied is usually called the **subject**. In anthropological terms, the person being studied is usually called the **informant**. Ethnographers also use the term **participants**. Feminists tend to use the term **coresearcher**, acknowledging the shared role between interviewer and person being interviewed. I have also heard the terms interviewee, discussant, partner, and conversational partner. Rubin and Rubin (2005) use "interviewees," "informants," and "conversational partners," depending on the situation. Now, you might ask why it matters what the individuals are named. I think it matters a great deal. In traditional research, the term *subject* is meant to be informative and neutral. Yet, some have interpreted this term in a negative manner, suggesting that the relationship between the interviewer and the person being interviewed is hierarchical—I am the king; you are my subject. Feminist research describes a dilemma regarding power and the position of the researcher. Although there are many terms used to refer to the person being interviewed, it is interesting to me that I have not read about alternative names for the interviewer.

The Structured Interview. You can conduct a structured or standardized interview in which the questions and format are the same for each individual. This type of interviewing is more often associated with survey research rather than qualitative research. I think most qualitative researchers would not recommend that you use this approach. The purpose of a structured interview is to eliminate the role of the researcher and to introduce objectivity. You will remember that I do not believe that qualitative research is about objectivity and the elimination of bias. I want you to be aware of this type of interviewing technique, but I do not recommend you use it when conducting qualitative research.

The Guided Interview. Another type of interview is the semistructured or guided interview. This type of interview involves your developing a general set of questions and format that you follow and use with all participants. Although the general structure is the same for all individuals being interviewed, the interviewer can vary the questions as the situation demands. I find that some individuals like this format because they feel uncomfortable with not having a clear set of guidelines to follow. Most new interviewers seem to like to have something to use for guidance.

The In-Depth Interview. My preference is to use in-depth, unstructured interviewing techniques. I first encountered this kind of interviewing when I read McCracken's (1988) *The Long Interview.* I was so drawn to his writing. For once, someone laid out a style of interviewing that did not recommend a specific set of questions. You might think of this as an informal conversation. Although McCracken suggested that a formal set of biographical questions should be used, he recognizes that "the first objective of the qualitative interview is to allow respondents to tell their own story in their own terms" (p. 34). He reminded us that the investigator should remain unobtrusive and ask questions in a general and nondirective manner. Rubin and Rubin (1995) spoke to me when they said that qualitative interviewing "is a great adventure . . . [it] brings new information and opens windows into the experiences of the people you meet" (p. 1). One year later, Kvale (1996) reminded me that qualitative interviewing is a "professional conversation" (p. 5). In keeping with the intent of letting the respondent talk, Boeree (1998) suggested that you should not force the person in any one direction.

Casual or Unplanned Interviews. Often, when you are in the field conducting either a case study or ethnography, opportunities arise for you to talk to some of your participants. The data are often useful, but because these interviews are unplanned, I do not discuss them further here.

General Issues in Interviewing

Identification of Participants. Who should be interviewed, how should they be identified, and how should they be contacted? Typically, the researcher has identified specific characteristics of individuals to study. She might want to study young pregnant middle school girls, or boys in gangs, or students from homes of divorce, or students who are highly successful in school, or first-year teachers, or women principals. After identifying the type of person to be interviewed, the researcher needs to contact individuals who meet the criteria. One method researchers have used to identify additional participants is to ask those already contacted to name others with similar characteristics. This technique, called **snowball sampling**, is quite useful when studying hidden or hard to reach participants. Atkinson and Flint (2001) provided many examples of the use of the technique. Bunch and Panayotova (2008), in their research on Latinos, used snowball sampling to identify appropriate community college personnel. Koerber and McMichael (2008) concluded that "our field (qualitative research) has not yet developed a systematic, transferable vocabulary" for evaluating appropriate samples (p. 458). They suggested that qualitative researchers develop frameworks for sampling that are similar to those in the quantitative domain—in part, I think, for others to evaluate the rigor of the design.

Another issue is determining how many participants should be interviewed. You may know that in quantitative research, determining a suitable sample size depends on how much variation there is in the population and how much sampling error you are willing to accept. Because your goal in qualitative research is to describe and interpret rather than to generalize, there are no hard rules about how many participants you should study. Sandelowski (1995) suggested that determining sample size is a matter of judgment. For her, there are times when a sample of 10 might be seen as adequate (p. 179). Most qualitative research studies use a small number of individuals and cover material in depth. It is quite common to see studies with fewer than 10 respondents; sometimes only a single person is studied. I know that the issue of sample size is not fully resolved in the literature. There are those who apologize that the sample is too small and not representative. There are others who do not see this as a problem. Those using the framework of grounded theory talk about theoretical sampling but do not specifically address sample size. My sense of the prevailing viewpoint is that those who take a fairly traditional and conservative view of qualitative research would prefer larger and more representative samples. In contrast, those who see qualitative research in a freer fashion are less concerned with the issue. Johnson and Christensen (2008), in their recent text on mixed approaches to research, addressed sampling in qualitative research (pp. 243–245), but they did not address sample size.

Developing Rapport. It is important that you learn to develop rapport in order to conduct an interview that generates meaningful and useful data. Ultimately, you seek cooperation and participation of the person you are interviewing. I don't think that I can stress too much that you should include time at the beginning of each interview to establish rapport. We all talk about this and assume that we know how to do it. You could probably develop your own list of what you should do: Be relaxed, make the interviewee feel comfortable, be accepting.

Selecting a Setting. Most interviews you conduct will be in a mutually agreed location. It is obvious that the location should be quiet and private, to the extent possible. If you go to the home or office of your participant, you can learn a considerable amount of information. I like to look around and take notes. If it is an office, does the participant display photographs? What other personal items are around? How does the individual office relate to the larger setting in which it is located? If you are in a school, you may have to "settle" for less than ideal circumstances because there is not usually a private room available for your use.

Observing Surroundings. It is a good idea to pay attention to physical surroundings and to the person you are interviewing. Keep notes about your observations. Does the person appear comfortable or fidgety? Does he look at you? Of course, if you are conducting your interviews in cyberspace, you would need to begin to develop a sense of what to look for online. Does the person use shorthand in writing? What time constraints exist between your questions and the participant's responses?

Interviewing Adolescents and Children. Bassett, Beagan, Ristovski-Slijepcevic, and Chapman (2008), in their study of reflections by interviewers of issues related to interviewing teenagers, suggested that recruiting teens and getting them to discuss complex abstract concepts presents special challenges. Lahman (2008) concluded that children are always "Othered" or unfamiliar in research. She reminded us that there is little methodology on interviewing children and that the child may say what he or she perceives the researcher wants to hear (p. 294). From my own viewpoint, I suspect that many participants—children or adults—give what they perceive to be the desired or correct response. Alternatively, adolescents might give the shocking response.

■ In-Depth Interviewing

As I said, there are many different kinds of interviews. I prefer in-depth interviews. I feel strongly that in an in-depth interview, you will get information from your participant that is not slanted toward what you want to hear or investigate. I have chosen to talk about what works for me in conducting this type of interview. Individual in-depth interviews are a type of qualitative interviewing that is described by some as a conversation between interviewer and participant (McCracken, 1988; Rubin & Rubin, 1995, 2005). The purpose in this style of interviewing is to hear what the participant has to say in his own words, in his voice, with his language and narrative. In this way, participants can share what they know and have learned and can add a dimension to our understanding of the situation that questionnaire data or a highly structured interview does not reveal. Individual in-depth interviewing is a process, not just a predetermined list of questions. I want to talk, here, about the interviewing process. The process builds in several stages.

The Interview Process

Planning. Because you will not be using a standardized set of questions, you need to think about what you will be doing prior to the actual interview. Here are some ways to get your thoughts organized.

- Identify 5 to 10 topic areas that you want to make sure you will cover in your interview. I like to put them on a single piece of paper with space between each one. Remember, these are to be used as guidelines. In fact, you may not actually need all these topics; sometimes you need only one question and the interview rolls right along.

- You can look in the literature about the topic, but I believe that it tends to put blinders on you and that it is better to conduct your literature review at a later time. Use your knowledge of the topic and your common sense to generate your topic areas.

- Identify some demographic areas that you think you will want to cover with each participant (e.g., for adults, marital status, children, or work history; for children, age, grade in school, number of siblings, or favorite activity). Often, these come up in the course of the interview, but you should make them explicit. I also put these on a single piece of paper with space between each one. Of course, the areas to cover are directed by the purpose of your research.

- Inexperienced researchers are often nervous without specific questions to ask. In the planning stages, I find it helpful to think about the questions I might start with and how I would phrase them. There are three kinds of questions that you can use to begin: (1) personal questions ("Tell me a little about yourself."); (2) concrete questions ("Tell me something that happened to you last week in your class"; "Tell me your thoughts when you learned last week that you were going to lose your job."); and (3) feeling questions ("What is it like to be a student at this school?"). Notice that all three questions are personal and immediate. They are not "yes" or "no" questions. They usually get the respondent to open up somewhat.

This plan will help get you ready to do an in-depth interview. Notice that you do not have a formal set of questions or a structured interview schedule to follow, but you will be well on your way to conducting a successful interview. Of course, practice is critical.

Getting Started. I think it is important to give considerable thought to how you will begin an interview. Your demeanor and tone will set the stage for what is to come. The first few minutes should be devoted to developing rapport and getting the participant to trust you and to open up to you. You might do this by talking in generalities about neutral topics—the traffic, the weather, or sports events. If you get started on a positive note, the interview will proceed smoothly.

Before you begin the interview, you have to provide some preliminary information: (1) why you are there, (2) your purpose, (3) what you will do with the information, (4) how you will treat the information, and (5) how long the interview will take.

- You will need to obtain permission to conduct the interview. You might have to obtain a signed permission form or agreement. Different institutions have different requirements; you should determine the requirements of the IRB (Institutional Review Board) at your institution. If you are interviewing children, you will need to get permission from an adult.

- In addition to having your respondent give you permission to conduct an interview, you should ask for permission to use a recording device.

- I talked earlier about the importance of developing rapport. I have found that you can develop rapport by introducing chitchat. While it may seem to you that you are wasting time that you would more profitably use to get at the crux of information, this time is invaluable for getting your respondent to cooperate with you.

- Make the person feel comfortable. You can do this by using laughter, smiles, and nods. You can offer some personal story about yourself, for example, how long it took you to drive to the site, what fun you had at a recent sporting event, how you get your own children ready for school. I stress that you should try to remain connected to your respondent rather than stay aloof.

- One way to get people to feel comfortable is to ask them to say a little bit about themselves (if they say, "What?" say, "Anything you want to share"). Because you have already shared some personal information, they may be more inclined to do so. All these preliminaries are used to help your respondent feel comfortable with you.

The Body of the Interview. You are now ready to continue with your interview.

- Use your semi- or unstructured guidelines to make the interview progress more smoothly. Remember, you will have a list of 5 to 10 topic areas that you expect to investigate.

- Don't try to take complete notes; it is almost impossible. But do take notes of questions or comments that you want to follow up. Sometimes you will want to probe more fully, but do not interrupt as the interview progresses.

- Concentrate on listening to what is said and planning your next questions. Perhaps it is like a game of chess; you have some moves and plans, but your opponent may fool you.

The End of the Interview. Stay aware of the time.

- My favorite final question is "Do you have anything you want to add that we have not talked about?" You will be so surprised at what you learn.

- Thank them for their participation.

- Upon completion of interview, take some time to get your materials in order. Mark the tapes, put your notes away, and record the length of the interview or stop time.

- Write down your thoughts and reactions in your journal after the interview is over.

Interviewing Techniques

Conducting in-depth interviews takes a considerable amount of planning and experience. It may look easy, but it really takes quite a bit of forethought. Now that you have considered the main components of an in-depth qualitative interview, I want you to begin to think about the interview questions. I have found that many people focus on the content of the questions. They are inclined to develop a list of questions that they think they want to ask. In my experience, this is a very rigid format and narrows the interview rather than expanding it. I would like you to think about questioning in two ways. One way involves the type of questions you might ask; I offer you several types below with some specific examples. The second way is to consider questioning strategies. I provide specific examples of such strategies below. This section concludes with some special areas of concern.

Types of Questions

Below, I describe and provide examples of several different types of questions. Although you can choose the order to follow, I almost always begin either with a Grand Tour question or a specific or concrete example question.

Grand Tour Question. This type of question is very general. It is a good way to begin because it gets the participant talking to you. Your stance should be open and nonjudgmental. The Grand Tour question comes from Spradley's (1979) work on ethnographic interviewing. It continues to be used in much qualitative research today (Brown & Holloway, 2008; Van Oord, 2008). This type of question will take the form "Tell me about yourself," or "Tell me what being in school is like for you," or "What can you say about going to the X school?" For the adult, you can ask, "What is it like to work at the X organization?" It is important to remember that you want to capture the words and ideas of the person you are interviewing. This will be a rich source of data as you begin your qualitative analysis.

Examples

- Very general—What is it like to be a graduate student?

- More specific—How stressful is it to be a graduate student?

- Very general—Tell me about your school.

- More specific—What kinds of things does your teacher do that you find helpful?

- Very general—What is it like to work in this organization?

- More specific—How are minorities treated in this organization?

- Very general—Tell me some of the things you feel as a new teacher.

- More specific—What are concerns you have as a new teacher in terms of working with parents (with other staff members, with troubled students)?

- Very general—How would you describe a day in the life of a principal (student, retired person)?

- More specific—Your challenge as a principal is to modify the discipline at your school. What are some things you have been thinking about along these lines?

Specific or Concrete Example Question. This type of question gives the participant an opportunity to be concrete and specific and provide relevant information. A concrete example works well because it is personal and immediate. It is important to ask for a specific story rather than a general statement. It helps to prevent jargon or responses that the participant thinks you, the researcher, want to hear. People like to talk about their experiences. If you are interviewing students, one way that works well is to have them relate stories about their school experiences. If you are interviewing adults, you might ask them about a recent experience that was meaningful. This use of the concrete guarantees a rich source of data. The less you become involved in abstract concepts, the richer your data will be.

Examples

- Tell me something that happened at this school that you think is a direct result of the new Site-Based Management plan.

- What was something that happened last week that you think contributes to your stress?

- What did you see (or hear) in your office that indicates that there is sexual harassment?

- Tell me something that happened to you last month that made you annoyed with your boss.

- When your teacher asked you to work with a new student who was transferred, what kinds of things made you happy or sad?

Comparison/Contrast Question. This type of question challenges the participant to think about other times, situations, places, events, or people and draw comparisons between them. Choose comparisons that are meaningful to the respondent; it helps them put their current situation into a meaningful framework. Contrasts and comparisons provide additional insight and serve to highlight what you are studying.

Examples

- How are things at this school now compared to when Mr. X was principal?

- Remember when you were a child. How do you feel now compared to then, in terms of your ability to accomplish and meet your own standards?

- Imagine you could choose to have a work setting any way you want. What would it be like compared to the way it is now?

- How does this situation compare with where you worked previously?

- In what ways does what you describe differ from your previous experience?

- How could you compare what you are doing now to what you did in the past?

- Does the situation with Mr. X differ from the situation with Mr. Y? In what ways?

- This year you say you are doing (or feeling) _____. How is that like the way you felt last year? How is it different from the way you did it last year?

- How do you think things will be in the future regarding _____?

New Elements/Topics Question. Shifting to a new topic must be done in a very subtle manner. You might feel during an interview that the participant is "stuck" on a particular thing and keeps repeating information. Here is a chance for you, as interviewer, to introduce a new topic. You are interested in covering areas that may not have been considered in previous questions. (Note: Some qualitative researchers are opposed to this approach and feel that the areas of interest should emerge from the data.) You might draw from the research literature and your own background topics of importance to the problems at hand. You can introduce topics not previously mentioned by the respondent. Avoid leading the respondent to say what you want him to say. Use transition statements to move from one area to another. Use "why" and "how" questions for completeness.

Examples

- We've talked for a while about discipline in the schools. Are there other aspects of working in a school you would like to discuss?

- You've talked about many challenges you face as a new teacher. What can you say about having a mentor?

- Can you think of some other things about the nature of your work life that you think are important?

- We've talked quite a bit about _____. Are there other issues you would like to discuss?

- Let's look at some other areas we haven't yet covered. What do you think about _____?

- Our time is somewhat limited and I want to be sure we've covered everything of interest to you; let's move on to some other areas. I'd like to talk about _____.

- What else is important to you about _____? Can we talk about some other areas (issues, factors, topics)?

- You mentioned _____ as being an important area for you. What about _____? Do you see _____ as something that you consider important? In what ways?

- Why do you think _____ has an influence in this organization?

- How does _____ work in this school?

- Can you clarify what you mean by _____? How are you thinking of it in this context?

Closing Question. A closing question provides a chance for the participant to add anything else that has not been mentioned.

Examples

- Can you think of anything else you would like to say about working in a school?

- Is there anything else you would like to add to what you have already said?

Strategies for Questioning

Strategies for questioning are techniques you can use to get the respondent to talk and reveal what he or she thinks or believes about something. I discuss six different techniques or strategies that you can use to get your respondent to respond more completely.

Elaboration. This strategy provides an opportunity for the participant to say more, to clarify and elucidate his or her responses, and allows for additional input by the participant. It may reveal other ideas that the participant has thought about.

Examples

- You've talked about your frustration working with your new principal. What else can you say about why you feel so frustrated?

- You said that you feel so happy working with a new group of classmates. What kinds of things have made you happy?

- What else can you tell me about being in the X school?

Probing. This strategy provides the interviewer a chance to try to get the underlying meaning of what is said. Sometimes you think you know what is meant, but it is always better to follow up because words take on many different meanings. Repeat the words that are said or raise an eyebrow. This idea is closely related to elaboration, but here, the emphasis is on digging down deeper into the feelings. Use the person's own words when restating, use nonverbal cues, and provide encouragement.

Examples

- Can you tell me some more about that?

- What do you mean when you say it is challenging as a teacher?

- I see. What do you mean by_____?

- Yes. Go on.

- Hmm. What else can you say about _____?

- That's good. I'm not sure I understand when you say _____. Can you explain more fully?

- Let's talk about that in more detail.

- I'm trying to find out what you think about _____. Tell me more.

- It's not clear to me. Can you give an example of what you mean when you say _____?

- Look at the person, nod your head yes, or use your eyes or eyebrows to indicate that you want the person to continue.

- That's interesting. Give me some additional information.

- I have heard you say during this interview that you feel frustrated. Why do you think you feel so frustrated?

- Happiness means different things to different people. I want to get at what it means to you. Tell me some more about it.

Nondirectional. This strategy puts the interviewer in a neutral position, neither for nor against something. Very tricky. Avoid letting your nonverbal and verbal cues lead the participant in a particular direction.

Examples

- Good: We have talked about being a graduate student. What is the experience like for you?

- Avoid: We have talked about being a graduate student. Don't you agree with me that it is frustrating because you have so little time to do everything?

One Question at a Time. Ask one question at a time. Stop and give the participant a chance to respond. Not giving the respondent time to respond is the biggest mistake I see even experienced interviewers make.

Examples

- Good: Let's talk about being in graduate school. Tell me about the experience.

- Avoid: Let's talk some more about being in graduate school. What courses are you taking? What is your major? Why do you think you decided to return to graduate school?

Wait Time. After you ask a question, be quiet and let the participant think and then talk. Use nonverbal cues. In an individual interview, you might look down at your paper or fiddle with your recording device to give the participant a chance to formulate his or her thoughts. If you add something right away, he or she may lose his or her train of thought. Trust me; your participant will talk if you remain quiet.

Examples

- Good: Look down at your notes. Do not tap your pen on the table or look at your watch. Try to remain neutral.

- Avoid: Jumping in too soon and repeating the question or asking a different question.

Special Areas of Concern. Encourage the respondent to tell her story in her own words. Don't assume that you know what she means when she says something. Be aware of when to cut the respondent off (when he's talking too much) and when not to cut the respondent off (when he is saying something you want to hear).

Examples

- Tell me what you think about _____.

- Take some time to tell me in your own words what you think about or how you feel about _____.

- What do you mean when you say successful? I'm not sure I understand. Can you tell me some more?

- You've said that when your boss does _____ that creates problems for you. Can you give me an example?

- Do you think _____ is important in this school? If so, in what ways?

- Avoid: Don't you think _____ is important in this school?

- Well, you've given me a lot of examples of _____. Let's talk about some other areas. What do you think about _____ ?

- That sounds interesting. Keep telling me about it.

Some Dos and Don'ts of In-Depth Interviewing

Now that you have thought about different types of questions and strategies for questioning, I have a few more reminders for you.

Do

- develop rapport.

- use a recorder and have a note pad to jot down notes.

- make eye contact.

- ask open-ended questions.

- provide an atmosphere for respondents to tell their own story in their own terms.

- remain unobtrusive. Do not put your own thoughts into your questions.

- phrase questions in a general and nondirective manner.

- avoid leading questions.

- use some questioning strategies, such as repeating the last word of the response or lifting an eyebrow.

- make sure you get specific and detailed information.

- avoid jargon or situations that are too technical.

- make sure you have enough discussion about the key issues to use later for data analysis.

Don't

- depend on your memory. Write it down.

- answer questions for respondents.

- ask three or four questions at the same time.

- ask a question and then provide the answer ("I agree that such and such is a good thing").

- stop the respondent in the middle of a conversation.

- allow the respondent to spend too much time on one topic.

- act nervous or uninterested.

Qualitative interviewing is challenging. It opens new doors to learn what others think and feel. It does not rely on a single set of questions; rather, it addresses ways to listen to respondents speak in their own words. I recommend two ways of thinking about asking questions: question types and question strategies. Question types are Grand Tour questions, comparison/contrast questions, and so on. Question strategies are techniques you can use to get your respondents to talk more, answer in greater depth, and ultimately lead you to their underlying meanings. I continue to believe that the best way to learn about how to interview is to practice. Practice with your friends and family. Practice with your classmates. Practice with your coworkers. Listen to yourself on tape and try to determine what strategies you use and what you want to avoid. You should now be well on your way to mastering one of the most important techniques for gathering data in any kind of qualitative research you choose to do.

■ Focus Group Interviewing

I was in a large comfortable room, having been invited to participate in a focus group discussion. I wasn't quite sure what was going to happen, but I had agreed to come. I arrived at the scheduled time, got a cup of coffee, and found my name tag. I was not precisely sure what I would be doing, but I had agreed to participate because someone called me, asked if I would, and offered me $100 for my time. I took a place at the table and chatted with others around me. I did not see anyone I knew. Soon an individual entered the room, took a seat, and got the group's attention. She thanked everyone for coming and said that we would begin shortly and that we would spend about an hour in a discussion. After getting our permission to record the session, she began. I should tell you that when I was called, I was told that someone had recommended me because I had had breast cancer. I confirmed the fact with the telephone interviewer, so I knew that we would be talking about that topic. Anticipating the actual meeting, I had been reflecting on my experience. How could I not begin thinking about the topic, especially one so painful and personal?

This is how we began. The moderator said, "I am Mary Jones and I work for the Cancer Foundation. We are here tonight to listen to your views on a topic you know only too well. I am married, have two children, and have been working with the Cancer Foundation for about five years. We're going to begin this evening by learning a little bit about each of us and then share our own journeys. I was diagnosed with breast cancer eight years ago. I didn't know how I would survive or what my life was going to be like, but here I am to tell the story." Mary paused and looked around the room. "Now it is your turn to share your stories. Who wants to begin?" Mary turned her attention to some papers in front of her. She did not look at anyone. The assembled body was silent. I wondered who would lead us off. Soon, one of the women sitting across from me began to speak. "I am Ann Spencer. I am not working now, but I used to teach elementary school. My boyfriend and I live together and are trying to decide whether to marry or not." She continued, sharing with us how she discovered that she had a tumor and the treatment she received. When Ann finished, Dianne spoke up. Mary was listening but not talking. She seemed intent on what we were saying, occasionally taking notes. As Dianne spoke, one of the other women—Kelly—asked Dianne a question. She responded. And then I chimed in as well. All the women in the room shared their stories. Mary listened intently but rarely spoke. Toward the end of the hour, Mary said, "We've talked from our hearts about this experience. Let's finish up by talking about how our lives have changed." There was no holding the group back. After we were well into the second hour, Mary indicated that we had to stop and thanked us all for coming. Some of us left the room. Others lingered, talking about our experiences.

I have told you this story because it illustrates one type of focus group interview. It illustrates what Morgan (1988) called a "self-managed group." The moderator introduces the topic, often by sharing personal information herself. The group essentially runs itself. When the moderator senses that the group has run out of ideas, she either introduces a new topic or reminds the group to reflect on why they are there. The group interaction is critical. It emerges because individuals who share a common experience stimulate each other to talk. The moderator's role is minimal. She knows that the group will talk and react to each other. For me, this is the best kind of focus group interview to conduct; the data are rich and varied.

A special type of interviewing technique, focus group interviewing had its origins in the late 1930s. One view is that this technique shifted the emphasis from the interviewer to those being interviewed, and it became more of a nondirective approach. Merton, a social scientist who studied response to wartime propaganda during World War II, is also credited with its development (Merton & Kendall, 1946). It has been widely used as a technique in market research by Lazarsfeld and in gauging political viewpoints (M. Lewis, 1995).

Just as qualitative interviewing takes many forms, so, too, does focus group interviewing. Some see it as a highly structured activity in which participants and leader follow a predetermined set of questions. Others see the technique as much less structured. In the latter type, the leader plays the role of facilitator and lets the group process evolve into questions and responses.

Whatever levels of structure, however, there are common elements to focus group interviewing. All agree that a focus group consists of a set of people (anywhere from 6 to 12) who come together for approximately one hour. The purpose is to discuss a specific topic. The leader/ facilitator may play a very directive role, by leading the group toward specific ends, or he or she may be very indirect and let the group take the leadership role. It is believed that by participating in a group discussion, members of the group may stimulate others to comment or react in ways that do not occur in individual interviews.

The Purpose of Focus Group Interviewing

The purpose of using focus groups is to gather information from participants about the topic of interest. A focus group is basically a group interview. Kitzinger (1994) refers to an "organized discussion."

What is critical about the group involvement is that there is group interaction. What distinguishes focus group interviewing from qualitative interviewing with a single individual is that the group interaction may trigger thoughts and ideas among participants that do not emerge during an individual interview. M. Lewis (1995) talked about putting individuals in a nurturing environment so that they disclose their views while at the same time they are influenced by their interactions with others.

Another advantage of focus group interviews is they save time. You can interview 6 to 12 people in one hour in a focus group. If you were conducting individual interviews, you might need to spend up to 12 hours to hear the voices of 12 people.

Your goal might be to learn how individuals think or feel about a particular topic that is common to each of them. I vividly recall interviewing parents in military schools in Panama who had experienced site-based school management. I asked them what changes they noticed in their school after site-based management was introduced. They were able to provide specific and concrete examples of changes that they had tried for years to achieve but had not been able to accomplish until management was turned over to the local school. By participating in the group, individuals were stimulated and thought of examples and ideas that might not have emerged during individual interviews.

Sometimes your goal might be to talk to individuals who have a common experience. Morgan (1988) suggested that although not everyone may want to state an opinion about something, most are willing to share their experiences.

The Structured Focus Group. Focus groups can be highly structured, self-directed, or fall somewhere between the two extremes. M. Lewis (1995) and Stewart and Shamdasani (1990) took the position that a formal interview guide should be developed, with questions moving from the general to the specific, placing those of greater importance at the beginning. Krueger (1988) suggested the number of questions to be included: no more than 10 and usually about 5 or 6. Other details about the moderator's specific role in the group are part of a structured approach. My preference, however, is not to practice such an approach. I believe it limits the nature of the discussion and is used in an attempt to lend a patina of objectivity to the task.

Semistructured or Guided Focus Group. As with individual qualitative interviews, focus groups can rely on a semistructured approach. In such an approach, the moderator/interviewer has developed a list of questions and has a preconceived plan for proceeding. Many researchers use such a plan as a guide and are willing to modify it as needed. In my experience, many new researchers find it much more helpful to have a list of questions or question areas that they wish to follow. They seem to need this almost as a crutch. I think it is important, however, that the group lead the way, to the extent possible. With practice, moderators can move into a less structured, less directive approach to conducting focus groups.

Issues Regarding Focus Groups

Deciding on the Size of the Group. Most who write about focus group interviewing recommend a group of 6 to 12 people. I agree with this. If there are more than 12, the session takes too long, and group interaction becomes more difficult to achieve; if there are fewer than 6, there may be insufficient interaction. On a related note, I often schedule more than 12 people because, in my experience, several participants will fail to appear on a given day, even though they have agreed to participate. This is particularly true if you are not compensating the participants. When I conducted focus groups on a military base, some were called away on temporary assignment and had to miss the session. When I conducted focus groups with students, some were not available due to scheduling conflicts or illness.

Deciding on the Number of Groups. I think you need to remember that goals specific to quantitative research, such as generalization, are not applicable to qualitative research, so it is not important to interview a large number of groups. At the same time, however, researchers often seem to be more comfortable having several groups that address the same topic. If you are conducting your own research, you might be limited by time and budget constraints as well as availability of participants. I have heard it said that if, as the moderator, you can anticipate responses and you find yourself being accurate, then you have listened to a sufficient number of groups.

Deciding on the Composition of Groups. How should you choose who will participate? You will not be choosing a **random sample.** In most cases, you will select participants who meet your predetermined criteria. If you are studying those who have survived heart attacks, then, of necessity, you will need people who are survivors. If you are considering those who like a particular brand of soup, then you need to choose people who have used that soup, unless you plan to have a taste test during the focus group. In most cases, researchers recruit participants by advertising, word of mouth, or nomination. The key consideration is that the participants have experience or expertise with regard to the topic. Again, because you are not trying to generalize in a traditional sense, it is not necessary to make sure that the group represents the population in terms of gender, race, ethnicity, or educational level. Some believe it is best to have homogeneous groups, while others want a greater mix. Some believe that it is better to have participants who do not know each other; others find that a discussion might go more smoothly if participants do know each other. There is no scientific research that speaks to group size, group number, or group composition.

Deciding on the Role of the Moderator. The moderator plays a key role prior to the actual focus group interview. He or she will be instrumental in deciding what questions will be included; whether there will be high, moderate, or low structure; and how the group will be conducted. I have found it very helpful to have co-moderators because they can help keep the flow going and make sure all group members participate. My husband and I worked as co-moderators when he had groups of both men and women.

Locating Facilities and Arranging for Recording. Ideally, it is best to use a space that is designated as a focus group facility. This type of space usually has oval tables, comfortable furniture, video cameras and recorders, and one-way windows. But most new researchers have to use whatever space they can find. If you plan to conduct focus groups in school settings, you can request quiet and private space, but there is no guarantee that you will get it. I remember conducting focus groups with middle school students in a library. My colleague and I were studying a federally funded program. One of the tasks was to listen to what students thought about the program, the materials, and the staff. We identified what type of student we needed, and at the assigned time, they were sent to the library. We had no video equipment; our audio equipment worked reasonably well; we were constantly interrupted with announcements over the loudspeaker system; and others were using the library. But we had a lively discussion, and the children shared their views about the program.

Transcribing. You are used to transcribing when conducting individual interviews. While time consuming, it is a fairly straightforward task. You might even use voice recognition software that will facilitate your transcription. But imagine that you have an audio- or videotape with about a dozen voices. Some speak at the same time; others interrupt. Others are so quiet that you cannot really hear them. And you do not know the voices well enough to be able to distinguish one from another. I have personally transcribed some of these discussions, and it is daunting. I suspect that most researchers do not make transcriptions of focus groups; rather, they listen and then extract themes.

Example of a Focus Group Interview

The purpose of this focus group was to collect opinions from various constituents about how their school changed as it adopted a new form of management and control. The schools in this district had long operated from a centralized location. Decisions were made at the central office level, and needs and desires of local schools were largely ignored. A new superintendent decided to implement a plan to move the governance, budget, and decision making to the local level. The building principal, while initially somewhat skeptical about the decision, decided it would be best to implement it. Two years after the plan was implemented, an outside team of evaluators was called in to assess the effect on the staff, teachers, and students. This focus group discussion is illustrative of various discussions that were held. I use it to illustrate how focus groups can yield a large volume of data in a relatively short time.

Prior to the appointed day, I asked the principal to identify a dozen or so parents who might have knowledge of how the new plan had affected the school. She nominated parents, and 12 of them agreed to come. We were to meet in the library of the building at approximately 3:30 P.M., after students had been dismissed. I moved some tables together, arranged my equipment, and waited for the parents to arrive.

As parents began to trickle in after 3:00, I asked them to wait until all had assembled. I was not surprised that at 3:30, only eight people were there. I had been through this many times before and knew that other activities or emergencies tended to interfere with schedules. We sat down around the table and I wrote my name in large letters on a tent card and put it in front of me so that all could see. The others followed without my saying anything.

I reminded them that the principal had nominated them and that we were gathered together to talk about the effects they were aware of since the new plan had been implemented. I reviewed details such as the amount of time we would spend together, that no names would be used in the reports, and that all reports would be written and distributed to the principal and to them without identifying which individual gave which response. I asked permission to tape record and all agreed. I tested the tape and made sure it was working. We were ready to go.

I have found it extremely effective to begin with specific and concrete questions. In this way, you get comments that are authentic. People do not try to impress you with what they know. Jargon is avoided. So I began with, "I understand that this school has had two years to move from a centralized administrative structure and to implement the plan to turn budget and management over to the school. Can you think of anything that is different about the school since this plan was adopted?" I finished my comment and looked down at my notes. No one said anything. I waited what seemed like an interminable time. Still no one said anything. Finally, I heard a voice from across the table. "Well, I know that Timmy's teacher says that she finds it much easier to get materials now than before." The woman seemed to pause. I encouraged her to continue. "What do you mean? Can you give me an example?" She thought for a moment. "The teacher was planning a special art project and she needed a certain kind of paper and paint. It was approved almost immediately and the following week the students began the project." "A good example," I commented. "Can you think of other things that have happened?" I said to the group in general. Two people began to speak at once. One mentioned new equipment for the playground. Another mentioned sending teachers to special training. One parent asked another, "Do you remember when Mr. Miller tried to get approval for his class to travel to an athletic event? Not until last year was he ever able to get the funds in time." The conversation proceeded in this way for about 20 minutes. I really did not introduce new questions at this point. I indirectly led the group by looking at one person or another. I did not specifically call on anyone. I evaluated the comments mentally as they were made. I determined that it was time to change the direction of the comments and so offered the following question. "We've talked a lot about funds and equipment. Can we shift gears a little and talk about other things that might have been affected by the program?" I waited for people to comment, and they did.

After interjecting several other comments that changed the direction of the conversation, I determined that our time was up. I then went around the table and asked if anyone had anything else to add to the conversation. I was quite surprised when one very quiet man chimed in. He had said virtually nothing throughout the past hour, but here was his chance. He expressed some concern about the time that it took and about the many meetings that were held when he thought someone should just decide. I suspect participatory management was not his preference. Finally, I thanked everyone for participating, gathered my materials, and took a much-needed break before my next group came in.

With this somewhat long account, I hope to illustrate that a lively conversation can occur when people have some experience and thoughts about a particular topic. You do not have to have a predetermined set of questions to get people to talk. I used a general question to begin the conversation, added a comparison question to change the nature of the discussion, and offered opportunities for all to speak.

■ Online Interviewing

I first read about the possibilities of doing research online in the very late 1990s. Markham (1998) described her experiences in cyberspace—she calls them "ethnographic adventures." When Markham decided to pursue this idea, she had virtually no experience with going online. Only a few years later, Markham's work, which she called "researching real experience in virtual space," takes you on a wonderful journey. Markham and Baym (2008) have edited a book about inquiry on the Internet.

The Purpose of Online Interviewing

The purpose of any type of interview is to gather information from a participant on a particular topic. I have stressed the idea that the interviewer is the vehicle or conduit through which information is passed. Mann and Stewart (2000) reminded us what we know so well. A good interviewer begins by building rapport and making a participant feel comfortable. She is a careful, nonjudgmental, and perceptive listener. Many interviewers know the importance of nonverbal cues: the wink of an eye or a small smile. Pauses and silent time also appear in face-to-face interviews. But without the face-to-face experience, and perhaps without even being online at the same time as his or her participants, an online interviewer might need to develop a new set of techniques or skills.

Online sampling provides some interesting challenges. If e-mail is used as a means of interviewing, there are no issues regarding traveling, recording, or transcribing. Online sampling also makes possible interviewing people who are geographically dispersed. Mann and Stewart (2000) spoke of "the challenges of presenting self online" (p. 59). The general idea has to do with getting a sense of the other. In theory, this leads participants to trust the interviewer and, hopefully, share their private and social worlds. Online interviewing may present special problems because none of the usual cues are available. However, there is not general agreement about how and whether online rapport can be established.

Issues and Challenges With Online Interviewing

There are both technological and substantive issues connected with online interviewing. Technological issues involve such concerns as deciding how the two people should communicate with each other. At the current time, e-mail would seem to be the most logical avenue for communication, but other issues might emerge, such as connection speed (Do the interviewer and participant have access to a high-speed connection?); computer glitches (unexpected disconnects or files being lost); participants' lack of skill in typing or spelling (which sometimes leads to reluctance on the part of a participant); wait time (How do you know whether the person is thinking of what to write or did not really get the question?); lack of nonverbal cues (no look of puzzlement, no smiles); sufficient time for an interview (Do you and the participant really have 30 minutes or more of uninterrupted time on the computer?); and difficulties in providing follow-up or probing questions (the interviewer may be unfamiliar with the process and need much more experience). Substantive issues might also raise a problem. Shepherd (2003) spoke about difficulty establishing rapport and interpreting meaning. She suggested that it is difficult to interpret the emotional tone in which messages are written, for example, when common online abbreviations are used (e.g., "LOL"). James and Busher (2006) explored issues they faced when using e-mail to conduct Web-based online interviews. In particular, they questioned the credibility and trustworthiness of the design and the authenticity of participants' voices. They concluded that asynchronous discussions are valuable. Hamilton and Bowers (2006) also addressed issues regarding e-mail interviewing and recruitment. Suzuki, Ahluwalia, Arora, and Mattis (2007) presented an interesting discussion about observation, interview, and physical data using electronic data with the Internet. They commented that few have written about data collection methods via electronic means. Among the benefits they mentioned are data accuracy, recruiting participants in a variety of remote locations, and potential comfort in discussing various topics because of anonymity. I agree with their concern that visual cues often used to develop rapport are missing. Ethical issues regarding consent and confidentiality are raised by them and by Markham (2005), who questions issues of privacy and informed consent.

Synchronous, Preplanned Interview. A synchronous interview involves the selection of a participant who agrees to be interviewed at a particular time and with the use of a particular technology. Both interviewer and participant agree to be online at the same time, and interview questions are posed by the interviewer and responded to by the participant.

E-mail, Instant Messenger (IM), and Online Chat. This type of interviewing is relatively new. Because it is not planned, you will need to think about how you can capture ideas that are available. Flowers and Moore (2003) provided a detailed account of how to conduct interviews using AOL Instant Messaging.

Focus Groups on the Internet

As the Internet becomes more available and as high speed connections link many people to the Web and potentially to each other, conducting focus groups online offers a new alternative to the traditional type of focus group setting. Rezabek (2000) used online asynchronous discussions that lasted for more than two months. Sweet (1999) distinguished between virtual focus group rooms and asynchronous online bulletin boards. She reported on studies to evaluate online and offline advertising, evaluate mock Web sites, critique existing Web sites, test and evaluate new products (products mailed in advance of the groups), uncover competitive Web site information, evaluate training programs, explore decision making, uncover imagery, evaluate concepts, evaluate package images, generate ideas, and to ascertain customer and employee satisfaction. Sweet identified issues specific to the technical aspect of focus groups. My impression is that little research has been done on the topic, but suggestions come from practical experience. Much of what is written about this topic is related to market research. Some distinct advantages are lower cost, immediate transcription, and global participation. Disadvantages might include difficulties with technology, inexperience of participants with the format, inability of participants to key in entries and to communicate in this manner, and lack of support for the researcher who is working on her or his own.

I believe there is great potential for online focus groups. It is too early to say what methodological issues may arise. For example, what role should the moderator play? Should the moderator submit a list of questions in advance of the online discussion? Must all participants be present at the same time? Can asynchronous focus groups accomplish the same goals as those that meet at the same time? How does the nature of the group interaction change when the group is not present physically or even at the same time? Do we need eye contact, nonverbal cues, and other aspects of face-to-face meetings? Can we begin to think about alternative ways to elicit information? Does online participation limit the type of person who will participate? Are older people less likely to participate? Are those with limited language skills less likely to participate?

I hope by the time you read this book you will have had the opportunity to participate in one or more online discussions. I believe that the technology is there. It is up to you to avail yourself of it.

CHECKLIST FOR CONDUCTING INTERVIEWS

I have conducted many interviews. Sometimes I have been on a tight schedule and have had to complete three to five interviews or focus groups in a single day. This takes careful planning and coordination. This checklist contains specific suggestions that will make your interviews or focus groups run more smoothly. If you plan to conduct your interviews online, you will need to address a number of other issues not discussed herein. McNamara (n.d.) provides an excellent overview of interview techniques.

(Continued)

(Continued)

Goal: Get the Story in the Participant's Own Words

Before You Go

- Schedule appointments. Confirm the day before by phone or e-mail. Leave your contact information for emergencies.
- Identify a suitable location. Make sure it is quiet and affords privacy. If interviewing in a school, you may have to make compromises.
- Arrange for recording (video or audio) equipment. Ensure appropriate microphones, batteries, and extension cords are available.
- Bring sufficient discs or other devices for recording information.
- If focus groups are online, make sure you accommodate different time zones.
- Anticipate technical problems with computer connections and have an alternate plan.
- Prepare a one-page handout indicating the purpose of your study and how the participants can contact you if they have additional comments. You will leave this with the participants, so if you are doing multiple interviews be sure to bring sufficient copies.
- If your interview is highly structured, you will want to prepare the questions in advance. If you choose to conduct a more unstructured interview, you will probably be comfortable with some general topic areas rather than formal questions. In any case, have several copies available.
- Three forms to prepare: permission form, response recording form, record form.

  1. Permission form. You need to obtain a signed permission form for each individual who will participate in your study. Refer to examples available through your university IRB office.

  2. Form for recording responses. Even if you tape an interview, you will probably try to record the responses participants provide. Many people like to use a form with either the question or the topic area at the top of each page and then space to record responses.

  3. Record form with participant's name, location, date of interview, and other pertinent information.

- Bring paper, pens, and a watch or clock.
- Bring your journal for making memos and notes.
- Check yourself to make sure you are prepared.

When You Arrive

- Confirm appointments. This is especially important with focus groups. If you are doing several focus groups in one day, arrange for a waiting area.
- Set up and check your equipment before you begin.
- Review your tasks. Make sure you feel ready. Review major areas you plan to cover that are on the advance question sheet.

During the Interview

- Obtain a signed permission form.
- Record the time you start.
- Check recording equipment after two or three minutes to make sure everything is working. Be prepared with extra batteries or additional discs.
- Watch your time and gauge what you are doing.
- Be prepared to deal with interruptions.
- Maintain a high level of interest in the participants even if you find what they say boring.

When You Complete the Interview

- Record the time you completed the interview. Label the disc with a number so you will be able to locate it later. Put the same number on your supplementary forms.
- Make notes or observations that you have learned from this interview that you want to remember. Record your thoughts in your journal. It is always easier to do this right after the interview than later; our memories can really play tricks on us.
- Remember, conducting successful interviews without detailed questions is very difficult. Each successive one will be easier.
- Give yourself a 10-minute break if you are conducting multiple interviews. Interviewing of this type is quite intense, and you need some time to recover and unwind.
- Prepare for the next interview. Have your materials ready and check your equipment.

■ Summary

Whether you are conducting individual, focus group, or online interviews, the purpose is to gather information from your participants about the topic you are studying. Interviews may be structured with set questions, semistructured or guided interviews with a list of topics or question areas, in-depth or unstructured interviews, or even casual or unplanned interviews.

When conducting in-depth interviews, it is important to look at the components of the interview process. I describe and provide examples of different types of questions. I also illustrate strategies for asking questions. I also address issues related to conducting focus group interviews and online interviews. Planning and practice are critical elements to consider as you develop skills of successful interviewing.

GROUP ACTIVITY

Purpose: To develop skill in interviewing.

Activity: Identify a coresearcher. Select a topic of interest to you. Identify an individual who is willing to be interviewed and who has some knowledge about this topic. Set aside at least

30 minutes at a mutually agreed time and place. Practice the mechanics of interviewing. Your coresearcher will serve as an observer. Identify at least three types of questions and three questioning strategies to practice. After you complete the interview, meet with your coresearcher to debrief on the extent to which you were successful in varying your question types and question strategies. Repeat the process with another individual, changing places with your coresearcher.

Evaluation: Determine which areas are comfortable for you and which ones you need to refine.

INDIVIDUAL ACTIVITY

Purpose: To become comfortable with online interviewing.

Activity: Identify a topic of interest to you. Contact a friend and ask whether he or she is willing to engage in an e-mail interview at a designated time. Practice varying types of questions and questioning strategies via e-mail.

Evaluation: Comment in your journal about your comfort level with interviews that are not face to face.

Chapter 10

Learning About Others Through Observations and Other Techniques

FOCUS YOUR READING

- Many techniques to gather data are available to you. Often, researchers combine more than one technique.

- The Internet offers fantastic opportunities to interact with groups and gather data in ways not previously considered.

There is an art to living life fully and paying attention to the details.
—Anne Copland

I hear and I forget. I see and I remember. I do and I understand.
—Confucius

When I began teaching courses in qualitative research in the late 1980s, there were very few materials available. I decided that I wanted students to observe the same situations as a group. I decided to focus on family interactions at mealtimes. I located a number of films that illustrated my point. The films I used were *Ordinary People*, *Haywire*, *Witness*, and *Moonstruck*. I took very brief clips from these films. I tried several ways for students to begin the observations. Some students were given the assignment to look for different ways in which women were treated; others were asked to look at nonverbal communication; others focused on exploring differences among cultural groups; a final group had no direction. At the time, I thought the activity afforded many opportunities to illustrate points about conducting observations. We could review the films endlessly; I could stop and start the clips in order to become involved in discussion. We could all view the same thing in the same setting. While I knew that the films were exaggerated and some-what contrived, they served the purpose. Today, of course, with the wonders of television, instant reruns, and all the capabilities of the Internet, this type of activity can be used and adapted to the world we now know.

In this chapter, I explore techniques of collecting data in the qualitative research field other than interviewing and focus groups. I have chosen to discuss four different techniques of gathering data. First, I consider observations and provide examples. Next, I examine using the written word and visual images to gather data. I conclude with a discussion about using information obtained online. Often, researchers combine several methods of gathering their data. Jackson's (2008) one-year study of schooling in the small town where she grew up illustrates her use of interviews with former classmates and community members, review of historical documents, and the shadowing of six seniors who had been in the school since kindergarten. You can get an excellent sense of the writer and the specific issues of power and pleasure when you read this interesting account.

Observing in Natural Settings. Observations usually occur in settings that already exist, rather than in contrived settings. You can observe naturally occurring groups either at work or in informal set-tings. You can also observe individuals in their home, educational, or work settings. Observations were originally associated with ethnographic studies.

Writing: What Exists, What You Get Others to Create, What You Create. There are various types of written documents that you can use in qualitative research. Qualitative researchers often use exist-ing documents to gather information. These can include official documents such as minutes of meetings or curriculum guides. They can also include newspaper accounts, letters, diaries or jour-nals, and online course descriptions. You can get others to create written material in the form of e-mail messages, responses to questions, or student journals. Finally, you may create written material in the form of **field notes,** memos, or a **researcher journal**. In some cases, you will make notes of your observations; in other cases, you will make notes that are self-reflective or introspective.

Images. You can use images such as photographs, films, or videotapes. They can be either existing images or ones made specifically for your research. With digital cameras, images are both easy to cre-ate and instantly available. You can also use drawings or sketches. Images can be created by you, by the participants, or by both together. Images from YouTube or other Internet sources can also be used.

Chat Rooms, Online Discussion Groups, Online Teaching, and Other Online Resources. There is a growing body of literature about the use of data from these sources.

■ Observing in Natural Settings

Many of the ideas about observation in qualitative research are drawn from anthropologists who immersed themselves in remote cultures. Sometimes they tried to remain unobtrusive; however, they more often became participant observers. They often spent months listening to and looking at those around them. They took notes. Critical to their work was the study of individuals and groups in their own environment. The anthropologists' goal was to try to gain a deep understanding of the social interaction and cultures of these groups. Early in the 1900s, it was fashionable to study individuals in cultures that were completely remote and different from our own, so anthropologists traveled to New Guinea, Samoa, Mexico, or other remote locations. Of course, you need to remember that access to these cultures was very limited. There was no television, and few Americans had actually traveled to such faraway places. These early types of observations were called *nonparticipant observations.* In some cases, observers found themselves interacting with the people and their roles shifted to participant observers.

Did You Know

Observation of human interaction, seemingly so simple, is incredibly complex. Your perspective on what you see and hear and how you make meaning of it is critical.

It was not until the late 1980s that ethnography began to be used to any extent in education (LeCompte, 2002). Borrowing from the early anthropologists, qualitative researchers worked to adapt this tradition to the study of schools and education. Researchers immersed themselves in classrooms and conducted extensive observations and took field notes. As interest in the technique increased, modifications were made to the length of observations, and shorter observation times became more widely used. Beginning in the 21st century, researchers became interested in online cultures and adapted techniques to the study of online chat rooms or other online communities. Kawulich (2005) offered an excellent overview of the topic.

In 2006, a special session of seven senior researchers was held at the International Congress of Qualitative Inquiry at the University of Illinois. An assignment for one group of students was to perform an ethnographic study of the conference by conducting informal interviews and observations. Students also had to obtain signed consent forms from the participants. What resulted was a publication based on the informal discussions among the researchers and the observations and comments by Carolyn Ellis, the organizer (Ellis et al., 2008). I believe you will enjoy reading about how these researchers traveled on their journey. One thing you will come away with is how open to new ideas these researchers are. I urge you to take a similar open stance as you explore alternative means of gathering data.

The Purpose of Observations

Gathering data through observation has long been associated with anthropologists. Observing humans in natural settings assists our understanding of the complexity of human behavior and interrelationships among groups. When they visited groups of people in remote lands, anthropologists' goals were to study the culture of these groups. One definition of **culture** is that it is a system of shared beliefs, values, customs, and behaviors that individuals use to cope with their world and with each other. In the early years, non-Western people were studied, and their values were often compared to our values.[1] Although not necessarily made explicit, the assumption was that the values of Western culture were somehow better than those of others. When educators decided to use anthropological methods to study classrooms, I believe many of the ideas about culture were largely ignored. Some of the observational studies in classrooms were done to get a sense of what it was like in a classroom. I recall Kidder's 1989 study of a fifth-grade classroom in Massachusetts. He spent nine months with 20 children and their teacher. His moving account includes sections on homework, discipline, and the science fair. I do not believe he knew which topics he would write about prior to his immersion in the class. Although not written as qualitative research per se, this is one of the earliest detailed accounts of a classroom that provides a rich context for the children and their teacher. Geertz (1973) reminded us that a thick description is to be valued in ethnography. I think he would agree that Kidder does just this.

But even as educators began to spend extended time in classrooms, there seemed to be a desire to study groups of children who were quite different from those who were the observers. Because most researchers who do these kinds of studies are highly educated, they usually are members of the middle class. Yet, they tended to study children who were not of the middle class. The greater the difference between those observing and those being observed, the more likely it was that ethnocentric ideas came into play. So, for example, when middle-class white observers studied working class black students, they saw many differences and, I suspect, found themselves making comparisons that were quite judgmental. Other anthropologists studied groups who were outside the mainstream culture. If you read the anthropological literature, you will see many references to studies of groups that could be seen as outsiders: motorcycle gangs, the homeless, homosexuals, pregnant teenagers, drug addicts, and the like.

Many researchers do not have the luxury of studying for such a long time or in such depth. And many schools and teachers are reluctant to give permission for outsiders to come into their schools and classrooms for such an extended time. Using observation to gather qualitative data has moved away from the kind of immersion practiced by anthropologists to a shorter and less intense activity. So, now you have to rethink what is meant by observing. In my experience, it is an activity that is much narrower in scope. I recall a student who studied kindergarten classrooms to determine how rules were formed. McIntyre (2002) studied violence in the lives of Northern Irish women. I remember reading a study of teenagers in malls and how groups interacted. In all these examples, the researchers limited themselves to a particular aspect of human interaction. They targeted that information and limited the scope of their observations to a predetermined area.

Issues Regarding Observations

Deciding Who Is to Be Studied and in What Situations. Do you want to study children in bilingual classrooms? Do you want to study high school athletes on the playing field? Do you want to study first-year teachers in their classrooms? Do you want to study girls in advanced math classes? Do you want to study nurses in emergency rooms? Often, qualitative researchers select one or several key demographic characteristics of a group of people and decide to study them by observing them in their natural settings. Usually, they first decide on the type of individual to study. Observations then can occur in a number of places. If school children are selected, then the observations might occur inside a classroom, on the playing field, on the bus, in the cafeteria, or in the hallways.

Fordham (1988) studied successful inner-city poor minority children and observed them at church, at home, and in social situations. Glass (2001) studied families of autistic children and studied them in their homes. Berger (2004) studied wheelchair athletes. Cocks (2008) studied the peer culture of disabled children. Condell (2008) reported on writing field notes while studying collaborative experiences of peers.

Formal Groups, Informal Groups, or Occasional Groups. You might not have thought about this before, but there are different kinds of groups you can study. A *formal group* is stable, with the same people serving as a nucleus, such as a class, a family, a team, a gang, or a work unit. These same people come together regularly for either work or play. There are usually formal or informal rules and boundaries that are known by all members of the group. *Informal groups,* on the other hand, are in contact with each other, but members may move in and out, and they do not meet regularly. Examples of informal groups are a card-playing group, members of an online chat room, a play group with mothers and children, a community action team, or members of a club or a support group. An *occasional group* consists of people who might come together once or a number of times but whose membership is constantly shifting. All types of groups can be observed, but you might look for different things in each.

Gaining Access. If studies are conducted in schools, gaining access is often difficult. In the current climate, many school officials are reluctant to let outsiders enter the schools. Often, researchers have to submit detailed plans outlining what they want to do and how much time they will take doing it. They may be asked to speak of how the research will benefit those studied. Large school systems are very difficult to penetrate and often receive many more requests than they can handle. If studies are to be conducted with specific subgroups, it is often difficult to get access to these groups. Almost 40 years ago, Liebow (1967) studied black men on street corners in Washington, D.C., and had to overcome the participants' reluctance to let him into their subculture. Gaining access when you are an outsider continues to be challenging, as Berger (2004) remarked about his surprise as he faced difficulties gaining access to observe people with disabilities. As you think about conducting your own observations, sensitivity and awareness of these issues are important considerations.

What to Study. In my experience, what is most difficult about conducting observations is knowing which of the many things to look at. There is so much going on when humans are together. Should you concentrate on a single person? If so, who? If you try to take in the whole setting, it becomes overwhelming. I find that beginning students are more comfortable with some guidelines. In the next section, I offer you some concrete suggestions. Boeree (1998) distinguished between the physical nature of human interaction and the meaning of interactions. As the observer, it is up to you to decide when an interaction is meaningful. In my experience, the distinction begins to emerge as you process the data you have collected. It is not evident during an observation which interactions are meaningful and which are—to use Boeree's term—physical.

Frequency and Length of Time. Obviously, this varies depending on what you are studying, who you are studying, and how much time you have available. I suggest that you conduct your observations several times and allocate between 30 minutes and an hour for each observation. Some settings are routine and predictable, while others are extremely varied.

Your Role. Observers take on different roles. If you are part of the group you observe, or if you become part of the group, you are called a **participant observer**. If you are not known to those you are studying, you are a surreptitious or **unobtrusive observer**. If you observe in cyberspace, you might be a completely unknown or unnoticed observer. In postmodern ethnography, the observer's role is an interaction in which his or her voice is made explicit. This contemporary position reflects the new thinking about power and privilege and the relationship between those being studied and those doing the studying. Lugosi (2006) suggested that, in certain situations, the observer might need to remain concealed.

How to Conduct an Observation

Qualitative observations differ tremendously, depending on the concepts and issues to be studied, location of observation, length of time and number of each observation, and type of group studied.

Planning

- Most people prefer to begin observations by deciding on a particular aspect to study. It is difficult to just "go in and look" without knowing what you will look at or what is important. I suggest you identify a specific aspect of human interaction to study. Many educators find it difficult to study culture in general and are better able to identify a particular dimension of human interaction to study. I have looked at interactions of aides with children, families interacting during different occasions (e.g., meals, parties, and leisure time), teachers in faculty meetings, and teacher-parent meetings. I have had students study staking out space in the library, motorcycle gangs in bars, and female athletes in the locker room.

- Identify three to five areas to look at, such as who initiates a conversation, reactions of participants to a particular issue, or nonverbal signals shown by participants. These should be seen as freeing, not limiting. Sometimes observers go into a situation with no agenda and this works well, but other times, students report being overwhelmed and being unable to focus on a particular thing because so much is going on.

- Decide whether you will take notes, use videos or digital technology, or rely on your memory. If the latter, then make sure that you allow sufficient time immediately after the observation to record your impressions.

- Decide how much time you will allow for your observation. I suggest at least 30 minutes initially. I would then follow up with a one-hour observation.

- For your initial observations, I suggest that you choose public spaces where individuals interact with each other. This way, you do not need to obtain permission and you can blend in with those you are studying. I use cafes, fast-food restaurants, playgrounds, shopping malls, airports, religious institutions, or any other place where people congregate.

Conducting the Observations

- Once you arrive at your destination, you need to settle down in a place where you will be able to look and listen. I frequently observe at a fast-food restaurant. I get some coffee and choose a table where I can be comfortable and can see and hear plenty of people. I find it helpful to drink my coffee and survey the space. I need to take notes and so I use a notebook; however, in some situations, you might find this gets in the way and you will have to rely on your memory.

- I find it very helpful to begin my observations with a look at the surroundings. I often draw a sketch or take a picture as a memory aid. If I am in a school or classroom, I note how the chairs are arranged, what kind of art is displayed, the lighting, and the air quality. If I go to the same classroom regularly, I make note of any changes in the physical space.

- Because your study is about individuals, you may decide you want to describe the main characters in the setting. What are they wearing? Is their speech formal or casual? How well do the players know each other?

- Because your goal is to observe human interaction, you need to decide what to focus on. In some settings, there may be several different things happening at the same time, and you will need to set some priorities. There is no right thing to look at. You just need to decide what is challenging or interesting to study.

Other Issues

- What is your role? Do you want to participate in the interactions or do you want to remain aloof? Is there a right or best way to behave? Can you behave one way one time and another way another time? I suspect you know that it is up you to choose what you want to do. I have observed in many classrooms where I was silent and sat in the back of the room. I have also found myself helping children who needed help. Should you disclose your role to members of the group or keep it hidden? It depends on the situation.

- Things are not always as they seem. If people know you are observing them they might want to look good, so you might not be seeing underlying human experience. Or, people might decide to behave as they think you want them to behave. If you are in a public setting, this is less likely to occur.

- Should you reveal to people what you are doing and why, should you keep it quiet, or should you tell a fictitious story? These are decisions you will need to make once you begin an actual research study. For now, because you are practicing and honing your skills, this is less critical.

- Should you have a very narrow focus, or should you look at everything? Here, you need to strike a balance. It should be obvious that you can't look at everything, but you may not know what is important until you have spent some time looking and listening and thinking about the underlying meaning of what you see and hear.

- How much is enough? You can only get a slice of life, so how large a slice should you get? You can answer this question by beginning your data analysis while you are observing. That means you will have to take notes either while you are observing or when you complete an observation. Sometimes circumstances dictate how long you can observe. I recall being at a preschool in Japan for about a week. I studied several classrooms, met with the principal, and observed children on the playground. Although I would have preferred to be there a longer time, it was not possible.

- Can you really get at the essence of the culture of the group? This is a difficult question to answer. I believe you can come to understand how individuals interact with each other and develop new insights through observation. A word of caution, however. As individuals become more sophisticated and worldly, they may learn to mask underlying meanings. Your task is to uncover deep meaning rather than surface structure.

- I am not sure that practice makes perfect, but I believe you can train yourself to be more observant. Exercises that involve observing the same phenomenon—for example, looking at films or videos, discussing what you observed with others, and then looking again at the same videos—will heighten your powers of observation. You can train yourself to focus on details or look at the whole and ignore the details. You can train yourself to look for the emotional content and meaning expressed in everyday language.

Examples of Observations

I have found it very effective to prepare some ideas in advance before I actually conduct an observation. I think of these as scenarios. Consider one of the following scenarios before you actually begin an observation.

Scenario 1

Topic: Using television families to study power.

Your role: Observer

Setting the stage: Select several current television series that concern a family. I suggest you pick several different kinds of programs and that you choose traditional and nontraditional situations. Choose at least three different episodes of the programs.

Providing focus for your observation: You are interested in studying power as it manifests in families. Prior to observations, you need to develop a working definition of power from your point of view. As a start, you might ask yourself these kinds of questions: What are the signs of power? How is it manifested? Who exhibits power in a specific family? What are ways in which it is accomplished? Are there power issues that are appropriate (from your perspective) or inappropriate in the families you observe?

Conducting the observation: The first time you watch the program, you may just want to get used to looking at different interactions and taking notes. After you feel comfortable, return to your question and try to jot down an example and evidence related to your focus. Continue this process through several episodes of the program.

Making sense of what you found: Because you are only practicing, you cannot conduct more than a tentative analysis. Write down your general thoughts about the topic.

Advantages: By using a television program, you can review your data many times. You can also do this observation in conjunction with other students and compare your comments.

Limitations: Television programs do not really reflect real life; most things are exaggerated. You may not find any evidence related to your topic.

Scenario 2

Topic: Examining the effects of parental cultural expectations on children's behavior.

Your role: Unobtrusive observer

Setting the stage: Identify a fast-food restaurant near your home where you might encounter families from many cultural backgrounds. Choose a weekend mealtime for your observation. Go to the restaurant prior to your actual observations to determine whether you can sit and observe. You might want to talk to the manager, who may become suspicious and ask why you are there.

Providing focus for your observation: You are aware that family expectations differ dramatically based on cultural backgrounds. You might look at such things as whether expectations for family members are based on gender. Are the adult men and women behaving in ways that might influence their daughters to be more traditional, to act out, or to be subservient? What kinds of rules do you think girls would learn in different cultural settings? Do parents behave differently toward their male or female children?

Conducting the observation: This is a much greater challenge than observing a television program. People might wonder why you are looking at them. You might not really be able to take notes while you look. In my experience, however, you should find some interesting things in public places.

Making sense of what you found: You can try your hand at writing some general thoughts about the different styles of cultural groups as they interact over a family meal. You may also want to restate your question because you might not be clear about your focus.

Advantages: Understanding different styles among cultural groups is a critical topic, especially as our culture becomes increasingly diverse.

Limitations: Conducting an observation in a public place without drawing suspicion may be a problem, in light of increased concerns about security.

Scenario 3

Topic: Examine the discrepancies between verbal behaviors and nonverbal cues.

Your role: Participant observer

Setting the stage: Identify locations where you are able to observe adults interacting with each other. If you choose an office, the people might be more careful of their behavior. If you choose a social situation, you might see different kinds of behaviors.

Providing focus for your observation: You have long had an interest in the relationship between verbal behaviors and nonverbal cues. You've suspected that what one says and what one does may often be at odds. You've noticed that when talking to people (e.g., in your office), you are struck by the abundance of comments that are socially acceptable. Yet, when you observe the way people behave, they often act in ways contrary to their words. You decide to observe people interacting in natural settings and look specifically for nonverbal cues, especially those that contradict verbal statements. You might begin by asking, "Do I see discrepancies? What kinds of discrepancies do I observe? Do people misunderstand the meaning of what others say and do?"

Conducting the observation: This observation can be conducted in any social or work setting. It can be a party, a social gathering, a work environment, or an informal get together. Your role is participant observer; you are actually part of the setting. Practice before you actually observe by paying special attention to certain words and behaviors, then identify several settings where you can see evidence of these behaviors. When you leave the setting, write down your thoughts in your journal because it would be awkward to do so while attending an event.

Making sense of what you found: Again, you have insufficient data to make any meaningful statements. However, you can try to organize your notes into themes.

Advantages: You have immediate access to a natural setting because you are part of the group.

Limitations: You might not see what you are looking for, or you might forget what you see because you are not able to take notes while you are interacting.

Scenario 4

Topic: Study gender differences in a math classroom.

Your role: Postmodern observer

Setting the stage: Identify a classroom that meets the criteria.

Providing focus for your observation: You are aware of many issues regarding the different behaviors of and expectations for males and females. Rather than identify a particular scenario or area of focus, in this observation you will gather data to target your observations. You will enter the situation with predetermined ideas about teachers' different expectations of performance. Because you have already adopted a stance, you might find it difficult to keep an open mind as you observe.

Conducting the observation: I usually find, with a general idea such as this, that several observations are in order. Once you select a classroom, you might find yourself moving from unobtrusive observer to one who takes an active role. I have seen observers in such classes help students with homework or explain different ideas. In fact, sometimes they forget to do their observations. It takes a good deal of skill to focus your attention and not get caught up in a particular situation.

Making sense of what you found: As with the other examples, you might find yourself having difficulty determining what it is you really have gathered.

Advantages: You are not limited to looking at a particular situation and may discover that new insights emerge.

Limitations: By not having a focus, you might find yourself struggling to determine what it is you should look for, or you might discover that you see what you want to see.

These illustrations should give you some ideas of places to observe and ways in which you can engage in observations. Many students who are just beginning their experiences with qualitative research find that targeted practice helps them begin to refine their observation skills.

Astute observing is an excellent way to gather information in your qualitative study. While it is fairly unstructured, it offers endless possibilities for learning how humans interact. You can increase your observational skills through practice, feedback, and discussion with others. Using television and film enables you to look and look again. Today, with sophisticated technology readily available, we find observation taking on entirely new dimensions. For example, we have video ethnography, a technique suggested by Genzuk (2003), who recommends that you begin by watching people at school, work, or leisure. I agree with him. Tutt (2008) provided a fascinating account of a yearlong study of living room interactions using video ethnography.

■ Existing Writing, Your Writing, and Writing You Generate

In addition to interviews, focus groups, and observations, there are various other excellent sources of information. Some of this information exists, and you have to identify it and gain access to it. Other information comes from participants. A third type is written by you. All types are legitimate and useful as you gather data for your qualitative study.

We have only just begun to tap what is available out there. The Internet is an incredible source of written information; I believe it will revolutionize the type of data we collect and use in our qualitative studies. Whether it is a blog written by one individual, a group blog with contributions from many, the discussion in a chat room, online class discussions, dialogue in Listservs, or some other ideas not yet imagined, the power of this source just beginning to be used in a systematic way. I can only mention again its immediacy, its availability for use in your study, its universality, and its ease of use.

I do not want you to think that the only source of written information is the Internet, however. I discuss some fairly common sources in the section titled "Issues Regarding Written Material."

The Purpose of Written Material

Documentation is one of the watchwords of historical research. Whether it is a primary source, such as the Declaration of Independence, or a secondary source, such as a biography of Benjamin Franklin, documents teach us about history. They are evidence of what people did and said and what they thought.

Written material created by participants—either in direct response to your requests or created for other purposes—captures the thoughts, ideas, and meanings of participants. Consequently, such material provides a window into the human mind.

Written material you create—a journal, a diary, field notes, or a poem—provides insight into your thinking and reactions to what you are studying and its effect on you and others.

I cannot stress how important such written material is to a study. Of course, one enormous advantage is that its form permits easy storage in a computer and easy use in data analysis.

Issues Regarding Written Material

What material should you use? How do you find it? What might be valuable and what might be trivial? The first type of material I want you to think about is written material already in existence. I suspect that there is no written material that you should reject without looking at it, but it is likely that some sources, more than others, might prove relevant to your topic. If you were studying teenage pregnant girls, you might find their diaries of interest. Getting access to these is unlikely, however. If you were interested in teachers serving as mentors, teacher training documents prepared by a school system might be valuable. If you were interested in how parents and children interact with each other around homework, you might find the homework itself of interest, or you might find directions for homework given by the teacher valuable. Obviously, your question is critical, but here are some other examples of written information that you might find useful: documents provided by schools, including school newsletters, school board meeting minutes, curriculum guides, teacher lesson plans, e-mail messages, school Web sites, or notes of observations by principals; documents in the public domain, including newspaper accounts or editorials; documents provided in a work setting, including interoffice memos, reports, or performance evaluations; documents provided by individuals, including letters, diaries, or stories.

Written material you ask participants to create might include e-mail responses to your questions. In a study of beginning teachers, I have used a weekly e-mail format with three simple questions: How was your week? What problem did you face? How did you solve it? By keeping the format consistent, I minimized the time it took for participants to respond, and I was able to capture many responses over time. Information was already on my computer, so I had little to do before data analysis. You might ask students to keep a journal of their thoughts about being in Mr. Smith's class or about learning a challenging subject. You might ask superintendents to dictate their ideas about school violence into voice recognition software that transfers the material to the computer.

Written material you create might include your online journal, **memos** regarding your thoughts about the qualitative data you collect, field notes that you develop after an extensive observation, or a poem you write to express your thoughts on a particularly challenging aspect of learning to become a qualitative researcher. You should not ignore class work or papers you create for a class in qualitative research.

Extracting the Essence

Just like any other data you collect, written material challenges you to find underlying meaning in the words of others and in your own words. Reacting to metaphors is especially exciting because they reveal what is beneath the surface meaning of the words you read. I recall asking students to write a short paper describing one of their parents by using metaphors. One student referred to her father as Santa Claus. She wrote, "In my family we had a wonderful Christmas tradition. Sometime during the month of December, Santa would come in the night and decorate our Christmas tree and fill our stockings. One such night was to be very different, for one of those nights, Santa kissed me good-night."

Another woman wrote about her father in a poem titled *The Perfect Southern Gent—My Daddy*. She described "his color of rich mocha chocolate with a hint of cream." Another student described his father as "a horse that wears blinders." And another student wrote,

Boy, write about your parents using metaphors she says. This sounds simple enough, but for the last 24 hours I've agonized over doing it. Seems this assignment has forced me to think about my Mom and Dad in ways that I haven't (or have avoided) during the last 10 years or so. Forgive me as my submission will probably resemble some postmodern stream of consciousness, but that's how things are bubbling up.

And finally, from one of my Middle Eastern students, "My father is the ocean who gives a life to the sand and the rocks that surround him and then retreats to let them nourish with what he gave." We used these submissions as we began our exploration of the meaning given by metaphors. Things are not always as they seem, we began to learn.

■ Images

I have emphasized throughout that qualitative research relies on the written word; it is the written word that forms the basis of all your data. But I also suggest to you that visual information is very powerful. Just as with written information, visual information can come in various forms: that which exists already (found images), that which you ask participants to create, the images that you create, or images created by groups of people either acting together or responding to each other.

Found images can serve several purposes: They document aspects of social interaction, they can be used as stimuli for interviews, and they can be used in presentations. I would be remiss if I did not mention again the power of the Internet. Images are widely available and easy for you or others to create and display online. A digital camera or video camera can be used to transfer information in fractions of seconds. You can display visual information in your written reports and use hyperlinks to take your reader to photos, videos, or art. You are only limited by your imagination.

If you become interested in this topic, you may want to read about the hermeneutics of seeing. Davey (1999) suggested that hermeneutics can embrace visual phenomena as well as the written word.

The Purpose of Images

"A picture is worth ten thousand words." I assume you've heard this many times. Did you know that the quotation is actually phony? The "Chinese" quotation in Figure 10.1 was fabricated by an advertising executive representing a baking soda company. The executive assumed that consumers would be compelled to buy a product that had the weight of Chinese philosophy behind it. The ad was most often seen on streetcars, on which customers did not have much time to read advertising copy.

Lester (n.d.) reminded us,

> With digital hegemony, visual messages have reasserted their position as an important communication medium, but at the cost of not recognizing the combination of words and pictures as vital in communication. With the correct interpretation of the proverb, words and pictures live in harmony as they are both used equally in order to understand the meaning of any work that uses them both. (¶ 4)

I believe images enhance and embellish and make alive the words we use to express our thoughts. Whether the images are created by us, our participants, or others, they send powerful messages.

Visual images are central to our culture and our communication. They provide another avenue of meaning. They represent a kind of reality captured by the researcher. However, I think that you need to remember that images, while an apparent representation of reality, are

Figure 10.1 Fabricated Chinese Quotation

actually created or used by the researcher to reflect a particular stance or point of view. Nevertheless, the power and seductive nature of images cannot be ignored.

Examples of Images

Some research asks participants to recreate scenes from their earlier life. Kelly and Kerner (2004) described how they used the photographic exhibition *Positive Lives* and personal snapshots to document the death of a loved one from HIV/AIDS. In a study of childhood sexual abuse, the researcher asked the participant to provide illustrations of the abuse. Kearney and Hyle (2004) discussed how they used drawings by participants to examine the emotional impact of change. La Jevic and Springgay (2008) used visual journals in a preservice education course. I use an exercise in which students are asked to represent themselves by drawing images on a large piece of paper. Some choose to be literal and often draw a timeline of significant events in their lives; others choose more abstract and metaphorical representations. A number of research projects involve giving participants disposable cameras and asking them to photograph a day in their lives. I have asked participants to bring in photographs of their families and to use these as a jumping off point to initiate interviews. Online images can be created and expanded and disseminated to serve as discussion points for online chats. You only need your imagination to think of how images can be used.

Issues Regarding Images

Quality of the Image. One important issue to consider is the quality of the visual representation. If you are going to use an image as part of your document, then how it looks becomes important. Of course, software to enhance or modify images is readily available and fairly easy for even the novice to use.

Manipulation of the Image. Most people used to believe an image was a literal representation of an event or a person. But whether you choose to manipulate an image with a computer program or to present an image to highlight a particular aspect of it, what you, as a researcher, see and subsequently represent visually is your interpretation of what you study.

Relationship of the Image to Your Words. I think it is important that your choice of images and words enhance each other. A photograph must have a purpose, in the same way that a quotation from a participant must have a purpose.

■ Using the Internet in Qualitative Research

There are a variety of ways to use the Internet in qualitative research. One way is to use group online environments, chat rooms, or discussion groups to study online cultures. Another idea is to convene focus groups using online technology. Online teaching is now possible, and courses in qualitative research are becoming increasingly available. Researchers have begun to examine visual diaries, blogs, Webinars, and vlogs as sources of information. The Internet is also being used to make available data that other researchers can use for secondary analyses (Lichtman, 2005). Finally, the Internet can facilitate discussions and exchanges among researchers. But conducting research with online communities is not without problems. Shepherd (2003) discussed some challenges she faced in using e-mail and chat rooms. In her blog, Anand (2006) discussed her brush with online qualitative research; she cautioned about the judicious use of such techniques.

Persistent Online Environments

Brown and Bell (n.d.) suggested that online environments, such as multiplayer gaming sites, constitute a complex social organization. These environments usually involve a large number of participants and elaborate behaviors. I have seen my teenage grandson play on these gaming sites for hours at a time. When I ask about them, he tells me he plays with kids all over the world. Thousands of young people play these games and interact with each other 24/7. Working with these types of environments requires skills in accessing and manipulating data.

Chat Rooms and Discussion Groups

Researchers see new arenas for studying culture. Instead of traveling to remote physical locations, they can now travel to cyber-locations and study online cultures. Some do this by studying existing chat rooms and discussion groups. I recall first reading about studying life online when Markham's (1998) book reached my desk. In this book, she explored how "users create, negotiate, and make sense of their social experience in computer-mediated contexts" (p. 9). Markham spends time online to study the experience of chat rooms, support groups, and virtual communities. Her goal is to experience the meanings of life online. More recently, Markham (2005) raised several issues about doing research of this kind. Although there are no clear guidelines, she suggests that the research should be both epistemologically and methodologically sound. She defines the Internet as a communication medium, a global network of connections, and a scene of social construction. "As social life becomes more saturated with Internet-based media for communication, researchers will be able to creatively design projects that utilize these media to observe culture, interact with participants, or collect artifacts." Online ethnographies, or "netnographies" (Kozinets, 2002) observe the textual discourse that is available on the Internet.

Using the new technology requires researchers to be creative and diligent as they chart new ground. Identifying individuals to study online is something of a challenge. Flowers and Moore (2003) discussed how they identified participants for online qualitative research studies. Robbins

(2001), a graduate student of mine, combined online interviews, reviews of Web sites, and postings from online message boards to gather her data about adolescent girls' use of the Internet.

Dholakia and Zhang (2004) spoke about using data from e-commerce data sites, such as bulletin board systems, newsgroups, chat rooms, server log files, and Web sites. They suggest that we no longer are looking at an oral culture or a written culture, but rather computer-mediated communications.

Focus Groups

Another idea for using the Internet is to convene online focus groups. Some organize focus groups in which participants are available in real time (synchronous groups). Rezabek (2000) described using online asynchronous focus groups in a Listserv to generate topics for future in-depth discussions. Issues to be addressed are the different hardware and software capabilities of participants, role of the researcher, ability of participants to type rapidly, and participants' reluctance to put their words in a permanent form online.

One challenge is to identify participants and to get them to participate. Some research suggests that computer users tend to be predominantly male and young. While this may have been true in the past, I do not think it will be so in the future. Researchers continue to develop new ideas about how to locate people and get them to participate. But I believe opportunities will present themselves as use of technology becomes easier, information travels faster, and more people have access to computers.

You can imagine a number of advantages to using online chat rooms or conducting online focus groups. First, you can capture a wide and varied audience. Data from discussions are easy to download and readily available. The anonymous nature of the online environment may result in participants being more open. New technologies provide readymade written transcripts that can be imported into your personal computer with little cost and fuss.

Online Teaching

The data from courses taught online can be used to study student cultures and interactions. I also find it especially helpful to understand how students process information, especially when it relates to the topic of qualitative research. I began putting my own courses online in the late 1990s. I knew very little about the technology but learned how to make Web pages and how to put together the rudiments of a discussion forum. By putting these courses online, I enabled others to locate them, and the information reached a larger audience than my own students. Several qualitative researchers began to search the Web and collect information about such courses. You can easily see what is out there by using a search engine and searching for "qualitative research courses." I hesitate to send you to a particular location because one drawback of using the Internet is that there is little permanence, and sites that were operational yesterday may have disappeared today.

One unfortunate consequence of newer technologies, such as the teaching tool Blackboard, is that courses are restricted to registered students and the larger community of scholars cannot gain access. I found that although my later courses worked better technologically, they were not available to anyone other than students at my university.

The traditional ways we think about teaching have been turned on their heads with the ready availability of computers for many students and software programs that facilitate discussions and comments. Most of us are used to providing education face to face. In this section, I illustrate some of the things you can do with computer technology that facilitate comments and thought. This first group of comments addresses the way students have taken the material they read and tried to apply it to their own thinking and practice. Online comments and discussions offer a variety of types of information. Here, for example, is a concern and a response about interviewing offered by someone belonging to a Listserv on qualitative research:

> Everyone, I just finished an interview for my qualitative research class, and it went horribly wrong. My participant, who is usually very talkative, locked up completely when the tape recorder went on. I asked him to not even think about it and just focus on our conversation, but his answers were very short and vague. He responded poorly to many of the open-ended questions I was asking him. When I asked him to elaborate, he didn't. I even strayed from the topics and talked with him about video games to loosen him up, and when I went back to the interview he did the same things again. Any thoughts and/or suggestions on what I should do for next time? *Mike M.*

One response followed:

> I have found that interviewing someone you know well—friend or grandparent, for example—is difficult. Often students pick someone they know as their first interview as they think the person will be more supportive. But it is really much easier to interview someone you don't know, particularly if you have a couple of open questions to ask. *Lesley M.*

Here are further examples of students' online comments. Students were asked to describe how they planned to analyze a set of interview data. Although they were given some guidelines to follow and had read information in their text, this was their initial attempt to analyze real data. They were asked to analyze several interviews. Each student conducted one of the interviews. After transcription, they were to transmit the interviews to all other classmates via the computer. I asked them to consider the process of data analysis and to plan what they would do as they began to think about the data they had received.

I also asked them to respond to my online questions: What are some steps you will follow in beginning your data analysis of the grad student interviews? Why did you select these steps?

> I began by reading each interview in its entirety. As I read, I thought about the questions that were being asked and how the subject responded, in order to gain overall, *initial perspective* [italics added] for the interview. Before I began taking any type of notes, I wanted to get a general idea of the direction/intent of the questions that were being asked and how/why the subject responded the way that he/she did. My next step was to read the interview transcriptions again to try and get some general direction and think about how the subjects actually responded/what they actually said. During my second reading, I made some general notes that I hope will aid in the identification of themes that will be amenable to additional analysis. Paul

> My first few steps in the data analysis process have been to *bracket my own thoughts* [italics added] and feelings regarding the graduate school experience; to organize each of the interviews provided by the class, and then to read through each interview a couple of times highlighting or circling key words or phrases that "speak to me"—at times even memoing in the margin of the interview transcripts.

I decided on each of these steps based on my readings of Creswell's text and numerous websites, as well as our class discussion. I believe these steps will provide me some initial reflection to prepare me to begin the coding process that comes next.

As I review the above statements, I realize that I'm portraying this as a linear process. Yet, I expect much of this experience of data analysis to be iterative and simultaneous based on my readings and our discussions. *Leanne*

My approach to this analysis is similar to that of my classmates. However, in reading the interviews, it seems to me that as I read each one sequentially, my thoughts tend to be more of a *forward-leaning spiral* [italics added]. In other words, with each interview read, I learn more for my "database," but also start drawing (perhaps jumping to) conclusions. This is the bane of a "scientific method"-based education . . . we always want to get to the (a?) conclusion. Thus, I agree with Leanne when she says that she tries to bracket as she reads. What I am attempting to do as I follow the sequential, linear approach to reading is to practice spiral thinking that characterizes some aspects of South Asian (i.e., Indian) thought. Thus, as I read I try to bracket while allowing my thoughts to loop back and appreciate and integrate what I learned from the earlier interviews read. Quite a trick . . . but that is the approach I am attempting. I am taking this approach/these steps (indeed, is not the very idea of "steps" a bit linear?) so as to get a good feel for the data. *Frank*

I originally thought that I would approach reading and data gathering from the interviews much like I do reading and data gathering for my other academic work. I sat down with a highlighter, notebook, and pencil and prepared to "dissect" the interviews. I ended up reading all of the interviews all the way through without making a single note or highlight. This gave me a better overall perspective to simply get an understanding (and enjoyment) of the interviews.

After reading them through, I reviewed them a second time. I began to take notes in the margins of the interviews, but in doing so, I would recall other interviews that had similar patterns (or themes). Thus I ended up putting all of my notes in my notebook. I used a two-column approach: on one side, I noted generalized themes of interviewer questions, and on the other I noted themes that the interviewee responded (although not necessarily questioned about). In some instances, I could draw a line across the column, as to which questioning concept led to which response concept. Yet at other times, I noted that the response concepts developed independently of questioning or as a result of different question concepts. This approach was the easiest for me to use in organizing the data in my mind. *Heather*

I illustrate here how this information can be used to understand how students process information about qualitative research. You can review the various topics that students suggested, which I have italicized in the transcripts. Paul looked at an initial perspective, Leanne knew about bracketing her thoughts (because she was following a phenomenological tradition), Frank spoke of a forward-leaning spiral (because he knew we were thinking about nonlinear analysis), and Heather got practical with developing a structure. In so many ways, these thoughts are reflective of these students. It is quite uncanny. We would never know these things in a regular classroom discussion, in which our discussions are not recorded, because our comments and questions disappear as soon as they are made.

The culture of an online classroom is also revealed by the data. Some transcripts might reveal issues about authority and hierarchy, who is in charge, and dynamics of interaction.

Opening up our courses for all to review and comment upon is a very new idea for teachers at any level. Most teachers are used to closing their doors and working with a confined group of students who they see and with whom they come in personal contact. There is something in it for the students and for the teachers as well. Teaching on the Internet poses new challenges, some of which are described by Joy (2004) in her dissertation about online teaching from the point of view of professors. She concluded that a new culture is established in such courses. I believe there is much more to study on this front.

Visual Diaries, Wikis, Blogs, and Vlogs

Technology, ready availability, and low cost have resulted in an enormous quantity of information presented on the Internet. As new technologies become increasingly popular, responsible researchers need to develop ways to access such environments in an ethical manner.

A *wiki* is a collection of Web pages designed to let anyone modify the information. The first wiki, WikiWikiWeb, was developed in 1994. Wikipedia, a free encyclopedia, is available in many languages, and the topics and material are increasing exponentially. *Blog* is short for Web log and *vlog* is short for visual Web log. I found several course syllabi asking students to create a blog as part of their class assignments; I suspect you might be able to locate student vlogs as well.

I have read several blogs by individuals who are pursuing degrees in qualitative research. They are like diaries, although open for all to see. Typically, a writer makes daily entries and posts them online. Some blogs permit others to make comments. Group blogs, in which a number of individuals post on the same blog, are also becoming popular.

Below are excerpts from several blogs related to qualitative research. Someone who calls herself "Profgrrrl" reveals her frustration with qualitative research in her blog of February 26, 2005:

> I entirely understand why qualitative research is often treated like the redheaded stepchild when people have these beliefs AND even worse act on them. There are a lot of crappy qualitative studies that have been published. But there are some truly wonderful ones as well. . . . But the bottom line is that it requires a clear, systematic plan that is followed with checks in place at regular intervals. And all too often I don't see people paying attention. Grrrr. End of rant. For now.

Read "Zapisal/a marysia o godz" in a 2003 blog:

> A friend of mine advised me not to focus on quantitative researches and results but to switch directly to qualitative studies, especially if I wanted to study the possible psychological profile of the bloggers—"you don't need demography to do it." Is it true? I don't know. My latest observations make me think that bloggers in Poland (I am mainly thinking about those who write diaries online) have some features in common that are related both to the personality and to the sex, age, or place of living. Is there a solution that I am not able to notice?

"Anand," in her 2006 blog, said

> The difference between online and offline is, I reckon, like the difference between meeting a friend in person and talking vis-à-vis talking over the phone or talking using a webcam. I am

assuming one would on most days prefer a meeting in flesh and blood over a virtual one unless of course distance separates them and there is no choice but to meet in the virtual world.

We learn about visual ethnography using Flickr in an April 2005 blog:

Last year, when I was offered the opportunity to teach a course on anthropology and photography at Haverford College, I immediately knew I wanted to do something with Flickr. I have to admit that it was exhausting correcting papers with dozens of hyperlinks to photos on Flickr. But it was also fun. I especially enjoyed seeing the various ways students used Flickr's tags to come up with interesting paper topics. . . . One student looked at how people interact with art on camera. Comparing art in the museum with public art. Someone looked at the "what's in my bag" meme, comparing it to John Berger's discussion of oil painting as a depiction of wealth. Another student looked at depictions of the disabled, which raged from offensive, to inspiring, to practical. Similarly, another student found offensive pictures of fat people presented as social commentary. She also had interesting things to say about pictures of fat cats.

I am not quite sure what can be done with this information, but I believe it to be useful. It may take the creative mind of a new qualitative researcher to examine how such postings can serve as data in a qualitative research study. "Where else can we learn so much that is so new, so rapidly?" I ask you. Keep your minds open.

Available Data and Communication

Have you considered what to do with the data you have collected and stored in your computer and analyzed with your software? Most of us keep close tabs on our raw data and will release it if pressed to do so, but researchers are beginning to call for placing data online so that others may gain access to it and use it for subsequent analyses. For example, in an issue of *FQS,* transcripts of interviews or the audio version of interviews were made available as part of the journal articles (Lichtman, 2004).

Another advantage of the Internet in qualitative research is the potential for scientific exchange. According to the editors of *FQS,* the Internet provides opportunities for flexible publication times; flexible publication space; and direct interaction among authors, editors, and readers.

■ Summary

Observation occurs in natural settings and provides data about individuals, interactions, and culture. Issues include deciding who to study and in what situations; whether to study formal, informal, or casual groups; how to gain access; what to study; the frequency and length of time for observations; and the role of the observer.

Written sources of data for qualitative studies include existing written documents, responses from participants, and your own written notes and reflections. Issues include deciding which materials to use and how to extract the essence of the writing.

Images are less frequently used as data, but they are potentially powerful, poignantly telling a story. Issues regarding images include the quality of the image, manipulation of images, and the relationship of images to words.

The Internet (chat rooms, wikis, blogs and vlogs, online course records) is a potential source of rich data. A positive aspect is that these data need no transcription, but no clear guidelines for use exist.

GROUP ACTIVITY

Purpose: To develop skill in looking more carefully.

Activity: Select video or film clips showing families at mealtimes. I have used different ethnic groups showing different families. An Italian family setting can be seen as Cher plays the starring role in the 1987 movie *Moonstruck.* An excellent example of a Jewish family meal can be found in Barry Levinson's 1990 film *Avalon.* The Amish culture is depicted by Harrison Ford's 1985 movie *Witness.* My last selection shows a Christian family, as Mary Tyler Moore and Donald Sutherland depict the standoffish nature of the parents in the 1980 movie *Ordinary People.* I show the videos in class and ask students to take notes on how the members of the family interact with each other. We usually see the entire set and then have a discussion. The discussion serves to simulate students to look and listen more closely.

Evaluation: Explore the ways in which class members focus on certain things and how they are influenced by the discussion.

INDIVIDUAL ACTIVITY

Purpose: To refine observational skills.

Activity: Select a television show that involves a family or members of a group. Pick at least two or three episodes. The class can identify the show they want to watch. Get a class member to videotape the shows so that you can discuss them in class at a later time. Make detailed notes on three aspects of the show. One area to observe is the things that are visible, such as the physical surroundings, how members are dressed, what props are used, and what makes the setting into a home or family setting. A second area to observe is the content of the show and the verbal and nonverbal interactions of the cast. A third area is the underlying meaning of the interactions. What are the dynamics of the interactions? What is the emotional content? Organize your notes into a one-page handout for the entire class.

Evaluation: Examine the extent to which class members are able to move from the concrete to the abstract, from the inductive and immediate nature of the show to a deeper meaning behind the surface.

Writing in your journal should now be part of your regular routine. I hope you make some comments about new technologies.

■ Note

1. This ethnocentric view was modified by Boas, who developed the concept of cultural relativism, which states, among other things, that cultural aspects of human behavior are learned and not biological. It was thought that through immersion in the society over an extended time, the researcher could somehow describe and understand the society's culture.

PART III

Putting It All Together

There are four chapters in this section. They are grouped together because they deal with organizing and presenting the data you have collected. Chapter 11 deals with how to draw meaning from the data you have collected. While I touch on the use of computer programs to assist you, I want you to recognize that you would need to spend a considerable amount of time with such programs. Ultimately, what you present is what others will know about your research. Today, most qualitative research is presented in written form. Thus, Chapter 12 discusses various ways to communicate your ideas. I urge you, however, to consider alternative ways to communicate, and some ideas are presented for you to consider. You will read about how others grapple with judging the quality of the work in Chapter 13. In Chapter 14, I speculate on where we are now and where we might travel.

Chapter **11**

Making Meaning From Your Data

FOCUS YOUR READING

■ In general, qualitative data analysis involves coding data and looking for themes or concepts.

■ Some researchers prefer to use narratives rather than themes.

■ Many researchers have moved beyond verbal data and use videos or visuals in their analyses.

Qualitative research takes time to constantly review where you are in the research process; what you have accomplished, what you have not accomplished, what challenges you have overcome and what new challenges you may have to deal with in the future. Once I was confident that I had captured my study participants' perceptions, then I organized, analyzed, and interpreted my data. I began writing my findings and observations as I went along. I found that presenting the feelings and perceptions of study participants can be difficult, especially when you are trying to be an objective observer and recorder of other people's thoughts, feelings, and perceptions. Capturing the experience through the images of your study participants requires good in-depth interviews, accurate transcriptions, and unbiased reporting. None of which is an easy task. A well-organized and conducted qualitative research study will enable you to make valuable contributions to the literature like these from my study.

—Warren Snyder

Qualitative research, no matter which approach you select or type of data you gather, uses an inductive strategy. Its purpose is to examine the whole, in a natural setting, to get the ideas and feelings of those being interviewed or observed. As a consequence, data analysis in qualitative research is also inductive and iterative. Some people like to collect data and analyze it simultane-ously; the analysis can lead to further questions that might be asked of subsequent participants. Others find that they collect the data and then begin the analysis; while this is not advised, it often happens. You can make the process iterative by proceeding through the steps below with some of your data and then testing it on additional data.

I see data analysis as being about process and interpretation. Whether you analyze your data using statistics or choose some other method, there is a process you follow and interpretations to be made from that process. The process in quantitative research is straightforward—at least, once you determine what statistics to run. When I was in graduate school, the process was very diffi-cult. You entered your data on 80-column cards and sorted the cards in the appropriate order. You wrote a program or selected a program to run your data, and you had your university run the program on a behemoth of a computer. How you interpreted the data you ran was also straightfor-ward; it was primarily a matter of testing hypotheses and rejecting (or failing to reject) them.

Analyzing the qualitative data you collect is a daunting enterprise. One of the dilemmas is that qualitative researchers do not agree on how the data should be analyzed. Many approaches or paradigms are silent about what analysis should be performed. Li and Seale (2007) reported on a project involving teaching and supervising their students in conducting qualitative analyses. Their students had difficulty knowing where to start coding, and they faced problems with ambiguities in definitions of codes, inaccuracies in reporting, and overinterpretation of the evidence.

If you have done any quantitative research, you likely have gathered numerical data, chosen one or several statistical approaches, selected a statistical software program, entered your data, and used statistics. While you may not have been entirely clear about which statistical approach to use or precisely how to enter your data, or even how to make meaning from your data once it was run, you felt comfortable that the results you obtained were objective and scientific. Once you selected the various statistical tests to run, the process was easy: You entered or imported your data and ran the program. You also expected that those who read your research would be comfort-able with your results and find them objective and believable.

I suspect, however, that you were left somewhat dissatisfied when you tried to organize your thoughts and put words to paper. What did those numbers really mean? Why were you rejecting the null hypothesis? Could you even be sure that you understood the null hypothesis? What did it mean to test at the .05 level of significance? But you were usually able to get guidance from a pro-fessor or tutor, who helped you interpret what you did.

Analyzing qualitative data is an entirely different matter. The data are not numerical. There are not agreed-upon ways of analyzing the data you have. And whether you have a theoretical compo-nent to your research or not, you have the practical dilemma of doing something with the data. Most qualitative approaches provide very general information about how to do this. With the exception of grounded theory, you are pretty much left on your own. Thorne (2000) reminded us that "qual-itative data analysis is the most complex and mysterious of all of the phases of a qualitative project, and the one that receives the least thoughtful discussion in the literature" (p. 68). There is a lack of standardization and few universal rules. Basit (2003) commented that qualitative data analysis is the most difficult and most crucial aspect of qualitative research (p. 143). In 1994, Morse com-mented that the actual process of analysis remains mysterious. Writing today, Morse (2008) consid-ers the issues of collaboration in qualitative inquiry and particularly comments that the researcher must "get inside the data," which makes collaboration somewhat problematic.

Did You Know

Steven Johnson (2004), in *Mind Wide Open,* helped us understand our inner workings and psyches in his fascinating book about the brain and the neuroscience of everyday life. By now, I shouldn't have to remind you that I want you to keep your mind wide open!

Whether you approach data analysis via a generic coding strategy or select one of several specific strategies, and whether you use computer software or not, I believe you will have the most success with a systematic approach. A systematic approach to analysis and interpretation brings order and understanding to your qualitative research project. You will also need creativity and discipline as you embark on your data analysis. The challenge is that the way you do this is flexible and open to discussion and interpretation. Unlike quantitative research, there are no agreed-upon statistical tests. In this chapter, I discuss several key issues.

I begin this chapter by providing you brief definitions of some of the analytic strategies that researchers use. I introduce these for your reference; however, unless you have been given an assignment to use one of them, I find that most qualitative researchers (whether novices or experienced) actually use a generic coding strategy. Many also like to use computer software packages to facilitate handling, organizing, and drawing meaning from the data. It is important to remember that ultimately, the researcher draws the meaning and insight from the data.

Next, I introduce the idea of data analysis as a process. What constitutes data? When should you do your analysis? How should you get started? What about coding and themes, or would you prefer to focus on the stories and narratives of those you study? How do you know when you are finished? Are you ever finished? I suspect that you will find those questions in any discussion of qualitative analysis.

Then, I discuss clarification of your philosophical stance. What do you believe qualitative research can do with and for data? What is your belief regarding what I call "who is right"? Do you need to verify what you have done with an expert? After all, who is an expert?

I then introduce a concrete example of what I refer to as the three Cs of analysis. This six-step approach should provide you with enough detail to start your own analysis.

Another topic I cover is whether, and in what ways, you should make use of computer software to analyze your data. Although most of you will have your data on your laptop computer, this is different from using analytical software. If you choose to use software, which program should you choose? How do you learn the software? Many faculty members are not qualified to assist you. Many of the instructional manuals cannot be used without additional workshops or tutoring. I conclude with new trends, especially in the area of secondary analysis.

■ Myriad Techniques or Procedures

Just as various disciplines have influenced the approaches qualitative researchers take in designing their research and gathering data, so, too, have a variety of disciplines influenced ways in which such researchers deal with their data.

Constant-Comparative Method. The **constant-comparative method** is a method closely associated with grounded theory. Its steps involve open coding, axial coding, and selective coding. Codes are developed and subsequently organized around concepts. Categories are developed from the concepts. Ultimately, theory is derived from the concepts. Strauss and Corbin (1990) provided specific examples of how to use this procedure. Eich (2008) provided more details of how to use this method in his grounded theory study of student leadership development programs. Connolly (2003) has adapted and simplified this method, which she refers to in general terms as Qualitative Data Analysis. She identifies three phases: generative, interpretive, and theorizing.

Content (Textual) Analysis. **Content analysis** has been around since Lasswell introduced the idea of studying the content of communication. Krippendorff wrote about it in 1980 (see also Krippendorff, 2004). Some qualitative researchers are drawn to it, I suspect, because it has a structure and is more in keeping with the position of looking for rigor and acceptance. Hsieh and Shannon (2005) identified three approaches to content analysis. In what they called a conventional content analysis, coding categories were derived directly from text. In a direct approach to content analysis, a theory or prior research is used to guide the analysis in the initial coding. A third type is summative analysis; in this latter approach, counting categories precedes the interpretation. It seems to me that these three approaches are a continuum, from less to more conservative. Sonpar and Golden-Biddle (2008) used content analysis of qualitative archival data to elaborate on theories of adolescence.

Discourse Analysis. **Discourse analysis** is a technique with several interpretations. It was originally interpreted as analyzing structure of text content in terms of syntax and semantics. When influenced by poststructural or postmodern views of the world, this procedure "is concerned with the way in which texts themselves have been constructed in terms of their social and historical 'situatedness'" (Cheek, 2004, p. 1144). Prins and Toso (2008) employed discourse analysis in their analysis of a widely used parent profile instrument.

Qualitative Comparative Analysis (QCA). QCA was developed by Ragin (1987) when dealing with comparison across cases. According to Greckhamer, Misangyi, Elms, and Lacey (2008), its purpose is to preserve the complexity of a single case while making comparisons across cases. It has primarily been used in sociology and political science and is more closely associated with conservative or traditional approaches to qualitative analysis.

Relational Data Analysis (RDA). Among the newer approaches, RDA is a multidimensional framework for unifying data analytic strategies across dimensions and phases. It is useful when using mixed methods research (Kurtines et al., 2008). In their feminist study of nursing unit managers, Paliadelis and Cruickshank (2008) used this analytic method to uncover multiple layers of meaning.

I believe that many of these methods were developed to systematize the analysis of qualitative data. All assume that the data are represented by words. They are not as well-established as quantitative procedures and, as you can see, current researchers are still modifying many of the techniques. My philosophy is that, unless you are following a grounded theory approach, you will be best served by using a generic approach and following the steps I outline below.

■ The Process

There are various ways to conceptualize data analysis in qualitative research. I want to discuss two of them: identifying themes and telling stories.[1] Much of the writing about analysis deals with identifying themes. Here is the idea in a nutshell: You gather a large amount of data. It might come from one individual over a long time; it might come from several individuals; it might come from one or a number of settings; or it might be derived from other sources (chat rooms, interviews, observation notes). All data are gathered in order to answer your research questions. Now, the data are usually so voluminous that they make no sense without some thought and organization. As a researcher, it is your task to provide that step. I have provided detailed information below on some steps you can follow to move from the data to development of themes. I see this as a process of sorting and sifting. Imagine that you have a large sieve. Some holes are square, some round, and some irregularly shaped. You put into the sieve a number of objects—some round, some square, and some irregularly shaped. You shake the sieve. The round ones drop through the round holes. The square ones drop through the square holes. Some of those irregularly shaped drop through the odd-shaped holes, while others stay in the sieve. You have sorted your objects based on a system. Some fit well while others do not. I hope you can see the parallel with the sorting and sifting I describe below.

One limitation of this type of analysis is that it operates from a reductionist perspective. Do we really believe that we can capture so much of what a person thinks and feels and portray it in five or six simple concepts? Some would argue that by doing this, we are trying to move into an analytic mode that is more closely allied to principles of quantitative paradigms. An alternative approach to an analysis that identifies themes is the emphasis on finding the narrative or telling stories (Coffey & Atkinson, 1996). The intention is to examine how such stories can be used as structured or formal ways to transmit information. You can read in greater detail Denzin's (1989) account of interpretive biography. Baumgartner (2000), in her study of HIV-positive adults, shed light on exploring how stories can be used as a source of data. I must caution you, however, that as with so much of qualitative research, the details are not explicit. Guy and Montague (2008) analyzed the personal narratives about men's friendships. Zilber, Tuval-Mashiach, and Lieblich (2008) stressed the importance of context in the construction and understanding of life stories. I particularly like Coffey and Atkinson's (1996) admonition:

> There are no formulae or recipes for the "best" way to analyze the stories we elicit and collect. . . . Such approaches also enable us to think beyond our data to the ways in which accounts and stories are socially and culturally managed and constructed. That is, the analysis of narratives can provide a critical way of examining not only key actors and events but also cultural conventions and social norms. (p. 80)

I am suggesting that you can either conduct an analysis in which your goal is to identify themes or conduct an analysis in which your goal is to provide an interpretation of the data by telling a story. Neither way is "right." The process you follow to get to the end depends on your goal.

Writing about the process is linear; in contrast, actually doing the analysis is anything but. You will be faced with many questions you need to answer and decisions to make. It is often the case that you know in advance the main types of data you will collect. However, as your project develops, you might discover that additional data become available. You may decide in advance that you will use a computer software program to analyze your data. However, the program you want may not be readily available, or you may think you can learn how to run a program that turns out to be much more complicated than you anticipated. You may decide that you are going to concentrate on one aspect of a problem and then find that the data you collect lend themselves to exploring totally different arenas. You may decide to incorporate images in your data, but you are not really able to determine how best to include the visual data and how to incorporate them into an analysis. The process may appear to be relatively clear and systematic; however, in reality, you might find yourself getting bogged down in details you did not expect. You might find that you want to capture information from the Internet (e.g., chat room discussions, Listserv comments, the blogosphere, YouTube), but you do not know enough about the logistics to do this effectively.

What Is Qualitative Data?

I think most would agree that qualitative data generally take the form of words, not numbers. Modern writers include visual, audio, or graphic data in the definition, as well as verbal or textual data. While some argue that qualitative data can be transformed into quantitative data, I think it is those who practice a traditional or fundamentalist paradigm who take this position. If you support a more inclusive position, then almost any data you gather from, by, or about your study can be seen as qualitative data.

Suppose you are interested in studying single-sex classrooms. Some schools have adopted the practice of organizing classrooms by gender. There are merits and disadvantages on both sides. The American Civil Liberties Union opposes the idea but advocates see that teaching can be targeted and distractions reduced. You are interested in going beyond the statistical data. You want to determine what is going on in the classrooms and how various participants see the experience. Let's look at the kind of qualitative data you might collect: interview data with students, teachers, and parents; observational data recorded in note form of classroom practices and student behaviors; shadowing of selected students; photographs or videos of students interacting; your notes regarding your thoughts about the practice; student work products, either on the computer or in hard copy; student chat room comments regarding their feelings about participating in this type of class; and your observations about the classroom's physical appearance and the appearance of the students. All are legitimate types of data. No one form of data is better or more legitimate or more meaningful than another type. You are limited only by your creativity and the available technology.

I use this example to help you see that the kind of data you might collect can be enormous and take different forms. When doing your data analysis, it is your job to organize the data and ultimately draw meaning from it.

As you can imagine, you will have an enormous quantity of data in somewhat different forms. You will most likely transcribe your interviews and observations into a word processing program. You may have some data already on your computer, taken from chat room discussions or student work products. All your verbal data can be organized in a word processing program; you will have to devise a way to organize your visual or graphic data. Some qualitative software programs incorporate visual and audio data and provide ways to analyze them. The most recent iteration of NVivo, launched in 2008, allows you to link audio and video files with text files.

I want to stress that the data will be collected not at one time but at several times across the life of your research project. In the same way, your analysis should cover the life of the project and should begin as you begin collecting your data. Planning how you will do your analysis might precede actual data collection. Let me emphasize that your plan should represent a general guide and should be modified as necessary, depending on the data you collect and the available tools for analysis.

Process and Traditions

I want to comment briefly on how the different approaches you have learned have somewhat different expectations in data analysis. For the most part, the process I will describe can be followed with any of the traditions. However, the emphasis may differ, depending on the tradition. I have found it very frustrating to try to determine specifically how to conduct analyses. Almost all of the material you read will leave you with more questions than answers. I know many of you will be looking at a particular approach, so I provide you with a general sense of what each emphasizes. But by no means are there specifics associated with any of the methods, with the exception of grounded theory.

If you were following an ethnographic approach, no specific guideposts are suggested, but you would focus on an understanding of the culture. Often, your data will include field notes based on observations. You might also have data from informal interviews. Your analysis would typically involve coding and looking for themes.

If you were following a grounded theory approach, you would follow a very specific three-part coding approach: open, axial, and selective. This is also referred to as the constant-comparative method. If you choose this approach, it would be helpful to review Strauss and Corbin's (1990) detailed explanation for this multistep coding process.

If you were following a phenomenological tradition, you would be interested in the lived experiences of the individuals. You would need to explore some of the philosophical underpinnings of phenomenology, but your data analysis would be facilitated if you bracketed your views.

If you were following a case study approach, you might use single cases and then multiple cases treating each case separately and then comparing cases.

If you were following a feminist tradition, you would concentrate on examining power disparities.

If you were following a generic approach, you would look for general themes or use narratives.

If you were following narrative analysis, biographical, autobiographical, or oral history traditions, you might concentrate on the gathered stories and narratives and look for epiphanies. You might choose content analysis or discourse analysis.

If you were following a postmodernist or critical theoretical approach, you might look at issues of sexuality and gender. Because these approaches are more theoretical than practical, analyses are very general.

If you were using mixed methods, you would tend to organize your data and construct tables as well as look for themes. You might select RDA for data analysis.

What About Transcribing?

There is a considerable discussion in the literature and on Listservs about transcribing your interviews. Some equipment on the market that transcribes audiotapes is not yet perfected. Perhaps, by the time you begin your research, better equipment will be available. But for now, you will need to transcribe your interview data—not write a summary. This is, of course, time consuming and quite difficult, especially if you have focus group data. Some will hire a person to transcribe their data, but, in my view, it is worth the effort to do it on your own. Bailey (2008) argued that because transcribing is not just a straightforward and simple task, but involves judgment questions about the level of detail to include, the work should be done by the researcher.

When Should You Do Your Analysis?

I see analysis as an ongoing process, not a linear process following the collection of data. A circular model of gathering and analyzing data is proposed. This is referred to as an iterative process. Often, a researcher will enter data into a computer program—a word processing program or qualitative software program—in concert with collecting additional data. Even when a researcher makes a decision not to conduct analyses using a computer, he or she organizes the data on the computer. Having entered the first piece of data—an interview, some field notes, or the current teaching unit—a researcher begins the process of analysis. Some do this informally while others proceed in a more formal manner.

Coding and Themes or Concepts

In many traditions, there appears to be general agreement that the goal of analyzing the text and words collected is to arrive at common themes. (In the remainder of this chapter, I use the term *concepts* in place of themes.) Most procedures involve a process in which the researcher chooses to code words, phrases, segments, or other portions of text. Some people believe that the codes should be determined a priori. However, most take the position that the codes emerge from the data via a process of reading and thinking about the text material. Aside from a specific process identified with grounded theory, coding is usually done through a careful reading of the text. I have seen some people read the text and mark large chunks of material with codes. Others work from a micro level and code text chunks or segments. Whatever the process, and I believe it varies by individual and perhaps even by type of data, the goal is to arrive at a manageable number of codes.

I see the process as one of organizing and categorizing. You begin with a large amount of material, for example, the text of an interview. That material is dissected and categorized into codes. Next, you proceed to a second interview. Again, dissect and categorize the data into codes; you can use the previous codes or add new codes. This iterative process continues until you have coded all your interviews. By this time, you have reviewed many interviews and coded them. You can now review your codes and look for ones that overlap or are redundant. You might find that you will rename some of your codes. You will likely generate many codes. These codes can then be organized into hierarchical categories, in which some codes will be subsets of larger categories. You might have 80 to 100 codes that you then organize into 15 to 20 categories and subcategories. These categories can then be organized into five to seven concepts. As a general rule, even large data sets do not reveal more than this small number of central and meaningful concepts about the topic of interest.

Narratives or Stories

In contrast to the process described above, some researchers believe that the analysis process involves identifying salient stories that either emerge from the data or are constructed as composites from bits and pieces of several data sources. For them, the meaning is in the story and in the interpretation of the story by the researcher. This process works best if you have interview data from a number of individuals, although I have also used it with detailed and extensive interviews from one or two individuals. Those who adopt this stance take the position that coding raw data into concepts is a reductionistic practice and detracts from the meaning of what is said (see Chase, 2005, and Riessman, 2005, for additional details about the process).

How Do You Know When You Are Finished?

Unlike statistical analysis, qualitative analysis has no defined end. You do not create statistical tables or statements about hypotheses. Rather, the process you follow seems to reach a logical saturation point. You collect your data and analyze your data at the same time. At some point, you complete collecting data. That point is often dictated by time or availability of people to interview or scenes to observe. I believe that you will know when you have sufficient data. Glaser (1978) referred to this as "theoretical saturation"; you find that you are not learning anything new. Well, your analysis follows the same idea. You read through your text. You code chunks, whether large or small. You reread your data. You change your codes. You combine your codes. You add codes. You delete codes. You combine your codes into categories. Your concepts come out of the categories. You reread your data. You look at new data. And so it goes.

You begin to see some common elements among the various interviews or observation notes. You might also see some inconsistencies, what statisticians often call *outliers.* Do not discard these; they are important, but they do not discredit the coding and categorizing you have done.

Now, it is time to combine these codes into categories and then into concepts. You begin your sifting and sorting process anew, but you are working from the codes, not the raw data. You look to see whether the codes can be combined into categories. You try to winnow the number of codes down to a manageable number of categories. You restructure your codes into major categories and subcategories. Again, you work through a distillation from which concepts emerge from your categories.

Your final step is to select supporting evidence for the concepts you have developed. This evidence is often in the form of quotations from the raw data. Once done, you are ready to write.

■ Philosophical Stance

I agree with many writers who say that qualitative analysis is the least understood and most complex of all aspects of conducting qualitative research. I think it is important for you to clarify your views about the process of analysis, but first I want to reveal mine.

As the researcher, you are the best equipped to make sense of the data. Using others to verify your interpretations assumes that there are "right" concepts to find or that some "findings" are better than others. Get rid of that notion. Unlike statistical analysis, in qualitative research analysis there is nothing that says that one set of interpretations is better than another. Now, that does not mean that you might not make a case for one set of interpretations over another based on your raw data, but "experts" are not needed here. You should be closer to your data than anyone else.

Using computer software makes the process easier; it does not give more reliable or believable results. The hard work of sifting, sorting, coding, organizing, and extracting remains yours.

The analysis is an integral part of the process of qualitative research. As such, it must begin early in your project. You should not wait until all your data are collected before you begin to think about your analysis. There are various procedures that you can choose to follow; whichever you choose, you need to document how you carried out your analysis.

It is important not to get to the end too quickly. The data need to be looked at several times. Don't jump to conclusions and concepts too quickly. That often leads to superficial analyses that don't really add much new information to the literature.

■ Conducting an Analysis

The goal of qualitative analysis is to take a large amount of data that may be cumbersome and without any clear meaning and interact with it in such a manner that you can make sense of what you gathered. You should not be surprised that there is no right way to do this. In fact, there is less written about the mechanics of doing such analysis than about any other topic in qualitative research. When authors do write about the process, they are quite vague. I propose here a process that I have used over many years. I suggest you think about it as a starting point, rather than a prescription. I hope you will find the ideas useful.

Getting Started

Qualitative research is usually a solo activity. You collect data on your own, analyze it on your own, write it on your own, and are responsible for what you say. But we know that much research benefits from interacting with others, trying your ideas out on others, and learning about the reaction of others to your ideas.

I know that students learn by doing and practicing. I encourage you to work with small groups of students as you embark on looking for meaning in what you have gathered. Here is an exercise from Barbara Kawulich (personal communication, 2008) that she calls "Hot Monkey Sex": Students are given three Post-it Notes each. On the first, they write their answer the to question "Given all the money you need, where in the world would you like to go for a month's vacation?" On the second, they write down who they want to go with. On the third Post-it Note, they indicate what they want to do on the vacation. Students work in pairs to analyze the data by organizing the Post-it Notes in various ways to tell a story generated by the responses. Kawulich chose the title for the exercise while working with a class consisting of several young teachers and one older, quiet teacher who did not get involved in the class. This activity really got the quiet teacher involved: Her Post-it Notes revealed that she wanted to go to Hawaii with Brad Pitt and have hot monkey sex. "The younger teachers roared with laugher, loving her openness and appreciating the fun-loving side we had never before seen." Kawulich reports that once she renamed the exercise, students would bring cameras to class because their friends wanted to see what "Hot Monkey Sex" looked like. Exercises like this can help you see how the codes emerge from the data and how no single scheme is better than another.

Preparing and Organizing Your Data

Once you have gathered your data, you need to put it into a format that is useful for analysis. In most cases, you will need to find a way to transcribe interviews, capture online discussions, or otherwise put words and text in a useful format. You will also need to think about visuals and audio that is not transcribed. I recommend that you place each item in a separate file, using a word processing package. It is helpful to insert your comments in brackets in a different font or color.

Make a folder and label it My Qualitative Research Project. You will place several files in this folder, depending on how much data you have collected. These files can be individual interviews and/or your observation notes and your researcher journal. At the very least, you will place your data and your journal files in the folder. It is helpful if you label each file in a systematic manner. For example, suppose you have four interviews: two with the same person and two additional ones. You would create the following four files: DonaldInt1, DonaldInt2, DavidInt1, DanielInt1. In a large project, you might have observation data as well: DonaldObs1, DavidObs1, and so on. Of course, your choice of file names depends on the type of data you collect. Some researchers like to incorporate a date in the file name.

In addition to these data files, you will want to create your researcher journal. Make another file and label it Researcher Journal. Some people also put information collected from a literature review in this folder. This folder should be created when you begin your research, not when you finish it. You should plan to keep adding to it as you move along.

Make sure you save a copy of this folder in a location other than your hard drive. There are too many horror stories of people who have lost everything because of computer glitches. I remember many years ago, when data were collected on 80-column IBM cards. I had a friend who had two copies of her data in boxes. Unfortunately, she kept both copies in the trunk of her car. One day, after a hard rain, she discovered the trunk inundated with water. Of course, both copies were ruined. A sad lesson. In today's computer world, keeping copies of your files is somewhat easier.

But I encountered a serious problem and lost an entire book chapter recently when my file became corrupted and I could no longer save it. An external hard drive became the savior.

Reviewing and Recording Your Thoughts

Most people find it helpful to read through all the material in their folder. In keeping with the iterative nature of the process, you should begin by reading a transcript. Add your thoughts and comments to your Researcher Journal file. It is okay to use informal writing here. Remember to date your notes. Your comments might look something like this:

9/15/2008. Read through the transcript of DanielInt1. Daniel certainly had a lot to say. I wish I had asked him more about why he decided to leave the field of teaching. I will need to remember to do that in my next interview and if I go back with him as well.

9/20/2008. Finished my second interview of DanielInt1. Glad he clarified his thoughts on this topic. Not sure I would have picked this up unless I had read what he said.

The Three Cs: Coding, Categorizing, and Identifying Concepts

You are now at a point where you can see how to move from raw data to meaningful concepts. I call this the three Cs of analysis: from Coding to Categorizing to Concepts.

Coding conversation and text into meaningful chunks is a challenging task. Whether you work with a word processing program or with other software, it is your responsibility to generate the codes. Do not expect that a computer program will generate codes or organize them; rather, you will need to provide the input. I have broken down this process into six steps (see Figure 11.1).

Figure 11.1   Three Cs of Data Analysis: Codes, Categories, Concepts

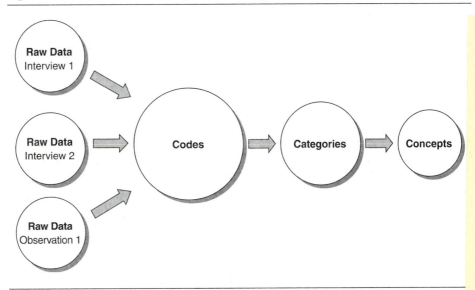

> *Step 1.* Initial coding. Going from the responses to some central idea of the responses.
>
> *Step 2.* Revisiting initial coding.
>
> *Step 3.* Developing an initial list of categories or central ideas.
>
> *Step 4.* Modifying your initial list based on additional rereading.
>
> *Step 5.* Revisiting your categories and subcategories.
>
> *Step 6.* Moving from categories to concepts (themes).

Step 1. Initial Coding. Even if you have only collected a small amount of data, it is not too early to begin coding. Select any transcript. Read the initial page or two. Use the "Comment" function in your word processing program to insert your initial codes (in Microsoft Word, you will find the function on the "Insert" menu). Enter your initial codes. Continue reading the transcript while entering different codes. Upon completion of initial coding with one transcript, select another transcript and continue the same process. Box 11.1 is an example that might help you see this more clearly. The researcher's codes are in brackets.

Box 11.1   Examples of Initial Coding

Transcript 1. Partial Interview: Cross-Gender Friendship

It was sophomore year in college. We knew each other—or at least who each other were—from freshman year. Sophomore year on the first day of classes, we met during some orientation. She was orientating freshmen. I was probably hanging around, looking for something or other to get into around campus. About four months after that we started hanging out constantly. [Maintenance as friendship only.]

We just—or at least I tried to—stay out of situations where it could have turned, become physical. [physical attraction] And we tried not to talk about it—those kind of things. [Evolution into something more.] After about eight months or so, things shifted. We both realized our feelings had changed. We tried to hold off as long as we could and keep the friendship as long as we could. But we started going to the next step.[potential problems]

One of the main things is that since I'm not actively seeing another person or actively engaged, is that when I meet a girl, any girl, is potentially more than a friend. [tensions/barriers]

Transcript 2. Partial Interview: Cross-Gender Friendship

Someone that I can talk to intimately. Someone that I can tell just about anything. [intimacy, talk to] . . . It's just a spark similar to physical attraction [physical attraction] but it's different. You know, when you talk to them that, you know, you may not agree on things necessarily, but you can understand each other. . . natural progression. [something more]

Step 2. Revisiting Initial Coding. By now, you will have developed a large number of codes. Some of them will be redundant and you will need to collapse them and rename codes. I have observed that some people tend to code almost every phrase or sentence, while others code larger chunks of information. You need to choose whatever works best. You may want to modify your codes based on an examination of what you have already collected and new raw data.

Step 3. Initial List of Categories. Now that you have modified your codes, it is time to organize them into categories. I have found that certain codes become major topics, while others can be grouped under a major topic and become subsets of that topic. In essence, you have moved from one long list of codes into several lists of categories, with related codes as subsets of the categories (see Box 11.2).

Box 11.2 Example of Initial Categories

(Subcategories have been omitted.)

- Maintenance
- Physical attraction
- Intimacy
- Tensions/barriers
- Problems
- Issues with boyfriend/girlfriend
- Meaning of friendship
- Issues of homosexuality

Step 4. Modifying the Initial List. At this point, you will need to continue the iterative process. You may decide that some of your categories are less important than others, or you may see that two categories can be combined. Remember that your goal in the Three Cs analysis is to move from coding initial data through identification of categories to the recognition of important concepts.

Step 5. Revisiting Categories. I would suggest that at this point, you revisit your list of categories and see whether you can remove redundancies and identify critical elements. In my experience, most new researchers tend to see everything as important. They appear reluctant to say that one area might reveal more interesting ideas than another. This is where you can exercise your judgment about what is important and what is not.

Here is an example taken from an entirely different context. Suppose you have 100 books and you want to arrange them into 5 piles. Well, there are a number of ways you can do this. You can sort by color—all blue-covered books together, all green-covered books together, and so on. You can sort by size, grouping all oversized books together. You can sort by topic—all books on science together, all books on humor together, and so on. Or you can sort by author—all books by Roth together, all books by Faulkner together, and so on. You could arrange by publication date—all books published after 2000 together, all from 1990 to 2000 together, and so on. Obviously, some categories make more sense than others, depending on your purpose. Further, you could place the books in subsets within each of the major categories. To continue with my example, you could place light blue books together, navy blue together, and so on. If you arranged by author, you could put major works together and minor works together.

Step 6. From Categories to Concepts. The final step in the process is to identify key concepts that reflect the meaning you attach to the data you collect. While there are no definitive rules for the number of concepts you might identify, I believe very strongly that fewer well-developed and supported concepts make for a much richer analysis than many loosely framed ideas. As you read and reread your data, you will see that some ideas appear richer and more powerful than others. It is up to you to determine that. I would suggest, as a rule of thumb, that five to seven concepts should be the maximum number that you can find in a set of data. Some information is unimportant even though it is there.

When organizing your codes into concepts, it is your task to decide the most informative or logical manner of sorting. You need to determine from the data what meaning you think can be found. Sometimes your initial thoughts are quite superficial. You will find that reorganizing and rewriting and rethinking often lead to more powerful ideas.

Additional Ideas

By now, you will have completed the six steps in the movement from codes through categories to concepts. To add texture and depth to your analysis, you may want to return to your documents to look for other things that will enhance your interpretation. One promising area to explore is the use of metaphors. Our language is rich with metaphorical allusions and they often reveal much about what others mean. To what extent were metaphors used? Are there sufficient metaphors to incorporate as part of your written paper? If so, can you code them according to certain criteria that may emerge? You might look for type of language, metaphor chosen, or gender-related metaphors.

You could also explore the use of stories. To what extent were stories used? Are there stories that might lead to epiphanies? Are some better than others? Other kinds of things to look for in your data are the richness of detail, conflicting ideas from the same respondent, unusual or unique experiences, or ideas that contradict current thinking on the topic.

I want to reemphasize that making meaning from qualitative data is a process that moves between questions, data, and meaning. Figure 11.2 provides a summary of the data analysis process. Key elements in the model are that it is iterative, circular, and can be entered at any point. You need to try to think of your own work in this way as well.

■ Data Analysis With Computers

By now, you are probably asking yourself how you will manage all of this. I remember one student telling me that she made 3" × 5" cards with codes and hung them on the wall in her basement. She placed some codes under others, thereby creating categories with subcategories. She could move these around and regroup in order to organize them into concepts. Another way to organize into

Figure 11.2 Relationship Between Questions, Data, and Meaning

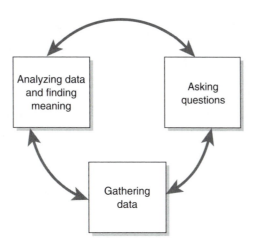

categories is to use markers or pencils of different colors and to sort like colors together. If you have a small amount of data this works pretty well. But even with a small amount of data, you lose the links between the raw data you have coded, the codes and categories you have developed, and your concepts. And what happens if you have a large amount of data? This is where computer programs enter the arena.

As I said earlier, I expect that you will have entered your data into a word processing program. This is, of course, valid for data that are in words. At a basic level, you can use a word processing program to find a given word or phrase in the text. For example, Microsoft Word has a "Find" feature that searches text and indicates each instance of a particular word or phrase. You could begin to code your raw data by asking the program to find a given phrase, then highlight it, and change the text color. Next, you could give each of those phrases the same code. You could do this for each set of raw data you have. Of course, you would have to keep track of the color and coding scheme that you have developed. There are several advantages to this simple process: (1) the ability to locate terms in text quickly, (2) the ability to identify text associated with the terms, and (3) the ease of storing and accessing information in comparison to the old way of color coding or sorting on the dining room table.

Several sophisticated computer programs have been developed that permit a more elaborate system of coding, searching, and retrieval of information. QSR International has been the leader in the movement. You can read about several of their programs on their Web site (http://www .qsrinternational.com/).

When I began teaching qualitative research, I was very reluctant to use computers. It seemed to me that by using computers I was buying into a paradigm that valued numbers, tables, and precision, yet I recognized that much of qualitative research took a different approach. What was I to do? I thought a qualitative software program might be too structured; in fact, I was not even sure what they did.

Some of the early programs were quite modest in their capabilities. They allowed you either to enter your data directly into a program or import your data from a word processing program. Most of the functions involved word counts. It was believed that by counting the number of occurrences of a given word you would be able to conduct an analysis. Somehow, I thought that magically the program would do my analysis for me. I wasn't quite sure how, but I continued to resist because that was not what I wanted.

I began to examine some of the newer programs and discovered a software package called NUD*IST. An unfortunate title, I thought. Were the writers trying to be cute? I did not know. I convinced my university that we should buy several copies, and I had them placed in our computer lab. First hurdle accomplished. How was I to learn this program? The user's manual left much to be desired. During the 1990s, the only training in the software was based in London. I was fortunate to be able to attend several seminars where we worked on our own data in conjunction with the software. I did incorporate some of the ideas into my courses but in general did not ask students to use the software.

As of 2008, NUD*IST has been replaced by the program NVivo 8. Developed by Lyn and Tom Richards from Australia, NVivo has an enormous capacity to do many things with data. The user's manual is still somewhat daunting, and most students are not able to learn the software without a workshop or course. But if you are fortunate to have access to NVivo and some training to accompany it, let me tell you what it will do for you and why you might want to explore it further.

Importing Files Into a Project. You can import any text material into the program directly from your word processing program. You can bring in one or many files at the same time. This saves an incredible amount of time. You can also link any other material that is nontextual through a process of External Links. Thus, if you have photographs or audio material that you do not want to lose, you can make links directly to your master file. New material can easily be added. You can also bring in results of your literature review. Thus, all of your data—whether interview data, photographs, references, or notes—can be organized and placed in the same project. This is a tremendous advantage, even if the program does nothing else for you. NVivo 8 has the capacity to handle videos and audio. It is also available in Chinese and Spanish.

Coding Information in Your Project. You can begin coding the various files you have in your project. Some simple keystrokes will enable you to mark a word, line, sentence, or section and code that piece of data with whatever term you want. The program makes a list of the various codes you have chosen. As your coding progresses, you might find that you have used terms that are similar. The program will let you combine several codes if you wish. New codes can always be added and others deleted. You can also code demographic information and develop tables and charts. If desired, the data can be exported into SPSS or a spreadsheet for display or analysis.

Organizing Codes in Your Project. You can begin organizing the various codes you have developed into a series of nodes with branches. This is similar to putting codes into categories and subsets. In a way, this is how you begin to take your raw data, code them, and develop concepts. The program has enormous flexibility with these nodes.

Searching in Your Project. One of the great strengths of this program is that you can conduct complex searches once you have coded your data. There are more than a dozen types of searches that you can conduct. Once you decide what you want to do, the program will locate information from any of your files and bring it into a new file and provide ready access.

Building Models. You can develop models representing your theoretical position, either prior to your analysis or subsequent to it. Attractive graphics facilitate this task.

Other Capabilities. You can create a file for your personal memos or self-reflections and add these to your project at any time. You can manage an enormous amount of data in a single project. You can work on your project with others and share your ideas. Training has now reached the United States; the developers are readily available to answer your questions. The Web site is very accessible. Although based in Australia, they often are in England at workshops and presentations. QSR provides online support and runs a Listserv where most of your questions can be answered.

Limitations. As you can tell, I really like this program. But I will be the first to admit that it is very difficult to learn. I don't think you can learn it on your own, so you need to decide whether it is worth the effort. A student version is available at a reduced cost. If you get it and use it, I believe it will open up many ideas to you that you have not thought of before.

You can read about other computer software programs such as Ethnograph, AtlasTI, and so on. I write about QSR products to illustrate the best of what is out there in 2008. However, if you have a small amount of data and a small budget, go for the old-fashioned method. Make use of your computer word processing programs as best as you can.

■ New Trends

Secondary analysis of qualitative data is a fairly new idea. Heaton's thoughtful book on reworking qualitative data highlights some important issues (Lichtman, 2005). Corti (2007) provides information about a project conducted in Finland dealing with archived qualitative data. Mruck (2005) comments on this and issues of data archiving and data protection in her editorial in a special issue of *FQS* on qualitative secondary data analysis.

A number of issues have surfaced recently regarding the use of the Internet and qualitative data. Can you use qualitative data that is found on the Internet for your study? How can you organize and process data you collect on the Internet? Are there available tools to facilitate this process? What about blogs, plogs (photo logs), and vlogs?

A number of online journals make qualitative data available to the marketplace. How can you gain access? How useful is it? Is secondary analysis of qualitative data legitimate?

Should data be archived? What about the quality of the data? Who should have access? Who should maintain the files? The Faculty of Social Sciences Committee on Ethics (FSSCE, n.d.) at Lancaster University has published a paper on the legal aspects of archiving qualitative data that addresses such issues as who holds the copyright, the potentially sensitive nature of some of the data and the potential harm to participants, and the issues of anonymity and privacy (see also Bryman & Burgess, 1994).

■ Summary

Unlike quantitative research, qualitative research—with the exception of grounded theory—lacks prescriptive guides to data analysis, although several approaches are suggested: constant-comparative method, content analysis, discourse analysis, qualitative comparative analysis, and relational data analysis. Most approaches are based on identifying concepts or telling stories. Regardless of which approach you use, you are a key tool in the analysis process, and you need to document your process.

The three Cs of data analysis are coding, categorizing, and concepts. I suggest a six-step process: initial coding, revisiting initial coding, developing an initial list of categories or central ideas, modifying your initial list based on additional rereading, revisiting categories and subcategories, and moving from categories to concepts.

For larger data sets, computer programs such as NVivo 8 can increase efficiency.

■

GROUP ACTIVITY

Purpose: To move from coding to concept development.

Activity: Select a piece of writing from the Internet. You can use a blog, a newspaper article, or other current topic. Have each class member provide codes of the text. Form small groups to review the codes together and categorize the codes into concepts. Compare concepts from different small groups.

Evaluation: Explore the extent to which individuals are able to move from codes to concepts.

■

INDIVIDUAL ACTIVITY

Purpose: To practice narrative analysis.

Activity: Write a short paper using metaphors to describe an important event in your life. Share your paper with class members. Compare analysis using coding and concepts with analysis using narratives.

Evaluation: Determine in what ways class members are able to make meaning from each method of analysis.

■ Note

1. Simons, Lathlean, and Squire (2008) wrote about the use of two techniques for analyzing data and present interpretations using each technique. First, they used thematic content analysis, in which they looked for themes across the data set based on content. Then, with the same data, they used narrative analysis. They described a technique developed by Riessman (2005) in which the analyst considers the social position of the narrator.

Chapter 12
Communicating Your Ideas

Focus Your Reading

■ Communicating your ideas in qualitative research is demanding and exciting. You are free to expand your horizons and present many ideas.

■ Writing that captures the reader's attention is extremely important.

■ Resist the temptation to write in a stilted fashion.

This life isn't bad for a first draft.

—Joan Konner

I wished I had had more direction as to how I was to write up the results of the dissertation. . . . I found that I really enjoy that sort of research and I can see myself doing more of it. My writing has improved a lot. I learned that I can do a whole lot more than I would have believed five years ago. I found that doing it in simple steps helps a whole lot. I think it's best to focus on small doable steps. Break the dissertation up into goals. Find someone else in the process to pace you with.

—Donna Joy

In this chapter, I discuss ways to write your qualitative research projects. I talk about several topics: structure of qualitative writing; the use of first person; integrating literature reviews into your writing; acknowledging the voice of informants; the value of the data; truth and fiction in writing; and alternative forms of presentation such as poetry, theater, blogs, vlogs, videos, and audio. I also present an illustrative outline and samples from student work.

As a student in college or graduate school, you have been taught a number of characteristics of technical writing. It should be objective. It should be formal. You should not use first-person voice; third-person voice is preferred. It should be passive. It should be nonjudgmental. You should just report the facts. If you have an opportunity to look at a dissertation or a thesis, you will likely see a five-chapter account that includes the research problem, the related literature, methods, results, and conclusions or interpretations. Most traditional dissertations will have statistical tables and charts and graphs as well; few will have photographs or other images. With the widespread availability of computers, there is some tendency in the United States to present these works in online formats. Such formats enable the writer to use hyperlinks and other online tools. For the most part, however, the style is formal, cool, and crisp. This style is in keeping with a foundationalist or traditional view of research.

In this book, I have presented arguments for alternative research approaches or paradigms. These alternative approaches often use alternative styles of presentation. You may encounter writing that is personal, involves the researcher, and makes use of first person. It is likely to be less formal; a traditional five-chapter account is often abandoned, and many structures and formats can be found. Headings are often derived from the voices of the informants. Many readers of this type of writing report being drawn to the accounts they read. Those studied take on a life of their own and are not just "subjects" in a research study. But unlike traditional research, there is no standard form for writing qualitative research.

Chenail (1995) asked us to consider several ideas when writing. Openness is critical because it builds trust between the reader and the researcher. Consequently, the writer should include information that is self-disclosing. I agree with him and recommend a section that I call "Self-Reflection." Chenail suggested focusing on the richness and depth of the data. He commented that a detailed and tight description should precede any generalizations.[1] He introduced the idea of juxtaposing the data you collect with your explanations, analysis, and commentaries. I believe that the strength of what you write is revealed in your ability to convince the reader that your interpretations are reasonable and supported by the data. Whether your writing is accepted depends, in part, on how you weave your data into concepts. Van Maanen (1988), talking specifically about writing about cultures, suggested that the writer reconstruct in dramatic form an impressionistic tale as a way to crack "open the culture and the fieldworker's way of knowing it" (p. 102). He saw this as a way to "braid" the knower with the known (p. 102). In their award-winning study, Ewick and Silbey (2003) used stories of citizen's resistance to authority.

■ First Steps

Your task as a writer of qualitative research is, as Liu (2000) suggested, to transform collected words into a piece of writing. Writing is not just putting down the words; it is making meaning of those words (Coffey & Atkinson, 1996; Liu, 2000). It would be a fairly simple task if you just needed to put down the words.

I want you to think about this idea carefully. How do you make meaning from the words you have collected? The writing act is inextricably woven with the task of organizing and making sense of your data. I wrote about that extensively in Chapter 11. Here, we focus on the representation or presentation based on your analysis.

Did You Know

Lyn Richards of QSR International (http://www.qsrinternational.com/) and Jan Morse (2007) have written *Readme First for a User's Guide to Qualitative Methods,* a book you definitely will want to read if you become involved in qualitative research. They speak about the dramatic changes in the qualitative research landscape over the last decade and how they have "altered the qualitative research world forever."

Let's first examine the structure of what you write. I suggest that there should be a structure in what you write, but there is no single structure. So you are obliged to develop a structure that fits the data you have collected, the ideas you are trying to convey, and your personal style. It might be easier for me to explain this by telling you what it is not. First, there are no agreed-upon guidelines for the organization or format of what you write. If you were writing a quantitative research article to be published in a journal, or if you were writing a traditional master's thesis or doctoral dissertation, or if you were writing a paper for a research class and the information you were presenting was based on a quantitative or experimental study, you would know just how to proceed. A journal would typically expect you to have headings such as Purpose, Related Literature, Methods, Results, and Discussion. A thesis or dissertation would usually follow a five-chapter format. A class research paper would generally use similar headings. You would usually include some tables summarizing your statistics. You would write in third-person, objective fashion.

I want you to take yourself out of that mindset now and imagine that you are free to develop your own structure and style. You ask yourself, How should I do that? What should I include? How much of myself can or should I include? How much of my participants' voices should be heard? Must my writing be dry and factual? Can I use metaphors and other rhetorical devices? How long should it be? How can I justify my interpretation of what I learned? Will my work be judged acceptable? Are there clear lines between fact and fiction? Should there be?

Before I ask you to suspend your current mindset, let me tell you about what is out there now, as I write this in 2008. I have seen qualitative research representation as theater (Bagley, 2008; Garcia, 2008), as art (Hatch & Yanow, 2008), as film or video (Downing, 2008; Woo, 2008), as dance (Fraser, 2008), and as blogs or digital ethnography (Hookway, 2008; Murthy, 2008). Of course, these approaches are quite extreme for someone just beginning, but you need to know they are out there.

I have seen all manner of written work varying by length, by format, by font, and so on. Variation by content is all too common. I suspect this is somewhat more than the mind can tolerate. People tend to want guidelines; they want some structure; they want authorities to suggest how to do things. With that in mind, accept my guidelines and admonitions. They are meant to serve as guidelines only—they should not be seen as rigid. You are to make the decisions.

■ Guidelines for Writing and Presenting Qualitative Research

Your Audience: What Do They Expect?

One of the first things you need to think about as you begin to write your research is the audience you are addressing. It might be your professor in a class you are taking. It might be the editors of a journal. It might be the readers of an online journal. It might be your thesis or dissertation committee. It might be a funding agency or the administration of a school system reading a project you completed. Academic journals seem to have the greatest number of rules and regulations and expectations. The best way to determine what they require is to read the guidelines for authors and to examine articles in current issues.

Different audiences and venues also have a different expectation in terms of length. Journal articles might be limited to a dozen pages or less. A final paper for a class might be limited to 25 to 30 pages. A thesis might be about 100 pages and a dissertation even longer.

What Are You Trying to Say?

Do you want to tell a story? Perhaps you are writing a biography or autoethnography. Your goal is to share the life of someone and describe the epiphanies in that life. Maybe you want to describe the lived experiences of individuals who have transferred to a new school. In such a phenomenological study, you might intend to identify a half dozen or so principles regarding such experiences, as they make themselves known to you through the details of the many experiences. Maybe you take a feminist perspective and your agenda is to give voice to girls in the sciences. It is up to you to decide, and you are the person who knows best. You need to trust yourself and not rely on others to tell you. Other students and professors can help you clarify your thoughts, even make suggestions, but you need to make the final decisions.

So spend some time getting your thoughts together. What is important about what you learned? What adds new insights or clarifies previously poorly understood concepts? What messages are important to share? Most think that you need to go beyond description. To repeat what people have said is interesting, but I don't think it represents research. Research takes you beyond what you heard and involves your interpreting the meaning of what you heard. It is necessary, but not sufficient, to describe; you need to go beyond description to give meaning. And you need to think about how what you learned informs us on the issues and takes us further than the prevailing wisdom or research.

The First Person

I urge you to adopt a style of writing that uses the first person. I have written this book with that in mind. First-person writing is engaging, it brings the reader into the story, and it acknowledges your role in doing the research. It makes your writing more personal. It takes the reader on a journey, and it is generally accepted by even the most conservative of writers today (see American Psychological Association, 2001, available online at http://www.apastyle.org/).

The notion that writing in third person gives what is written greater weight and is more authoritative is an old one and very difficult to overcome. The prevailing wisdom is that keeping the self outside what is being studied makes representations more believable. Atkinson posited the idea that a rhetorical device—not using first person in written presentations—would suggest that knowledge claims have greater authority (cited in Amir, 2005). But there is not sufficient evidence to suggest that this idea is believable.

Another reason often cited for not using first person in writing is that third-person writing ensures the material is seen as objective and scientific. In other words, the researcher has removed the self from the message. But we have already acknowledged that in most forms of qualitative research, that idea is inconsistent with the fundamental assumptions of a nonfoundationalist movement.

Some words of caution: Many of you will be working with advisers and faculty who were trained in traditional methods and writing styles. They will question some of your new ideas. I suggest that rather than becoming combative, you arm yourself with resources and references.

So, to get back to it, use "I." You and your readers will be more attentive and more accepting of what you have to say.

The Voices of Others

We all agree that we want to hear the voices of others. As technology develops, we are now able to hear or see others, but for most of us, the way we represent the voices of others is through the written word. The people we study are real people. In contrast to traditional experimental research that studies subjects or samples (nameless, faceless individuals who represent a particular category or type), our participants interact with us, and often their stories, thoughts, and feelings capture us in more ways than we can imagine.

I remember a number of years ago sitting in my office in Blacksburg, Virginia. Alice Weiping Lo, a student of mine from Hong Kong, entered my office in tears. "What is wrong?" I asked her. She proceeded to tell me about her encounter with the wives of Mainland Chinese graduate students and the difficulties they faced. She remarked that she felt guilty that life had so many hardships for these women and that she was powerless to do anything about it. She had taken on their struggles as part of her doctoral interviews. It became clear that these encounters were more than just data gathering. I encouraged her to consider working with these women after she completed her own doctoral work. I understand that she has remained in Blacksburg and provides a support network for what is now a large Asian population in the town (Lo, 1993).

I relate this example at length because it gives insight into the way in which the lives of a researcher and the people who are studied can become intertwined. Traditionalists would say this is bad and that it brings bias to the study. I need to remind you that you are not conducting traditional research on subjects. You are learning about the lives of individuals—what they think, how they feel, what motivates them, what challenges they face.

It is the goal of qualitative research to acknowledge the individuals studied and to reflect their voices. A parallel goal is to acknowledge that the writer/researcher has a voice that is tied intimately to what and who is studied and the interpretations drawn. Rather than keeping the voice in the distance or hidden, much of qualitative research anticipates and celebrates the voice.

Thus, there are dual voices: the voice of the writer and the voice of those studied. What is the relationship between the researcher and those studied? What should it be? Holliday (2001) suggested that this interaction creates a third culture: the interaction between the researcher and the participant. Holliday spoke of personal authorship by using first person to relate experience or to explain the author's perspective. This use of the personal reflects the role of the writer in the research. The writer's voice is revealed. This type of writing is associated with postmodern and critical thinking. Gilgun (2005) argued strongly that we need to give voice to informants.

By now, you understand that I want you to give voice to those you study. How you do that, how much you say, and how open you are is a matter of some debate. We are used to anonymity in quantitative research. This is not always the case in qualitative research. I can only say it depends. If you interview a public figure or one who chooses to keep his name confidential, that is understandable. But in my experience, many individuals you study like to have their names revealed. That is for discussion between you and those you study.

I find that using direct quotes is a generally accepted practice. I encourage you to do so. I recommend that you leave the language as it is given to you. You should not try to edit it or make it grammatically correct. After all, you are telling a story in the voices of those you studied. Let the voices be their own.

The Use of Metaphors

We use metaphors because they often reveal much about us as writers and our participants as speakers.[2] We use our metaphors and theirs as well. That is why it is so critical that we capture precise words and language from those we study. What is a metaphor? A **metaphor** is the use of one idea or term to represent another. It is used to assist with expression and understanding. We can trace the use of metaphors to very early language. Some have said that the stylized cave paintings in southern France are metaphors.[3] You can read extensively about different kinds of metaphors, including mixed metaphors, dead metaphors, or extended metaphors. Using metaphors adds variety, clarity, and illumination to your writing. And if you use metaphors spoken by your participants, you will extend your understanding of them and, by implication, our understanding of them.

Imagine how excited I was to have stumbled across Hatch and Yanow's (2008) article on ways of seeing in painting and research. In their recent study, they used contrasts between Rembrandt and Pollock, among others, as metaphors for seeing differences between realists and interpretivists. For them, metaphors are necessary and not just nice—not just decorative parts of speech. I find their comparisons between painting and research intriguing, in that they talk about seeing social realities through two modes of painting.

Koro-Ljungberg (2001) discussed metaphors and how they connect different layers of text, even by telling different stories using different fonts. For a detailed analysis of metaphorical analysis from a poststructural view, read Koro-Ljungberg (2004).[4] She used metaphorical data from interviews with successful international scientists. One conclusion is that the **epistemology** of a researcher, or her assumptions about knowledge, changes data and possible interpretations. In describing qualitative research, Shank (2002) stated that using metaphors is a powerful tool that can change the way we understand things. Shank used three metaphors in exploring the reasoning process in research. First, he used the metaphor of the mirror through which one can see sharply and reflectively. He saw the window as a metaphor for what is simple and elegant. Finally, he used the metaphor of a lantern, which is flexible and creative (p. 125).

I have spoken at length about using your voice and giving the voices of others a dominant place in your writing. In the next sections, I address some of the organizational and stylistic issues that you will face.

Creative Nonfiction

Here is a problem: Research writing is basically boring. I had always known that quantitative reports were boring—so many tables and charts. I couldn't understand them anyway. In the early days of qualitative writing, researchers found themselves emulating these boring quantitative reports. They thought, I suspect, that their reports would be seen as more credible, more scientific, and more acceptable. In contrast to this kind of writing, two books made a deep impression on me. Elliot Liebow published *Tally's Corner: A Study of Negro Streetcorner Men* in 1967.[5] As an anthropologist, he used extensive field methods to study these men. Here is a portion of the opening paragraph of Chapter 2:

> A pickup truck drives slowly down the street. The truck stops as it comes abreast of a man sitting on a cast iron porch and the white driver calls out, asking if the man wants a day's work. The man shakes his head and the truck moves on up the block, stopping again whenever idling men come within calling distance of the driver. At the Carry-out corner, five men debate the question briefly and shake their heads no to the truck. The truck turns the corner and repeats the same performance up the next street. In the distance, one can see one man, then another, climb into the back of the truck and sit down. In starts and stops, the truck finally disappears. (p. 29)

Liebow's (1967) writing vividly illustrates Caulley's (2008) principles. He immediately draws you into the narrative with concrete events. Although you don't know precisely what the white driver wants from the men, you know they don't want any part of it. You find yourself thinking about the men and why they are idling. I remember when I first read this; I was so surprised that it was based on his dissertation. It certainly was nothing like the dissertations I had read. My copy is brown with age and shows a price of $3.95.

Equally forceful is Tracy Kidder's (1989) *Among Schoolchildren.* It opens thusly:

> Mrs. Zajac wasn't born yesterday. She knows you didn't do your best work on this paper, Clarence. Don't you remember Mrs. Zajac saying that if you didn't do your best, she'd make you do it over? As for you Claude, God forbid that you should ever need brain surgery. But Mrs. Zajac hopes that if you do, the doctor won't open up your head and walk off saying he's almost done, as you just said when Mrs. Zajac asked you for your penmanship, which, by the way, looks like you did it and ran. (p. 3)

Like Liebow (1967), Kidder (1989) opens his narrative with information about those in the book. Liebow did not name his people initially, but does so as his story continues. Kidder, on the other hand, draws you in immediately with an interesting device: He uses the voice of Clarence, the presumed narrator. Although Kidder's work is not academic and is part of the popular literature, the year he spent in Holyoke, Massachusetts, living among these 20 children lends an air of verisimilitude to the writing.

Oliver Sacks (1985) knows how to draw you in as well. How could *The Man Who Mistook His Wife for a Hat,* his book of essays describing his work with neurological patients, be anything but fascinating? Here is a portion of the first essay:

> Dr. P. was a musician of distinction, well-known for many years as a singer, and then, at the local School of Music, as a teacher. It was here, in relation to his students, that certain strange problems were first observed. Sometimes a student would present himself, and Dr. P. would not recognise him; or, specifically would not recognise his face. The moment the student spoke, he would be recognised by his voice. (p. 7)

A little more formal, but nonetheless compelling. Sacks (1985) is particularly effective in providing immediate, detailed, and engrossing accounts of various cases he has investigated. He is able to take complex information—potentially dry and technical—and write about it in such a way that the reader can't put the essay down. One hallmark of Sacks' writing is the titles of his essays are humorous and nontechnical.

All the authors described here write their accounts in a way that draws you in, captures you, and makes you continue reading. They are certainly not boring. Flash forward to 2008: Caulley (2008) quotes Richardson's statement that so much qualitative research she reads is just boring. How have we come to this and what can we do about it?

Caulley (2008) makes a compelling case for using techniques associated with creative nonfiction (nonfiction that uses fiction techniques). According to Caulley, the idea originated in the 1960s with the New Journalism (p. 424).[6] He included many techniques and examples in his very interesting article and provided a clear discussion of the controversy surrounding this approach. Caulley suggested that written work should begin with a section that is "vivid and vital" (p. 424). I see the Introduction as a hook to get the reader involved, interested, and anxious to read more. You can imagine that this type of opening is not really possible if you are writing formal, objective, third-person text. Another way to get the reader involved and anxious to continue reading is to begin with an arrival or departure. Liebow (1967) and Kidder (1989) do this very well.

Caulley (2008) offered additional suggestions that you will find useful:

- *Dramatic or Summary Methods.* Caulley identifies two basic methods of writing, dramatic and summary. He prefers the dramatic (or scenic) method of writing to the summary method. Rather than provide a summary of what happened, Caulley suggests that you provide a specific account or slice of life.

- *Scene-by-Scene Writing.* Many writers of qualitative research offer several quotes, one after another. Caulley argues against this approach; rather, he prefers using a narrative of various scenes. In this way, readers get the sense that the action is unfolding in front of them. Of course, Caulley would not discourage the judicious use of quotes.

- *Use of Realistic Details.* Many writers speak of the use of realistic details. I suggest that you take extensive notes as you collect data. You may also use a digital camera to capture details that you then incorporate into your text.

- *Show, Don't Tell.* It is important to remember that what you write should incorporate an active voice and avoid abstract concepts.

- *The Active Voice.* In active voice, the subject of a sentence performs the action described by the verb. Caulley provides excellent examples from Cheney (2001): "He was enticed by her black hair" becomes "Her black hair knocked him for a loop." "She was embraced by the clown" becomes "The clown grabbed her and hugged her."

- *Captured Conversation.* Many qualitative writers use the words of participants. In my experience, however, novice writers tend to use participants' words to excess. A more effective way of using the voices of others is to interweave quotes with points that the writer wishes to emphasize.

Caulley (2008) suggested that you put some of these ideas into practice. I concur. I am indebted to Caulley for organizing and presenting this information in such an exciting manner. Now, we wait to see whether our writing will be less boring. Goodall (2008) provided examples of creative nonfiction in his recent book on the personal narrative and political consequences for the ethnographer.

Structure Is a Good Thing

I don't mean to imply that structure is bad. In fact, I think it is critical for a good piece of writing; it gives order and unity to what you write. I suggest that the structure you choose should be one you impose and develop based on the data you have, the audience you plan to address, and the meaning you want to convey. Chenail (1995) offered several alternative structures or formats for writing, including "natural, simple to complex, first discovered, theory guided, narrative logic, most to least important, dramatic presentation, no special order." Whatever structure you choose, most pieces of qualitative research include the following sections.

Opening Section. The opening section of your report should draw the reader in and set the stage. Traditional research writing often begins with a background, statement of the problem, and research questions. I think it is a good idea to include such topics near the beginning of what you write. You could include an opening paragraph that is personal and tells a little bit about who was studied or the data collected, or you could relay something one of your participants said. Because much of qualitative research follows an inductive approach, writing from the particular to the more general is consistent with that format. Here is an example:

> Sure there will be times when "I [find] myself wondering more and more why I [am] in the program." It is all too easy to find myself "feeling overwhelmed by the coursework, the workload." Still all in all, it has proven an experience beyond my wildest imagination. The personal and professional growth alone is amazing. I am actually learning (and unlearning) to "[be] open to opportunities and let the path take me to it." In all honesty and seriousness, "I would not change a thing!"
>
> In many respects, this paper is an ethnographic tribute to the graduate student journey. I have sought to share the cultural behaviors, language, and artifacts of the graduate student through a descriptive storytelling format that presents an "everyday" perspective. Of course, this topic also positions me as the researcher in the somewhat precarious position of "going native," as I am actively engaged in doctoral coursework. Certainly I am "immersed in the day-to-day lives of the people" (Creswell, 1997, p. 58). The bracketing cautions loom tremulously. Or perhaps my immersion merely positions me for the emic perspective of an insider's view of the graduate student culture (*Ways of Approaching Research: Qualitative Designs*, n.d.). While there are also admitted limitations in the variety of data sources, the nature of the research question, as well as the data itself, suggest the opportunity to provide a holistic portrait of the graduate student experience. Fully realizing that this qualitative effort may not generalize to the larger population, I acted on the opportunity to capture a glimpse of this world.

Methods and Procedures. While traditional research writing often expects this section to follow next, I have seen authors choose to include such information in an appendix or at the end of what they write. I believe they do this because they do not want to detract from the personal nature and deep description about the topic. Some qualitative writing is silent about methods and procedures.

Profiles of Participants. Much of qualitative research involves the study of individuals. I often see a description of each participant, including demographic characteristics. These are usually introduced with fictitious names. Sparkes and Smith (2003) introduced one of the three men in their study as follows:

> David is 28 years old and a teaching assistant, living in a large city in Northern England. His father, a headmaster at the local school, was the chairman of the local rugby club, and his mother was involved in the general catering for the club. (p. 302)

Harding (2005) introduced the city girl in her study with,

> The 30-year-old national board certified teacher is 5 feet 6 inches tall with a medium build. She has long, red hair that she keeps pulled back in a ponytail meant to harness her curls. She wears glasses when she teaches, and they add to her overall seriousness. She is not a person who starts out smiling—I get the sense that her laughter will have to be earned. Her speech is punctuated with "Ya know what I mean?" I am never sure if she is asking this question of herself or of me. (p. 55)

Concepts and Supporting Evidence. You may see a section that identifies the major concepts that emerged from the study. Usually, several short quotations that come directly from the data are used to support the concepts. The concept headings are often quotes directly from the participants.

Self-Reflection. You will often see self-disclosure in the writing. Here are some examples.

> While I have attempted qualitative research before, I have never felt myself being drawn into the data as I have with these interviews. The students became very real to me and I visualized them as I delved into the transitions that they experienced in their various graduate programs. Breuer, Mruck & Roth (2002) commented "that doing qualitative research makes the impact of the researcher far more obvious than in its quantitative [counterpart] . . . the interactional and constructional nature of epistemological processes become more than elsewhere evident and can be experienced in existential ways." As a student in adult learning, adult development and individual change are the lenses I use when examining data. As I reviewed the data, it helped me study individual transitions from a new perspective.

> I am feeling very anxious about doing the interview this afternoon. I feel like I have a good relationship with the participant. In some ways this causes more stress because I feel like I have to be very "formal" during this process and this is very different from our usual interactions. Also, I am worried about not having a "pre-set" list of questions. What will happen if I run out of things to ask or if she doesn't respond to the questions? For this reason, I have come up with several questions that I would like to ask her. I feel like at this point I am too inexperienced to "wing it."

> Conducting this study has allowed me to look back on my life as a graduate student. While working a full-time job, being a wife, mother, daughter, sister, friend, and trying to balance the demands of school are difficult tasks. I have missed, and will miss, many family gatherings and outings with friends. Sometimes it is a lonely experience, one that only another graduate student can relate, but the reward is going to be wonderful!

Research Literature. Very often the related research is integrated in the paper and not provided as a separate section.

■ Writing a Qualitative Research Proposal

By now, you know that there is no single way of doing something in the qualitative research field. New ideas emerge regularly. Your institution may have its own requirements. I offer a general outline that you should find helpful.

1. *Introduction and Research Problem.* You can think of this first section as addressing such questions as what the issues are, what you hope to focus on, and why it is of value. Your purpose is to convey to the audience the topic of your research, why it is important, and how it fits into our larger understanding of the issues. Headings might include Introduction, Central Research Question, Related Literature, and Potential Significance of your research. I do not think it is important to conduct an extensive review of the related literature; however, introducing key ideas is important. In a sense, this first section will be very similar to a traditional research proposal.

2. *Methodology of the Study.* In the second section, you address such issues as the research approach you plan to take, participants, the data you anticipate getting and how you plan to collect it, and the manner in which you anticipate dealing with your data. Headings might include Research Approach, Ways to Collect Data, Ways to Analyze Data. You will also address issues of the role of the researcher and how to judge value. While the headings for this section are similar to what you might find in a traditional proposal, much of the content will be vastly different.

Looking at the outline and comments that I made above does not really tell you what the underlying story is or the problems you might face. I think it important that I discuss some of the issues surrounding your proposal. Your purpose in writing a research proposal is to seek approval from a university or funding agency to conduct your research. The first task you face is to clarify in your mind what you plan to do and how you plan to do it. Haverkamp and Young (2007) believed that a first step is "gaining clarity on one's foundational framework for qualitative research, as reflected in the identification of a philosophy of science paradigm" (p. 266). I recognize that some of the details may not be clear to you because the research process is inductive and iterative. But to the extent possible, you need to decide what your study is about and how you plan to conduct it. I see this as a process between you and your mentors. Your colleagues can also play an important role in the process. So before you actually write anything, you will need to meet with others to clarify your thinking.

Once you decide on the general topic area and research purpose, these are some of the issues that you need to be thinking about. Will you select one of the approaches I discuss in Chapter 5? For example, are you interested in the lived experiences of children who have recently immigrated to the United States? If so, you would use a phenomenological approach. Are you interested in exploring ways in which beginning teachers interact with their students? If so, you might want to consider an ethnographic approach. Or would you like to see how a school that is scheduled to close deals with the myriad issues as they plan for the final year? If so, you might want to conduct a case study.

You will also need to consider a section on the role of the researcher. It is critical that you explain how qualitative research requires the researcher to move away from objectivity and take a reflective and subjective stance.

Often, sample sizes in qualitative research are small and are samples of convenience rather than random samples from which you can generalize to a larger population. You will need to defend this approach and speak about the goal of qualitative research as being description and understanding, rather than hypothesis testing.

Because you will probably not use a formal questionnaire (so there will be nothing that you can submit for approval), you will need to address how you plan to collect data. You can review Chapters 9 and 10 to get some ideas.

You will need to explain the process you anticipate using to analyze your data. If you plan to use a computer software program, you need to demonstrate either your expertise or how you plan to gain expertise by taking a course, a tutorial, or seeking outside assistance.

Because you may choose to write in a less formal style and use the first-person pronoun, you will probably need to address these issues and provide a justification.

Another area that review boards and committees often consider is the worth and value of your study. Refer to Chapter 13 for supporting evidence.

How should you write your proposal? You can choose to follow the fairly traditional style that I provide above. Or you can choose to weave a narrative addressing the topics I present. If you choose the latter, I strongly suggest that you seek approval from your adviser and committee members prior to presenting it to a larger group. You need an advocate on your side, and you need to know that what you plan to do is supported by someone at your institution.

In a Google search of the term *qualitative research proposal,* the first article that appears was written more than 10 years ago. It is interesting to look at the suggestions made then and compare them to suggestions that might fit today. Heath (1997) reiterated Morse's claim that there is no accepted outline for a qualitative research proposal. In those days, a proposal reflected the views of the time. Heath's outline included four parts plus references and a mini-bibliography. I think you can take away the following ideas that are relevant today.

Heath (1997) advised to begin with something interesting, such as a quote or story. Caulley (2008) suggested that the first paragraph is critical because it grabs the reader. Heath continues, "You should include a section on 'research paradigm' when you have unfamiliar readers." He also suggested that you include something on research method. Today, that would translate into including a section on your research approach, as I describe in Chapter 5. He also recommended that you include details about ways you plan to collect and analyze your data. In the final section, he recommended that you acknowledge your biases.

Given that this outline was written in 1997, I think it is a good launching point; however, there are several obvious omissions. The proposal does not recommend including a formal literature review, nor does it speak to commenting on any ethical issues. The proposal does not deal with informed consent or issues regarding IRBs, issues that were not relevant at that time. Finally, it does not specifically address how the final paper should be written. Munhall and Chenail (2007) offered additional suggestions. You can also read guidelines for proposals seeking funding (Penrod, 2003).

Sandelowski and Barroso (2003) described a proposal for a qualitative research study as a double challenge, due to the emergent nature of the research design and the need to describe a process to produce a process. They added the dimension of mutual respectful interaction between writers and readers. In their article, they outline a traditional quantitative research proposal and contrast it with their qualitative approach. They relied heavily on grounded theory, so their proposal addressed the relevant issues. They basically followed a general outline that could be used with both types of proposals. Differences were apparent when they spoke of theoretical sampling, data collection and analysis together, and the development of concepts and categories. I believe they were trying to educate the funders with their proposal.

The challenge of writing a research proposal is clear. You are a novice in this arena. The group to whom you are communicating may also be novices, or worse, they may have preconceived ideas of what a proposal should look like and how a study should be designed. A number of researchers recount their experiences in dealing with review boards and the political dynamics of such boards. There is clearly a power struggle here because a review committee may hold the power to approve or disapprove your research. It is your responsibility to convince yourself first of what you are doing, convince your committee, and finally convince an outside panel to support your idea. You will be extremely well served if you write clearly, are prepared with evidence of what constitutes appropriate or good practices in the arena in which you plan to work, and remain confident that your study is of value and will contribute to a better understanding of education.

■ Alternative Forms of Presentation

Most of you will write your results and present them as a class paper or project, as a thesis or dissertation, as a journal article, or as a report to a sponsor. I want you to be aware of some alternative presentation ideas that have surfaced recently.

LeftCoast Press, the brainchild of Mitch Allen, has recently embarked on a number of initiatives that are outside the mainstream. According to its Web site (http://www.lcoastpress.com/),

> [The series on] ethnographic narratives encourages novel and evocative forms of lived experiences, including autoethnography, literary, poetic, artistic, visual, performative, critical, multi-voiced, conversational, and co-constructed representations. We are interested in ethnographic narratives that depict local stories; employ literary modes of scene setting, dialogue, character development, and unfolding action; and include the author's critical reflections on the research and writing process, such as research ethics, alternative modes of inquiry and representation, reflexivity, and evocative storytelling.

Schwandt's (2001) *Dictionary of Qualitative Inquiry* noted alternative means of communicating through poetry, film, drama, and dance. Ethnotheatre is an art form that uses theatrical techniques to present real research findings. Curtis (2008) described his use of verbatim theater (somewhat different from ethnotheatre) as an alternative form of qualitative presentation. You can read Boudreau's (2002) account of how Soldana, a professor of theater, presented Wolcott's *Brad Trilogy*. Kabel (2002) wrote about using poems, photos, and people's voices; Butler-Kisber (2002) also used poetry. Robertson (2006) presented the results of her research as a panel discussion. P. J. Lewis (2008) presented a documentary film using digital video and computer software in his research on a good teacher.

I have seen a great deal of interest in autoethnography (writing emotionally about the self), in which the method and writing are intertwined (Bochner & Ellis, 2002; Holt, 2003). Bochner and Ellis have written extensively on the topic, and you can read many of their accounts in their edited volumes on alternative narratives. Ellis et al. (2008) are considered the driving force in what is called the alternative ethnography movement. I encourage you to explore these ideas; you will certainly read material that is stimulating.

■ Qualitative Writing

There are two excellent sources of qualitative writing that reflects current thinking; both are journals specifically designed to publish qualitative writing. *Qualitative Research,* from the United

Kingdom, issued its first volume in 2000 (http://qrj.sagepub.com/). The September 2008 issue's Table of Contents reflects the type of article it publishes. It is a fairly short issue, containing five articles and two book reviews. Topics reflect a broad range of interests, such as the relationship between policy research and practice and multiple standpoints. *Qualitative Inquiry,* from the United States, is much larger and includes many articles related to technology (http://qix.sagepub.com/). Its October 2008 Table of Contents includes topics such as global and local cyberselves, online teaching, and technology in a collaborative writing group. I urge you to look at both these journals to get a sense of how to write your own qualitative study.

I want to leave you with some examples written by students. This first excerpt is from a paper prepared by a student taking an introductory course in qualitative research. Notice how the writer uses a first-person, direct style. When she actually begins her story, she writes as a fictionalized journal.

January 15. It's time. Applications are due in a couple of months and if I'm going to go back to school, now is the time. Children are still a few years away. I can't even imagine how I could possibly balance young kids and an advanced degree program, although I'm sure some people do so successfully. And I don't want to wait the additional years until I actually have kids and then they reach school age. I've waited long enough. I mean seriously, how long can I drive around with "PRE PHD" on my license plate before actually taking action to make that a reality?

Do I consider relocating or are there viable options close to home? How to choose? I guess I need to get serious and go to the library (maybe online?) and start to weigh this out.

January 19. Just to make sure I am making an informed decision, I looked at everything—every school where my program is offered. There are very viable options locally, so I will continue to focus on these. Staying here rather than relocating is more attractive to me. Beyond cost and the application logistics of degree type (PhD or EdD), fees, requisites, prerequisites, and program size what else do I consider? What else is *important* to consider? The basic logistics in the Peterson's guide seem somewhat sterile—no real feel of what this will really be like. Maybe the websites offer more.

December 3. I need help! I can't do this alone. I need additional strategies next semester. Have to make time to reflect on this—after my papers are done! Why am I even stopping to comment in this journal?!?!

December 13. Ta da! Completion and success. Now can I sleep and de-stress??? YES!!!

December 20. Met up with a few folks from my class for coffee and tea. All are weary and we look it. But no pity or despair! We are also amazingly resilient and energized by our efforts. One person, a neophyte like me, commented that she had "rediscovered learning is very energizing to [her] and exciting." What an amazing testimony. I love it! I too love "to learn and have gotten a lot of enjoyment out of the people interaction in the . . . program." " . . . just the relationships with classmates—many of them have turned into friends and that's really enriched my life."

January 1. Ever a day of reflection and planning, at least for me. Here goes.

What worked? I continue to rely on my tried-and-true internal standards of commitment, perseverance, and time management (e.g., prioritization, organization). I expect I will continue to tap these in the many semesters ahead. (C. L. Wells, personal communication, 2002)

I chose this next excerpt to reveal how Talisha described in detail her approach to data analysis. She also used color and inserts to highlight the points she was trying to illustrate. Notice the use of self-reflection.

There was a lot of information collected in each person's interview that [*sic*] I was not quite sure how to tackle everyone's interview. I decided to begin data analysis by thoroughly reading everyone's interview and jotting notes in the margins about statements that I found surprising, interesting, or themes that were common in everyone's interview. After finding these things, I used Microsoft Excel to create a list for everyone in the class and their interview. The list was titled according to the person who conducted the interview and then interesting and similar statements were listed under the title.

I also color-coded similar themes in everyone's interviews. If a participant mentioned something about self-discovery or self-awareness, the statement would be colored green as in the above example of Heather's interview. Or if someone mentioned the support of family, a spouse, professors, or students, the statement would be colored yellow. Or if someone mentioned something about having to balance work and school, or organize or structure in order to participate in a graduate program, the statement would be colored red. Coding is a technique used in grounded theory's open coding. It allowed me to identify similarities and differences in the interviews. This project could be related to a grounded theory approach because, in the end, a theory could be derived regarding graduate student life from the data. (T. McAuley, personal communication, December 5, 2002)

■ Summary

You might design a wonderful study and collect important data; however, if the way in which you present your findings is unclear, abstract, or boring, you have been unsuccessful. It is critical that you present your study in such a way to draw in your audience and actively engage them in the process. In most cases, communication is written, although alternatives to the written word have occasionally been used. I recommend that you write in a direct style, using an active voice. Weaving quotes from participants into the fabric of your writing is a way provide support for your interpretations.

I recommend that you use some stylistic techniques drawn from the New Journalism and creative nonfiction. Caulley (2008) suggested some tools such as starting with a story, writing scene by scene, and including dramatic details.

Unlike traditional research, in qualitative research the writer is free to select from among a variety of presentation styles. For beginning researchers, I suggest including four basic elements: what your study is about, a profile of participants, ways you gathered and analyzed data, and major findings. An open style that communicates the role you played is also valuable.

------------------■------------------

GROUP ACTIVITY

Purpose: To practice a simple writing task using qualitative data. To learn about sharing with others and revealing about the self.

Activities: Combine a group observation with a simple writing exercise. During a break between classes, choose a location where you will meet or see other students. This could be in a cafeteria, bookstore, lounge, or hallway. You are to take about 30 minutes. You will be focusing on interactions among students. You can choose any aspect of interaction of interest. You will not be taking notes but rather making mental images and practicing your ability to look and listen.

Immediately upon returning to class, you will write three paragraphs. One paragraph will focus on your observation. What did you see? What do you think it means? What insights do you have about this human encounter? The second paragraph will describe your self-reflections. How did you feel? What did you understand about the task and about yourself? The last paragraph will be about the method you used. All writing should be in first person. If possible, you should write on your computer.

The final part of this task is sharing and getting insights from others. Depending upon the size of your class, you can either share with the entire group or split into smaller groups.

Evaluation: Determine the ease with which you can communicate some ideas to others, and note how others attend to this observation and writing experience.

INDIVIDUAL ACTIVITY

Purpose: To reinforce writing ideas by using what you wrote in the group experience and modifying it based on what others did and what you learned about yourself.

Activities: Take your writing assignment that you produced in the above Group Activity and rework it. Work on your writing style, your ability to communicate, and your ability to set the tone of what you are trying to say. Send it as an attachment to other class members. Choose one or two other examples you receive and examine how they have been changed. Begin to build a portfolio of your writing.

Evaluation: Continue to assess your ability to communicate. Judge what other information you need in order to move forward with your writing.

■   Notes

1. It was Geertz (1973) who used the term "thick description" to explain that context was important to an understanding of cultures. Geertz acknowledged that he adopted the term from the British philosopher Gilbert Ryle.

2. The seminal work in the field is by Lakoff and Johnson (1980).

3. I visited six of these caves a few years ago. The seemingly simple paintings took on various meanings to members of our group. One began chanting while the others were buried deep in their thoughts.

4. To gain a deeper understanding of the poststructuralist viewpoint, you will need to study the philosophical positions of Foucault and Derrida, among others. Foucault's 1972 and 1980 books are a good place to start. Derrida's writing from 1972, translated in 1982 may also be helpful. Neither is easy reading.

5. Originally, it was his dissertation from The Catholic University of America.

6. The New Journalism used unconventional literary techniques when writing about news. Tom Wolfe published a collection of such articles by Truman Capote, Norman Mailer, and Joan Didion, among others. This type of writing appeared most often in news magazines such as *The New Yorker, Rolling Stone,* or *Esquire.*

Chapter 13

Judging and Evaluating

FOCUS YOUR READING

■ Criteria for judging qualitative research continue to evolve as the field evolves.

■ Increasingly, review boards and journal editors recognize that standard criteria suitable for quantitative research may not apply.

■ A backlash reflected in a conservative movement in the United States regarding the No Child Left Behind initiative has led some to require more scientific approaches.

The nice thing about standards is that there are so many to choose from.
—Andrew S. Tannenbaum

A number of years ago, I wrote an article with some colleagues about the process of supervision for family therapists (Keller, Protinsky, Lichtman, & Allen, 1996). At the time, I believed we used a novel approach. We videotaped several supervisors and students. We then assigned four pairs (composed of a supervisor and a student) to observe each videotape and develop themes independently of each other. The various iterations resulted in common themes based on our individual and joint observations To our chagrin, the editors of a respectable journal in the field said that although they liked the article, it resembled our own reflections and was not sufficiently scholarly or scientific. We subsequently rewrote the article in light of the criticisms. But I believe the reason it was not accepted was that the reviewers were still developing their own criteria for judging research that did not fit traditional modes. Today, editors of various journals, while still differing on what constitutes acceptable qualitative research, are more open to alternative methods and approaches.

As you read this chapter, you will become aware that one of the most controversial areas surrounding qualitative research is how to evaluate what you read. There are currently several schools of thought regarding how qualitative research should be judged, what criteria should be used, and who should determine the criteria. I see these issues along a continuum. In Figure 13.1, conservative, more traditional views, especially those that emerged prior to 1990, are represented at the right. This view holds that the same criteria used for traditional research methods should be used for qualitative research. In the early 2000s, this view was in the minority. However, there has been a resurgence of interest in this traditional view and in adopting research designs that are quantitative and scientific in nature. This appears to be fueled, at least in part, by the political fervor of the No Child Left Behind Act of 2001 (NCLB), which requires "scientifically based research."[1] Moving along the continuum, there are those who want to make sure that qualitative research remains scientific. They adopted concepts supposedly parallel to those of the traditionalists. They suggest, for example, the use of triangulation to demonstrate reliability.[2] This faction adopts a postpositivist position, in which the researcher strives for an objective stance. But this point of view, too, is not necessarily one adopted by many qualitative researchers in the new millennium. Another view is one in which such terms as trustworthiness and verifiability come into play. Criteria developed in the 21st century represent differing points of view. They tend to emphasize the role of the researcher, for example. I find the criteria very much influenced by some of the newer ideas of poststructuralism, feminism, and postmodernism. Politics and power also play a critical role here.

I have identified a number of important issues. What should the criteria be to decide whether a piece of qualitative work is good, appropriate, or suitable? Who should determine these criteria? How do the criteria become modified as time and views change? Should there be a single set of criteria, or are several sets suitable, depending on the type of qualitative research conducted? Or should the criteria be continuously evolving to represent the dynamic nature of the field? In what ways do alternative modes of dissemination, such as the Internet, affect the criteria? Differing audiences may expect different things, so a conservative academic journal might look for one thing while a more avant-garde source may expect something else. There is the academic community, the government community, the educational community, the publishing community, and the general public. At times they overlap, but not always. Should the criteria be published? How specific should they be?

Figure 13.1   Key Issues Associated With Evaluating Qualitative Research

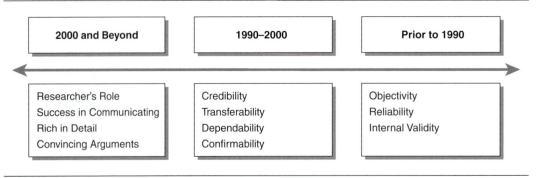

Did You Know

Whatever criteria are used to judge the quality of the research, Ball and Forzani (2007) believe that "until education researchers turn their attention to problems that exist primarily inside education and until they develop systematically a body of specialized knowledge, other scholars who study questions that bear on educational problems will propose solutions. Because such solutions typically are not based on explanatory analyses of the dynamics of education, the education problems that confront society are likely to remain unsolved" (p. 530).

You might understand some of these issues more clearly if you look outside your own field and into the world of art. You might know of Édouard Manet (born 1832), a great painter and one of the precursors of the Impressionists. But if not, I suspect that many of you have heard of Claude Monet (born 1840) and Edgar Degas (born 1834). Both artists are considered preeminent in their field of Impressionism. The Impressionist movement was popular in the mid- to late 1800s. It is generally considered one of the most popular and well-received artistic movements today. However, these artists were originally seen as outsiders. They departed from their predecessors by using light and color to depict visual reality. They worked outdoors (*en plein air*) and tried to capture how the light influenced what they saw.

But these artists were not always so well received. In fact, in order to show their work, artists' work had to be accepted in the Paris Salon. This Salon began in 1791 and eventually became a small group of people who determined the criteria for what was good and desirable in art. In 1863, the Salon refused a very important work that Manet had painted: *Déjeuner sur l'herbe* (*The Picnic*). The artistic community of France, supported by Napoleon III, formed an alternative to the traditional Paris Salon and called it the Salon des Refusés (Salon of the Rejected). Manet's painting created quite a scandal. Why? Because it didn't meet the criteria that were acceptable to those who ran the traditional Salons. One reason for the scandal was the content of the painting. Manet juxtaposed a female nude with males in modern dress as a gesture of provocation. Further, Manet's painting of Olympia (a nude courtesan) also shocked the viewers at the 1865 Salon. People jeered it. In fact, the first Impressionist exhibition was not held until 1874, although by this time Manet was no longer involved. By 1886, the eighth and last Impressionist exhibition was held, showing the work of 17 artists. Subsequently, the Impressionist movement fell into a sharp decline. Those who were judging realized that they had to expand their expectations of what was good and beautiful. Of course, this led to many other breaks with artistic tradition, such as Cubism in the early 1900s, Surrealism some years later, and Abstract Expressionism in post–World War II New York. By the next century, the artistic world had been knocked completely off its feet, and room was made for a vast range of work, ranging from video installations to performance art to readymades. No longer is it clear what art is, how to judge it, or what it should be like. What is clear is that the world has opened up to new ideas, to new expressions, and to new people who were not previously in the field.

I have gone into detail about the artistic community because I want you to understand that the issues the Impressionists faced are not so different from what you face. Just as "What is good art?" is a question that cannot easily be answered, "What is good research?" is a question that we consider now. With these ideas in mind, I want to begin with my personal criteria. I stress "personal" and yet want to make clear that the criteria are not presented without considerable thought, reading, and experience.

■ Personal Criteria

You can find many lists of what should be included in a good piece of qualitative research. However, you will find little or no evidence that these criteria are anything more than criteria generated by people who have worked in the field or who have read about the field. They seem to be based implicitly on the philosophy and assumptions made by the writers. Throughout this book, I have chosen to make my personal philosophy explicit. This is important as you begin to understand personal criteria. I will talk about three intertwined concepts: the self, the other, and the interaction of the self/other. Next, I discuss the importance of positioning what was studied and what was found in a larger context. How convincing is the researcher in arguing a case? A third issue is to make explicit the manner in which the study was done. Does the writer include rich detail and explanation so that others may decide its worth? Finally, I look at success in communication.

Researcher's Role: Revealing the Self and Other Connection

Why is the self so important? Shouldn't the self remain outside the research? If the self is involved, can you trust what you read? I believe strongly that the role of the researcher is critical to the work. He or she should not try to remain outside the system. He need not try to achieve objectivity because that is an assumption of quantitative research and not of qualitative research. He need not try to get "experts" to approve of what he writes because he is the expert in the situation. He needs to reveal himself through a process of self-reflexivity (see Chapter 7 for details on the topic).

In addition to revealing the self, the researcher should reveal what he or she learns about the other. By "the other" I mean those who are studied. Unlike quantitative research, where those who are studied are the subjects or the sample—nameless and faceless individuals who have been chosen at random to represent others with similar characteristics—those studied in qualitative research are real people with real needs, ambitions, fears, and desires. Their stories touch the researcher and touch the readers I believe that is why we are so captivated and energized by them.

I argue here that an understanding of the other does not come about without an understanding of the self and how the self and the other connect. I believe each is transformed through this research process.

I have chosen to divide my personal criteria along several dimensions. What was studied? What was found? How was the study done? How does the writer communicate?

Convincing Arguments:
What Was Studied and What Was Found

I see this concept as critical in an assessment of the worth of a piece of qualitative research, yet it is very difficult to get at its essence. What is important to one person may have no relevance to someone else. Yet, if the researcher does a good job, she convinces the reader that the topic is an important one to consider and fits into a larger context. You can assume that the topic that is studied is important to the researcher. Otherwise, why would she choose to write about it? But the strength of a qualitative study is the extent to which the writer convinces you that what she studied is important and that it fits into a larger context.

I perused topics covered in the most recent issues of several journals specifically devoted to qualitative research. I notice they cover a wide range. For example, Volume 13, Number 3, September 2008 of *The Qualitative Report* presents the following topics: vocative texts (poetic texts that show rather than tell—a suggestion that Caulley [2008] made when writing about creative nonfiction); issues facing a working class researcher; experience in creating a research-based drama; ethical dilemmas in a community-based project; and connections between prayer, faith, and forgiveness. This is only a portion of the topics. I am struck by how diverse they are.

I also looked at articles in the August 2008 issue of *Qualitative Inquiry.* Topics include living hymns and iterations (a spiritual search); notions of truth for trauma survivors using three modes of presentation (dissertation, memoir, and autoethnography); social and cultural problems of producing, consuming, and using technology; a multiyear case study of computer supported collaborative learning; and power relations of a multiyear study of information and computer technology.

Next, I looked at articles in the July 2008 issue of *Qualitative Research.* The issue seems to be devoted to narratives of one kind or another. The 17 articles covered a wide range: narratable subject, ethnographic and narrative research with eighth-grade students in New Hampshire, archival materials about fin-de-siècle prostitutes, the life of a poet and feminist, and men's written friendship narratives.

I concluded my search by looking at July 2008, Volume 21, Number 4, of the *International Journal of Qualitative Studies in Education* (*QSE*). Finally, I hoped to find articles that were specifically related to education. It contained six articles, an editorial, and a book review. The lead article by Denzin is a call to continue the paradigm dialogues begun by Guba in the 1980s and I think is a reaction to the NCLB movement calling for scientific studies in education. Other topics include middle school student appropriations of messages about democratic actions, autoethnographic study of race in the academy, young children enacting a community's fear and loss, multiple intelligences in South Korea, and understanding the impact of the Columbine shootings using oral history and poetic expression.

What do I take away about the current topics from this brief exercise? I am struck that they are so diverse. There is not a common theme. Their personal interests and agendas often drive researchers. Whether they are useful or of value to you as a reader is up to you. Are they of value to the larger educational community? We cannot know for sure.

I return to my original position. It is up to the writer to make a convincing argument that the topic is important and may be one from which we can learn about our situation. I am not speaking about generalizing to other situations; that is not something qualitative researchers claim to do.

The findings are meaningful in light of the questions asked; these two ideas are intertwined. "Lies, damned lies, and statistics," said Benjamin Disraeli and Mark Twain when speaking of using statistics and numbers to support weaker arguments. I would suggest that findings or interpretations tied to questionable topics are no better than using statistics to bolster questionable arguments.

Rich in Detail: How the Study Was Done

You can judge what you read by the information provided about how it was done. Can you determine what the researcher did, how she did it, and why it was done? Can you follow a path to how interviews were done or how those studied were selected? Can you determine why the researcher chose to conduct a phenomenology or ethnography? Does the researcher provide enough explanation? Does the researcher provide explanations for concepts that are often associated with qualitative research? For example, is the role of the researcher addressed? What about power? If the researcher chooses an approach to research that is not widely understood, is that approach and rationale explained? I think it is important that you are provided sufficient information to determine what was done.

Many of the studies that I cite above provide detailed descriptions of how the study was done. Often, when a new concept or idea is introduced, the researchers provide clear explanations.

Communication:
Are You Convinced by the Presentation?

Finally, we can only judge the worth of research by what we read or hear or see. You need to decide to what extent the writer reaches you by her presentation. Do the words convey a story? Does the play provide insight and meaning? Does the video clip provide a window into understanding a particular issue? Most of what you will encounter is the written word, so I want to say a few more things about what to look for.

- *Opening.* Are you drawn into the context or story immediately? Because qualitative research tends to be inductive in nature, I find that manuscripts that draw me in and take me on a personal journey are those that are most effective. I want to be grabbed when I begin to read. This is not to say that you are just reading a story, but a story is an excellent way to begin.

- *Engaging Style.* Does the writer use a style that is open and engaging while at the same time reflects thoughtfulness and scholarship?

- *Reflections.* Does the writer incorporate personal reflections and insights, thereby drawing the self into the writing?

- *Integration.* Does the writer clarify and draw connections between the extant research, what has been learned on the journey, and her own insights?

- *Rich Detail.* Does the writer provide sufficient detail regarding methods and findings so the reader can understand the message?

- *Voices of Others.* Does the writer use the voices of others to reach new insights and interpretations?

- *Justification.* If the researcher uses a particular approach, does he or she provide ample explanation?

- *New Meanings.* Does the writer offer new connections, interpretations, or insights based on her research?

These criteria are meant as a starting point for you as you begin to read what others have written and plan your own research. You might find that you will want to add to or modify what I have written; I hope you will. You should also find it helpful to examine criteria that have evolved over the past 25 years or so. In this next section, I offer a brief history so you can understand the context of the criteria.

■ What Do Others Have to Say?

Although I have offered my criteria for evaluating qualitative research, I think it is helpful for you to understand the larger field and what has gone before. I will begin this discussion with what is known already. What are the criteria for reviewing traditional research approaches? Most would agree that they are internal validity (in experimental studies, the degree to which the independent variable has an effect on the dependent variable), external validity (the degree to which the findings can be generalized), reliability (the degree to which the findings can be replicated), and objectivity (the degree to which the findings are free from bias). These are pivotal and expected of those conducting research based on positivist or postpositivist positions. I want you to remember these as you begin your journey to establish new criteria. A randomized control group design is said to be the gold standard of experimental research.

I am going to remind you again of some of the underlying assumptions on which these criteria are based. One assumption is that methods associated with the natural sciences are the best and can be used in the social sciences. Second, only observable phenomena are considered. The researcher seeks an objective reality; thus, the researcher's role is to find a way to observe the phenomena and remain outside the system. These assumptions underlie the criteria of traditional research.

Below, I also illustrate some criteria that have emerged as qualitative research has taken a more prominent place in the research domain. I think it will help you to see the historical and chronological evolution of these criteria. Prior to the 1990s, most qualitative researchers operated from a postpositivist perspective. Consequently, they found themselves in the traditional mind-set. But I think some researchers knew that something was amiss; they just weren't sure quite what.

Some criteria from these early years were generic and meant to apply to all types of qualitative research paradigms, while others were quite specific. Many involved explicit or implicit assumptions that qualitative research should be similar to quantitative research.

Prior to 1990

As qualitative research began to take hold, many were unsure how to judge this type of research. Journal editors tended to rely on traditional criteria, and many journals were reluctant to publish research that did not appear to fit the format of traditional research. There were not any journals that devoted themselves primarily to qualitative research. I recall when several of us submitted a qualitative research study to a marriage and family journal. The reviews came back: We found the study very interesting but did not see it as more than some ramblings from a few people. University researchers were just beginning to explore qualitative approaches. Those in education departments and schools were quite reluctant to approve research ideas that did not adopt a quantitative approach to answering questions that generated statistics.

Among the earliest to write about evaluating qualitative research studies were Lincoln and Guba (1985), who tried to develop criteria that were parallel to foundationalist criteria. They wrote about credibility, transferability, dependability, and confirmability. J. Smith and Heshusius (1986) criticized Lincoln and Guba and commented that Lincoln and Guba adopted the assumption that there is an external reality independent of the researcher. I think, in these early days, many were left wondering whether they should adopt criteria from the traditional scientific perspective even though what they were doing did not necessarily fit this traditional mode.

By the next decade, the winds of change were in the air and we began to see alternative criteria based on different assumptions.

The 1990s

During the 1990s, we saw alternative attempts to define criteria emerging. One camp developed criteria that were meant to be comparable to traditional criteria. Trochim (2001), using Guba and Lincoln's four terms, compared them to traditional criteria. Thus, internal validity was replaced by credibility, external validity by transferability, reliability by dependability, and objectivity by confirmability. In my view, on closer examination, these criteria are somewhat limited and limiting.

The term *credibility* suggests that the results should be evaluated from the point of view of the participants, and thus, they are the only ones capable of judging the credibility of results. I think this seems simplistic. The research is not written for the benefit of the participants. It should be set in a larger context and the interpretation of the term credibility expanded. I would agree that the participants may be the only ones to judge the extent to which the researcher explained or captured the meaning of what he saw. However, they are not the only ones to determine the extent to which the researcher's interpretations make sense in a larger context (see Choudhuri, Glauser, & Peregoy, 2004, who speak to credibility).

Transferability, akin to generalizability, is the extent to which the results can be transferred to other settings. Here, Trochim (2001) suggested that the reader needs to decide whether the results transfer. But he offered no guidance as to how the reader should make such a judgment.

The term *dependability* emphasizes the need for the researcher to account for the ever-changing context within which research occurs. The researcher is responsible for describing the changes that occur in the setting and how these changes affected the way the researcher approached the study. I am not clear what Trochim (2001) meant when he spoke to the "ever-changing context." Does he mean the context in which the research is conducted? Does he mean the larger social context?

The term *confirmability* refers to the degree to which results could be confirmed or corroborated by others. I have the most difficulty with this criterion because it implies an attempt to describe an objective reality.

These four criteria are typical of some of the earlier attempts to establish criteria comparable to those used in traditional research. Glaringly omitted are comments about the researcher's role and self-acknowledgment. You will see these emerge as you read criteria established more recently.

In the 1990s, many peer reviewers' assessment of qualitative research also followed criteria often used to judge experimental research (Taylor, Beck, & Ainsworth, 2001). Taylor et al. looked at how peer reviewers judged qualitative research and, not surprisingly, found six themes to be essential to the publication of qualitative research: What is the purpose of the study? How does the purpose build on previous research? How thorough is the methodology? How are the findings presented? What are the contributions, implications, and significance of the study? Is the manuscript organized, edited, and well formatted? If you think these criteria sound familiar and represent a traditionalist stance, you are correct.

So you can see that during the last decade of the 20th century, scholars and researchers were struggling with how to evaluate these new products. Almost all accepted the idea that the traditional criteria of objectivity, reliability, validity, and generalizability were not appropriate. Some looked for parallel ideas, while others recognized that alternative criteria needed to be developed. Some hold the view that qualitative research should not be evaluated in the traditional manner but rather should be judged by the user. By the time you read this, I think you will find that the field is still in a state of evolution.

2000 to Present

As the calendar turned to the 21st century, I hoped that this issue would become less thorny. But that is not the case. As I write this section, 2008 is more than half over. I still find a state of change even in the years since the turn of the century. Some writers discuss such traditional criteria as study design, sampling and data collection, analysis, findings, interpretations, trustworthiness, and implications (Choudhuri et al., 2004). Morse (2003) acknowledged what she called the "uncertain exploratory nature" of qualitative research using a flexible design and emerging findings. Yet, she suggested that evaluators look for relevance (the worthiness of the question and its value), rigor (the adequacy and appropriateness of the method used to answer the questions), and feasibility (the ability of the researcher to conduct the research; p. 833).

Other approaches ask us to consider rigor by looking at five fundamental considerations: Does the researcher convey reflexivity or the ability to stay open to the participant's experience? Does the researcher show credibility or validity and accuracy (a concept of traditional research)? Is transferability observed or the ability to generalize (again a concept from traditional research)? Is there an audit trail? And is there confirmability or objectivity?

Some traditionalists use the concept of triangulation. However, I see this concept adopted primarily by those who take a very conservative view of qualitative research. In general, **triangulation** refers to the idea that multiple sources bring more credibility to an investigation. Guion (2002) offered an elaboration of the idea in that she identified five kinds of triangulation: data triangulation, investigator triangulation, theory triangulation, methodological triangulation, and environmental triangulation. Most writers think about data triangulation, in which data from different sources are collected. Investigator triangulation involves the use of different investigators, while theory triangulation involves the use of multiple perspectives. Multiple methods is the mainstay of methodological triangulation. Finally, using different locations or settings is the key element of environmental triangulation. I believe that triangulation was adopted as a way to make qualitative research more objective and less subjective— in other words, more scientific. If one view of something led to one interpretation, looking at that thing from two different vantage points, where all led to the same interpretation, made the interpretation more acceptable or more legitimate. Guion's concept, that there can be triangulation of different kinds of things besides data, is an elaboration of the same idea. In contrast to criteria that build on fairly traditional notions of what makes for good research, others take a somewhat different view.

Parker (2003, pp. 5–6) posed four questions regarding criteria that address issues relating to what is good, who is the audience, what is analysis, and the role of theory. Rather than answering these questions in a predictable manner, he suggested that there are no clear answers. Instead, he suggested that we explore three additional issues as well as their exceptions:

1. *How is the study related to existing research?* We know that a study does not exist in a vacuum and that we need to relate our research to existing research. But isn't it possible that there is no existing research out there, and the absence of research may be equally important?

2. *Does the narrative move in a linear fashion to reach its conclusion?* In general, we expect this to happen. Parker suggests that there may be times when a fragmented format is more appropriate and a traditional format may inhibit innovation.

3. *To whom is the research accessible?* He suggests that at times, issues are complex and arguments difficult to write, thus making writing less accessible.

I find it particularly interesting that he suggested that "the study should make clear by what criteria it should be evaluated" and when the rules should be followed or broken (Parker, 2003, p. 6). In encouraging innovation and flexibility, Parker suggested that criteria typically associated with quantitative research are not necessarily appropriate in qualitative research.

Devers (1999) and Hoepfl (1997) agreed that clear criteria are critical, but expressed the concern (as I have) that we have been relying on traditional criteria based on positivism. Devers wants criteria to address the voice of the researcher and alternative means of reporting. Denzin and Lincoln (2000) added the ideas of verisimilitude, emotionality, personal responsibility, caring, political praxis, multivoiced texts, and dialogues with subjects. I know you will agree that these ideas bear little resemblance to the criteria I mentioned earlier.

But Parker (2003) warned that using fixed criteria might limit innovation, as it has done with traditional psychological research, and risks making legitimate certain types of qualitative research at the expense of others (see also Elliott, Fischer, & Rennie, 1999). He continued, saying that there really are no overriding criteria that fit a particular situation. He suggested that new research questions call for a new combination of research methods.

Barbour and Barbour (2002) cautioned against using checklists that appeal to credibility and rigor and suggest that some of the most influential papers would not have been published if traditional criteria had been used. They concluded their thoughtful article with the suggestion that qualitative researchers and reviewers should look for suggestions from their own modes of collaboration and look for new ways of collaborating.

Other new ideas are emerging. For example, you will see such criteria as including thick description, prolonged engagement (this is primarily appropriate for ethnography), reflexivity (consideration of subjectivity and bias—an idea from traditional research), member checking (using respondents to check language—an idea that the researcher is trying to "get it right"), theoretical richness (incorporation of appropriate theory, which only works if theory is an issue), alternative structure for writing, and expressiveness (data and analysis should be interesting).

Morrow (2003) spoke to credibility/trustworthiness/rigor and validity in a syllabus for a qualitative course in psychology:

If necessary in your field, give rationale and educate a bit. DON'T do this if your program is accustomed to qualitative research, as you will bore them to tears. The 10th time one reads about Guba and Lincoln's parallel criteria they will want to cry. If using critical or feminist or other ideological theory, describe authenticity criteria and how you will accomplish them.

Briefly summarize components of rigor that you have already described (self-reflective journal, multiple data sources, immersion in the data, peer research team, etc.).

One final take on criteria for judging qualitative research comes from the United Kingdom. The list below reflects some of the thinking that has emerged as the new century is upon us.

- Owning one's own perspective, and reflecting on subjectivity and bias
- Producing coherent connection between theory and method
- Focusing on meaning
- Accounting for, and being sensitive to, context
- Open-ended stance on data collection and analysis
- Collection of, and in-depth engagement with, "rich" data
- Balancing description of data with interpretation of data
- Offering transparent analysis (e.g., grounded in example)
- Offering plausible/credible/meaningful (to reader or others) analysis
- Offering sense of what is distinct within account of what is shared
- Drawing out "resonant"/accessible conclusions (Larkin, 2002)

It is clear that criteria in the 21st century are not one-dimensional. Patton (2002) has suggested different criteria depending on the type of qualitative research being conducted. He suggested that a traditional, scientific type of qualitative research would involve the expected ideas of objectivity, rigor, generalizability, and triangulation. On the other hand, a study that used social constructivism would look at trustworthiness, reflexivity, particularity, subjectivity, and multiple perspectives, and a study based on critical change would identify the nature of injustice and inequality and issues of power and of taking action. Despite the diversity of views on the feasibility or desirability of criteria, some believe that several criteria need to be developed. However, it is clear that more discussion and debate should be conducted.

2008 and Beyond

At this point, I caution you to be careful as you review criteria for judging qualitative research. Several viewpoints are in play. One group contends that we need to return to research that is more scientific, but I believe that is not necessarily the majority viewpoint. Others see the field as still in a state of flux. Freeman, deMarrais, Preissle, Roulston, and St. Pierre (2007) laid out their interpretation of the problem. Savall, Zardet, Bonnet, and Peron (2008) talked about the emergence of implicit criteria. The climate of the world of educational research is such that there is increased accountability and standardization and control. The field has become more politicized than it once was. Savall et al's premise premise, like some other voices, is that it is not possible, nor is it desirable, to reach any kind of consensus about what standards should be adopted. Rather, they recommend a continued conversation. They cite the political movement across the United States related to the NCLB initiative and the emphasis on "mandating scientific method into law" as the reason for this discussion (p. 25). They are against this movement because they believe that "top-down efforts such as these to legislate scientific practice and mandate research design threaten to harden the boundaries of what counts as science, to devalue many qualitative research endeavors, and to limit creative research practice of all kinds" (p. 25).

D. Cohen and Crabtree (2008) reviewed published journal articles discussing criteria for rigorous research. They report seven criteria that emerged from their research: (1) conducting ethical research, (2) the importance of the research, (3) clarity and coherence of the final report, (4) appropriate and rigorous methods, (5) reflexivity and researcher bias, (6) importance of establishing credibility, and (7) importance of verification or reliability. But they point to the difficulties with using these criteria for all types of qualitative research: The assumptions underlying qualitative research—whether explicit or implicit—influence the manner in which the research is conducted and reported. As I have argued throughout this book, they conclude that the field is not unified and that reviewers of journals often embrace a kind of generic criteria. Although they review articles in the health field, the points they make are applicable to education.

Paulus, Woodside, and Ziegler (2008) explored what happens to their assumptions about qualitative research when they engage in a dialogic collaborative process:

> Assumptions about research are pervasive, and the need for qualitative research to compete with or position itself in relation to the positivist paradigm remains implicit and all too often unacknowledged. Collaborative research, as we have experienced it, addresses the concern that qualitative research methods need to be more transparent and public. The transparency begins with the researchers themselves, because they first must make the process visible to themselves through dialogue and writing. Through our collaborative process we have demonstrated how dialogue and writing blend to become inseparable parts of a transparent meaning-making process. (p. 239)

Paulus et al. (2008) addressed an important and novel topic: collaboration among researchers. They commented that the collaborative effort transformed some of their fundamental assumptions about qualitative research. I am struck by their acknowledgment that collaboration led them to see findings as part of an ongoing conversation. I think that by making their assumptions explicit to others, they began to question them and changed as a result.

That the issue of judging, quality, and rigor is very much alive can be seen in the report of a two-day workshop held in Norway in 2007 on the topic "Is there a 'legitimation crisis' in qualitative methods?" The workshop, sponsored by the European Scientific Foundation, was aimed at improving the quality of qualitative research. Speakers and presenters were prominent leaders in the field from Europe and the United Kingdom. I report this because it is clear that the issue of quality is not yet resolved (Weil, 2008).

■ Journals and Editorial Board Criteria

I think you might find it interesting to read about the criteria that qualitative journals use in evaluating studies. You can find a comprehensive list of journals that publish articles of a qualitative nature at http://www.slu.edu/organizations/qrc/QRjournals.html.

Today, some journal editors recognize that determining quality in qualitative research is a topic that continues to need examination. Easterby-Smith, Golden-Biddle, and Locke (2008) argue that methodological pluralism in qualitative research is a complicating factor in determining quality. What I find especially important is that they want to move away from what they refer to as a "list of static criteria."

I e-mailed the editors of several journals that focus on publishing qualitative research studies. All agreed that their journals did not publish specific criteria. Paul Atkinson (editor of *Qualitative Research*) commented that he was not convinced that "codification of such criteria" was particularly helpful (P. Atkinson, personal communication, 2005). Norman Denzin (editor of *Qualitative Inquiry*) suggested that I read the chapter in his book *Performance Ethnography*, on reading and writing interpretation (N. Denzin, personal communication, 2005). Jude Spier from the *International Journal of Qualitative Methodology* sent its editorial review form. The six review criteria included relevance to journal's purpose; quality of information, writing, and documentation; and adherence to ethical standards. Ronald Chenail (editor of *The Qualitative Report*) indicated they did not have a set of written criteria. He referred me to several journal articles with guidelines for publication (R. J. Chenail, personal communication, 2005).

■ Summary

Just as qualitative research encompasses a number of traditions, the criteria for judging and evaluating qualitative research are varied. By the 1980s, criteria began to appear that were patterned after the criteria used for traditional research. Credibility (internal validity), transferability (external validity), dependability (reliability), and confirmability (objectivity) were suggested criteria.

Multiple sets of criteria have recently been presented. Many of those suggestions inform my personal criteria. To what extent does the report contain the researcher's role, convincing arguments, rich detail, and communication? Communication is clarified by attention to the following hallmarks: intriguing opening, engaging style, reflections, integration, rich detail, voices of others, justification, and new meanings.

Guides are simply guides. The reader must choose his or her own criteria, whether self-developed or adopted from others.

GROUP ACTIVITY

Purpose: To compare students' criteria with Lincoln and Guba's four criteria—credibility, transferability, dependability, confirmability.

Activity: Select a qualitative research study that has been published in either *The Qualitative Report* or *FQS,* two journals that are devoted exclusively to qualitative studies and that are in the forefront of thinking in this area. Make sure the study represents a completed piece of research. Form groups of three, then compare group members' personal criteria with Lincoln and Guba's criteria, and decide how they are alike and how they differ. Now, read the study you selected and evaluate to what extent the study does or does not meet the criteria. Comment on what the authors might have done differently.

Evaluation: Gauge how students are able to select specific elements from a study to illustrate the extent to which it is judged "good."

INDIVIDUAL ACTIVITY

Purpose: To learn how to add your voice to what you are doing. By this time, you have begun to think about the field and have some ideas. I would like you to work on developing your own checklist.

Activity: Using the criteria for good qualitative research described in this chapter, react to each criterion and indicate what you like and what you would change. Share with the class, if time permits.

Evaluation: Here, you will begin to see how students are evolving and thinking on their own. You should get a range of comments and hopefully some that you can use as you develop new criteria or adapt what is out there.

Journal entries should continue even if I haven't reminded you to do so.

■ Notes

1. Coauthored by Democrats Representative Miller of California and Senator Kennedy of Massachusetts.
2. Triangulation is a concept coming from trigonometry and geometry. It is the process of finding a distance to a point by calculating the angles to it from two fixed points a known distance apart. It is used in surveying, navigation, and the aiming of weapons.

Chapter 14

Thinking About the Future

FOCUS YOUR READING

■ Qualitative research continues to grow in the field of education; however, some believe that the field should take a more conservative posture.

■ Review committees continue to play an important role as they wield power to approve student projects.

■ The Internet has made huge inroads in so many aspects of communication.

Some set great value on method, while others pride themselves on dispensing with method. To be without method is deplorable, but to depend on method entirely is worse. You must first learn to observe the rules faithfully; afterwards, modify them according to your intelligence and capacity.

—Lu Ch'ai, *The Tao of Painting,* 1701

It is approximately three years since I wrote this chapter about the evolving field of qualitative research. Much of what I wrote in 2005 is still relevant today. I begin the chapter discussing what I perceive to be some trends. Following that, I review aspects of how the Internet has changed the field. After addressing both theory and practice, I revisit the major journals publishing articles of a qualitative nature.

■ Trends

Sustained Growth, Yet Skepticism

Qualitative research has come to mean so much more than it did in the 1980s, when qualitative research in education was limited to a few ethnographers who studied schools and classrooms.

Ethnography itself has expanded and now includes the study of various Internet cultures. A variety of research approaches are used, alone or in combination, to investigate questions. Journals devoted to qualitative methods continue to thrive. Dissertations continue to be written at many universities.[1] Increasingly, journals publish articles that reflect alternative writing styles. Universities have increased their course offerings in qualitative research methods; Nova Southeastern University announced its new Graduate Certificate program in Qualitative Research.

However, there is still confusion about what constitutes "good" qualitative research. That a political agenda is tied to this position is evidenced in much writing. I see articles suggesting that we need to return to the gold standard of research design. Torrance (2008) argued that the international movement for what he calls "research that leads to evidence-based policy" (translation: randomized control trials) has led to a movement toward new standards and guidelines for qualitative research. He is not in favor of this and suggests that qualitative researchers and policy makers engage in dialogue. I don't think policy makers are interested in being educated by researchers, but perhaps I am just a skeptic. Amis and Silk (2008) took the position that we need a plurality of methods (foundational, quasifoundational, and nonfoundational) and space for alternatives.

Ethics review boards at universities have challenged many proposals that are qualitative in nature, and some have put so many obstacles in the way that researchers have been unable to get their proposals approved. Rather than being open to alternative ideas, boards expect researchers to conform to these presumed higher standards. Whiteman (2007) agreed that research ethics boards (or IRBs) have taken a more conservative posture at the same moment that Internet research requires more flexibility and broader ethical definitions. Patterson (2008) told a similar story from the viewpoint of a Canadian.

One alternative that qualitative researchers have adopted is to use a combination of methods, often referred to as a mixed methods approach. Newer books on the topic have placed qualitative research much more in the stance of traditional research styles. The writing is more formal. The analysis of data is more systematic.

Creativity Abounds

I never cease to be amazed at the topics, approaches to answering questions, and especially styles of presentation that I find in journals, Web pages, blogs, dissertations, course syllabi, and other avenues of communication. Just like artists who remain challenged by what they see around them and their inner spirits, so, too, are qualitative researchers continuing to amaze. Researchers have presented their views in the form of plays, artworks, and personal reflections. Of course, at times reality interferes, and student researchers recognize that in order to complete the work at a particular university, they need to abide by the rules. They often look for a sympathetic mentor who will champion their cause.

Blog posting has become very popular. Reshma Anand posted this message on her blog (http://www.reshmaanand.com) in November 2007: "I am just so bored." Well, I don't really know what this has to do with qualitative research, but this young woman from India really intrigued me. Her quote from Einstein says it best: "Everything that can be counted does not necessarily count. Everything that counts cannot necessarily be counted." This is certainly something to think about. John Schostak posted this challenging comment on his blog (http://methodologyblog.imaginativespaces.net/blog) in July 2008: "The issue with data is whether we all see the same thing." If you want to read some of my thinking that is not about qualitative research, you can read my art blog (http://arttalk-maril.blogspot.com) or my blog documenting my Grand Tour of three major art venues in Europe: Art Basel, Documenta 12, and the Venice Biennale (http://thegrandtour07.blogspot.com/).

Did You Know

Can you imagine your life without a computer, the Internet, and e-mail? E-mail actually began in 1965—before the Internet—as a way for users of a mainframe to communicate. Google was founded in 1998. Some 10 short years later, Google and similar search engines enable us to locate information almost immediately.

■ The Internet

I believe that more than anything else to date, the Internet has changed the way we access information, communicate with people, and learn about new things. It has also challenged qualitative researchers to rethink some of their tried and true methods.

Access to Information

Let me address access to information first. Of course, you all know that search engines provide the capability to access print, audio, and visual information in ways that we never dreamed of just a few years ago. Google remains the preeminent search engine. The company is now scanning in texts from major libraries. This is mind-boggling. It could give equal access to information to anyone around the world; all you need is a computer and a connection to the Internet. In the United States, most public libraries provide free Internet access. Wireless access is readily available in airports, coffee houses, and malls. Many new cell phones have Internet access built in. College students in many areas are required to have computers and to be linked to the Internet. Access is almost instantaneous. Many elementary and high schools teach students how to access information online. Many of these students are so well versed that they often teach the teachers and parents. You can post something on the Internet today and it will become available immediately to anyone who locates it. This has revolutionized how information is sent and received worldwide; no longer do we have to wait for material to be written, edited, and published in hard copy.

Wikipedia, the largest online free encyclopedia, has more than 2 1/2 million articles published in English and more than 1/2 million available in many other languages. You can search general terms like "qualitative research" and specific terms like "qualitative data." Because it can be edited by anyone, you need to be very cautious in its use. However, I have found basic information to be readily available and accurate.

But there are several problems associated with this instant access. Web sites are transitory. "Here today and gone tomorrow" may be quite common; some information that you locate today may not be there tomorrow. Other information might be old and never updated. There is no central clearinghouse that maintains what is on the Internet; rather, it is up to the Web site owner to keep files current and accessible. As a user, you must be ever diligent in locating and judging what is there and how useful it is to you.

But I want to offer a word of caution: More information does not necessarily mean good information. In the past, we used to rely on information in journals because a panel of peers reviewed it. So a student might rely on a published journal article because others had reviewed it. This is less true with material online; anyone can publish anything online and it may or may not be reviewed or even suitable. But I would not want to limit information just because one's peers do not review it.

Communication With Everyone

Communication has also changed. Instant messaging, blogs and vlogs, chat rooms, and other devices have facilitated discussions and interchanges among colleagues. Facebook, created in 2004 as a social networking Web site, was founded by a young Harvard student. YouTube, created in 2005 as a video sharing Web site, puts you in touch instantly with others. No longer is the United States the primary force in communication. The art of letter writing is in the dim past for all but the few stalwarts. People post their ideas and wait for others to respond. Sometimes discussions occur among people who would never before have come in contact with each other. And communication is not limited to written words: Pictures are posted, videos are available, audio discussions are presented. Some communication becomes interactive.

As a result of this new kind of communication, I find myself challenged by ideas that I would not ever have encountered previously. I find many people offering comments that would not have had a venue in the past. By opening up communication, the playing field has been leveled. Power issues seem less important. Voices can be heard from those who otherwise were silenced.

New Ideas

Learning about new things has also changed. Online journals demonstrate how the old process of lengthy peer reviews and delayed publication dates can be shortened. An individual can submit a paper, have it reviewed online, and publish it in a very short turnaround time. And as an aside, enormous numbers of trees have been saved, use of storage space in homes and offices is reduced, and information can be organized and accessed on one small flash drive or DVD.

New ideas for doing and promoting qualitative research can also be found. Chenail (2008) described several ways in which YouTube can be used as a qualitative research asset. I had never thought of studying doing laundry in public places; Chenail offers many links to these laundry and other projects. Cynthia Russell offers a TiddlyWiki, a kind of nonlinear personal Web notebook, that deals with the qualitative research field (http://technology-escapades.net/qualitative.htm). Created in 2007, it offers a dynamic and growing resource.

Online focus groups are being conducted, with opportunities for interaction between participants who might never have seen or heard each other before. For example, you can set up your own chat room for free by going to Parachat (http://www.parachat.com), Anexa (http://www.anexa.com), or Talk City (http://www.talkcity.com). You can set up your own Listserv for free by going to Yahoo Groups (http://groups.yahoo.com), Tight Circle (http://www.tightcircle.com), or Topica (http://www.topica.com). These sites I mention are free but do include paid advertising; if you want to avoid that, you can set up a Listserv for a small cost at Listhost (http://www.listhost.com), Sparklist (http://www.sparklist.com), or Lyris (http://www.lyris.net).

Hookway (2008) addressesed issues of using the "blogosphere," or what he calls an online extension of diaries. In particular, he deals with several ethical issues. Online cultures are being studied, and the traditional issues of gaining access and the role of the researcher are only some of the things to consider. Blogs are being posted with ideas about qualitative research and what writers think.

Presentation of research can be only as challenging as the skill of the writer in using the new technology. I have seen writers use pictures and audio, link to other sites on the Web, and take the reader in new directions not possible with traditional writing in journals or term papers. Some universities are now requiring students to post their theses and dissertations online rather than in a traditional format. So what we study and how we study are changing as a result of the new technology.

The voices of all can be heard. No longer is the field dominated by the culture of Western Europe and the United States. Influences from Asia, South America, and Africa are beginning to be felt. Qualitative research in education has reached beyond the purview of departments of educational research and ethnography. Nurses are among the forefront of those voices as I write, but perhaps others will emerge as well.

■ Greater Acceptance by the Field

In 1990, *The Qualitative Report* was launched as a traditional paper journal. By 1994, it went online and reached a worldwide audience. According to Chenail, St. George, and Wulff (2004), there has been a much greater acceptance of qualitative research in a variety of disciplines. In fact, this journal has even shifted its approach from peer review to a process in which authors are aided in developing their research into acceptable articles. I recently completed this type of review and found myself contemplating the value of what the authors had to say rather than being critical of what they omitted. This process is facilitated, in part, by the availability of technologies that permit multiple reviewers to comment directly on the manuscript.

I see traditional disciplines such as psychology, sociology, family studies, nursing, and education being more accepting of qualitative research than in the past. More journals offer opportunities for publishing and have modified or revised criteria for submissions. More universities offer courses in qualitative research than ever before. More publishers are publishing books directly related to qualitative research. I anticipate that this trend will continue as researchers and readers see the benefits and rewards of conducting qualitative research.

■ About Theory

Many qualitative researchers believe that holding a particular theory about something before we gather data is severely limiting. Thomas Jefferson reminds us that "the moment a person forms a theory, his imagination sees in every object only the traits which favor that theory."

You might be interested in some of what I learned about linking theory and practice. The Jones and Barlett Nursing Theory Art Gallery (http://nursing.jbpub.com/sitzman/artGallery.cfm) exhibits students' artistic impressions of nursing theory. In this series, students create art works to illustrate a particular theory.

As you know by now, I have a very strong interest in art. I believe many artists operate without a clear theory. Here is some evidence to support this idea. Brancusi says, "Theories are patterns without value. What counts is action." Kazantzakis supports this notion: "The ultimate most holy form of theory is action." Felix Cohen says, "Generally the theories we believe we call facts, and the facts we disbelieve we call theories" (The Painter's Keys, n.d.).

For a very long time, I have viewed theory and practice as separate. It seems as though university people consider theoretical issues, and out in the field, the focus is on practice. Many of the articles I read continue to stress practice and pay little attention to theory. I don't mean to suggest that we can or should have practice devoid of theory, but I do not see much evidence that theoretical issues regarding practice are evident in published research. How to bridge the gap? I am not really sure.

■ About Practice

In terms of practice, I see some compromise. A number of researchers have adopted a mixed methods approach rather than choosing either qualitative or quantitative approaches exclusively. Although supposedly both approaches are treated evenly, I often find that qualitative research takes a back seat to quantitative research. I believe that those interested in mixed methods focus on the means of gathering data and do not always address different assumptions.

Increasingly, I see researchers taking risks with new methods of gathering and analyzing data. Fueled in part by the Internet, researchers find themselves in chat rooms, using blogs, and looking for alternative ways to display data and make meaning from what they have found.

As the field develops, greater opportunities are available for researchers to experiment with alternative ways of gathering and presenting information. Live performances at national conferences, Web-based information, and the use of visual representations will no doubt become more common.

New technologies, demands on students, and increased costs have led to an increase in online teaching. I have taught online classes in qualitative research for several years. For a transcript from one section of an online class, see the resource "Teaching Qualitative Research Online," which can be found at www.sagepub.com/lichtman2estudy.

■ Journals With a Qualitative Focus

I want to call your attention to the following journals.

International Journal of Qualitative Studies in Education (QSE). ISSN 0951–8398. Publisher: Taylor & Francis, Ltd. First volume: 1988. This is the first journal that was devoted to articles of a qualitative nature and the only one that targets education. Originally four issues annually, but now six issues annually. Editors: James Scheurich and M. Carolyn Clark, Texas A&M University. Its editorial policy states that the purpose is to enhance the practice and theory of qualitative research in education. Beginning with Volume 10 (1997), the Table of Contents is available online. Topics in 2008 include an autoethnographic study of race, a special issue on emergent methodologies that include storytelling, writing as blurred reflection, and painting. You might find the qualitative study of children's conceptualization of their school especially interesting. The authors are international. My impression is that this journal publishes fairly nontraditional articles on a wide range of topics.

Qualitative Research. ISSN 1468–7941. Publisher: Sage Publications. First volume: 2001. Three issues annually. Editor: Paul Atkinson. Their editorial statement in the first issue sets the tone of their endeavor: "As qualitative research methods achieve ever-wider currency in the social and cultural disciplines, we need constantly to apply a critical and reflective gaze. We cannot afford to let qualitative research become a set of taken-for-granted precepts and procedures. Equally, we should not be so seduced by our collective success or by the radical chic of new strategies of social research as to neglect the need for methodological rigour. We see this new journal as a forum where innovations will be explored and celebrated, without in any sense deserting the more established values and disciplines" (p. 5). Their intention is to encourage debate between the orthodox (the familiar) and the heterodox (the innovative). Topics in 2008 are quite disparate. A special issue is devoted to narrative analysis. Other topics for the year range from performance art to the process of sample recruitment.

Qualitative Inquiry. ISSN 1077–8004. Publisher: Sage Publications. First volume: 1995. Six issues annually. Editor: Norman Denzin. This journal is "the first interdisciplinary, international journal to provide a forum for qualitative methodology and related issues in the human sciences" (p. 3). The editors make several important points that indicate their points of view. They describe qualitative research as an umbrella term; they acknowledge the political nature of the field; and they state explicitly that the researcher is not a neutral observer. Topics in 2008 include ethics and ethics boards (academic freedom and research ethics boards, disciplinary power and IRBs, and a review of narrative ethics) and issues about race (experiences of doctoral students of color, writing against racism, straight and white). Almost all the articles are by single authors. Many have titles that reflect an openness with language, for example, "Reflections on the Realization That I Have Been Holding My Breath" or "At the Eye of the Storm: An Academic('s) Experience of Moral Panic."

The Qualitative Report. ISSN 1052–0147. Publisher: Nova Southeastern University. First volume: 1990. Four issues annually. Free online since 1994. Editors: Ron Chenail, Sally St. George, and Dan Wulff. The editorial in the first issue indicates that this is a "narrative of qualitative and critical inquiry" that rejects "absolute, finality, and authority and embraces ambiguities, uncertainties, and diversities of human experience." Topics in 2008 cover a wide range. You can read about physical activity in intermediate schools relating to school culture and athletic elitism. Or you might be interested in a case study of rewards of qualitative research in assessment. Of special interest might be the qualitative paper on teachers who left the teaching profession. You might find it interesting to read a book review of the first edition of this book as a dialogue between a student and her professor (Dawson & St. George, 2008).

Forum Qualitative Social Research. ISSN: 1438–5627. Publisher: Freie Universität Berlin. First volume: 1999. Editor: Katja Mruck. Peer-reviewed multilingual online journal. Aim is to promote discussion and cooperation among researchers from different countries and different disciplines. Most issues are special topics. Topics in 2008 include differences in interviewing elites and experts, the role of the researcher in the narration of life, and a special issue devoted to performative social science. This journal has a new "look" that makes it easier to read and access. I find it especially helpful for a global perspective and with regard to thoughtful methodological issues.

International Journal of Qualitative Methods. ISSN: 16094069. Publisher: International Institute for Qualitative Methodology at the University of Alberta, Canada. First issue: 2002. Four issues annually. Founding Editor: Janice Morse. Aim is to heighten the awareness of qualitative research; to advance the development of qualitative methods in varying fields of study; and to help disseminate knowledge to the broadest possible community of academics, students, and professionals who undertake scholarly research. By keeping the journal free, they hope to reach an audience who, for whatever reason, do not read traditional, subscription-based journals. Some of the topics for 2008 include lessons learned from children about research, methodological issues about writing an ethnography, case studies and qualitative interviewing, and an article about research ethics and cyberspace. This journal is very open to feminist topics.

Qualitative Research in Psychology. ISSN: 1478–0887. Publisher: Taylor and Francis, UK. First issue: 2004. Editor: David Giles. This journal has recently changed publishers and can only be accessed with a subscription.

Of course, many other journals publish articles either about qualitative research or of a qualitative research nature. You will find many articles that address topics of education in nursing journals, health journals, business journals, and others as well.

Perhaps the most challenging, yet frustrating, part of writing this book has been to keep on top of what is out there. When I began teaching qualitative courses in the early 1990s, I could not find an appropriate book to use; my students used articles I located and put into a study packet. Few of my colleagues were talking about qualitative research, and even fewer were willing to encourage students to embark on such an endeavor. Education faculty in many universities were trained in traditional modes of experimental research and were often reluctant, or too busy, to learn alternative ways of doing research. For some, it meant a challenge to their own basic tenets of what is good and right. For others, qualitative research methods were the ramblings of those who were "touchy-feely" and not real scientists. This has now changed. Qualitative research is a discipline that has reached its legitimate place in the research hierarchy. It is no longer second best. It no longer needs apologists. It no longer is a stepchild.

I stay current by belonging to discussion groups and chat rooms online, by reading online journals, by being on the editorial boards of two prestigious online journals, and by using search engines to see what else is out there.

■ For the Future

In an ideal world, qualitative research will continue to grow and challenge those who find it exciting. Questions will be posed and insight gained that takes us in directions not yet conceived. Legitimacy and acceptance by the larger scientific community and scholars worldwide will not lead to conservatism and complacency. The voices of all who want to study and those from whom we gain knowledge and understanding will be heard.

You, as students, are on the forefront of this movement. I know some of you will make meaningful contributions in your chosen fields. Perhaps you may even make contributions to how we learn about others and ourselves.

■ Note

1. Bloomberg and Volpe (2008) have just published a guide to completing your qualitative dissertation. Meloy's 1993 book on the same topic was revised in 2001.

Glossary

Action research: A type of qualitative research that focuses on a solution to a specific local problem.

Anthropology: The systematic study of cultures and groups of people.

Axiology: A branch of philosophy related to values and judgments. See also Epistemology, Ontology.

Bias: In quantitative research, a researcher attempts to minimize bias by remaining objective and outside the system. In qualitative research, researcher bias and subjectivity are accepted and inevitable—it is not seen as negative.

Bracketing: A process used by phenomenologists to identify the researcher's preconceived beliefs.

Case study: A type of qualitative research focusing on the study of a single individual or organization.

Codes: Terms supplied by the researcher to identify chunks of the data.

Coding: A first step in data analysis in which text is sorted and organized to identify recurrent themes and concepts.

Concept: In qualitative data analysis, an idea that builds on coding and categorizing of raw data. See also Themes.

Constant-comparative method: A technique of data analysis associated with grounded theory.

Constructivism: A theory or philosophical doctrine that says that knowledge is constructed by the researcher and is affected by the context. It is a belief in multiple truths and a belief that the interaction of the researcher with what is being studied affects the determination of truth. It was originally associated with Kant, and more recently associated with Lincoln, Guba, and Denzin.

Content analysis: A technique of data analysis in which detailed review of text content leads to themes.

Coresearcher: An individual who provides information about the research and sometimes participates in analysis of data. See also Informant, Participant.

Critical theory: A philosophical movement that began in 1923 and was associated with the Institute of Social Research, part of the Frankfurt School. It combined psychoanalysis and Marxism. Prior to World War II, it was connected with Columbia University and subsequently moved to California.

Culture: Attitudes and behaviors associated with a particular social group or organization.

Deductive reasoning: A type of reasoning that moves from the general to the specific or from the abstract to the concrete. It is associated with quantitative research. See also Inductive reasoning.

Discourse analysis: A technique of data analysis dealing with naturally occurring written discourse.

Emic perspective: A term associated with ethnography to refer to an insider's view. See also Etic perspective.

EndNote: Computer software published by Thomson with three purposes: online search tool, reference and image database, and bibliography and manuscript maker.

Epistemology: A branch of philosophy dealing with the theory of knowledge, the nature of knowledge, or how we know what we know. See also Axiology, Ontology.

Ethnography: A qualitative research approach emanating from anthropology and focusing on the study of the culture of groups.

Ethnomethodology: The study of how group members make sense of their surroundings. See also Ethnography.

Etic perspective: A term associated with ethnography to refer to an outsider's view. See also Emic perspective.

Feminist theory: A philosophical movement related to postmodernism that emphasizes power disparities and inequalities between the genders. Some feminists see bias in both quantitative and qualitative research approaches.

Field methods: The procedures used to collect and analyze data.

Field notes: Notes, often informal, made by a researcher during and after observations or visits to a setting. See also Memos, Researcher journal.

Focus group interviewing: A technique of data collection that relies on group interaction and discussion.

Foundationalist: A synonym for traditional experimental research.

Generic approach: An approach to qualitative research that does not rely on any particular tradition but utilizes elements of many.

Grounded theory: A qualitative research approach from which theories may emerge. It emphasizes theoretical sampling and uses open, axial, and selective coding. It is associated with Strauss, Glaser, and Corbin.

Hermeneutics: A technique or discipline of data analysis involving detailed analysis of transcripts and textual material. It is associated with phenomenology.

Hypothesis: A formal statement about the relationship between variables. It is commonly associated with quantitative research.

In-depth interview: A technique of data collection that relies on long and probing questions and does not use formal questionnaires. It is also called a depth interview.

Inductive reasoning: A type of reasoning that moves from the specific to the general or from the concrete to the abstract It is associated with qualitative research. See also Deductive reasoning.

Informant: An individual who provides information relative to the research. See also Coresearcher, Participant.

Interpretivism: A theory or philosophical doctrine that emphasizes analyzing meanings people confer on their own actions.

Literature review: An integration and interpretation of research on one's topic of interest.

Memos: Comments and notes written by the researcher, usually after reading a transcript. It may be a separate document or interspersed in the transcript.

Metaphor: A figure of speech in which a word or phrase that means one thing is applied to another in order to suggest an analogy. It is often used in qualitative writing to vividly describe ideas.

Methodology: The various techniques, methods, and procedures used in conducting research.

Mixed methods: A type of research that combines both quantitative and qualitative designs.

Naturalistic inquiry: A type of qualitative research or a method of studying phenomena as they exist in the world.

NVivo: A powerful computer software program available from QSR. Useful for storing, organizing, and managing complex qualitative data.

Objectivity: A goal of quantitative research in which a researcher attempts to remain outside the system.

Observation: A technique of data collection in which the researcher observes the interaction of individuals in natural settings.

Online interviewing: A technique of data collection in which the researcher "talks" to informants online. Data may be collected from a pre-identified informant or from one who appears by chance. It can include individuals or groups in chat rooms or Listservs.

Ontology: A branch of metaphysics concerned with the nature of reality. See also Axiology, Epistemology.

Paradigm: A way of seeing the world. The term was popularized by Thomas Kuhn. It is also a set of interrelated assumptions about the world that provides a philosophical and conceptual framework.

Participant: An individual who provides information for the research. See also Coresearcher, Informant.

Participant observer: The role a researcher takes when observing a group. Researchers are either already part of the group being studied or become part of the group.

Phenomenology: A type of qualitative research with philosophical roots that emphasizes the study of lived experiences.

Positivism: A theory or philosophical doctrine in which science deals only with observable entities and objective reality. It involves belief in one truth and was originally associated with Comte.

Postmodernism: A philosophical movement popularized in the 1990s. Postmodernists question institutional authority and seek greater power.

Postpositivism: A philosophical doctrine that acknowledges the shortcomings of positivism but strives to attain objective reality. It includes belief in the approximation of one truth.

Poststructuralism: Poststructuralists (associated with Derrida) react to structuralism and suggest that meaning is constantly in motion and resistant to closure. These researchers define the present cultural climate and differentiate it from positivism.

Qualitative interviewing: A technique of data collection that ranges from semi-structured to unstructured formats. Interviewing is seen as a conversation in which an informant and a researcher interact so that the informant's thoughts are revealed and interpreted by a researcher.

Quantitative research: A term describing traditional methods of hypothesis testing, determining cause and effect, and generalizing.

Queer theory: Grew out of gay/lesbian studies of the 1980s. Suggests that sexual and gender identity are socially constructed. Deals with understanding sexuality in terms of shifting boundaries, ambivalences, and cultural constructions.

Random sample: A sample drawn from a population in such a way that each population element has a chance of being selected. Useful for generalizing.

Reflexivity: A researcher's capacity to reflect on his or her own values both during and after the research.

Research: A systematic investigation of phenomena.

Research approach: A design or plan to conduct research, for example, using case study, phenomenology, or grounded theory.

Researcher journal: A researcher's written thoughts during the life of a project. Journals tend to be self-reflexive, as distinguished from field notes or memos, which are usually about the data. See also Field notes, Memos.

Scientific method: A systematic way of testing hypotheses and determining cause and effect. It is presumed to be objective, but some critics question its assumptions.

Self-reflection: Originally associated with phenomenology, self-reflection is now seen as awareness of self and one's influence on the research process as well as the influence of the process on the self.

Snowball sampling: A technique for identifying informants in which the original group of informants is asked to identify additional individuals with similar characteristics. Lillian Rubin suggests that you ask informants to identify acquaintances rather than close friends.

Sociology: The study of social lives and behaviors.

Subject: An individual who is studied in an experiment. The term is associated with quantitative research; *participant, informant,* or *coresearcher* replaces this term in qualitative research.

Symbolic interactionism: A sociological term for the examination of how individuals and groups interact as process of symbolic communications.

Themes: Central issues or concepts that a researcher identifies based on coding original data. Most research data can be organized in five or six themes. See also Concept.

Theory: A substantiated explanation of some aspect of the world. A proposed explanation of a phenomenon. Not a fact, but an attempt to explain facts.

Thick description: Used by ethnographers to emphasize providing a detailed description of a culture. A term associated with Clifford Geertz.

Triangulation: The use of several methods or strategies to gather data with the purpose of increasing the credibility of findings or of obtaining a more substantive view of reality.

Unobtrusive observer: A type of observation in which the observer is not known to those being studied.

Voice: A term related to privileged position and self-disclosure. With self-disclosure comes potential vulnerability of the researcher.

References

Adkins, L. (2004). Passing on feminism: From consciousness to reflexivity. *European Journal of Women's Studies, 11*(4), 427–444.

Agar, M. (1973). *Ripping and running: A formal ethnography of urban heroin addicts.* New York: Seminar Press.

Aggleton, P. (1987). *Rebels without a cause: Middle class youth and the transition from school to work.* London: Falmer Press.

Ahern, K. (1999). Ten tips for reflexive bracketing. *Qualitative Health Research, 9,* 407–411.

Aldridge, M. (1995). Scholarly practice—ethnographic film and anthropology. Beyond ethnographic film: Hypermedia and scholarship. *Visual Anthropology, 7*(3), 233–235.

American Educational Research Association. (2005). *Ethical standards.* Retrieved September 5, 2008, from http://www.aera.net/aboutaera/?id=222

American Psychological Association. (2001). *Publication manual of the American Psychological Association* (5th ed.). Washington, DC: Author.

Amir, D. (2005). The use of "first person" writing style in academic writing. An open letter to journals, reviewers, and readers. *Voices: A World Forum for Music Therapy.* Retrieved November 1, 2008, from http://www.voices.no/columnist/colamir140305.html

Amis, J., & Silk, M. (2008). The philosophy and politics of quality in qualitative organizational research. *Organizational Research Methods, 11,* 456–480.

Anand, R. (2007). *The qualitative research blog.* Retrieved December 8, 2008, from http://www.reshmaanand.com/.

Aparicio, F. R. (1999). Through my lens: A video project about women of color faculty at the University of Michigan. *Feminist Studies, 25*(1), 119–130.

Armstrong, G. (1998). *Football hooligans: Knowing the score.* New York: Berg.

Arvay, M. (1998). Struggling with re-presentation, voice and self in narrative research. In J. Anderson & C. Miller (Eds.), *Connections.* Victoria, British Columbia, Canada: University of Victoria.

Atkinson, R., & Flint, J. (2001). *Accessing hidden and hard-to-reach populations: Snowball research strategies.* Retrieved November 1, 2008, from http://www.soc.surrey.ac.uk/sru/SRU33.html

Bagley, C. (2008). Educational ethnography as performance art: Towards a sensuous feeling and knowing. *Qualitative Research, 8*(1), 53–72.

Bailey, J. (2008). First steps in qualitative data analysis: Transcribing. *Family Practice, 25*(2), 127–131.

Ball, D., & Forzani, F. (2007). What makes educational research "educational"? *Educational Researcher, 36*(9), 529–540.

Barbour, R., & Barbour, M. (2002). Evaluating and synthesizing qualitative research: The need to develop a distinctive approach. *Journal of Evaluation in Clinical Practice, 9*(2), 176–186.

Barnacle, R. (2001). *Phenomenology and education research.* Paper presented at the Australian Association for Research in Education, Fremantle, Australia.

Barrett, S. (1996). *Anthropology: A student's guide to theory and method.* Toronto: University of Toronto Press.

Basit, T. (2003, Summer). Manual or electronic? The role of coding in qualitative data analysis. *Educational Researcher, 45*(2), 143–154.

Bassett, R., Beagan, B., Ristovski-Slijepcevic, S., & Chapman, G. (2008). Tough teens: The methodological challenges of interviewing teenagers as research participants. *Journal of Adolescent Research, 23*(2), 119–131.

Baumgartner, L. (2000). *Narrative analysis: Uncovering the truth of stories.* Adult Education Research Conference Proceedings, Vancouver, British Columbia, Canada. Retrieved November 21, 2005, from http://www.edst.educ.ubc.ca/aerc/2000/baumgartnerl-web.htm

Becker, H. (1976). *Boys in white: Student culture in medical school.* New Brunswick, NJ: Transaction Books.

Behar, R. (1996). *The vulnerable observer: Anthropology that breaks your heart.* Boston: Beacon Press.

Bell, R. (1992). *Impure science: Fraud, compromise, and political influence in scientific research.* Somerset, NJ: John Wiley & Sons.

Belousov, K., Horlick-Jones, T., Bloor, M., Gilinskiy, Y., Golbert, V., Kostikovsky, Y., et al. (2007). Any port in a storm: Fieldwork difficulties in dangerous and crisis-ridden settings. *Qualitative Research, 7*(2), 155–175.

Bennett, C. (2002). Enhancing ethnic diversity at a Big Ten university through project TEAM: A case study in teacher education. *Educational Researcher, 31*(2), 21–29.

Berger, R. (2004). Pushing forward: Disability, basketball, and me. *Qualitative Inquiry, 10*(5), 794–810.

Bergman, M. (2005). *Mixed methods: Keynote abstract.* Retrieved November 28, 2005, from http://www.health-homerton.ac.uk/research/files/ka_03.pdf

Bertaux, D. (1981). *Biography and society: The life history approach in the social sciences.* Beverly Hills, CA: Sage.

Bertaux, D., & Delacroix, C. (2000). Case histories of families and social processes. In P. Chamberlayne, J. Bornat, & T. Wengraf (Eds.), *The turn to biographical methods in social sciences: Comparative issues and examples* (pp. 71–89). London: Routledge.

Bissell, M. (2001). 1938: B. F. Skinner publishes *The behavior of organisms: An experimental analysis.* In D. Schugurensky (Ed.), *History of education: Selected moments of the 20th century.* Retrieved November 2, 2008, from http://www.oise.utoronto.ca/research/edu20/moments/1938skinner.html

Bloomberg, L., & Volpe, M. (2008). *Completing your qualitative dissertation: A roadmap from beginning to end.* Thousand Oaks, CA. Sage.

Blumenfeld-Jones, D. S. (1995). Dance as a mode of research representation. *Qualitative Inquiry, 1*(4), 391–401.

Blumer, H. (1969). *Symbolic interactionism: Perspective and method.* Englewood Cliffs, NJ: Prentice Hall.

Bochner, A., & Ellis, C. (Eds.). (2002). *Ethnographically speaking: Autoethnography, literature, and aesthetics.* Walnut Creek, CA: AltaMira Press.

Bodovski, K., & Farkas, G. (2007). Do instructional practices contribute to inequality in achievement? The case of mathematics instruction in kindergarten. *Journal of Early Childhood Research, 5*(3), 301–322.

Boeree, G. (1998). *Qualitative methods.* Retrieved November 1, 2008, from http://www.ship.edu/~cgboeree/qualmethone.html

Bogdan, R., & Biklen, S. (1992). *Qualitative research for education: An introduction to theory and method.* Boston: Allyn & Bacon.

Boman, J., & Jevne, R. (2000). Ethical evaluation in qualitative research. *Qualitative Health Research, 10,* 547–554.

Bordwell, D., & Thompson, K. (2004). *Film art: An introduction.* New York: McGraw-Hill.

Bottorff, J. (2003). *Workshop on qualitative research.* Retrieved November 1, 2008, from http://www.vchri.ca/i/presentations/QualitativeResearch/

Boudreau, D. (2002). *The drama of data.* Retrieved November 2, 2008, from http://researchmag.asu.edu/stories/ethnotheatre.html

Bowen, G. (2008). Naturalistic inquiry and the saturation concept: A research note. *Qualitative Research, 8*(1), 137–152.

Brayton, J. (1997). *What makes feminist research feminist? The structure of feminist research within the social sciences.* Retrieved November 2, 2008, from http://unb.ca/PAR-L/win/feminmethod.htm

Breuer, F., Mruck, K., & Roth, W.-M. (2002, September). Subjectivity and reflexivity: An introduction [10 paragraphs]. *Forum Qualitative Sozialforschung/Forum: Qualitative Social Research, 3*(3). Retrieved July 4, 2004, from http://www.qualitative-research.net/fqs-texte/3-02/3-02hrsg-e.htm

Breuer, F., & Roth, W.-M. (2003, May). Subjectivity and reflexivity in the social sciences: Epistemic windows and methodical consequences [30 paragraphs]. *Forum Qualitative Sozialforschung/Forum: Qualitative Social Research, 4*(2). Retrieved November 3, 2005, from http://www.qualitative-research.net/fqs-texte/2-03/2-03intro-3-e.htm.

Brown, B., & Bell, M. (n.d.). *Social interaction in "there."* Retrieved September 1, 2008, from http://www.equator.ac.uk/var/uploads/Brown-There.pdf

Brown, L., & Holloway, I. (2008). The adjustment journey of international postgraduate students at an English university: An ethnographic study. *Journal of Research in International Education, 7*(2), 232–249.

Brown, S., Stevens, R., Troino, P., & Schneider, M. (2002). Exploring complex phenomena: Grounded theory in student affairs research. *Journal of College Student Development, 43*(2), 1–11.

Bryman, A. (2006). Integrating quantitative and qualitative research: How is it done? *Qualitative Research, 6*(1), 97–113.

Bryman, A., & Burgess, R. G. (1994). Reflections on qualitative data analysis. In A. Bryman & R. G. Burgess (Eds.), *Analysing qualitative data* (pp. 216–226). London: Routledge.

Bulmer, M. (1984). *The Chicago school of sociology: Institutionalization, diversity, and the rise of sociological research.* Chicago: University of Chicago Press.

Bunch, G., & Panayotova, D. (2008). Latinos, language minority students, and the construction of ESL: Language testing and placement from high school to community college. *Journal of Hispanic Higher Education, 7*(1), 6–30.

Butera, K. (2006). Manhunt. *Qualitative Inquiry, 12*(6), 1262–1282.

Butler, S. (2008). Performance, art and ethnography [39 paragraphs] *Forum Qualitative Social Research, 9*(2), Art 34. Retrieved August 30, 2008, from http://nbn-resolving.de/urn:nbn:de:0114-fqs0802346

Butler-Kisber, L. (2002). Artful portrayals in qualitative research: The road to found poetry and beyond. *The Alberta Journal of Educational Research, XLVIII*(3), 229–239.

Byers, D. (2003). *Intentionality and transcendence: Closure and openness in Husserl's phenomenology.* Madison: University of Wisconsin Press.

Byrne, M. (1998). *Hermeneutics 101.* Paper presented at the QUIG98, Athens, GA. Retrieved November 2, 2008, from http://www.coe.uga.edu/quig/byrne.html

Caelli, K., Ray, L., & Mill, J. (2003). "Clear as mud": Toward greater clarity in generic qualitative research. *International Journal of Qualitative Methods, 2*(2). Retrieved November 1, 2008, from http://www.ualberta.ca/~iiqm/backissues/2_2/html/caellietal.htm

Camic, P., Rhodes, J., & Yardley, L. (Eds.). (2003). *Qualitative research in psychology: Expanding perspectives in methodology and design.* Washington, DC: American Psychological Association.

Campbell, A. (1984). *The girls in the gang: A report from New York City.* Oxford, UK: Clarendon Press.

Campbell, B. (n.d.). *Phenomenology as research method.* Retrieved November 1, 2008, from http://www.staff.vu.edu.au/syed/alrnnv/papers/bev.html

Campbell, D., & Stanley, J. (1963). *Experimental and quasi-experimental designs for research.* Boston: Houghton Mifflin.

Campbell, P., & Sanders, J. (2002). Challenging the system: Assumptions and data behind the push for single-sex schooling. In A. Datnow & L. Hubbard (Eds.), *Gender in policy and practice: Perspectives on single-sex and coeducational schooling* (pp. 31–46). New York: Routledge.

Cannella, G. S. (2004). Regulatory power: Can a feminist poststructuralist engage in research oversight? *Qualitative Inquiry, 10*(2), 235–245.

Cannella, G. S., & Lincoln, Y. S. (2007). Predatory vs. dialogic ethics: Constructing an illusion or ethical practice as the core of research methods. *Qualitative Inquiry, 13*(3), 315–335.

Caulley, D. (2008). Making qualitative research reports less boring: The techniques of writing creative nonfiction. *Qualitative Inquiry, 14*(3), 424–449.

Chamberlayne, P., Bornat, J., & Wengraf, T. (Eds.). (2000). *The turn to biographical methods in social science: Comparative issues and examples.* London: Routledge.

Chapter II: Investigations of the objectives of the curriculum. (1931, January). *Review of Educational Research, 1*(1), 9–21.

Chase, S. E. (2005). Narrative inquiry: Multiple lenses, approaches, voices. In N. K. Denzin & Y. S. Lincoln (Eds.), *Handbook of qualitative research* (pp. 651–679). Thousand Oaks, CA: Sage.

Cheek, J. (2004). At the margins? Discourse analysis and qualitative research. *Qualitative Health Research, 14*(8), 1140–1150.

Chenail, R. (1995, December). Presenting qualitative data. *The Qualitative Report, 2*(3). Retrieved November 21, 2005, from http://www.nova.edu/ssss/QR/QR2–3/presenting.html

Chenail, R., St. George, S., & Wulff, D. (2004). A new beginning. Editorial statement. *The Qualitative Report.* Retrieved November 27, 2005, from http://www.nova.edu/ssss/QR/Editorial/editstm.html

Chenail, R. J. (2008). YouTube as a qualitative research asset: Reviewing user generated videos as learning resources. *The Weekly Qualitative Report, 1*(4), 18–24. Retrieved November 1, 2008, from http://www.nova.edu/ssss/QR/WQR/youtube.pdf

Childers, S. (2008). Methodology, praxis, and autoethnography: A review of *Getting lost. Educational Research, 37,* 298–301.

Choudhuri, D., Glauser, A., & Peregoy, J. (2004). Guidelines for writing a qualitative manuscript for the *Journal of Counseling and Development. Journal of Counseling and Development, 82*(4), 443–446.

Clark, M. (2008). Blog on sociological research methods. Retrieved August 30, 2008, from http://blog.lib.umn.edu/clar0514/class/2008/08/qualitative_and_quantitative_a.html

Clayton, P. (1997). Philosophy of science: What one needs to know. *Zygon: Journal of Religion and Science, 32*(1), 95–105.

Clinchy, B. (n.d.). *Tales told out of school: Women's reflections on their undergraduate experience.* Retrieved November 1, 2008, from http://www.podnetwork.org/publications/essayseries.htm

Cocks, A. (2008). Researching the lives of disabled children: The process of participant observation in seeking inclusivity. *Qualitative Social Work, 7*(2), 163–180.

Coffey, A., & Atkinson, P. (1996). *Making sense of qualitative data: Complementary research strategies.* Thousand Oaks, CA: Sage.

Cohen, D., & Crabtree, B. (2008). Evaluative criteria for qualitative research in health care: Controversies and recommendations. *Annals of Family Medicine, 6*(4), 331–339.

Cohen, R. (2007, November 18). Bad grad, good grad. *New York Times.* Retrieved December 9, 2008, from http://www.nytimes.com/2007/11/18/magazine/18wwln-ethicist-t.html

Colyar, J. (2008). Becoming writing, becoming writers. *Qualitative Inquiry.* Retrieved from http://qix.sagepub.com/cgi/content/abstract/1077800408318280v1

Condell, S. (2008). Writing fieldnotes in an ethnographic study of peers—collaborative experiences from the field. *Journal of Research in Nursing, 13*(4), 325–335.

Connolly, M. (2003). Qualitative analysis: A teaching tool for social work research. *Qualitative Social Work, 2*(1), 103–112.

Constas, M. (2007). Reshaping the methodological identity of education research: Early signs of the impact of federal policy. *Evaluation Research, 31,* 391–400.

Conteh, J. (2003). *Succeeding in diversity: Culture, language and learning in primary classrooms.* Stoke-on-Trent, UK: Trentham Books.

Cook, T. D., & Campbell, D. (1979). *Quasi-experimentation: Design and analysis issues for field settings.* Boston: Houghton Mifflin.

Correll, S. (1995). The ethnography of an electronic bar: The lesbian café. *Journal of Contemporary Ethnography, 24*(3), 270–298.

Corti, L. (2007). Re-using archived qualitative data—where, how, why? *Archival Science, 7*(1), 37–54.

Coyne, I., & Cowley, S. (2006). Using grounded theory to research parent participation. *Journal of Research in Nursing, 11,* 501–515.

Crabtree, B., & Miller, W. (Eds.). (1992). *Doing qualitative research.* Newbury Park, CA: Sage.

Creese, A., Bhatt, A., Bhojani, N., & Martin, P. (2008). Fieldnotes in team ethnography: Researching complementary schools. *Qualitative Research, 8*(2), 197–215.

Creswell, J. (1997). *Qualitative inquiry and research design: Choosing among five traditions.* Thousand Oaks, CA: Sage.

Creswell, J. (2003). *Research design: Qualitative, quantitative, and mixed methods approaches* (2nd ed.). Thousand Oaks, CA: Sage.

Creswell, J. (2007). *Qualitative inquiry and research design: Choosing among five approaches* (2nd ed.). Thousand Oaks, CA: Sage.

Creswell, J., Hanson, W., Clark, V., & Morales, A. (2007). Qualitative research designs: Selection and implementation. *The Counseling Psychologist, 35*(2), 236–264.

Crotty, M. (2003). *The foundations of social research: Meaning and perspective in the research process.* Thousand Oaks, CA: Sage.

Crump, R. E. (1928). *Correspondence and class extension work in Oklahoma.* New York: Columbia University, Teachers College.

Curtis, A. (2008). How dramatic techniques can aid the presentation of qualitative research. *Qualitative Researcher, 8,* 8–10. Retrieved September 2, 2008, from http://www.cardiff.ac.uk/socsi/qualiti/QualitativeResearcher/QR_Issue8_Jun08.pdf

Custer, R. L. (1996). Qualitative research methodologies. *Journal of Industrial Teacher Education, 34*(2), 3–6.

Daalen-Smith, C. (2008). Living as a chameleon: Girls, anger, and mental health. *The Journal of School Nursing, 24*(3), 116–123.

Davey, N. (1999). The hermeneutics of seeing. In I. Heywood & B. Sandywell (Eds.), *Interpreting visual culture: Explorations in the hermeneutics of the visual* (pp. 3–29). London: Routledge.

Davidson, A. L. (2002). *Grounded theory.* Retrieved November 1, 2008, from http://az.essortment.com/groundedtheory_rmnf.htm

Davis, O. L. (2002). Editorial: Educational research in the foreseeable future. *The Journal of Curriculum and Supervision, 17*(4), 175–178.

Dawson, K., & St. George, S. (2008). A book review of Marilyn Lichtman's *Qualitative Research in Education: A User's Guide. The Qualitative Report, 13*(1), 26–29. Retrieved December 9, 2008, from http://www.nova.edu/ssss/QR/QR13-1/dawson.pdf

Day, E. (2002, September). Me, my*self and I: Personal and professional re-constructions in ethnographic research [59 paragraphs]. *Forum Qualitative Social Research, 3*(3). Retrieved December 9, 2008, from http://www.qualitative-research.net/index.php/fqs/article/view/824

Denny, T. (1978). *Story telling and educational understanding.* Retrieved November 1, 2008, from http://www.wmich.edu/evalctr/pubs/ops/ops12.html

Denzin, N. K. (1989). *Interpretive interactionism.* Newbury Park, CA: Sage.

Denzin, N. K. (1997). *Interpretive ethnography: Ethnographic practices for the 21st century.* Thousand Oaks, CA: Sage.

Denzin, N. K. (2008). The new paradigm dialogs and qualitative inquiry. *International Journal of Qualtiative Studies in Education, 21*(4), 315–325.

Denzin, N., & Lincoln, Y. (Eds.). (1994). *Handbook of qualitative research.* Thousand Oaks, CA: Sage.

Denzin, N., & Lincoln, Y. (Eds.). (2000). *Handbook of qualitative research* (2nd ed.). Thousand Oaks, CA: Sage.

Denzin, N., & Lincoln, Y. (Eds.). (2005). *Handbook of qualitative research* (3rd ed.). Thousand Oaks, CA: Sage.

Dermot, M. (2000). *Introduction to phenomenology.* London: Routledge.

Derrida, J. (1982). *Margins of philosophy* (A. Bass, Trans.). Chicago: The University of Chicago Press. (Original work published 1972)

Deutsch, N. (2004). Positionality and the pen: Reflections on the process of becoming a feminist researcher and writer. *Qualitative Inquiry, 10*(6), 885–902.

DeVault, M. (1990). Talking and listening from women's standpoint: Feminist strategies for interviewing and analysis. *Social Problems, 37*(1), 96–116.

Devers, K. (1999, December). How will we know "good" qualitative research when we see it? Beginning the dialogue in health services research. *Health Services Research,* 1–12.

De Welde, K. (2003). The brouhaha of ethnography: Not for the faint-hearted. *Journal of Contemporary Ethnography, 32*(2), 233–244.

Dholakia, N., & Zhang, D. (2004, May). Online qualitative research in the age of e-commerce: Data sources and approaches [27 paragraphs]. *Forum Qualitative Sozialforschung/ Forum: Qualitative Social Research, 5*(2). Retrieved November 1, 2008, from http://www.qualitative-research.net/fqs-texte/2-04/2-04dholakiazhang-e.htm

Dick, B. (2002). *Grounded theory: A thumbnail sketch.* Retrieved November 1, 2008, from http://www.scu.edu.au/schools/gcm/ar/arp/grounded.html

Diekelmann, N. (2002). *Interpretive research: Postmodernism.* Retrieved November 7, 2005, from http://www.son.wisc.edu/diekelmann/courses/701/schedule6.htm

di Gregorio, S. (2000, September). *Using NVivo for your literature review.* Paper presented at the Strategies in Qualitative Research: Conference, Institute of Education, London.

Dillman, D. (1978). *Mail and telephone surveys.* New York: Wiley.

Dillon, M. (1997). *Merleau-Ponty's ontology.* Evanston, IL: Northwestern University Press.

Dixon-Woods, M., Bonas, S., Booth, A., Jones, D. R., Miller, T., Sutton, A. J., et al. (2006). How can systematic reviews incorporate qualitative research? A critical perspective. *Qualitative Research, 6*(1), 27–44.

Donmoyer, R. (1990). Generalizability and the single-case study. In E. Eisner & A. Peshkin (Eds.), *Qualitative inquiry in education: The continuing debate* (pp. 175–200). New York: Teachers College Press.

Downing, M. (2008). Why video? How technology advances method. *The Qualitative Report, 13*(2), 173–177.

Draucker, C., Martsolf, D., Ross, R., & Rusk, T. (2007). Theoretical sampling and category development in grounded theory. *Qualitative Health Research, 17*(8), 1137–1148.

Duncombe, J., & Jessop, J. (2005). "Doing rapport" and the ethics of "faking friendship." In M. Mauthner, M. Birch, J. Jessop, & T. Miller (Eds.), *Ethics in qualitative research* (pp. 107–122). London: Sage.

Easterby-Smith, M., Golden-Biddle, K., & Locke, K. (2008). Working with pluralism: Determining quality in qualitative research. *Organizational Research Methods, 11,* 419–429.

Efinger, J., Maldonado, N., & McArdle, G. (2004). PhD students' perceptions of the relationship between philosophy and research: A qualitative investigation. *The Qualitative Report, 9*(4), 732–759. Retrieved November 17, 2005, from http://www.nova.edu/ssss/QR/QR9-4/efinger.pdf

Eich, D. (2008). A grounded theory of high-quality leadership programs: Perspectives from student leadership development programs in higher education. *Journal of Leadership & Organizational Studies, 15,* 176–187.

Eisenhart, M. (2001). Educational ethnography past, present and future: Ideas to think with. *Educational Researcher, 30*(8), 16–27.

Eisenhart, M. (2006). Qualitative science in experimental time. *International Journal of Qualitative Studies in Education, 19*(6), 697–708.

Eisner, E., & Peshkin, A. (1990). *Qualitative inquiry in education: The continuing debate.* New York: Teachers College Press.

Elliott, R., Fischer, C. T., & Rennie, D. L. (1999). Evolving guidelines for publication of qualitative research studies in psychology and related fields. *British Journal of Clinical Psychology, 38,* 215–229.

Ellis, C. (1995). *Final negotiations: A story of love, and chronic illness.* Philadelphia: Temple University Press.

Ellis, C., & Bochner, A. (2000). Autoethnography, personal narrative, reflexivity: Researcher as subject. In N. Denzin & Y. Lincoln (Eds.), *Handbook of qualitative research* (pp. 733–768). Thousand Oaks, CA: Sage.

Ellis, C., & Bochner, A. (2002). *Ethnographically speaking: Autoethnography, literature, and aesthetics.* Walnut Creek, CA: AltaMira Press.

Ellis, C., & Bochner, A. (Series Eds.) (2008). *Writing lives: Ethnographic narratives.* San Francisco: LeftCoast Press.

Ellis, C., Bochner, A., Denzin, N., Lincoln, Y., Morse, J., Pelias, R., et al. (2008). Talking and thinking about qualitative research. *Qualitative Inquiry, 14*(2), 254–284.

Embree, L. (2003). General impressions of our tradition today. In C.-F., Cheung, I. Chvatik, I. Copoeru, L. Embree, J. Iribarne, & H. Sepp (Eds.), *Essays in celebration of the founding of the Organization of Phenomenological Organizations* (pp. 1–4). Retrieved November 1, 2008, from http://www.o-p-o.net/essays/lesterintroduction.pdf

English, L., & Irving, C. (2008). Reflexive texts: Issues of knowledge, power, and discourse in researching gender and learning. *Adult Education Quarterly, 58*(4), 267–283.

Etherington, K. (2004). *Becoming a reflexive researcher: Using ourselves in research.* London: Kingsley.

Ewick, P., & Silbey, S. (2003). Narrating social structures: Stories of resistance to legal authority. *American Journal of Sociology, 108*(6), 1328–1372.

Eysenbach, G., & Till, J. (2001). Ethical issues in qualitative research on Internet communities. *British Medical Journal, 323,* 1103–1105.

Faculty of Social Sciences Committee on Ethics. (n.d.). *Collection, storage, and archiving of qualitative data.* Retrieved November 1, 2008, from http://www.lancs.ac.uk/fass/resources/ethics/storage.htm

Falk, E., & Mills, J. (1996). Why sexist language affects persuasion: The role of homophily, intended audience, and offense. *Women and Language, 19*(2), 36–44.

Faux, R. B. (2005, February). To reveal thy heart perchance to reveal the world. *Forum Qualitative Sozialforschung/Forum: Qualitative*

Social Research, 6(2). Retrieved November 2, 2005, from http://www.qualitative-research.net/fqs-texte/2-05/05-2-7-e.htm

Fetterman, D. (1982). Ethnography in educational research: The dynamics of diffusion. *Educational Researcher, 11,* 17–21, 29.

Fetterman, D. M. (1998). *Ethnography: Step by step* (2nd ed.). Thousand Oaks, CA: Sage.

Filmer, A. (2007). Bilingual belonging and the whiteness of (Standard) English(es). *Qualitative Inquiry, 13*(6), 747–765.

Fine, M. (1992). *Disruptive voices: The possibilities of feminist research.* Ann Arbor: University of Michigan.

Flowers, L., & Moore, J. (2003, Winter). Conducting qualitative research on-line in student affairs. *Student Affairs On-Line, 4*(1). Retrieved November 1, 2008, from http://www.studentaffairs.com/ejournal/Winter_2003/research.html

Fook, J. (1996). *The reflective researcher.* St. Leonards, Australia: Allen & Unwin.

Fordham, S. (1988). Racelessness as a factor in black student school success: Pragmatic strategy or Pyrrhic victory? *Harvard Educational Review, 58*(1), 54–84.

Foreword. (1931, January). *Review of Educational Research, 1*(1), 2.

Foucault, M. (1972). *The archeology of knowledge* (A. M. Sheridan-Smith, Trans.). London: Tavistock.

Foucault, M. (1980). *Power/knowledge: Selected interviews and other writings, 1972–1977* (C. Cordon, Ed.; C. Cordon, L. Marshall, J. Mepham, & K. Soper, Trans.). New York: Pantheon Books.

Frank, C., & Uy, F. (2004). Ethnography for teacher education. *Journal of Teacher Education, 55*(3), 269–283.

Fraser, J. (2008). Dancing with research. *Canadian Medical Association Journal, 179*(5), 450–451.

Freeman, M. (2000). Knocking on doors: On constructing culture. *Qualitative Inquiry, 6*(3), 359–369.

Freeman, M., deMarrais, K., Preissle, J., Roulston, K., & St. Pierre, E. (2007). Standards of evidence in qualitative research: An incitement to discourse. *Educational Researcher, 36*(1), 25–32.

Friedan, B. (1963). *The feminine mystique.* New York: Dell.

Garcia, D. (2008). Culture clash invades Miami: Oral histories and ethnography center stage. *Qualitative Inquiry, 14*(6), 865–895.

Garfinkel, H. (1967). *Studies in ethnomethodology.* Cambridge, UK: Polity Press.

Garson, G. D. (2002). *Case studies.* Retrieved November 9, 2005, from http://www2.chass.ncsu.edu/garson/pa765/cases.htm

Gearing, R. (2004). Bracketing in research: A typology. *Qualitative Health Research, 14,* 1429–1452.

Geertz, C. (1973). *The interpretation of cultures.* New York: Basic Books.

Geiger, S. N. (1986). Women's life histories: Method and content. *Journal of Women in Culture and Society, 11,* 334–351.

Genzuk, M. (2003). *A synthesis of ethnographic research.* Retrieved November 1, 2008, from http://www-rcf.usc.edu/~genzuk/Ethnographic_Research.html

Giddings, L. (2006). Mixed-methods research: Positivism dressed in drag? *Journal of Research in Nursing, 11*(3), 195–203.

Gilgun, J. (2005). "Grab" and good science: Writing up the results of qualitative research. *Qualitative Health Research, 15,* 256–262.

Giorgi, A. (1989). One type of analysis of descriptive data: Procedures involved in following a scientific phenomenological method. *Methods: A Journal of Human Science, Annual Edition, 1,* 39–61.

Glaser, B. G. (1978). *Theoretical sensitivity: Advances in the methodology of grounded theory.* Mill Valley, CA: Sociology Press.

Glaser, B. G. (1992). *Basics of grounded theory analysis: Emergence vs. forcing.* Mill Valley, CA: Sociology Press.

Glaser, B. G. (1998). *Doing grounded theory: Issues and discussion.* Mill Valley, CA: Sociology Press.

Glaser, B. G., & Holton, J. (2004, March). Remodeling grounded theory [80 paragraphs]. *Forum Qualitative Sozialforschung/Forum: Qualitative Social Research, 5*(2). Retrieved November 3, 2005, from http://www.qualitative-research.net/fqstexte/2-04/2-04glaser-e.htm

Glaser, B. G., & Strauss, A. (1967). *The discovery of grounded theory: Strategies for qualitative research.* Chicago: Aldine.

Glass, P. (2001). *Autism and the family.* Unpublished doctoral dissertation, Virginia Polytechnic Institute and State University, Falls Church.

Golden, D., & Mayseless, O. (2008). On the alert in an unpredictable environment. *Culture Psychology, 14,* 155–180.

Goodall, H. (2008). *Writing qualitative inquiry: Self, stories, and academic life.* San Francisco: LeftCoast Press.

Goode, D. (1994). *A world without words: The social construction of children born deaf and blind.* Philadelphia: Temple University Press.

Goodson, I. (Ed.). (1992). *Studying teachers' lives.* London and New York: Routledge.

Greckhamer, T., Misangyi, V., Elms, H., & Lacey, R. (2008). Using qualitative comparative analysis in strategic management research. *Organizational Research Methods 11,* 695–726.

Guion, L. (2002). *Triangulation: Establishing the validity of qualitative studies.* Retrieved November 3, 2005, from http://edis.ifas.ufl.edu/pdffiles/FY/FY39400.pdf

Gültekin, N., Inowlocki, L., & Lutz, H. (2003, September). Quest and query: Interpreting a biographical interview with a Turkish woman laborer in Germany [55 paragraphs]. *Forum Qualitative Sozialforschung/Forum: Qualitative Social Research, 4*(3). Retrieved November 17, 2005, from http://www.qualitative-research.net/fqs-texte/3-03/3-03guel-tekinetal-e.htm

Guy, L., & Montague, J. (2008). Analysing men's written friendship narratives. *Qualitative Research, 8*(3), 389–397.

Haig, B. (1995). *Grounded theory as scientific method.* Retrieved November 1, 2008, from http://www.ed.uiuc.edu/EPS/PES-yearbook/95_docs/haig.html

Hamill, C. (1999). Academic essay writing in the first person: A guide for undergraduates. *Nursing Standard, 13*(44), 38–40.

Hamilton, R., & Bowers, B. (2006). Internet recruitment and e-mail interviews in qualitative studies. *Qualitative Health Research, 16,* 821–835.

Hansen, S., & Rapley, M. (Eds.). (2008). Teaching qualitative methods. *Qualitative Research in Psychology, 5*(3), 171–232.

Harding, S. (1987). *Feminism and methodology.* Bloomington: Indiana University Press.

Harding, S. (1998). *Is science multicultural? Postcolonialism, feminism & epistemologies.* Bloomington: Indiana University Press.

Harding, S. (2005). *Science and social inequality: Feminist and postcolonial issues.* Champaign: University of Illinois Press.

Harper, D. (2003). Framing photographic ethnography: A case study. *Ethnography, 4*(2), 241–266.

Harré, R. (2004). Qualitative research as science. *Qualitative Research in Psychology, 1*(1), 3–14.

Haskell, J., Linds, W., & Ippolito, J. (2002, September). Opening spaces of possibility: The enactive as a qualitative research approach [96 paragraphs]. *Forum Qualitative Sozialforschung/Forum: Qualitative Social Research, 3*(3). Retrieved November 4, 2005, from http://www.qualitative-research.net/fqs-texte/3-02/3-02haskelletal-e.htm

Hatch, M., & Yanow, D. (2008). Methodology by metaphor: Ways of seeing in painting and research. *Organizational Studies, 29*(1), 23–44.

Haverkamp, B., & Young, R. (2007). Paradigms, purpose, and the role of the literature: Formulating a rationale for qualitative investigations. *The Counseling Psychologist, 35*(2), 265–294.

Heath, A. (1997). The proposal in qualitative research. *The Qualitative Report, 3*(1). Retrieved December 9, 2008, from http://www.nova.edu/ssss/QR/QR3-1/heath/html

Hèbert, T. (2001). *Jermaine: A gifted black child living in rural poverty.* Paper presented at the QUIG-Qualitative Interest Group Conference, Athens, GA.

Hemmings, A. (2006). Great ethical divides: Bridging the gap between institutional review boards and researchers. *Educational Researcher, 35*(4), 12–18.

Henson, M. (2001). Cultural imperialism: A case study of football in Bath in the late-Victorian era. *The Sports Historian. The Journal of the British Society of Sports History, 21*(2), 20–34.

Hey, V. (1997). *The company she keeps: An ethnography of girls' friendships.* Philadelphia: Open University Press.

Hoepfl, M. (1997, Fall). Choosing qualitative research: A primer for technology education researchers. *Journal of Technology Education, 9*(1). Retrieved November 3, 2005, from http://scholar.lib.vt.edu/ejournals/JTE/v9n1/hoepfl.html

Holliday, A. (2001). *Doing and writing qualitative research.* London: Sage.

Holliday, A. (2007). *Doing and writing qualitative research* (2nd ed.). Thousand Oaks, CA: Sage.

Hollway, W., & Jefferson, T. (2000). *Doing qualitative research differently.* London: Sage.

Holman Jones, S. (2004). Carolyn Ellis and Art Bochner: Building connections in qualitative research [113 paragraphs]. *Forum Qualitative Sozialforschung/Forum: Qualitative Social Research, 5*(3). Retrieved December 9, 2008, from http://www.qualitative-research.net/index.php/fqs/article/view/552

Holt, N. L. (2003). Representation, legitimation, and autoethnography: An autoethnographic writing story. *International Journal of Qualitative Methods, 2*(1). Retrieved November 1, 2008, from http://www.ualberta.ca/~iiqm/backissues/2_1/html/holt.html

Hookway, N. (2008). Entering the blogosphere: Some strategies for using blogs in social research. *Qualitative Research, 8*(1), 91–113.

Hopkins, B., & Crowell, S. (Eds.). (2003). *The new yearbook for phenomenology and phenomenological philosophy.* Madison: University of Wisconsin.

Hsieh, H., & Shannon, S. (2005). Three approaches to qualitative content analysis. *Qualitative Health Research, 15*(9), 1277–1288.

Humphreys, L. (1970). *Tearoom trade: Impersonal sex in public places.* New York: Aldine.

Husserl, E. (1981). Pure phenomenology, its methods and its field of investigation (R. W. Jordan, Trans.). In P. McCormick & F. Elliston (Eds.), *Husserl: Shorter works* (pp. 9–17). Notre Dame, IN: University of Notre Dame Press. (Original work published 1917)

Ihde, D. (1995). *Postphenomenology: Essays in the postmodern context.* Evanston, IL: Northwestern University Press.

Imel, S. (1998). *Race and gender in adult education.* ERIC Clearinghouse Trends Alert. Retrieved November 2, 2008, from http://ericacve.org/docs/race-gen.htm

Imel, S., Kerka, S., & Wonacott, M. (2002). *Qualitative research in adult, career, and career-technical education. Practitioner file.* Columbus, OH: ERIC Clearinghouse on Adult, Career, and Vocational Education. (ERIC Document Reproduction Service No. ED472366)

Intrator, S. (2000). *Eight text devices useful in writing qualitative research.* Paper presented at the American Educational Research Association, New Orleans, LA.

Jackson, A. (2001). Multiple Annies: Feminist poststructural theory and the making of a teacher. *Journal of Teacher Education, 52*(5), 386–397.

Jackson, A. (2008). Power and pleasure in ethnographic home-work: Producing a recognizable ethics. *Qualitative Research, 8*(10), 37–51.

James, N., & Busher, H. (2006). Credibility, authenticity, and voice: Dilemmas in online interviewing. *Qualitative Research, 6*(3), 403–420.

Jang, E., McDougall, D., Pollon, D., Herbert, M., & Russell, P. (2008). Integrative mixed methods data analytic strategies in research on school success. *Journal of Mixed Methods Research, 2*(3), 221–247.

Jensen, J. L., & Rodgers, R. (2001). Cumulating the intellectual gold of case study research. *Public Administration Review, 61*(2), 236–246.

Jewett, L. (2004). *A delicate dance: Autobiography, ethnography and the pedagogical lie of autoethnography.* Paper presented at the American Educational Research Association, San Diego, CA.

Johnson, B., & Christensen, L. (2008). *Educational research. Quantitative, qualitative, and mixed approaches* (3rd ed.). Los Angeles: Sage.

Johnson, R., & Onwuegbuzie, A. (2004). Mixed methods research: A research paradigm whose time has come. *Educational Researcher, 33*(7), 14–26.

Johnson, S. (2004). *Mind wide open: Your brain and the neuroscience of everyday life.* New York: Scribner.

Johnson, T. S. (2008). Qualitative research in question: A narrative of disciplinary power with/in the IRB. *Qualitative Inquiry, 14*(2), 212–232.

Jones, K. (2004). Mission drift in qualitative research, or moving toward a systematic review of qualitative studies, moving back to a more systematic narrative review. *The Qualitative Report, 9*(1), 95–112. Retrieved September 1, 2008, from http://www.nova.edu/ssss/QR/QR9-1/jones.pdf

Josselson, R. (Ed.). (1996). *Ethics and process in the narrative study of lives* (Vol. 4). Thousand Oaks, CA: Sage.

Joy, D. (2004). *Instructors transitioning to online education.* Unpublished doctoral dissertation, Virginia Polytechnic Institute and State University, Blacksburg.

Kabel, C. J. (2002). *Qualitative research, now there are choices: My study used photos, poems, and people's voices.* Retrieved November 3, 2005, from http://www.coe.uga.edu/quig/proceedings/Quig02_Proceedings/choices.pdf

Karp, K., & Shakeshaft, C. (1997). Restructuring schools to be math friendly to females. *NASSP Bulletin, 81*(586), 84–93.

Kawulich, B. (2005). Participant observation as a data collection method [81 paragraphs]. *Forum Qualitative Sozialforschung/ Forum: Qualitative Social Research, 6*(2). Retrieved December 9, 2008, from http://www.qualitative-research.net/index.php/fqs/article/view/466

Kearney, K., & Hyle, A. (2004). Drawing out emotions: The use of participant-produced drawings in qualitative inquiry. *Qualitative Research, 4,* 361–382.

Kearsley, G. (2002). MEPP: A case study in online education. *The Technology Source.* Retrieved November 1, 2008, from http://technologysource.org/article/mepp/

Keller, J. F., Protinsky, H. O., Lichtman, M., & Allen, K. (1996). The process of clinical supervision: Direct observation research. *Clinical Supervisor, 14*(1), 51–63.

Kelly, A., & Kerner, A. (2004). The scent of positive lives: (Re)memorializing our loved ones. *Qualitative Inquiry, 10*(5), 767–787.

Kerlinger, F. (1964). *Foundations of educational research.* New York: Holt, Rinehart & Winston.

Kerlinger, F. (1973). Statement from the editor. *Review of Research in Education, 1*(1), v–viii.

Kerlinger, F. (2000). *Foundations of educational research* (4th ed.). New York: Harcourt.

Kevles, D. J. (1998). *The Baltimore case: A trial of politics, science, and character.* New York: W. W. Norton & Co.

Kidder, T. (1989). *Among schoolchildren.* New York: Avon Books.

Kitzinger, J. (1994). The methodology of focus groups: The importance of interaction between research participants. *Sociology of Health, 16*(1), 103–121.

Koerber, A., & McMichael, L. (2008). Qualitative sampling methods: A primer for technical communicators. *Journal of Business and Technical Communication, 22*(4), 454–473.

Koro-Ljungberg, M. (2001). Metaphors as a way to explore qualitative data. *International Journal of Qualitative Studies in Education, 14*(3), 367–379.

Koro-Ljungberg, M. (2004). Displacing metaphorical analysis: Reading with and against metaphors. *Qualitative Research, 4*(3), 339–360.

Koro-Ljungberg, M. (2008). Positivity in qualitative research: Examples from the organized field of postmodernism/poststructuralism. *Qualitative Research, 8*(2), 217–236.

Koro-Ljungberg, M., Gemignani, M., Brodeur, C. W., & Kmiec, C. (2007). The technologies of normalization and self: Thinking about IRBs and extrinsic research ethics with Foucault. *Qualitative Inquiry, 13*(8), 1075–1094.

Kozinets, R. (2002). The field behind the screen: Using netnography for marketing research in online communities. *Journal of Marketing Research, 39*(1), 61–72.

Kozleski, E., Engelbrecht, P., Hess, R., Swart, E., Eloff, I., Oswald, M., et al. (2008). Where differences matter: A cross-cultural analysis of family voice in special education. *The Journal of Special Education, 42,* 26–35.

Krippendorf, K. (1980). *Content analysis: An introduction to its methodology.* Beverly Hills, CA: Sage.

Krippendorff, K. (2004). *Content analysis: An introduction to its method.* London: Sage.

Krueger, R. A. (1988). *Focus groups: A practical guide for applied research.* London: Sage.

Kurtines, W., Montgomery, M., Lewis Arango, L., Kortsch, G., Albrecht, R., Garcia, A., et al. (2008). Promoting positive youth development: Relational data analysis (RDA). *Journal of Adolescent Research, 23*(3), 291–309.

Kvale, S. (1996). *InterViews: An introduction to qualitative research interviewing.* Thousand Oaks, CA: Sage.

Lagemann, E. C. (2000). *An elusive science: The troubling history of education research.* Chicago: University of Chicago Press.

Lahman, M. (2008). Always othered: Ethical research with children. *Journal of Early Childhood Research, 6*(3), 281–300.

La Jevic, L., & Springgay, S. (2008). A/r/tography as an ethics of embodiment. *Qualitative Inquiry, 14*(1), 67–89.

Lakoff, G., & Johnson, M. (1980). *Metaphors we live by.* Chicago: University of Chicago Press.

Landman, M. (2006). Getting quality in qualitative research: A short introduction to feminist methodology and methods. *Proceedings of the Nutrition Society, 65,* 429–433.

LaRaviere, T. (2008). Chairman Fred Hampton Way: An autoethnographic inquiry into politically relevant teaching. *Qualitative Inquiry, 14*(3), 489–504.

Larkin, M. (2002). *Features of a good qualitative project.* Retrieved November 1, 2008, from http://www.psy.dmu.ac.uk/michael/qual_good_project.htm

Lather, P. (1991). *Feminist research in education: Within/against.* Geelong, Victoria, Australia: Deakin University Press.

Lather, P. (2007). *Getting lost: Feminist efforts toward a double(d) science.* Albany: State University of New York Press.

LeCompte, M. (2002). The transformation of ethnographic practices. *Qualitative Research, 2*(3), 283–299.

Lemke, J. L. (1994). Semiotics and the deconstruction of conceptual learning. *Journal of Accelerative Learning and Teaching, 19*(1), 67–110.

Lemke, J. L. (2003). Analysing verbal data: Principles, methods, problems. In K. Tobin & B. Fraser (Eds.), *International handbook of science education.* Retrieved November 1, 2008, from http://academic.brooklyn.cuny.edu/education/jlemke/papers/handbook.htm

LePage-Lees, P. (1997). Struggling with a nontraditional past: Academically successful women from disadvantaged backgrounds discuss their relationship with "disadvantage." *Psychology of Women Quarterly, 21*(3), 365–385.

Lester, P. (n.d.). *A picture's worth a thousand words.* Retrieved November 1, 2008, from http://commfaculty.fullerton.edu/lester/writings/letters.html

LeVasseur, J. (2003). The problem of bracking in phenomenology. *Qualitative Health Research, 13,* 408–420.

Lévi-Strauss, C. (1968). *Structural anthropology* (M. Layton, Trans.). New York: Penguin Press. (Original work published 1958)

Lewis, M. (1995). *Focus group interviews in qualitative research: A review of the literature.* Retrieved November 1, 2008, from http://www.scu.edu.au/schools/gcm/ar/arr/arow/rlewis.html

Lewis, P. J. (2008). A good teacher [18 paragraphs]. *Forum Qualitative Sozialforschung/Forum: Qualitative Social Research, 9*(2), Art. 41. Retrieved December 9, 2008, from http://www.qualitative-research.net/index.php/fqs/article/view/399

Li, S., & Seale, C. (2007). Learning to do qualitative data analysis: An observational study of doctoral work. *Qualitative Health Research, 17*(10), 1442–1452.

Lichtman, M. (2004, September). "The future is here; it is just not widely distributed yet"—Adapted from William Gibson. Ron Chenail in conversation with Marilyn Lichtman [19 paragraphs]. *Forum Qualitative Sozialforschung/Forum: Qualitative Social Research, 5*(3). Retrieved November 7, 2005, from http://www.qualitative-research.net/fqs-texte/3-04/04-3-11-e.htm

Lichtman, M. (2005, August). Review: Mechthild Kiegelmann and Leo Gürtler (Eds.). (2003). Research questions and matching methods of analysis [22 paragraphs]. *Forum Qualitative Sozialforschung/Forum: Qualitative Social Research, 6*(3). Retrieved November 28, 2005, from http://www.qualitative-research.net/fqs-texte/3-05/05-3-16-e.htm

Lichtman, M., & Taylor, S. I. (1993). *Conducting and reporting case studies* (Report No. TM 019 965). Paper presented at the annual meeting of the American Educational Research Association, Atlanta, GA. (ERIC Document Reproduction Service No. ED 358 157)

Liebow, E. (1967). *Tally's corner: A study of Negro street corner men.* London: Routledge.

Liebow, E. (1993). *Tell them who I am: The lives of homeless women.* New York: Penguin Books.

Lincoln, Y. S., & Guba, E. (1985). *Naturalistic inquiry.* Beverly Hills, CA: Sage.

Lincoln, Y. S., & Guba, E. (2000). Paradigmatic controversies, contradictions, and emerging confluences. In N. Denzin & Y. S. Lincoln (Eds.), *Handbook of qualitative research* (pp. 163–188). Thousand Oaks, CA: Sage.

Lincoln, Y. S., & Tierney, W. (2004). Qualitative research and institutional review boards. *Qualitative Inquiry, 10*(2), 219–234.

Liu, Y. (2000, May). How to write qualitative research? A book review [9 paragraphs]. *The Qualitative Report, 5*(1/2). Retrieved November 21, 2005, from http://www.nova.edu/ssss/QR/QR5-1/liu.html

Lo, A. (1993). *Sojourner adjustment: The experience of wives of mainland Chinese graduate students.* Unpublished doctoral dissertation, Virginia Polytechnic Institute and State University, Blacksburg.

Lugosi, P. (2006). Between overt and covert research: Concealment and disclosure in an ethnographic study of commercial hospitality. *Qualitative Inquiry, 12*(3), 541–561.

Luykx, A., Lee, O., & Edwards, U. (2008). Lost in translation: Negotiating meaning in a beginning ESOL science classroom. *Educational Policy, 22*(5), 640–674.

Lye, J. (1996). *Some principles of phenomenological hermeneutics.* Retrieved November 2, 2008, from http://www.brocku.ca/english/courses/4F70/ph.html

Macbeth, D. (2001). On "reflexivity" in qualitative research: Two readings and a third. *Qualitative Inquiry, 7*(1), 35–68.

Maguire, P. (1987). *Doing participatory research: A feminist approach.* Amherst: University of Massachusetts.

Mann, C., & Stewart, F. (2000). *Internet communication and qualitative research: A handbook for research online.* London: Sage.

Markham, A. (1998). *Life online: Researching real experience in virtual space.* Walnut Creek, CA: AltaMira Press.

Markham, A., & Baym, N. (Eds.). (2008). *Internet inquiry: Conversations about method.* Thousand Oaks, CA: Sage.

Markham, A. M. (2005). Reconsidering self and others: The methods, politics, and ethics of representation in online ethnography. In N. K. Denzin & Y. S. Lincoln (Eds.), *The handbook of qualitative research* (pp. 793–820). Thousand Oaks, CA: Sage. Retrieved November 17, 2005, from http://faculty.uvi.edu/users/amarkha/writing/denzinlincoln.htm

Mauthner, M., Birch, M., Jessop, J., & Miller, T. (Eds.). (2005). *Ethics in qualitative research.* London: Sage.

Maxwell, J. (2004). Causal explanation, qualitative research, and scientific inquiry in education. *Educational Researcher, 33*(2), 3–11.

Mazzei, L. (2007). *Inhabited silence in qualitative research: Putting poststructural theory to work.* New York: Peter Lang.

McCarthy, A. (1999). *Getting serious about grounded theory.* Paper presented at the Western Australian Educational Research Forum.

McCarthy, A. (2001). *Educational choice: A grounded theory study.* Paper presented at the Western Australian Institute for Educational Research.

McCleary, R. (2007). Ethical issues in online social work research. *Journal of Social Work Values and Ethics, 4*(1). Retrieved December 9, 2008, from http://www.socialworker.com/jswve/content/view/46/50/

McCracken, G. (1988). *The long interview.* Newbury Park, CA: Sage.

McGinn, M., & Bosacki, S. (2004, March). Research ethics and practitioners: Concerns and strategies for novice researchers engaged in graduate education [52 paragraphs]. *Forum Qualitative Sozialforschung/Forum: Qualitative Social Research.* Retrieved November 4, 2005, from http://www.qualitative-research.net/fqs-texte/2-04/2-04mcginnbosacki-e.htm.

McIntyre, A. (2002). Women researching their lives: Exploring violence and identity in Belfast, the north of Ireland. *Qualitative Research, 2*(3), 387–409.

McLeod, J. (2000). *Qualitative research as bricolage.* Paper presented at the Society for Psychotherapy Research Annual Conference, Chicago, IL.

McNamara, C. (n.d.) General guidelines for conducting interviews. Retrieved August 25, 2008, from http://www.managementhelp.org/evaluatn/intrview.htm

McPhail, J. (1995). Phenomenology as philosophy and method. *Remedial and Special Education, 16,* 156–165, 177.

Mehra, B. (2002, March). Bias in qualitative research: Voices from an online classroom. *The Qualitative Report, 7*(1). Retrieved August 30, 2008, from http://www.nova.edu/ssss/QR/QR7-1/mehra.html

Meloy, J. (1993). *Writing the qualitative dissertation: Understanding by doing.* Mahwah, NJ: Lawrence Erlbaum Associates.

Meloy, J. (2001). *Writing the qualitative dissertation: Understanding by doing* (2nd ed.). Mahwah, NJ: Lawrence Erlbaum Associates.

Merriam, S. (1988). *Case study research in education: A qualitative approach.* San Francisco: Jossey-Bass.

Merriam, S. (2002). *Qualitative research in practice: Examples for discussion and analysis.* San Francisco: Jossey-Bass.

Merton, R. K., & Kendall, P. L. (1946). The focused interview. *American Journal of Sociology, 51,* 541–557.

Metcalfe, M. (2003). Author(ity): The literature review as expert witnesses [45 paragraphs]. *Forum Qualitative Sozialforschung/Forum: Qualitative Social Research, 4*(1). Retrieved November 1,

2008, from http://www.qualitative-research.net/index.php/fqs/article/view/761/1650

Metz, M. (1983). What can be learned from educational ethnography? *Urban Education, 17,* 391–418.

Mitchell, G. J., & Cody, W. K. (1993). The role of theory in qualitative research. *Nursing Science Quarterly, 6*(4), 170–178.

Mittapalli, K., & Samaras, A. P. (2008). Madhubani art: A journey of an education researcher seeking self-development answers through art and self-study. *The Qualitative Report, 13*(2), 244–261. Retrieved from December 9, 2008, http://www.nova.edu/ssss/QR/QR13-2/mittapalli.pdf.

Moreira, C. (2008a). Fragments. *Qualitative Inquiry, 14*(5), 663–683.

Moreira, C. (2008b). Life in so many acts. *Qualitative Inquiry, 14*(4), 590–612.

Morgan, D. (1988). *Focus groups as qualitative research.* Newbury Park, CA: Sage.

Morrow, S. (2003). *Qualitative research in psychology syllabus.* Retrieved November 4, 2005, from http://www.ed.utah.edu/psych/coursematerials/7420MorrowS03.pdf

Morse, J. (2003). A review committee's guide for evaluating qualitative proposals. *Qualitative Health Research, 13*(6), 833–851.

Morse, J. (2008). Styles of collaboration in qualitative inquiry. *Qualitative Health Research, 18*(1), 3–4.

Morse, J. M. (1994) "Emerging from the Data": The cognitive processes of analysis in qualitative inquiry. In J. M. Morse (Ed.), *Critical issues in qualitative research methods* (pp. 23–43). Thousand Oaks, CA: Sage.

Moustakis, C. (1994). *Phenomenological research methods.* Thousand Oaks, CA: Sage.

Mruck, K. (2005, January). Editorial: The *FQS* issue on "secondary analysis of qualitative data" [6 paragraphs]. *Forum Qualitative Sozialforschung/Forum: Qualitative Social Research, 6*(1). Retrieved November 21, 2005, from http://www.qualitative-research.net/fqs-texte/1-05/05-1-48-e.htm

Munhall, P., & Chenail, R. (2007). *Qualitative research proposals and reports: A guide* (3rd ed.). Sudbury, MA: Jones & Bartlett.

Murthy, D. (2008). Digital ethnography: An examination of the use of new technologies for social research. *Sociology, 42*(5), 837–855.

Nakamura, K. (2003). *Visual anthropology.* Retrieved November 7, 2005, from http://www.deaflibrary.org/nakamura/courses/visualanthro/index.shtml

National Science Foundation. (n.d.). *Interpreting the common rule for the protection of human subjects for behavioral and social science research.* Retrieved September 5, 2008, from http://www.nsf.gov/bfa/dias/policy/hsfaqs.jsp

Neuman, W. L. (2003). *Social work research methods: Qualitative and quantitative approaches.* Boston: Allyn & Bacon.

Nielsen, T. (2000). Hermeneutic phenomenological data representation: Portraying the ineffable. *Australian Art Education, 23*(1), 9–14.

Nightingale, D., & Cromby, J. (Eds.). (1999). *Social constructionist psychology.* Buckingham: Open University Press. Retrieved November 21, 2005, from http://www.psy.dmu.ac.uk/michael/qual_reflexivity.htm

O'Brien, T. (2007). Perils of accommodation: The case of Joseph W. Holley. *American Educational Research Journal, 44*(4), 806–852.

O'Loughlin-Brooks, J. (n.d.). *Literature review for human sexuality.* Retrieved November 1, 2008, from http://iws.ccccd.edu/jbrooks/chapter1.htm

Olson, L. (1995, April 12). Standards times 50. *Education Week,* pp. 14–20.

The Painter's Keys. (n.d.). *Resource of art quotations.* Retrieved November 27, 2005, from http://www.painterskeys.com/getquotes.asp?fname=sw&ID=307

Paliadelis, P., & Cruickshank, M. (2008). Using a voice-centered relational method of data analysis in a feminist study exploring the working world of nursing unit managers. *Qualitative Health Research, 18*(10), 1444–1453.

Pan, M. (2007). *Preparing literature reviews: Qualitative and quantitative approaches.* Los Angeles: Pryzak Press.

Parker, I. (2003). *Qualitative research in psychology: Criteria.* Retrieved November 5, 2005, from http://www.uel.ac.uk/cnr/documents/Parker.doc

Parry, O., & Mauthner, N. (2004). Whose data are they anyway? Practical, legal and ethical issues in archiving qualitative research data. *Sociology, 38*(1), 139–152.

patterson, d. (2008). Research ethics boards as spaces of marginalization: A Canadian story. *Qualitative Inquiry, 14*(1), 18–27.

Patton, M. Q. (2002). *Qualitative evaluation and research methods.* London: Sage.

Paulus, T., Woodside, M., & Ziegler, M. (2008). Extending the conversation: Qualitative research as dialogic collaborative process. *The Qualitative Report, 13*(2), 226–243. Retrieved December 9, 2008, from http://www.nova.edu/ssss/QR/QR13–2/paulus.pdf

Penrod, J. (2003). Getting funded: Writing a successful qualitative small-project proposal. *Qualitative Health Research, 13*(6), 821–832.

Perttula, J. (2000). Transforming experience into knowledge: The phenomenological method revisited. *The Finnish Journal of Education, Kasvatus, 31*(5), 428–442.

Peters, T. (2007, September 29). "Systems thinking" and me: Never the twain shall meet. Retrieved November 1, 2008, from http://www.tompeters.com/

Petrie, G. (2003). ESL teachers' views on visual language: A grounded theory. *The Reading Matrix, 3*(3),137–168.

Pillow, W. (2003). Confession, catharsis, or cure? Rethinking the uses of reflexivity as methodological power in qualitative research. *International Journal of Qualitative Studies in Education, 16*(2), 175–196.

Piper, C. (n.d.). *Case study of a multimedia CD-ROM dissertation web.* Retrieved November 7, 2005, from http://www1.chapman.edu/soe/faculty/piper/casestudy.htm

Plummer, K. (2004). Book review. Sneaky kid and its aftermath. *Qualitative Inquiry, 4*(1), 125–128.

Polan, D. (2004). *Brecht and the politics of self-reflexive cinema.* Retrieved November 1, 2008, from http://www.ejumpcut.org/archive/onlinessays/JC17folder/BrechtPolan.html

Prettyman, S., & Jackson, K. (2006). Ethics, technology, and qualitative research: Thinking through the implications of new technology. Retrieved June 13, 2008, from http://www.qual-strategies.org/previous/2006/papers/prettyman/

Priest, H. (2002, December). An approach to the phenomenological analysis of data (Issues in research). *Nurse Researcher,* 50–63.

Primeau, L. (2003). Reflections on self in qualitative research: Stories of family. *American Journal of Occupational Therapy, 57*(1), 9–16.

Prins, E., & Toso, B. (2008). Defining and measuring parenting for educational success: A critical discourse analysis of the Parent Education Profile. *American Educational Research Journal, 45*(3), 555–596.

Pyett, P. (2003). Validation of qualitative research in the "real world." *Qualitative Health Research, 13*(8), 1170–1179.

Ragin, C. C. (1987). *The comparative method: Moving beyond qualitative and quantitative strategies.* Berkeley, Los Angeles and London: University of California Press.

Ratcliff, D. (2003). Video methods in qualitative research. In P. Camic, J. Rhodes, & L. Yardley (Eds.), *Qualitative research in psychology: Expanding perspectives in methodology and design* (pp. 113–131). Washington, DC: American Psychological Association.

Ratner, C. (2002, September). Subjectivity and objectivity in qualitative methodology [29 paragraphs]. *Forum Qualitative Sozialforschun/Forum: Qualitative Social Research 3*(3). Retrieved November 7, 2005, from http://www.qualitative-research.net/fqs-texte/3-02/3-02ratner-e.htm

Reid, M., & Moore, J. (2008). College readiness and academic preparation for post-secondary education. *Urban Education, 43*(2), 240–261.

Reinharz, S. (1992). *Feminist methods in social research.* London: Oxford University Press.

Reinharz, S. (1997). Who am I? The need for a variety of selves in the field. In R. Hertz (Ed.), *Reflexivity & voice* (pp. 3–20). Thousand Oaks, CA: Sage.

Repass, M. (2002). *The professional woman's desire to retire: The process of transition.* Unpublished doctoral dissertation, Virginia Polytechnic Institute and State University, Falls Church.

Rezabek, R. (2000, January). Online focus groups: Electronic discussions for research [67 paragraphs]. *Forum Qualitative Sozialforschung/Forum: Qualitative Social Research, 1*(1). Retrieved November 4, 2005, from http://www.qualitative-research.net/fqs-texte/1-00/1-00rezabek-e.htm

Richards, L., & Morse, J. (2007). *Read me first for a user's guide to qualitative methods.* Thousand Oaks, CA: Sage.

Richardson, L. (1997). *Fields of play: Constructing an academic life.* New Brunswick, NJ: Rutgers University Press.

Richardson, L. (2008). My dinner with Lord Esqy. *Qualitative Inquiry, 14*(1), 13–17.

Riessman, C. K. (2005). Narrative in social work: A critical review. *Qualitative Social Work, 4*(4), 383–404.

Rist, R. (1980). Blitzkrieg ethnography: On the transformation of a method into a movement. *Educational Researcher, 9*(2), 8–10.

Robbins, J. (2001). *Making connections: Adolescent girls' use of the Internet.* Unpublished doctoral dissertation, Virginia Polytechnic Institute and State University, Falls Church.

Robertson, J. (2003). Listening to the heartbeat of New York: Writings on the wall. *Qualitative Inquiry, 9*(1), 129–152.

Robertson, J. (2006). "If you know our names it helps!" Students' perspectives about "good" teaching. *Qualitative Inquiry, 12*(4), 756–768.

Robinson, P. (2000). The body matrix: A phenomenological exploration of student bodies on-line. *Educational Technology & Society 3*(3). Retrieved November 1, 2008, from http://www.ifets.info/journals/3_3/c05.html

Rodriguez, D. (2006). Un/masking identity. *Qualitative Inquiry, 12*(6), 1067–1090.

Roman, L., & Apple, M. (1990). Is naturalism a move away from positivism? Materialist and feminist approaches to subjectivity in ethnographic research. In E. Eisner & A. Peshkin (Eds.), *Qualitative inquiry in education* (pp. 38–73). New York: Teachers College Press.

Rose, G. (1993). *Feminism and geography: The limits of geographical knowledge.* St. Paul: University of Minnesota Press.

Rosenberg, D. (1999). *Action for prevention: Feminist practices in transformative learning in women's health and the environment (with a focus on breast cancer).* Retrieved November 1, 2008, from http://www.oise.utoronto.ca/CASAE/cnf99/drosenb.htm

Rossman, G., & Rallis, S. (2003). *Learning in the field: An introduction to qualitative research* (2nd ed.). Thousand Oaks, CA: Sage.

Roth, W.-M. (2003, November). Autobiography as scientific text: A dialectical approach to the role of experience. Review essay: Harry F. Wolcott (2002). Sneaky kid and its aftermath [42 paragraphs]. *Forum Qualitative Sozialforschung/Forum: Qualitative Social Research, 5*(1). Retrieved June 13, 2008, from http://www.qualitative-research.net/fqs-texte/1-04/1-04review-roth-e.htm

Roth, W-M. (2004a, September). Political ethics, unethical politics [49 paragraphs]. *Forum Qualitative Sozialforschung/Forum: Qualitative Social Research, 5*(3). Retrieved June 13, 2008, from http://www.qualitative-research.net/fqs-texte/3-04/04-3-35-e.htm

Roth, W.-M. (2004b, February). Qualitative research and ethics [15 paragraphs]. *Forum Qualitative Sozialforschung/Forum: Qualitative Social Research.* Retrieved November 7, 2005, from http://www.qualitative-research.net/fqs-texte/2-04/2-04roth2-e.htm

Rubin, H., & Rubin, I. (1995). *Qualitative interviewing: The art of hearing data.* Thousand Oaks, CA: Sage.

Rubin, H., & Rubin, I. (2005). *Qualitative interviewing: The art of hearing data* (2nd ed.). Los Angeles: Sage.

Rufi, J. (1926). *The small high school.* Unpublished doctoral dissertation, Teachers College, Columbia University, New York.

Russell, G. M., & Kelly, N. H. (2002, September). Research as interacting dialogic processes: Implications for reflexivity [47 paragraphs]. *Forum Qualitative Sozialforschung/Forum: Qualitative Social Research, 3*(3). Retrieved November 4, 2005, from http://www.qualitative-research.net/fqs-texte/3-02/3-02russel-lkelly-e.htm

Rusu-Toderean, O. (n.d.). *In between positivism and post-positivism. A personal defence of empirical approaches to social sciences.* Retrieved November 4, 2005, from http://www.polito.ubbcluj.ro/EAST/East6/toderean.htm

Ryle, G. (1949). *The concept of mind.* Chicago: University of Chicago Press.

Sacks, O. (1985). *The man who mistook his wife for a hat.* New York: Summit Books.

Saldana, J. (2003). Dramatizing data: A primer. *Qualitative Inquiry, 9*(2), 218–236.

Sandelowski, M. (1995). Sample size in qualitative research. *Research in Nursing & Health, 18,* 179–183.

Sandelowski, M., & Barroso, J. (2003). Writing the proposal for a qualitative research methodology project. *Qualitative Health Research, 13*(6), 781–819.

Savall, H., Zardet, V., Bonnet, M., & Peron, M. (2008). The emergence of implicit criteria actually used by reviewers of qualitative research articles: Case of a European journal. *Organizational Research Methods, 11*(3), 510–540.

Schalet, A., Hunt, G., & Joe-Laidler, K. (2003). Respectability and autonomy: The articulation and meaning of sexuality among the girls in the gang. *Journal of Contemporary Ethnography, 32*(1), 108–143.

Scheurich, J. (1997). *Research method in the postmodern.* London: Falmer.

Schostak, J. (2008). *Qualitative research blog.* Retrieved December 8, 2008, from http://methodologyblog.imaginativespaces.net/blog

Schrage, M. (1999). *Serious play: How the world's best companies simulate to innovate.* Boston: Harvard Business School Press.

Schwandt, T. (2001). *Dictionary of qualitative inquiry.* Thousand Oaks, CA: Sage.

Schwandt, T. (2007). *The Sage dictionary of qualitative inquiry* (3rd ed.). Los Angeles: Sage.

Scown, A. (2003). *The academic as knowledge worker: The voices of experience.* Paper presented at the Third International Conference on Knowledge, Culture and Change in Organisations, Penang, Malaysia. Retrieved November 4, 2005, from http://2003.managementconference.com/ProposalSystem/Presentations/P000217

Secretan, L. H. K. (1997). *Reclaiming higher ground: Creating organizations that inspire the soul.* New York: McGraw-Hill.

Shank, G. (2002). *Qualitative research: A personal skills approach.* Columbus, OH: Merrill Prentice Hall.

Shapka, J., & Keating, D. (2003). Effects of a girls-only curriculum during adolescence: Performance, persistence, and engagement in mathematics and science. *American Educational Research Journal, 40*(4), 929–960.

Shepherd, N. (2003). Interviewing online: Qualitative research in the network(ed) society. *Association of Qualitative Research Sydney, Australia,* 17–19.

Simmons-Mackie, N., & Damico, J. (2003). Contributions of qualitative research to the knowledge base of normal communication. *American Journal of Speech-Language Pathology, 12*(2), 144–154.

Simons, L., Lathlean, J., & Squire, C. (2008). Shifting the focus: Sequential methods of analysis with qualitative data. *Qualitative Health Research, 18*(1), 120–132.

Skinner, B. F. (1938). *The behavior of organisms: An experimental analysis.* Englewood Cliffs, NJ: Prentice Hall.

Slattery, P. (2001). The educational researcher as artist working within. *Qualitative Inquiry, 7*(3), 370–398.

Smith, C. (1996). The use of research in local policy making: A case study of corporal punishment in public education. *Educational Policy, 10*(4), 502–517.

Smith, J. K., & Heshusius, L. (1986). Closing down the conversation: The end of the quantitative-qualitative debate among educational inquirers. *Educational Researcher, 15*(1), 4–12.

Snyder, W. (2003). *Perceptions on the diffusion and adoption of Skillsoft, an e-learning program: A case study.* Unpublished doctoral dissertation, Virginia Polytechnic Institute and State University, Blacksburg.

Sokolowski, R. (2000). *Introduction to phenomenology.* Cambridge: Cambridge University Press.

Sonpar, K., & Golden-Biddle, K. (2008). Using content analysis to elaborate adolescent theories of organization. *Organizational Research Methods, 11*(4), 795–814.

Sosu, E., McWilliam, A., & Gray, D. (2008). The complexities of teachers' commitment to environmental education: A mixed method approach. *Journal of Mixed Methods Research, 2*(2), 169–189.

Soy, S. (2006). *The case study as a research method.* Retrieved November 1, 2008, from http://www.ischool.utexas.edu/~ssoy/usesusers/l391d1b.htm

Sparkes, A., & Smith, B. (2003). Men, sport, spinal cord injury and narrative time. *Qualitative Research, 3*(3), 295–320.

Spradley, J. P. (1979). *The ethnographic interview.* New York: Holt, Rinehart & Winston.

Sprenkle, D., & Piercy, F. (Eds.). (2005). *Research methods in family therapy.* New York: Guilford Press.

Stake, R. (1995). *The art of case study research.* Thousand Oaks, CA: Sage.

Stanage, S. M. (1995). Lifelong learning: A phenomenology of meaning and value transformation in postmodern adult education. In S. B. Merriam (Ed.), *Selected writings on philosophy and adult education* (pp. 269–280). Malabar, FL: Krieger.

Starbuck, H. M. (2003). *Clashing and converging: Effects of the Internet on the correspondence art network.* Austin: University of Texas.

Starks, H., & Trinidad, S. (2007). Choose your method: A comparison of phenomenology, discourse analysis, and grounded theory. *Qualitative Health Research, 17*(10), 1372–1380.

Steinberg, L. (1972). *Other criteria: Confrontations with twentieth-century art.* New York: Oxford University Press.

Steinberg, S. (2000). The post-modernist wonderland [Review of the book *Intellectual impostures*]. Retrieved November 7, 2005, from http://www.wsws.org/articles/2000/ju12000/ post-j01.shtml

Stewart, D. W., & Shamdasani, P. N. (1990). *Focus groups: Theory and practice.* London: Sage.

Strauss, A., & Corbin, J. (1990). *Basics of qualitative research: Grounded theory procedures and techniques* (2nd ed.). Newbury Park, CA: Sage.

Suzuki, L., Ahluwalia, M., Arora, A., & Mattis, J. (2007). The pond you fish in determines the fish you catch: Strategies for qualitative data collection. *The Counseling Psychologist, 35*(2), 295–327.

Sweet, C. (1999). *Designing and conducting virtual focus groups.* Retrieved November 4, 2005, from http://www.sysurvey.com/tips/designing_and_conducting.htm

Szczelkun, S. (n.d.). *Preliminary thoughts on methodology: Reflexivity.* Retrieved August 30, 2008, from http://www.stefan-szczelkun.org.uk/phd002.htm

Tashakkori, A., & Creswell, J. (2007). Editorial: The new era of mixed methods. *The Journal of Mixed Methods Research, 1*(1), 3–7.

Tashakkori, A., & Teddlie, C. (Eds.). (2003). *Handbook of mixed methods in the behavioral and social sciences.* Thousand Oaks, CA: Sage.

Taylor, E., Beck, J., & Ainsworth, E. (2001). Publishing qualitative adult education research: A peer review perspective. *Studies in the Education of Adults, 33*(2), 163–179.

Taylor, E. B. (1871). *Primitive culture.* London: John Murray.

Tekinarslan, E. (2008). Blogs: A qualitative investigation into an instructor and undergraduate students' experiences. *Australasian Journal of Educational Technology, 24*(4), 402–412. Retrieved August 30, 2008, from http://www.ascilite.org.au/ajet/ajet24/tekinarslan.html

Tellis, W. (1997, July). Introduction to case study [68 paragraphs]. *The Qualitative Report, 3*(2). Retrieved November 4, 2005, from http://www.nova.edu/ssss/QR/QR3-2/tellis1.html

Thorne, B. (1993). *Gender play: Girls and boys in school.* Buckingham, UK: Open University Press.

Thorne, S. (2000). Data analysis in qualitative research. *Evidence-Based Nursing, 3,* 68–70.

Tierney, W. G., & Corwin, Z. B. (2007). The tensions between academic freedom and Institutional Review Boards. *Qualitative Inquiry, 13*(3), 388–398.

Tinelli, A. (2000). *Leaders and their learnings: What and how leaders learn as they transform organizations.* Unpublished doctoral dissertation, Virginia Polytechnic Institute and State University, Blacksburg.

Tolich, M. (2002, October 4). *An ethical iceberg: Do connected persons' confidentiality warrant vulnerable person status?* Paper presented at the joint IIPE/AAPAE Conference, Brisbane.

Torrance, H. (2008). Building confidence in qualitative research: Engaging the demands of policy. *Qualitative Inquiry, 14*(4), 507–527.

Tripp, D. (1992). Critical theory and educational research. *Issues in Educational Research, 2*(1), 13–23.

Tripp, D. (1993). *Critical incidents in teaching: Developing professional judgment.* London: Routledge.

Trochim, W. (2001). *Research methods knowledge base.* Cincinnati, OH: Atomic Dog Publishing. Retrieved July 2, 2008, from http://www.socialresearchmethods.net/kb/qualdeb.php

Tutt, D. (2008). Where the interaction is: Collisions of the situated and mediated in living room interactions. *Qualitative Inquiry, 14*(7), 1157–1179.

Ulichny, P. (1997). When critical ethnography and action collide. *Qualitative Inquiry, 3*(2), 139–168.

Vandenberg, D. (1996). *Phenomenology and educational discourse.* Durban: Heinemann Higher and Further Education.

Van der Mescht, H. (2004). Phenomenology in education: A case study in educational leadership. *Indo-Pacific Journal of Phenomenology, 4*(1), 1–16.

Van Maanen, J. (1988). *Tales of the field: On writing ethnography.* Chicago: University of Chicago Press.

van Manen, M. (1997). *Researching lived experiences: Human science for action-sensitive pedagogy.* London, Ontario, Canada: Althouse Press.

Van Oord, L. (2008). After culture: Intergroup encounters in education. *Journal of Research in International Education, 7*(2), 131–147.

Vargas, Y. V. (2008). Marco said I look like charcoal: A Puerto Rican's exploration of her ethnic identity. *Qualitative Inquiry, 14*(6), 949–954.

Wallace, T. (2003). *N. C. State ethnographic field school.* Retrieved November 4, 2005, from http://www4.ncsu.edu:8030/~twallace/Guate-Syllabus%202003.htm

Watt, D. (2007). On becoming a qualitative researcher: The value of reflexivity. *The Qualitative Report, 12*(1), 82–101. Retrieved August 30, 2008, from http://www.nova.edu/ssss/QR/QR12-1/watt.pdf

Weems, M. (2003). Poetry. *Qualitative Inquiry, 9*(1), 13–14.

Weil, S. (2008). Is there a "legitimation crisis" in qualitative methods? Conference Essay: ESF Exploratory Workshop on Improving the Quality of Qualitative Research [31 paragraphs]. *Forum: Qualitative Social Research, 9*(2). Retrieved December 9, 2008, from http://www.qualitative-research.net/index.php/fqs/article/view/438

Westrick, J. (2005). Phenomenology and meaning making: Student voices and understandings of cultural difference. *Journal of Studies in International Education, 9,* 105–120.

Whiteman, E. (2007). "Just chatting": Research ethics and cyberspace. *International Journal of Qualitative Methods, 6*(2), 95–105.

Wolcott, H. F. (1973). *The man in the principal's office: An ethnography.* New York: Holt, Rinehart & Winston.

Wolcott, H. F. (2001). *Writing up qualitative research* (2nd ed.). Thousand Oaks, CA: Sage.

Wolcott, H. F. (2002). The *sneaky kid and its aftermath: Ethics and intimacy in fieldwork.* Walnut Creek, CA: AltaMira Press.

Woo, U. (2008). Engaging new audiences: Translating research into popular media. *Educational Researcher, 37*(6), 321–329.

Wooden, H. Z., & Mort, P. (1929). Supervised correspondence study for high school pupils. *Teachers College Record, 30*(4), 447–452.

Wright, R. L. (2004). You were hired to teach! Ideological struggle, education, and teacher burnout at the new prison for women. *The Qualitative Report, 9*(4), 630–651. Retrieved November 21, 2005, from http://www.nova.edu/ssss/QR/QR9-4/wright.pdf

Yin, R. (2002). *Case study research: Design and methods.* Thousand Oaks, CA: Sage.

Yon, D. (2003). Highlights and overview of the history of educational ethnography. *Annual Review of Anthropology, 32,* 411–429.

"You've got to find what you love," Jobs says. (2005, June 14). *Stanford Report.* Retrieved December 9, 2008, from http://news-service.stanford.edu/news/2005/june15/jobs-061505.html

Zilber, T., Tuval-Mashiach, R., & Lieblich, A. (2008). The embedded narrative: Navigating through multiple contexts. *Qualitative Inquiry, 14*(6), 1047–1069.

Zou, Y., & Trueba, E. (Eds.). (2002). *Ethnography and schools: Qualitative approaches to the study of education.* Lanham, MD: Rowman & Littlefield.

Zucker, A. (1996). *Introduction to the philosophy of science.* Upper Saddle River, NJ: Prentice Hall.

Index

Academic journals, 208
Action research, xiv, 243
Active research, 64
Active voice, 212
Adolescents, 43, 143. *See also* Teens
Analyses:
    as individual, 108
    preliminary, 107–108
Anonymity, 54–55, 63
Anthropology, 8, 70–71, 243
Autobiography, 88
Autoethnography, 70–71, 217
Axial coding, 73
Axiology, 20–21, 23, 243

Baltimore, David, 59–60
Benedict, Ruth, 71, 90
Bias, 16–17, 116, 227, 230, 243
    See also Objectivity
Biography, 88
Blog, 181–182, 236–237
"Blogosphere," 239
Boas, Franz, 71, 90, 183
Bracketing, 75, 80, 100, 180, 213, 243
Bricoleur, 35
Burt, Cyril O., 60

Case, 81–83
Case study:
    definition of, 81, 243
    examples of, 83–84
    history of, 81–82
Casual interview, 141
Categories, for data analysis, 199–200
Chat rooms, 177–178
Chicago School, 28
Citations, 136
Classroom ethnography, 6
Closed places, 45
Closing questions, 148
Codes, 6, 194, 202, 243
Coding, 6, 73, 197–199, 243
Communication, 226–227, 238

Comparison/contrast question, 147
Computer:
    data analysis with, 200–203
    data organization using, 193
    literature review using, 136
Computer software packages, 98, 136, 202
Comte, Auguste, 7
Concepts, 15, 44–45, 194, 200, 243
Concrete example question, 146–147
Confidentiality:
    compromises in, 60–61
    description of, 55
    difficulties in maintaining, 61, 65
Confirmability, 228
Consent, informed. *See* Informed consent
Constant-comparative method, 73, 190, 193, 243
Constructivism, 11, 243
Content analysis, 190, 243
Coresearcher, 140, 243
Creative nonfiction, 210–213
Creativity, 34–35, 236–237
Credibility, 228
Critical theory, 89
Cultural relativism, 183
Culture, 90, 165–166, 243

Data:
    collection of, 182
    definition of, 192
    falsifying of, 60
    Internet, 203
    interpretation of, 57, 59, 195
    organization of, 97, 193, 196–197
    ownership of, 58
    preparing of, 196–197
    reviewing and recording your thoughts, 197
    themes developed from, 18
    variety of, in natural settings, 15–16
Data analysis:
    categories, 199–200
    circular model of, 193
    coding, 197–199
    complexity of, 188

computers for, 200–203
concepts, 200
conducting of, 195–200
constant-comparative method of, 190, 193
content analysis, 190
grounded theory approach to, 18, 193
individual nature of, 195–196
iterative process of, 188, 193
methods of, 189–190
process of, 188, 190–193
relational, 190
secondary, 203
systematic approach to, 189
themes, 190–191
Databanks, 58
Data triangulation. *See* Triangulation
Debriefing, 101–102
Deductive reasoning, 14, 243
Dependability, 228
Dewey, John, 27
Dialogic collaborative process, 232
Discourse analysis, 88, 190, 244
Discussion groups, 177–178
Dissertations, 209
    traditional, 236
Do no harm, 54, 59–60
Dramatic method of writing, 212

Editorial board, 233
Educational ethnography(s), 8, 29, 71
Educational psychology, 29
Educational research:
    demographics of, 26
    dissertations about, 27–28
    future of, 33–35
    in higher education, 27
    before 1980s, 26–31
    from 1980s to 2000, 31–32
    overview of, 25–26
    from 2000 and beyond, 32
Elaboration strategy, for questioning, 149
Elementary school teachers, 26
E-mail, 158
Emic perspective, 109, 244
EndNote, 136, 244
Environmental triangulation. *See* Triangulation
Epistemology, 210, 244
ERIC, 131
Essence of the experience, 79–80
Ethical conduct, 53–54, 56
    enforcement of, 58–59
    principles of, 54–58, 66
    violations of, 59–61
Ethical dilemmas, 62
Ethical standards, 63–65
Ethics review boards, 236
Ethnographers, 31

Ethnography:
    definition of, 70–71, 244
    description of, 30–31
    educational, 71
    examples of, 72
    growth of, 236
    history of, 70–71
    purpose of, 70
Ethnomethodology, 117, 244
Ethnotheatre, 217
Etic perspective, 109, 244
Evaluation of studies:
    before 1990, 227–228
    criteria used in, 223–224, 232
    editorial board criteria, 233
    issues associated with, 222
    in 1990s, 228–229
    personal criteria for, 224–227
    in 2008, 231–232
    in 2000 and beyond, 229–231
Exemplary case, 82–83
External validity, 227

Feminist research, 85–87
Feminist theory, 85–87, 244
Field methods, 71, 244
Field notes, 164, 167, 244
First-person writing, 208–209
Focus group(s):
    composition of, 155
    description of, 153–154
    facilities for, 155
    guided, 154
    on Internet, 159
    issues regarding, 154–156
    moderator's role in, 155
    number of, 155
    online, 159, 178, 238
    purpose of, 156
    semistructured, 154
    size of, 154–155
    structured, 154
    virtual, 159
Focus group interviewing:
    definition of, 139, 244
    elements of, 153
    example of, 152–153, 156–157
    history of, 153
    purpose of, 153–154
    qualitative interviewing vs., 154
    self-managed group, 153
    transcribing of, 156
Formal groups, 167
*Forum Qualitative Social
    Research,* 241
Foundationalist paradigms, 7, 244
Friendship, 56

Generalization, 96
Generic approach, 87–88, 244
Graduation degree programs, 27
Grand tour question, 146
Grey literature, 129
Grounded theory:
    coding methods in, 73
    data analysis, 193
    definition of, 244
    description of, 14, 18
    examples of, 74–75
    Glaser's view of, 73
    history of, 72–74
    purpose of, 72
    Strauss' view of, 74
Guided interview, 141

Hall, G. Stanley, 27, 36
Hermeneutical phenomenology, 78, 80, 89, 244
Humphreys, Laud, 60
Husserl, Edmund, 75–76, 79, 90
Hypothesis, 7, 128, 244

Images, 175–177
Inappropriate behavior, 57
In-depth interview:
    benefits of, 143
    body of, 145
    definition of, 244
    description of, 101–102, 141
    end of, 145
    getting started, 144–145
    process of, 143–145
    questions, 145–151
    techniques for, 145–151
    tips for, 151–152
In-depth study, 17–18
Inductive reasoning, 5, 244
Inductive strategy, 187–188
Inductive thinking, 14–15
Informal groups, 167
Informant, 140, 244
Information access, 34–35
Information overload, xvii–xviii
Informed consent:
    description of, 55–56
    for Internet-based studies, 64
    in public places, 64
Installation art, 34
Institutional review boards:
    challenges for, 65–66
    federal regulations that govern, 63
    origins of, 65
    politics of, 62, 66
    problems with, 65–66
    requirements of, 144
    research proposal preparation requirements, 63

International Journal of Qualitative Methods, 241–242
International Journal of Qualitative Studies in Education,
    225, 240
Internet:
    access to information, 237–238
    "blogosphere," 239
    blogs, 181–182, 236–237
    chat rooms, 177–178
    classrooms, 180–181
    communication using, 238
    data from, 203
    description of, 33
    discussion groups, 177–178
    ethical challenges for conducting studies on, 62–64
    focus groups on, 159, 178, 238
    online environments, 177
    scientific exchange using, 182
    teaching uses of, 178–181
    uses of, 177–182
    visual diaries, 181
    vlogs, 181
    wiki, 181, 238
    wireless access, 237
    written information available on, 173
Interpretivism, 20, 244
Inter-rater reliability, 17
Interview and interviewing
    adolescents, 143
    beginning of, 100–101
    casual, 141
    checklist for, 159–161
    children, 143
    description of, 13
    everyday examples of, 139
    examples of, 103–107
    focus group. *See* Focus group(s); Focus group
        interviewing
    goal of, 140
    guided, 141
    in-depth. *See* In-depth interview
    modeling of, 100–101
    online. *See* Online interviewing
    outside, 102
    participants, 141–142
    practicing of, 47, 101–102
    preparing for, 97
    preparing of papers after, 108–113
    purpose of, 140–141, 157
    qualitative. *See* Qualitative interviewing
    rapport, 142
    sample size, 142
    setting for, 142
    story-telling in, 40
    structured, 141
    surroundings, 143
    transcribing of, 193
    unplanned, 141

Intrusiveness, 57
Investigator triangulation. *See* Triangulation

Journals, xvi, 5, 49, 233, 240–242

Kerlinger, Fred, 29

Laboratory experiments, 10
Layered text format, 135
Legitimation crisis, 32
Life history, 88
Listserv, 178–179
Literature review:
    citations in, 136
    computer for, 136
    definition of, 126, 245
    examples of, 132–136
    importance of, 127–128
    limitation of, 127
    literature sources, 128–129
    locating of literature, 130–131
    middle ground approach, 126
    in qualitative research, 127
    relevancy, 131
    research topic, 129–130
    sorting, selecting, and organizing of information, 131–132
    steps involved in, 129–132
    suggestions for, 136
    traditional approach, 126–127
    viewpoints in, 126
    writing of, 126, 132
Lord, Frederic, 36

Malinowski, Bronislaw, 71, 90
Mead, Margaret, 71
Member checks, 17, 230
Memos, 174, 245
Metaphors, 210, 245
Methodological triangulation. *See* Triangulation
Methodology, 35, 245
Microethnography, 70
Misconduct:
    in qualitative research, 60–61
    in scientific community, 59–60
Mixed methods approach, 21, 32, 84–85, 245
Modeling of good practices, 100–101
Morgan, Lewis Henry, 71
Multiple realities, 14, 118
Multiple regressions, 118

Narrative analysis, 88
Narrative storytelling, 88
Narrative writing style, 98
Naturalistic inquiry, xv, 245
Natural settings:
    data from, 15–16
    ethical challenges for, 62
    research in, 31

Neopositivist movement, 8
New elements/topics question, 147–148
New Journalism, 219
No Child Left Behind Act, 222, 232
Nondirectional strategy, for questioning, 150
Nonparticipant observations, 165
NVivo, 19, 202, 245

Objective reality, 19
Objectivity, 19–20, 116, 227, 245
Observing/observations:
    access for, 167
    conducting of, 168–170
    definition of, 245
    description of, 15, 47
    duration of, 167
    examples of, 170–173
    frequency of, 167
    of groups, 167
    issues regarding, 166–168
    in natural settings, 164–173
    nonparticipant, 165
    planning of, 168
    purpose of, 165–166
    researcher's role during, 168
    what to study, 167–168
Online classrooms, 180–181
Online environments, 177
Online focus groups, 159, 178, 238
Online interviewing:
    definition of, 139, 245
    focus groups on Internet, 159
    issues and challenges associated with, 158
    purpose of, 157–158
    sampling, 158
    synchronous interview, 158
Online journals, 238
Online teaching, 178–181
Ontology, 20, 245
Open coding, 73
Openness, in writing, 206
Open places, 45
"Opt-out" letter, 64
Organization of Phenomenological Organizations, The, 78
Outliers, 195
Outside interviews. *See* Interviews

Paradigms, 7, 245
Participant:
    definition of, 20, 62, 140, 245
    identification of, 141–142
    number of, 142
    report description of, 213–214
Participant observer, 168, 245
Participation, voluntary, 63
Partner, 47–48
Passive research, 64

Phenomenologists, 17
Phenomenology:
    bracketing, 75, 80, 100, 180, 213
    definition of, 245
    in education, 77–78, 80
    elements of, 77
    essence of the experience, 79–80
    example of, 6
    hermeneutical, 78, 80, 89
    history of, 76–77
    lived experience, 79
    as method, 79–80
    overview of, 75–76
    as philosophy, 79–80
    purpose of, 75
    reductionist process, 80
    reinterpretations of, 79
    research approach and, 69
    theory-driven nature of, 128
    worldwide growth of, 77–78
Photoethnography, 70–71
Positivism, 7–8, 73, 245
Positivist paradigms, 7, 20–21
Postmodernism, 20, 88–89, 245
Postpositivism, 8, 245
Post-postmodernism, 89
Poststructuralism, 20, 88, 245
Preliminary analyses, 107–108
Privacy:
    description of, 54–55
    difficulties in maintaining, 61–62, 65
Probing strategy, for questioning, 149–150
Professional associations, xvi

Qualitative comparative analysis, 190
Qualitative Inquiry, 218, 225, 241
Qualitative Interest Group, 30
Qualitative interviewing:
    definition of, 139, 245
    focus group interviewing vs., 154
    purpose of, 140–141
Qualitative methods, xiv–x
Qualitative Report, The, 241
Qualitative research:
    acceptance of, 239
    background, 7–8
    challenges of, xvii–xviii, 22
    definitions, 5–7, 39, 245
    dynamic nature of, 13
    in education, 30
    elements of, 12–19
    examples of, 5–7
    finishing of, 194–195
    getting started, 46–49, 100
    goals of, 40, 209
    history of, xv
    holistic characteristics of, 15

    in-depth nature of, 17–18
    nonlinear nature of, 19
    purpose of, 12
    reasons for increased interest
        in, xv–xvi
    textbooks about, xvi
    varied approaches to, 13–14
Qualitative Research, 217–218, 225, 241
Qualitative Research in Psychology, 242
Quantitative research:
    definition of, 245
    description of, 7
    qualitative research vs., 9–12, 97
Queer theory, 86, 245
Questions:
    closing, 148
    comparison/contrast, 147
    concrete example, 146–147
    description of, 42–43
    elaboration strategy for, 148
    formulating of, 44
    grand tour question, 146
    in-depth interview, 145–151
    new elements/topics, 147–148
    nondirectional strategy for, 150
    probing strategy for, 149–150
    selection of, 38–39
    topics for, 44–45
    wait time between, 150

Randomized clinical trials, 8
Randomized control group studies, 34
Random sample, 155, 245
Rapport, 56, 142, 158
Reflexivity, 21, 121–122, 230, 245
Relational data analysis, 190
Reliability, 220, 225, 226, 227
Representational crisis, 32
Research. *See also* Educational research; Qualitative research;
    Quantitative research
    definition of, 38, 245
    recent trends in, 8
    traditional methods of, 8
Research approach, 69, 245
Researcher:
    as bricoleur, 35
    checklist for becoming, 41–42
    role of, 16–17, 20, 116, 224
    subjectivity of, 17
    traits of, 41–42
Researcher journal, 164, 196, 245
Research literature, 214
Research proposal, 215–217
Research study:
    example of, 99–113
    interrelated factors in, 69
    voluntary nature of participation in, 63

Research topic, for literature review, 129–130
Research writing. *See* Writing
Review boards. *See* Institutional review boards
Review of Educational Research, 25–26
Review of Research in Education, 29
Root metaphor, 126

Sample size, 142
Scaffolding, 15
Scene-by-scene writing, 212
Scientific method, 7, 26, 245
Selective coding, 73
Self, 121, 224
Self-awareness, 122–123
Self-disclosure, 122–123
Self-managed group, 153
Self-referentiality, 122
Self-reflection, 22, 98, 214, 245
Self-reflexivity, 117–120, 224
Semistructured focus group, 154
Skills development, 48–49
Skinner, B. F., 28–29
Snowball sampling, 13, 142, 245
Sociology, 7, 245
Software, 98, 136, 202
Stories, 194, 200
Strauss, Anselm, 28, 74
Structured focus group, 154
Structured interview, 141
Subjects, 20, 62, 140, 245
Summary method of writing, 212
Summative analysis, 190
Support group, 96
Symbolic interactionism, 14, 245
Synchronous interview, 158

Taylor, E. B., 71
Teacher training, 27
Teens, 6, 16, 48, 51–52, 66, 143, 166, 171
Testing movement, 29
Textual representation, 21–22
Themes, 15, 18, 245
Theoretical richness, 230
Theoretical sampling, 72, 73, 89, 142, 214, 242, 248
"Theoretical saturation," 194
Theory:
    critical, 89
    description of, 239–240, 245
    feminist, 85–87
    grounded. *See* Grounded theory
    in qualitative research, 128
Theory triangulation. *See* Triangulation
Thick description, 18, 245
Thorndike, E. L., 36
Transcribing of interviews, 193
Transferability, 228

Trends, 235–237
Triangulation, 17, 98, 222, 229, 245
    data, 229
    environmental, 229
    investigator, 229
    methodological, 229
    theory, 229
Tuskegee Experiment, 59
Twenty questions, 96–99
Tyler, Ralph, 28
Typical case, 82–83

Unobtrusive observer, 168, 245
Unplanned interview, 141
Unusual or unique case, 82–83

Verbatim theater, 217
Virtual focus groups, 159
Visual anthropology, 71
Visual diaries, 181
Visual images, 175–177
Vlogs, 181
Voice, 21, 33–34, 245

"Why" questions, 12, 100
Wiki, 181, 238
Wolcott, Harry, 60
Words, 18
Writing:
    active voice in, 212
    alternative presentations, 217
    audience for, 208
    creative nonfiction, 210–213
    dramatic method of, 212
    first-person, 208–209
    guidelines for, 208–214
    metaphors in, 210
    openness in, 206
    realistic details in, 212
    research proposal, 215–217
    scene-by-scene, 212
    sections, 213–214
    sources of, 217–219
    steps for, 206–207
    structure of, 207, 213–214
    styles of, 206
    summary method of, 212
    third-person, 206, 207, 209
    voices of others in, 209–210
Writing style, 10, 18, 126, 132, 207, 218, 234, 245
Written material:
    extracting the meaning of, 174–175
    Internet as source of, 173
    issues regarding, 173–174
    from participants, 174
    purpose of, 173

About the Author

Marilyn Lichtman is a retired professor of educational research and evaluation from Virginia Tech at both the main campus in Blacksburg, Virginia, and at the graduate campus in Falls Church, Virginia. After attending The University of Chicago as an undergraduate, she moved to Washington, D.C. She completed all her degrees at The George Washington University, receiving her doctorate in educational research. She taught both qualitative and quantitative research courses while at The Catholic University of America and Virginia Tech. She is a regular user of the Internet for teaching and was an early contributor to teaching qualitative courses online. She is currently on the editorial boards of *The Qualitative Report* and *Forum: Qualitative Social Research (FQS),* both online journals devoted to qualitative issues. She has served as a consultant to many school systems, private companies, and government agencies. Currently she is docent council chairman at the Corcoran Gallery of Art in Washington, D.C.